D0427405

PRAISE FOR

GHETTO KLOWN

JOHN LEGUIZAMO

"John's writing has always been cutting-edge. He is a pioneer in theater and comedy, not just for Latin people, but as much as any comic or playwright I've ever seen or read. No one makes me laugh louder than this man. We are better because of him."

—SOFÍA VERGARA

"The graphic novel of *Ghetto Klown* captures the infectious spirit of John Leguizamo's live performances with the same surprising humor and cultural insight. These pages make John seem like the coolest super hero in New York."

—JESSE EISENBERG

Editor: David Cashion
Designer: Pamela Notarantonio
Managing Editor: Jen Graham
Production Manager: Kathy Lovisolo

Library of Congress Cataloging-in-Publication Data
Leguizamo, John.
  Ghetto Klown / John Leguizamo, Christa Cassano and Shamus Beyale.
      pages cm
    ISBN 978-1-4197-1518-1 (hardback) – ISBN 978-1-61312-861-9 (ebook)
1. Leguizamo, John–Comic books, strips, etc. 2. Dramatists, American–20th century–
Biography. 3. Dramatists, American–20th century–Comic books, strips, etc.
4. Comedians–United States–Biography. 5. Comedians–United States–Comic books,
strips, etc. 6. Hispanic Americans–Biography. 7. Hispanic Americans–Comic books, strips, etc.
8. Graphic novels. I. Cassano, Christa. II. Title.
  PS3562.E424Z46 2015
  812'.54–dc23
  [B]
                                        2015006551

Text copyright © 2015 John Leguizamo
Illustrations copyright © 2015 Christa Cassano (pages 1–62) and Shamus Beyale (pages 63–181)

Published in 2015 by Abrams ComicArts, an imprint of ABRAMS. All rights reserved. No
portion of this book may be reproduced, stored in a retrieval system, or transmitted in
any form or by any means, mechanical, electronic, photocopying, recording, or otherwise,
without written permission from the publisher.

Abrams ComicArts is a registered trademark of Harry N. Abrams, Inc., registered in the
U.S. Patent and Trademark Office.

Printed and bound in the U.S.A.
10 9 8 7 6 5 4 3 2 1

Abrams ComicArts books are available at special discounts when purchased in quantity
for premiums and promotions as well as fundraising or educational use. Special editions
can also be created to specification. For details, contact specialsales@abramsbooks.com
or the address below.

THE ART OF BOOKS SINCE 1949

115 West 18th Street
New York, NY 10011
www.abramsbooks.com

To Justine

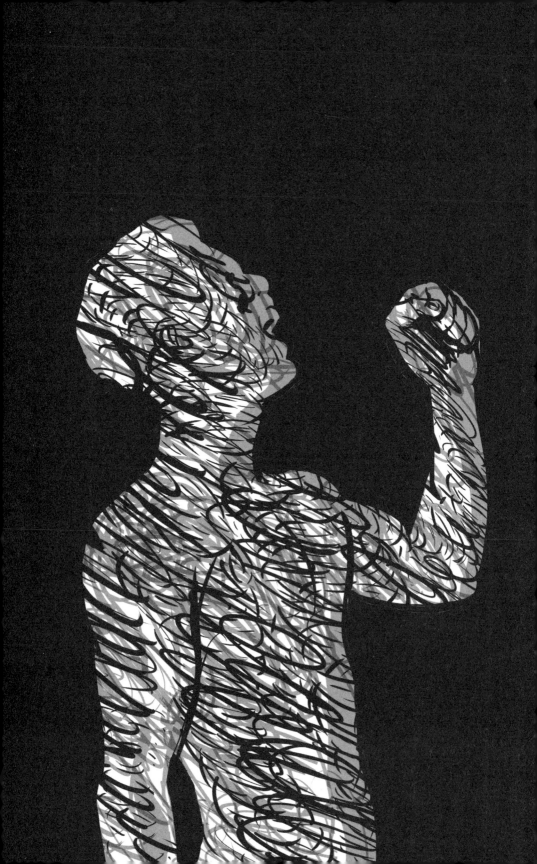

GHETTO KLOWN

JOHN LEGUIZAMO

A GRAPHIC NOVEL

ILLUSTRATED BY
CHRISTA CASSANO AND SHAMUS BEYALE

ABRAMS COMICARTS, NEW YORK

PREFACE

In 1998, I started on a journey to document and make sense of my life with my one-man stage show *Freak*, but ultimately I became interested in creating a comprehensive study of the life of an artist as a Latin man working in "Hollywouldn't." That impulse evolved into *Ghetto Klown*. Despite the various stage incarnations and the HBO television adaptation, the show seems best suited to the graphic-novel format, because it really needs to travel through a space-time continuum with fewer constraints than an in-person retelling. My story goes from me being a little kid all the way to a middle-aged man and jumps around to different states and countries, the action fast and very physical. You can travel to places visually with the graphic-novel medium that you can't achieve onstage, and experience inner states that even movies can't quite capture. This is the magic of putting pen to paper, and it's one of the most exciting ventures I've undertaken yet.

It's been fascinating to see the play evolve into a graphic novel. A play is always a highly visual medium, but in this new manifestation, being able to get to any perspective, any point of view, or any angle is amazing. It's even more freeing than film, because there you always have a budget to worry about. But when working with a graphic artist, whether you're going for a close-up of an eye or a New York City street filled with cabs, crowds, and tenements, it's probably going to cost you the same amount. On the page, the only limitation is your imagination.

I really lucked out with Christa Cassano and Shamus Beyale because they're both so exacting, and God is in the details. They're both meticulous and such naturals at creating likenesses of the large cast of my story, including my family members and the various actors and directors I've worked with. What really trips me out is that the earlier parts of my life are depicted with magical little drawings seemingly made by someone who'd been there with a camera; that's how on point Christa and Shamus are. It's a kind of alchemy to see the places—and sometimes the people—that I no longer have access to, except in my mind, right there on the page; they've been rendered as if I've simply taken a tour through my memories.

In addition to spookily channeling the visuals, Christa and Shamus's interpretation adds so much humor and reality to what I had originally written, because now you see the scenes with the actual characters in the actual spaces instead of having to imagine it all from my onstage pantomiming. The graphic-novel option changes and enhances the story from the play format, because I don't have to explain things the way I do in a staging that has only minimal sets or costumes. And I don't have to constantly remind people of who I'm playing. My work is evocative—through the power of suggestion— and what you had to imagine before is now manifested. The illustrations really concretize my play, and it's no longer just a theatrical impression but a visual documentation of my life.

I have to say, it is really weird to see myself portrayed as a character. While going through the process of creating this book and seeing it all realized, my emotions ran the gamut from amazement to pride to humiliation, because I finally had an objective POV of everything I've perpetrated in my life. I can now really see, in a crazy, therapeutic way, what I was capable (and culpable) of, and what I was not. I'm washed away of my sins. (Do I sound like I'm at Mass? I am a recovering Catholic.) My therapist said it best, though: "Artists rework their trauma through their art—what they could not control when the incident happened. Now they have control, and this eases the pain of it all." Amen.

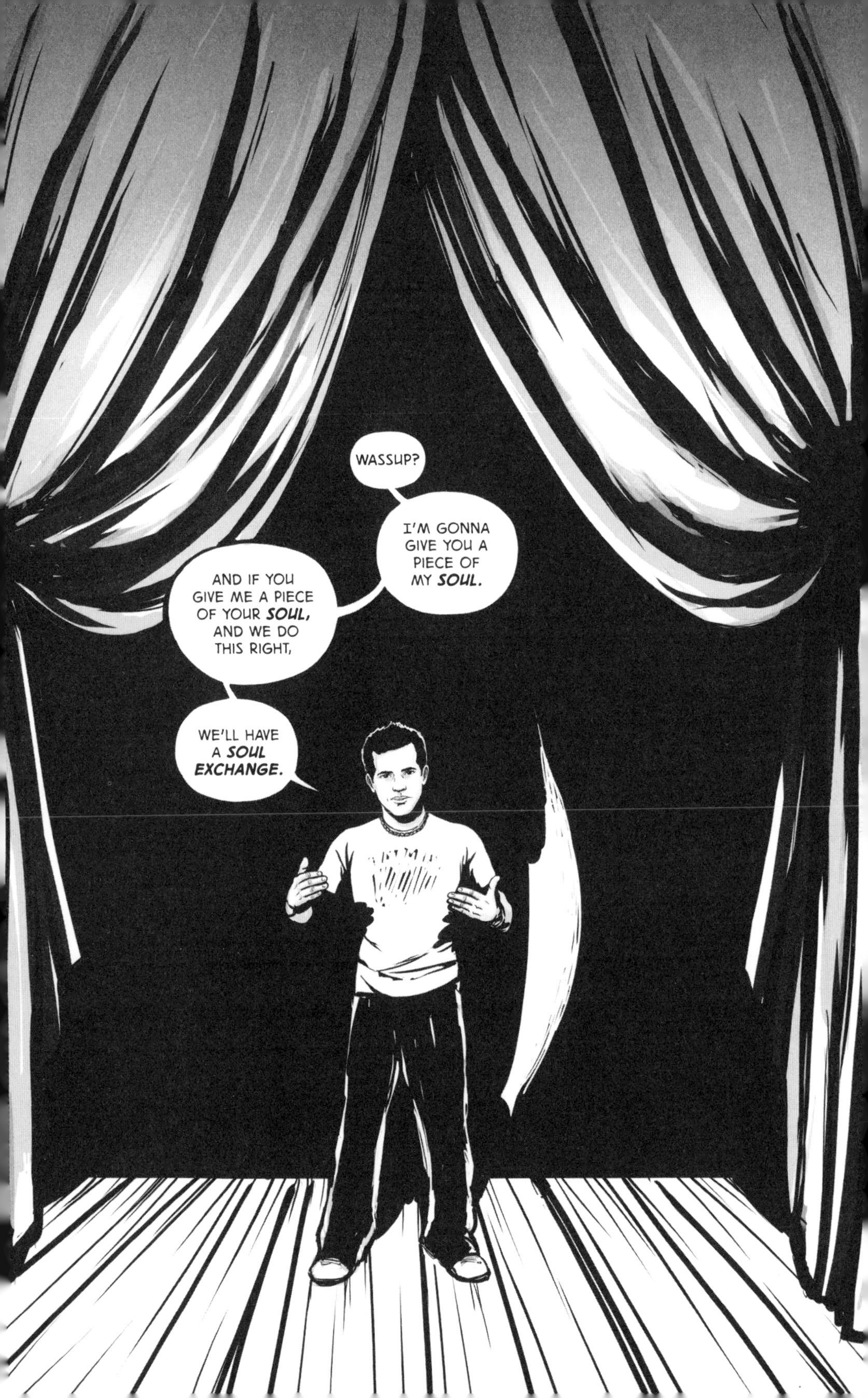
WASSUP?
I'M GONNA GIVE YOU A PIECE OF MY **SOUL.**
AND IF YOU GIVE ME A PIECE OF YOUR **SOUL,** AND WE DO THIS RIGHT,
WE'LL HAVE A **SOUL EXCHANGE.**

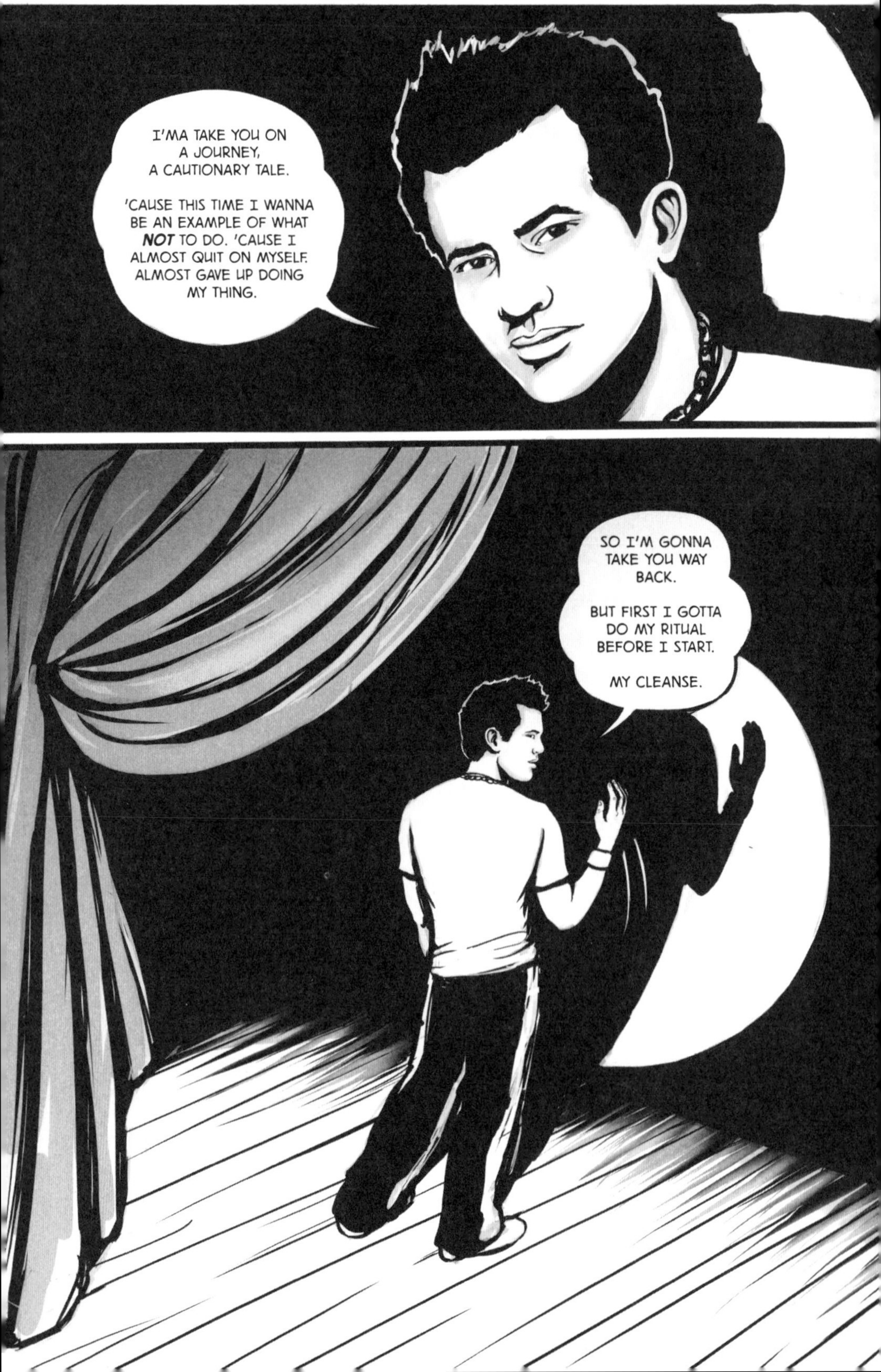
I'MA TAKE YOU ON A JOURNEY, A CAUTIONARY TALE.
'CAUSE THIS TIME I WANNA BE AN EXAMPLE OF WHAT **NOT** TO DO. 'CAUSE I ALMOST QUIT ON MYSELF. ALMOST GAVE UP DOING MY THING.
SO I'M GONNA TAKE YOU WAY BACK.
BUT FIRST I GOTTA DO MY RITUAL BEFORE I START.
MY CLEANSE.

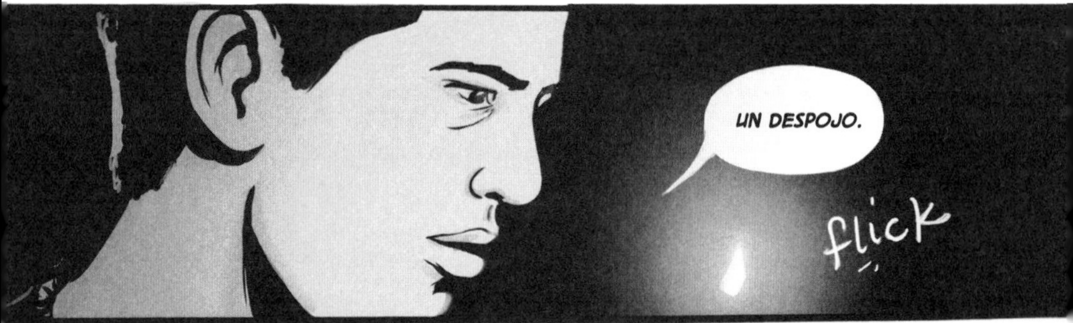
UN DESPOJO.
flick

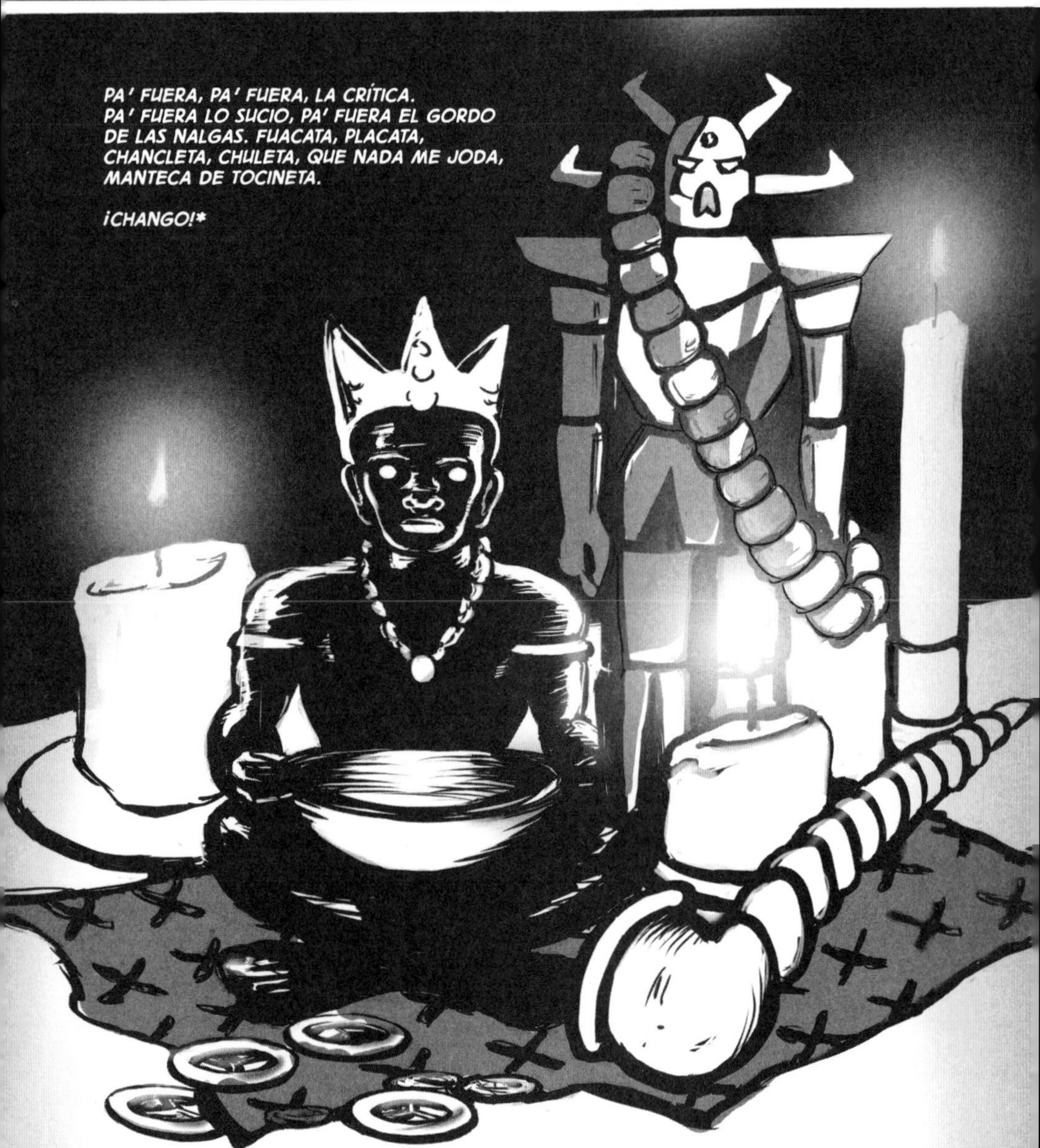
PA' FUERA, PA' FUERA, LA CRÍTICA.
PA' FUERA LO SUCIO, PA' FUERA EL GORDO DE LAS NALGAS. FUACATA, PLACATA, CHANCLETA, CHULETA, QUE NADA ME JODA, MANTECA DE TOCINETA.
¡CHANGO!*

*Cleansing spell. Get out! Get out! Criticism, filth, the fat in my butt. Omenapatia thwack! Plop! Flip-flop, pork chop, let nothing bother me, bacon lard! Chango [a god of Santería]!

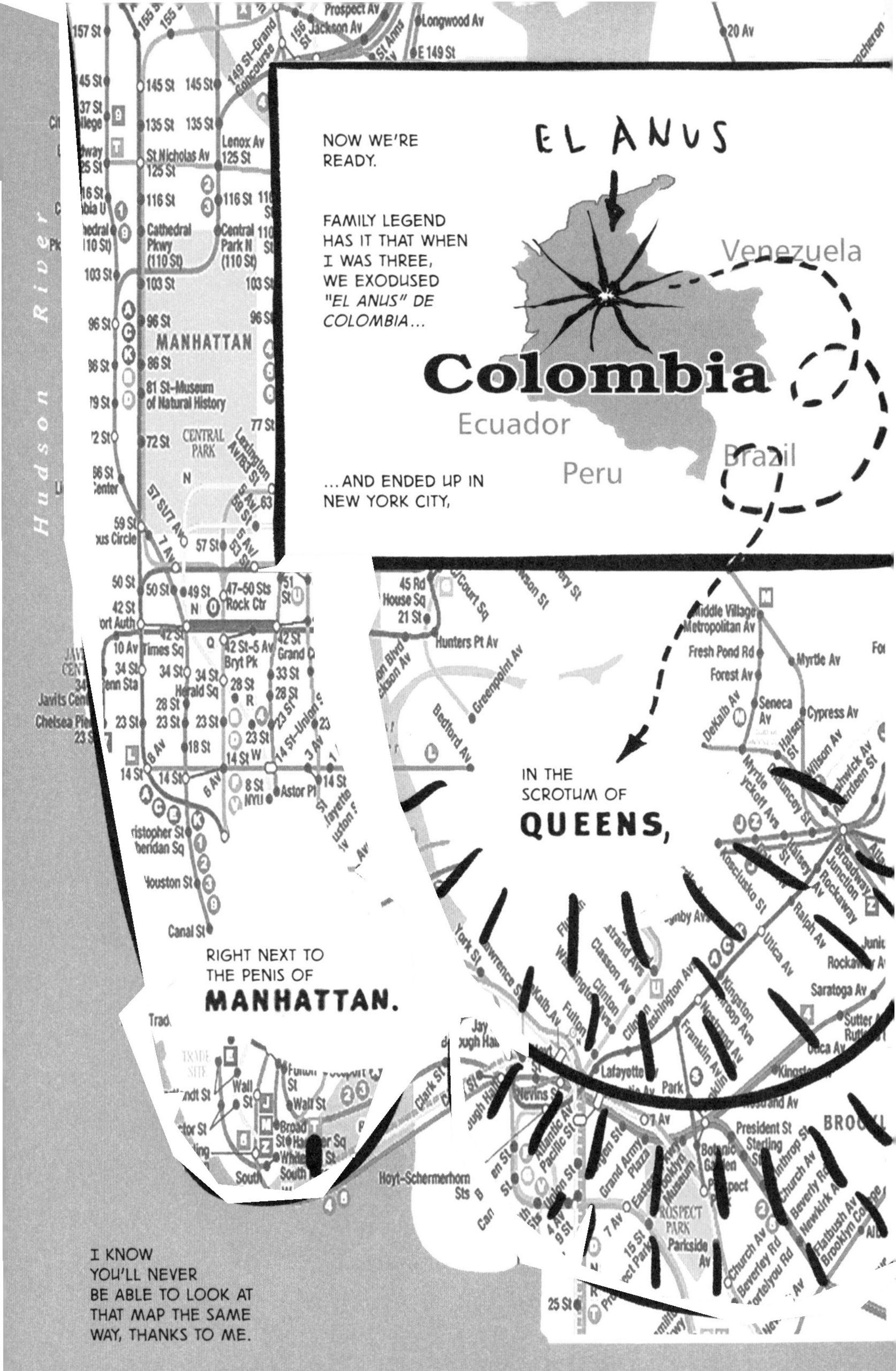
NOW WE'RE READY.
FAMILY LEGEND HAS IT THAT WHEN I WAS THREE, WE EXODUSED *"EL ANUS" DE COLOMBIA...*
EL ANUS
Colombia
Venezuela
Ecuador
Peru
Brazil
...AND ENDED UP IN NEW YORK CITY,
IN THE SCROTUM OF **QUEENS,**
RIGHT NEXT TO THE PENIS OF **MANHATTAN.**
Hudson River
MANHATTAN
CENTRAL PARK
I KNOW YOU'LL NEVER BE ABLE TO LOOK AT THAT MAP THE SAME WAY, THANKS TO ME.

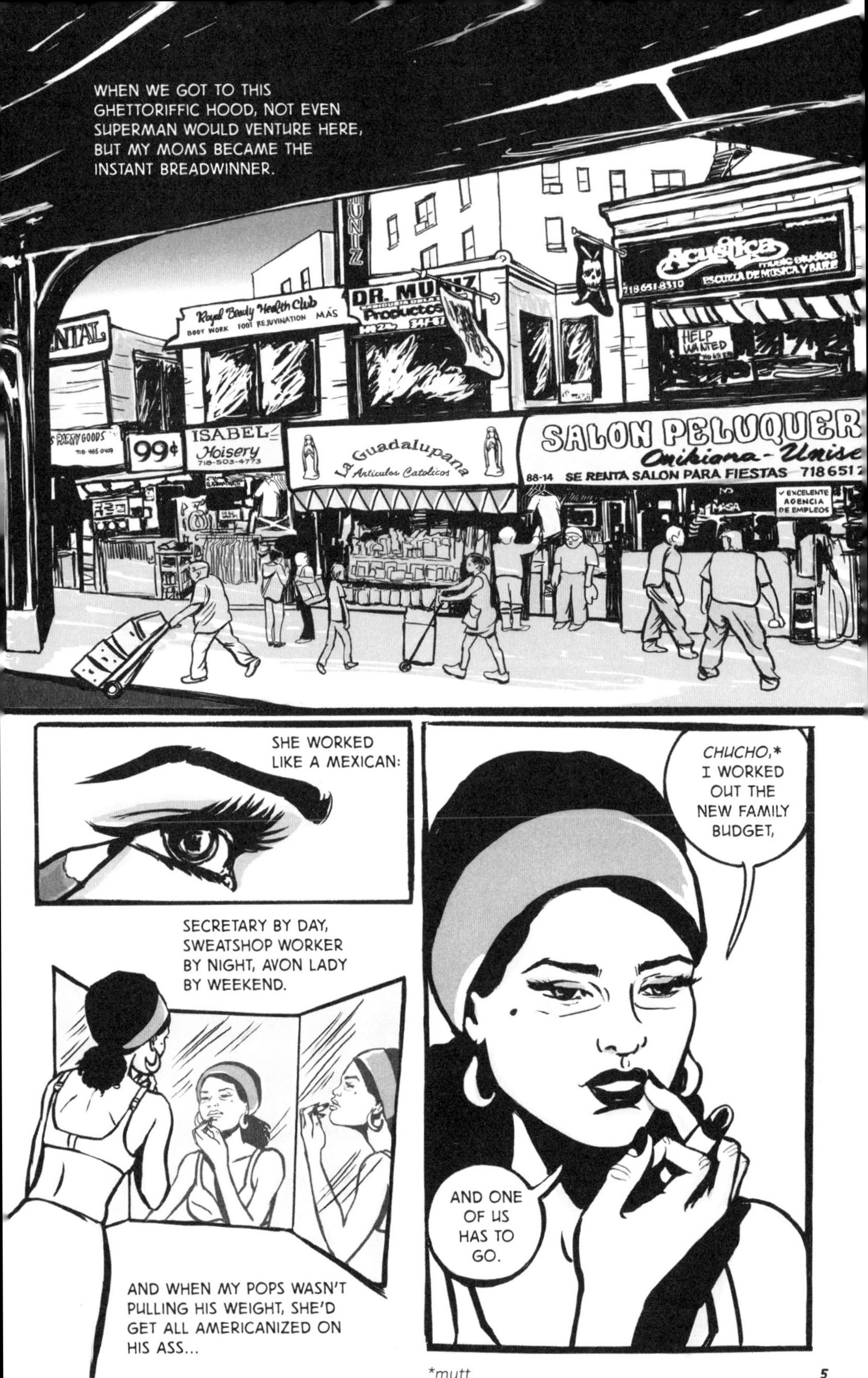
WHEN WE GOT TO THIS GHETTORIFFIC HOOD, NOT EVEN SUPERMAN WOULD VENTURE HERE, BUT MY MOMS BECAME THE INSTANT BREADWINNER.
Royal Beauty Health Club
BODY WORK FOOT REJUVINATION MÁS
DR. MU
Productos
Acustica
music studios
ESCUELA DE MUSICA Y BAILE
718 651 8310
HELP WANTED
99¢
ISABEL
Hoisery
718-503-4773
La Guadalupana
Articulos Catolicos
SALON PELUQUER
Omikiama-Unise
88-14 SE RENTA SALON PARA FIESTAS 718 651
EXCELENTE AGENCIA DE EMPLEOS
SHE WORKED LIKE A MEXICAN:
SECRETARY BY DAY, SWEATSHOP WORKER BY NIGHT, AVON LADY BY WEEKEND.
AND WHEN MY POPS WASN'T PULLING HIS WEIGHT, SHE'D GET ALL AMERICANIZED ON HIS ASS...
CHUCHO,* I WORKED OUT THE NEW FAMILY BUDGET,
AND ONE OF US HAS TO GO.

*mutt

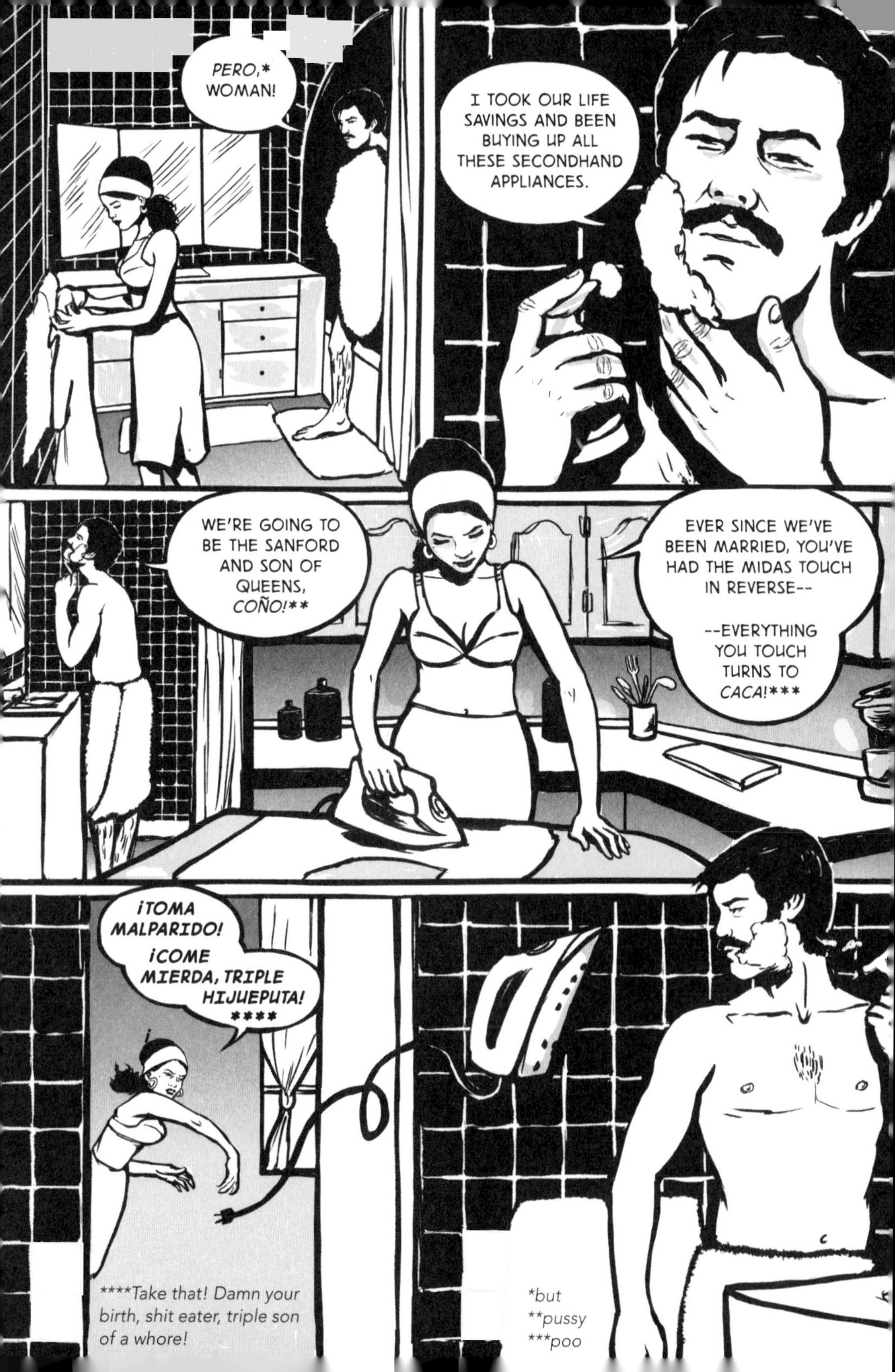
PERO,* WOMAN!
I TOOK OUR LIFE SAVINGS AND BEEN BUYING UP ALL THESE SECONDHAND APPLIANCES.
WE'RE GOING TO BE THE SANFORD AND SON OF QUEENS, *COÑO!***
EVER SINCE WE'VE BEEN MARRIED, YOU'VE HAD THE MIDAS TOUCH IN REVERSE--
--EVERYTHING YOU TOUCH TURNS TO *CACA!****
¡TOMA MALPARIDO! ¡COME MIERDA, TRIPLE HIJUEPUTA! ****
****Take that! Damn your birth, shit eater, triple son of a whore!
*but
**pussy
***poo

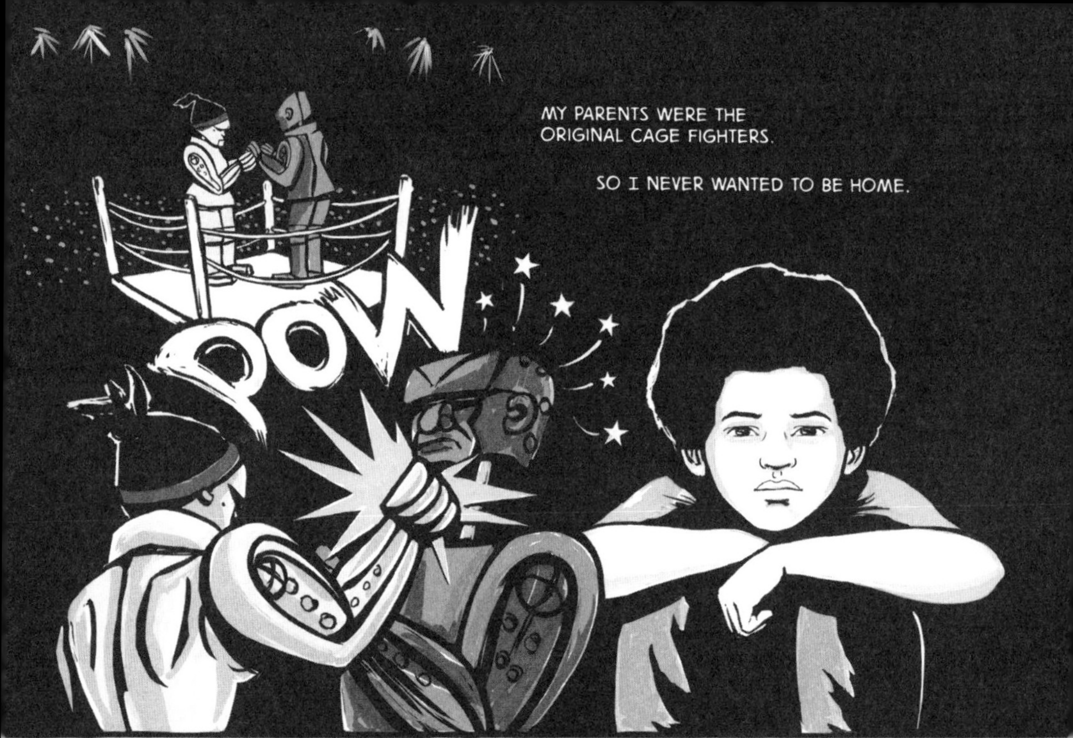
MY PARENTS WERE THE ORIGINAL CAGE FIGHTERS.
SO I NEVER WANTED TO BE HOME.
POW

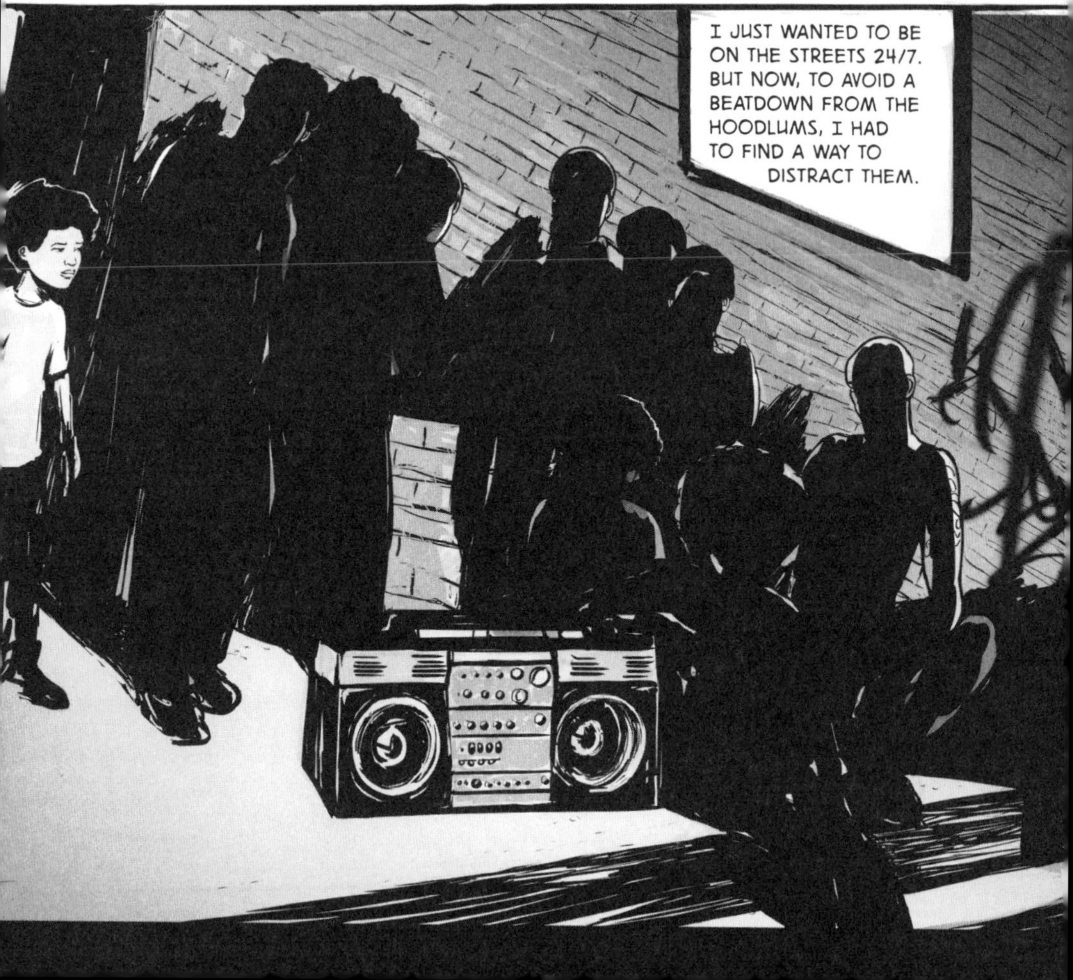
I JUST WANTED TO BE ON THE STREETS 24/7. BUT NOW, TO AVOID A BEATDOWN FROM THE HOODLUMS, I HAD TO FIND A WAY TO DISTRACT THEM.

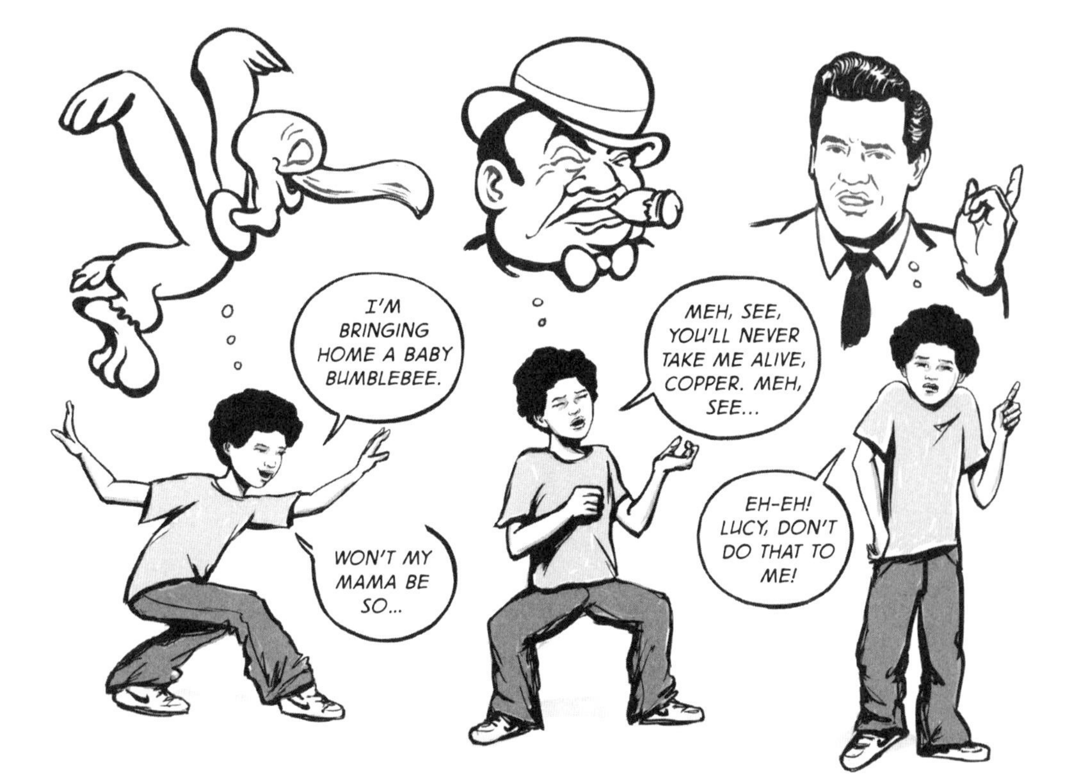
I'M BRINGING HOME A BABY BUMBLEBEE.
WON'T MY MAMA BE SO...
MEH, SEE, YOU'LL NEVER TAKE ME ALIVE, COPPER. MEH, SEE...
EH-EH! LUCY, DON'T DO THAT TO ME!

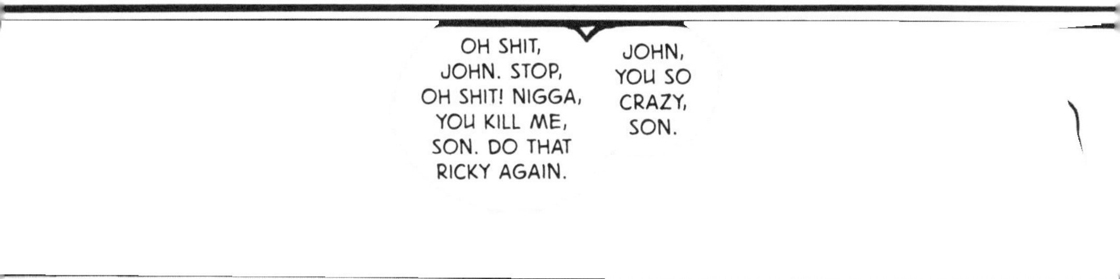
OH SHIT, JOHN. STOP, OH SHIT! NIGGA, YOU KILL ME, SON. DO THAT RICKY AGAIN.
JOHN, YOU SO CRAZY, SON.

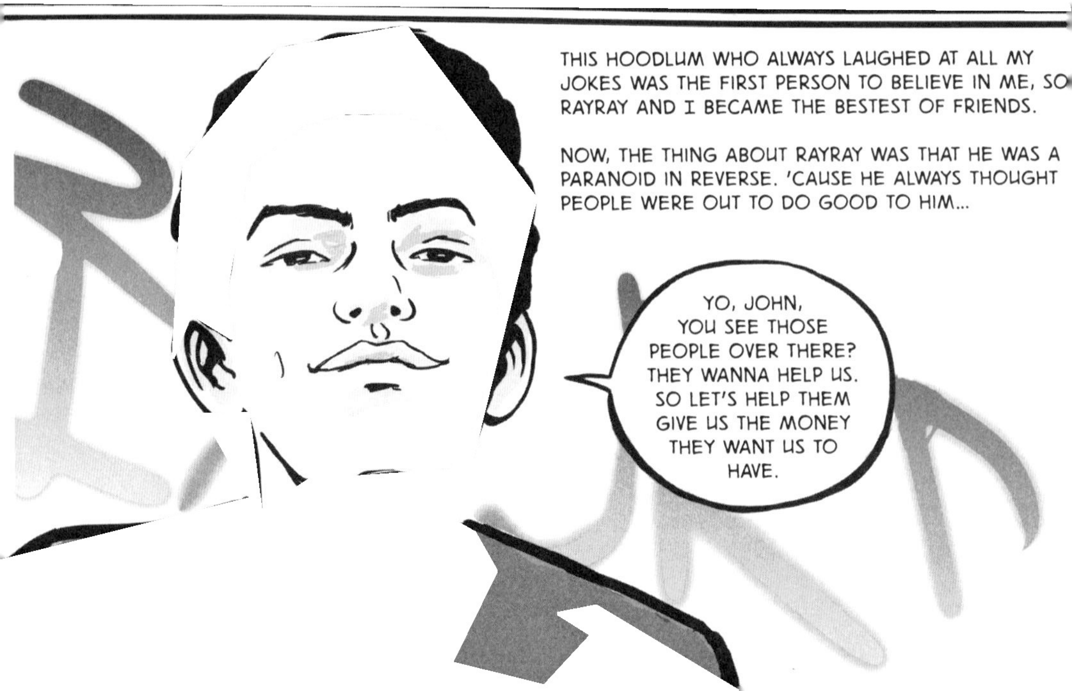
THIS HOODLUM WHO ALWAYS LAUGHED AT ALL MY JOKES WAS THE FIRST PERSON TO BELIEVE IN ME, SO RAYRAY AND I BECAME THE BESTEST OF FRIENDS.
NOW, THE THING ABOUT RAYRAY WAS THAT HE WAS A PARANOID IN REVERSE. 'CAUSE HE ALWAYS THOUGHT PEOPLE WERE OUT TO DO GOOD TO HIM...
YO, JOHN, YOU SEE THOSE PEOPLE OVER THERE? THEY WANNA HELP US. SO LET'S HELP THEM GIVE US THE MONEY THEY WANT US TO HAVE.

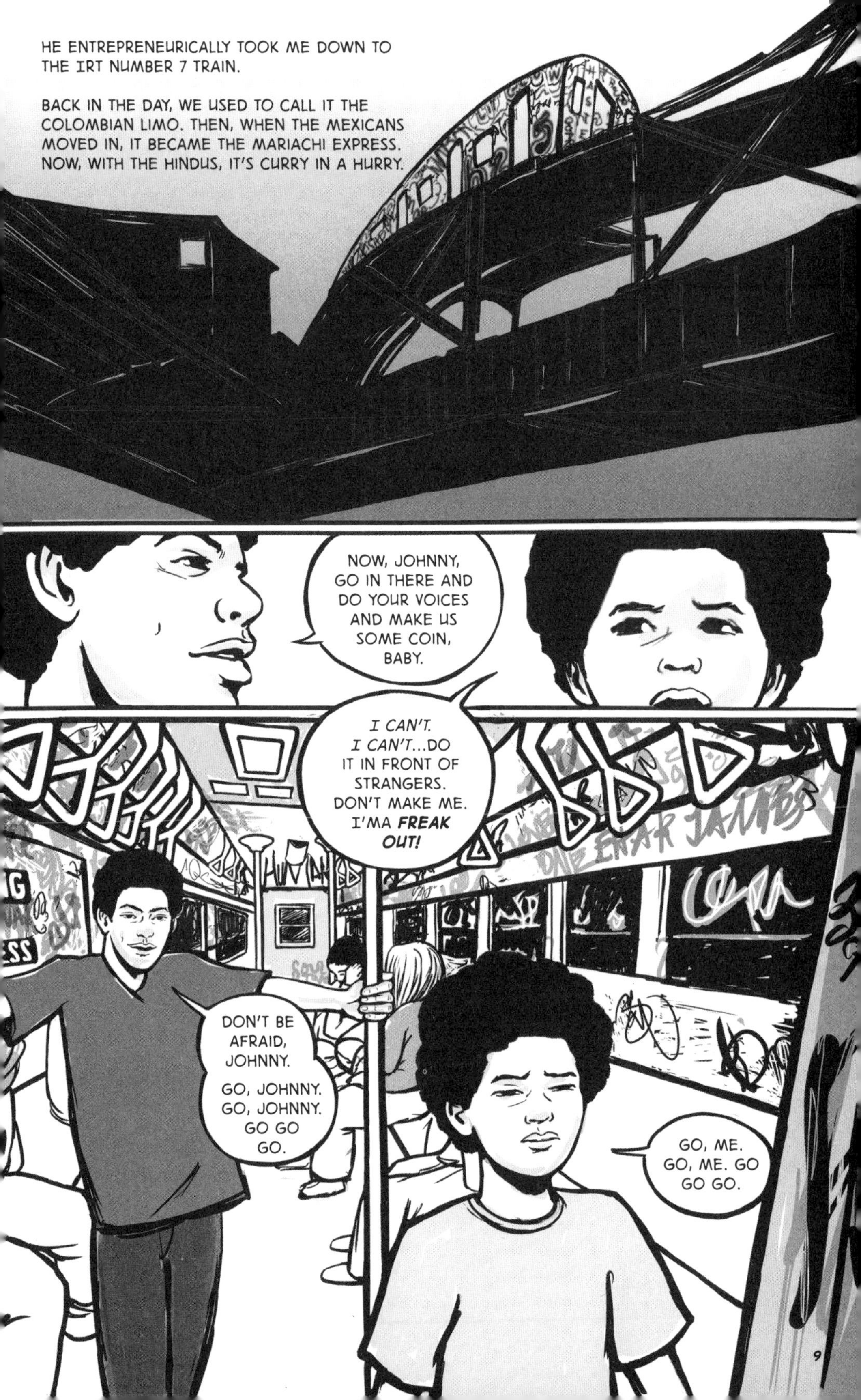
HE ENTREPRENEURICALLY TOOK ME DOWN TO THE IRT NUMBER 7 TRAIN.
BACK IN THE DAY, WE USED TO CALL IT THE COLOMBIAN LIMO. THEN, WHEN THE MEXICANS MOVED IN, IT BECAME THE MARIACHI EXPRESS. NOW, WITH THE HINDUS, IT'S CURRY IN A HURRY.
NOW, JOHNNY, GO IN THERE AND DO YOUR VOICES AND MAKE US SOME COIN, BABY.
I CAN'T. I CAN'T...DO IT IN FRONT OF STRANGERS. DON'T MAKE ME. I'MA ***FREAK OUT!***
DON'T BE AFRAID, JOHNNY.
GO, JOHNNY. GO, JOHNNY. GO GO GO.
GO, ME. GO, ME. GO GO GO.

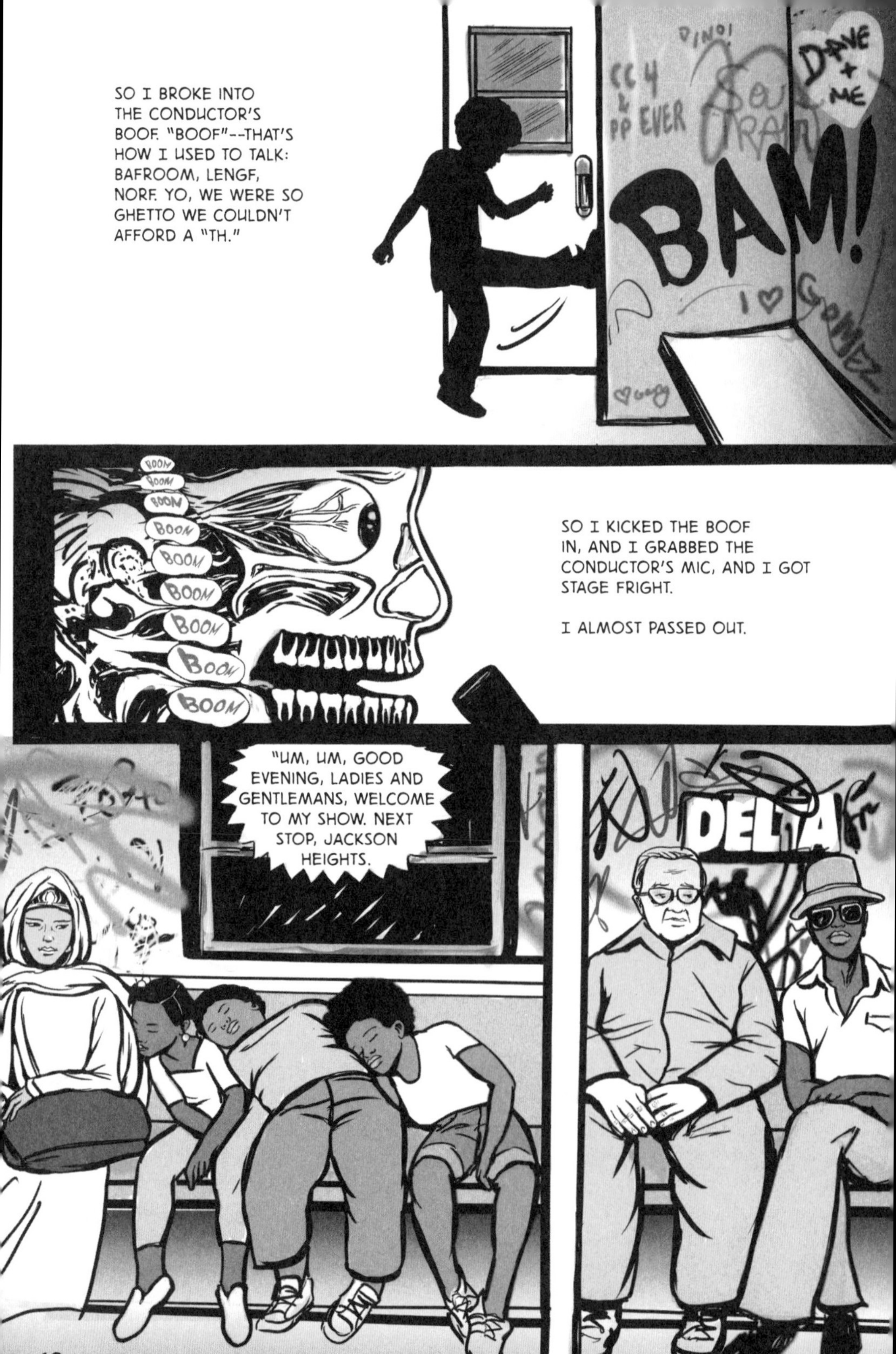
SO I BROKE INTO THE CONDUCTOR'S BOOF. "BOOF"--THAT'S HOW I USED TO TALK: BAFROOM, LENGF, NORF. YO, WE WERE SO GHETTO WE COULDN'T AFFORD A "TH."
DINO!
CC 4 & PP EVER
DAVE + ME
BAM!
BOOM
BOOM
BOOM
BOOM
BOOM
BOOM
BOOM
BOOM
BOOM
SO I KICKED THE BOOF IN, AND I GRABBED THE CONDUCTOR'S MIC, AND I GOT STAGE FRIGHT.
I ALMOST PASSED OUT.
"UM, UM, GOOD EVENING, LADIES AND GENTLEMANS, WELCOME TO MY SHOW. NEXT STOP, JACKSON HEIGHTS.
DELTA

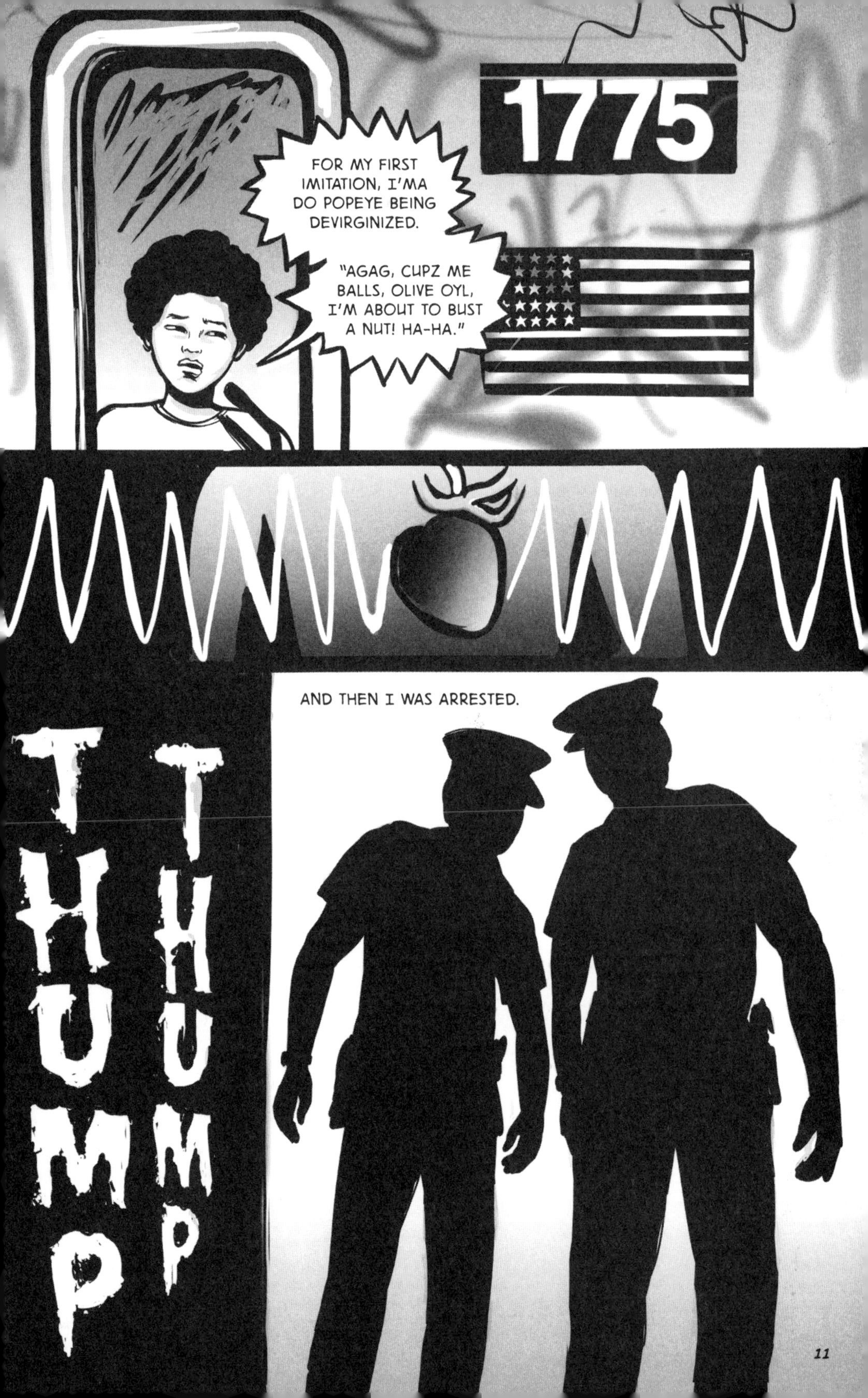
1775
FOR MY FIRST IMITATION, I'MA DO POPEYE BEING DEVIRGINIZED.
"AGAG, CUPZ ME BALLS, OLIVE OYL, I'M ABOUT TO BUST A NUT! HA-HA."
THUMP THUMP
AND THEN I WAS ARRESTED.

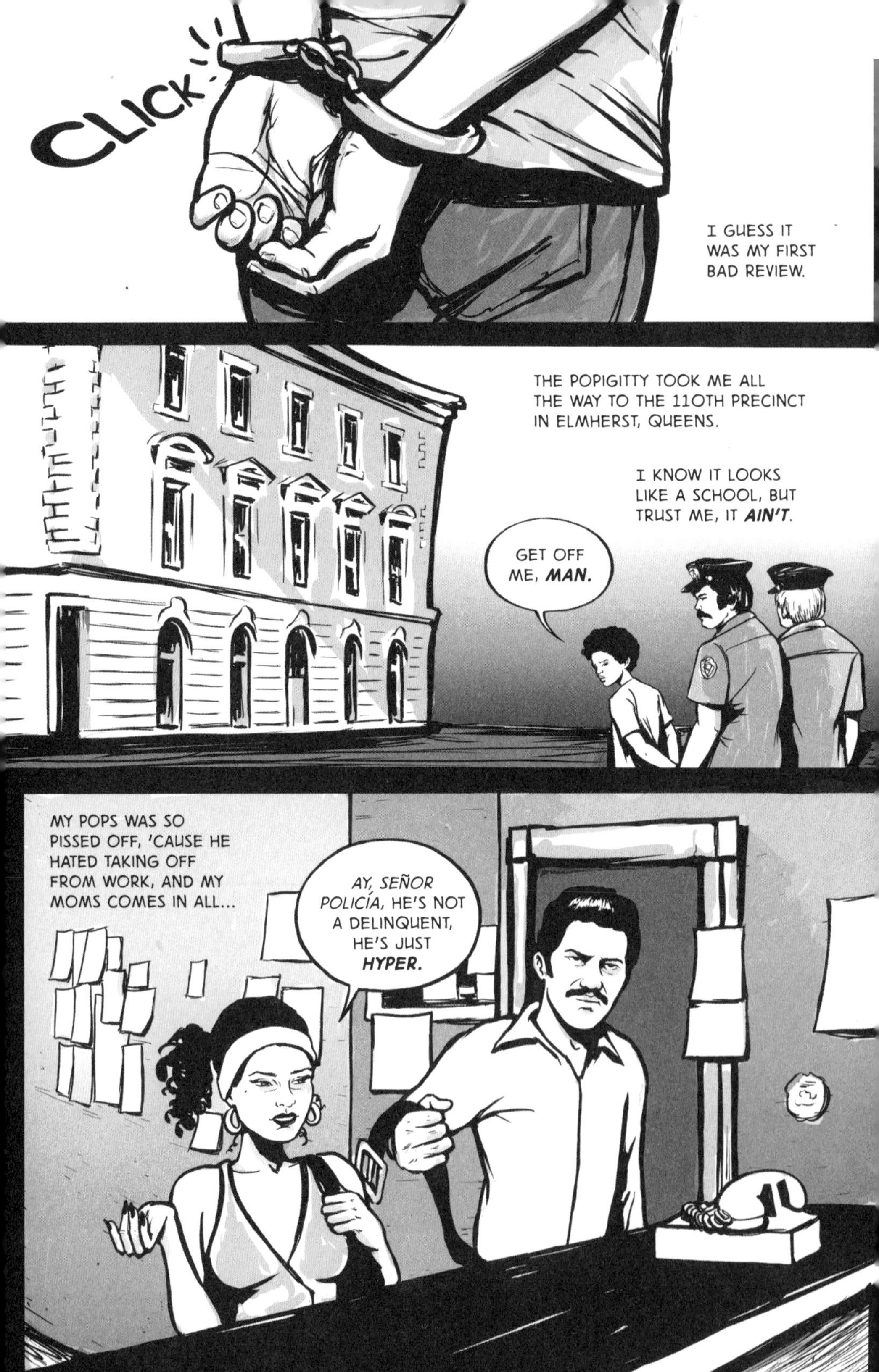
CLICK
I GUESS IT WAS MY FIRST BAD REVIEW.
THE POPIGITTY TOOK ME ALL THE WAY TO THE 110TH PRECINCT IN ELMHERST, QUEENS.
I KNOW IT LOOKS LIKE A SCHOOL, BUT TRUST ME, IT *AIN'T*.
GET OFF ME, *MAN.*
MY POPS WAS SO PISSED OFF, 'CAUSE HE HATED TAKING OFF FROM WORK, AND MY MOMS COMES IN ALL...
AY, SEÑOR POLICÍA, HE'S NOT A DELINQUENT, HE'S JUST *HYPER.*

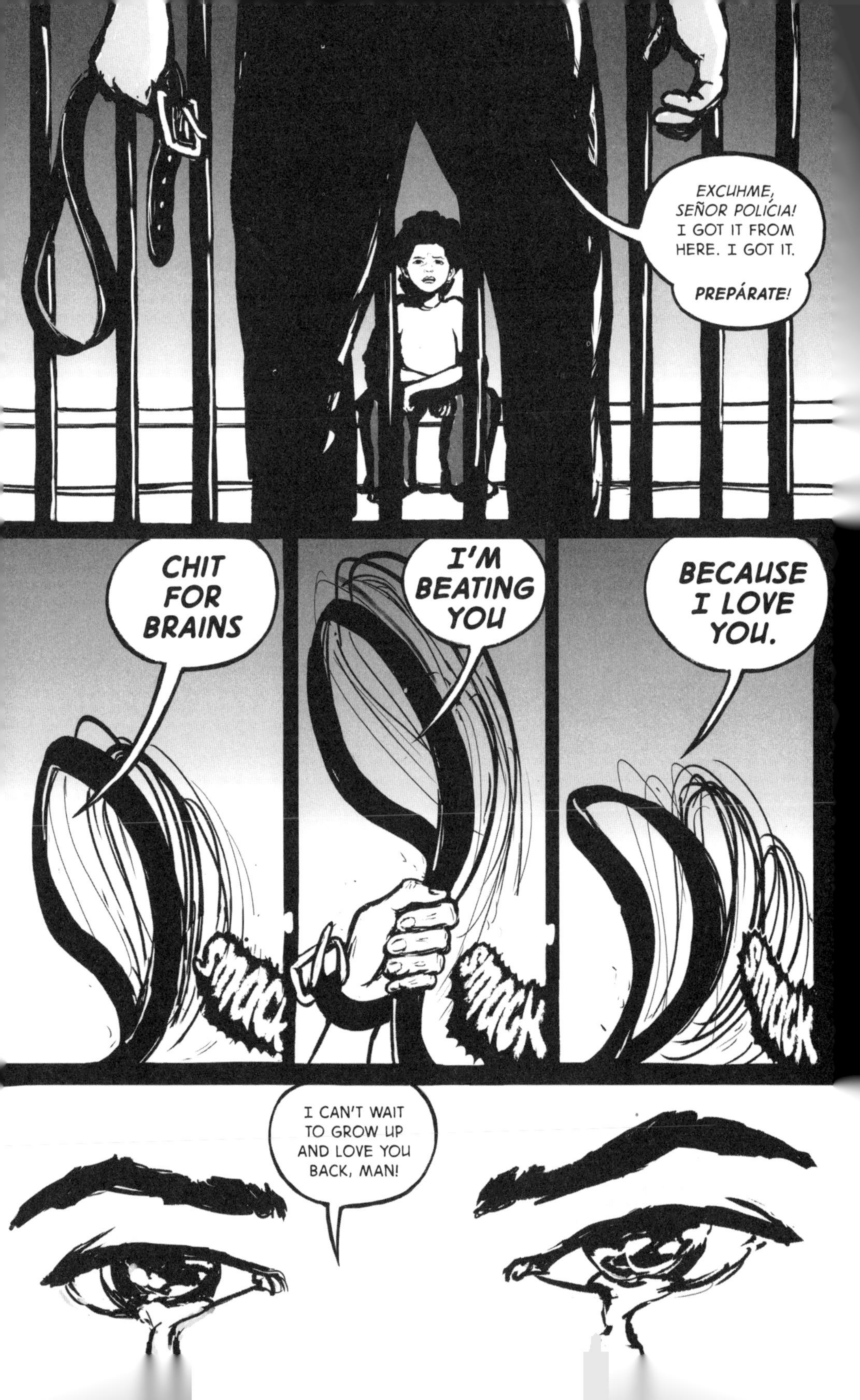
EXCUHME, SEÑOR POLÍCIA! I GOT IT FROM HERE. I GOT IT.
PREPÁRATE!
CHIT FOR BRAINS
SMACK
I'M BEATING YOU
SMACK
BECAUSE I LOVE YOU.
SMACK
I CAN'T WAIT TO GROW UP AND LOVE YOU BACK, MAN!

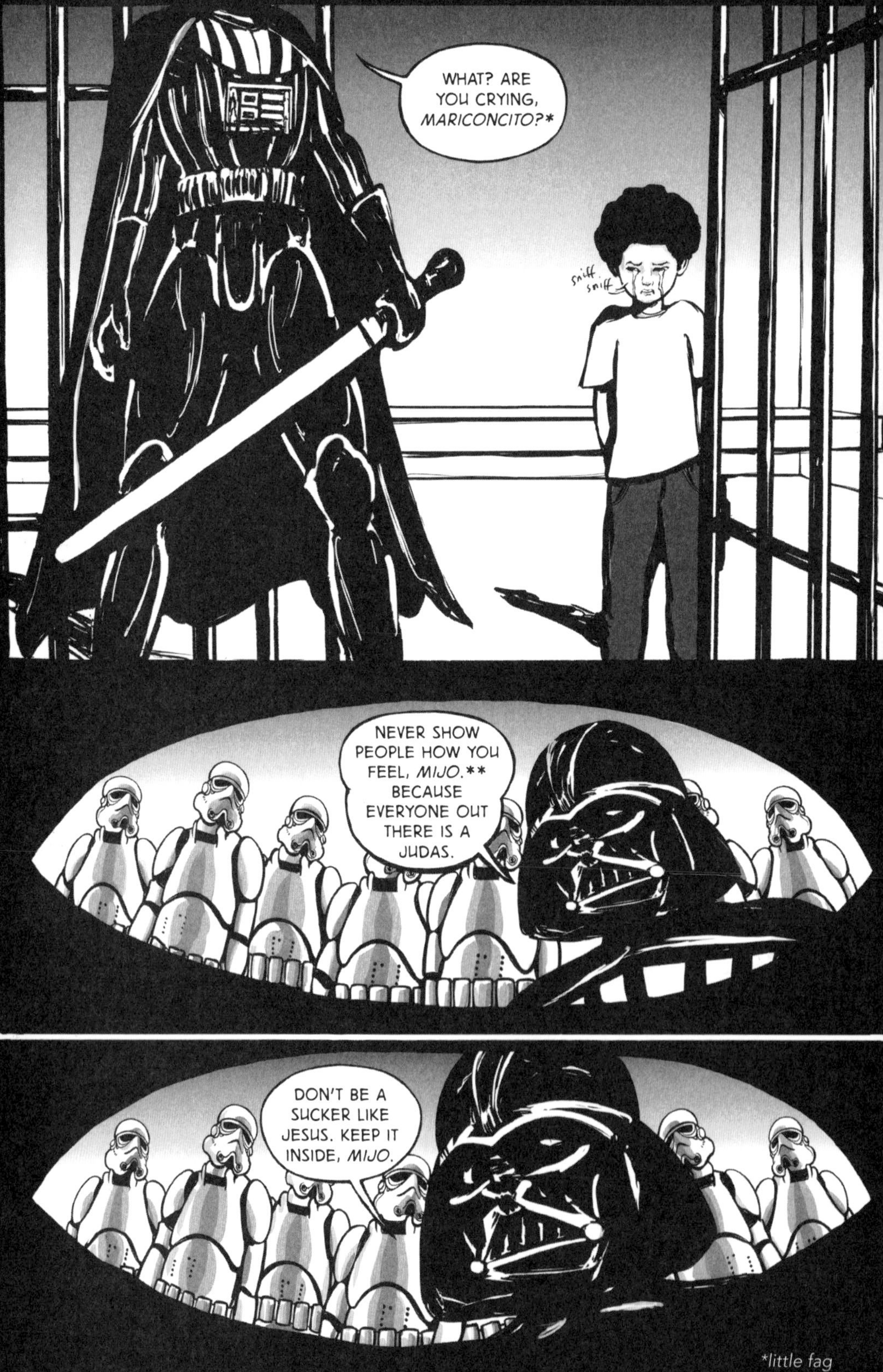
WHAT? ARE YOU CRYING, *MARICONCITO?**
sniff sniff
NEVER SHOW PEOPLE HOW YOU FEEL, *MIJO*.** BECAUSE EVERYONE OUT THERE IS A JUDAS.
DON'T BE A SUCKER LIKE JESUS. KEEP IT INSIDE, *MIJO*.

**little fag*
***kiddo*

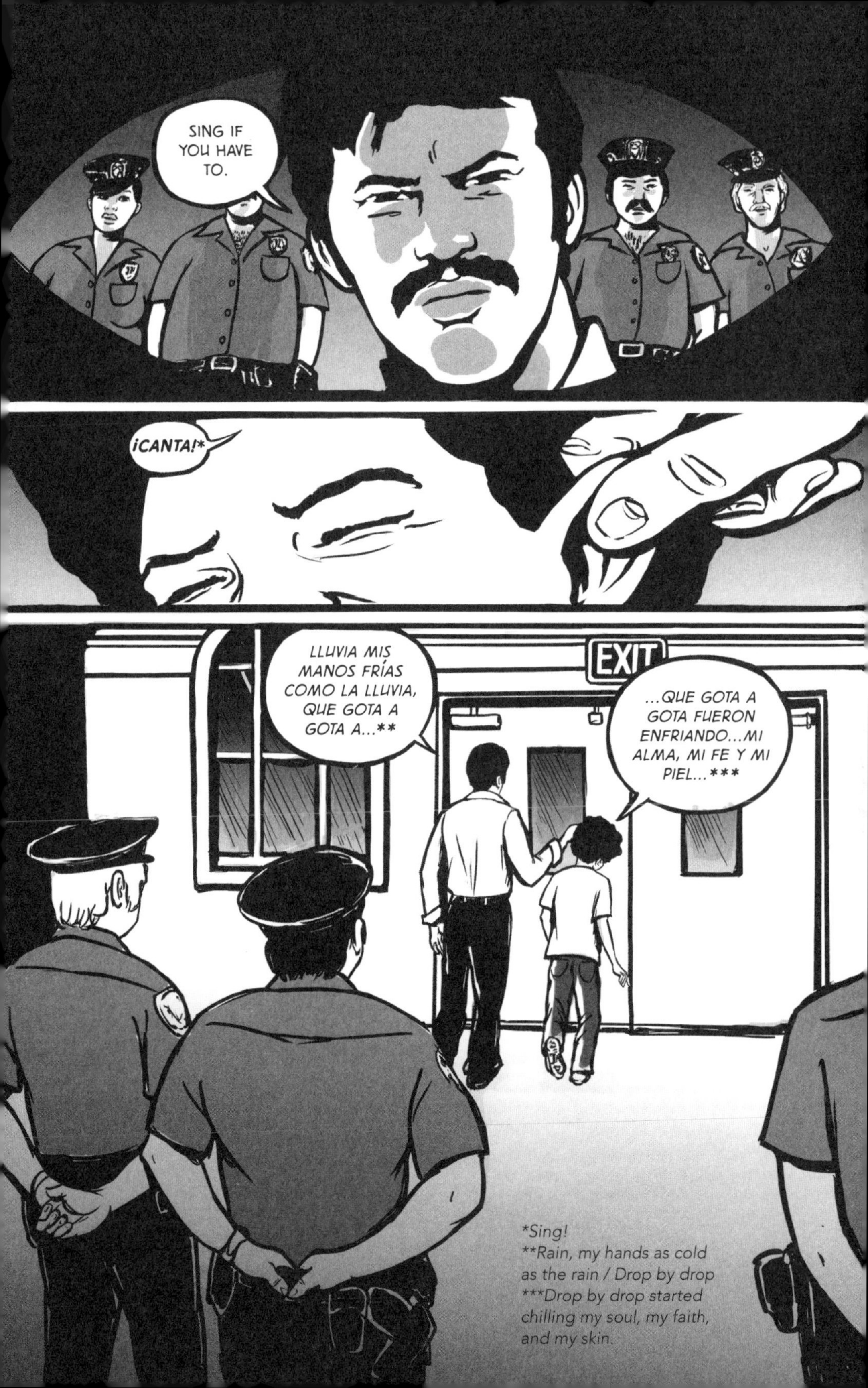
SING IF YOU HAVE TO.
¡CANTA!*
LLUVIA MIS MANOS FRÍAS COMO LA LLUVIA, QUE GOTA A GOTA A...**
EXIT
...QUE GOTA A GOTA FUERON ENFRIANDO...MI ALMA, MI FE Y MI PIEL...***
*Sing!
**Rain, my hands as cold as the rain / Drop by drop
***Drop by drop started chilling my soul, my faith, and my skin.

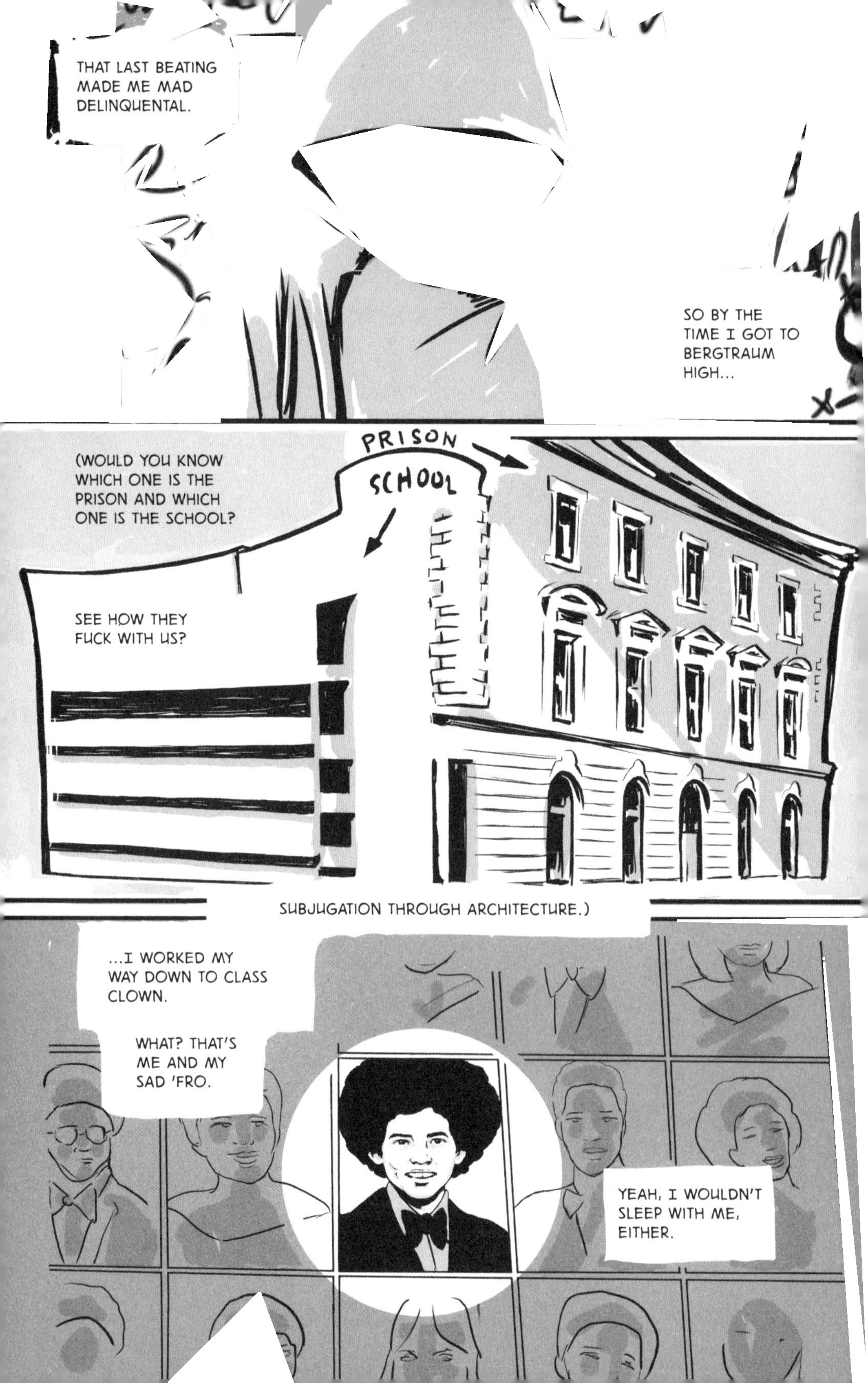
THAT LAST BEATING MADE ME MAD DELINQUENTAL.
SO BY THE TIME I GOT TO BERGTRAUM HIGH...
PRISON
SCHOOL
(WOULD YOU KNOW WHICH ONE IS THE PRISON AND WHICH ONE IS THE SCHOOL?
SEE HOW THEY FUCK WITH US?
SUBJUGATION THROUGH ARCHITECTURE.)
...I WORKED MY WAY DOWN TO CLASS CLOWN.
WHAT? THAT'S ME AND MY SAD 'FRO.
YEAH, I WOULDN'T SLEEP WITH ME, EITHER.

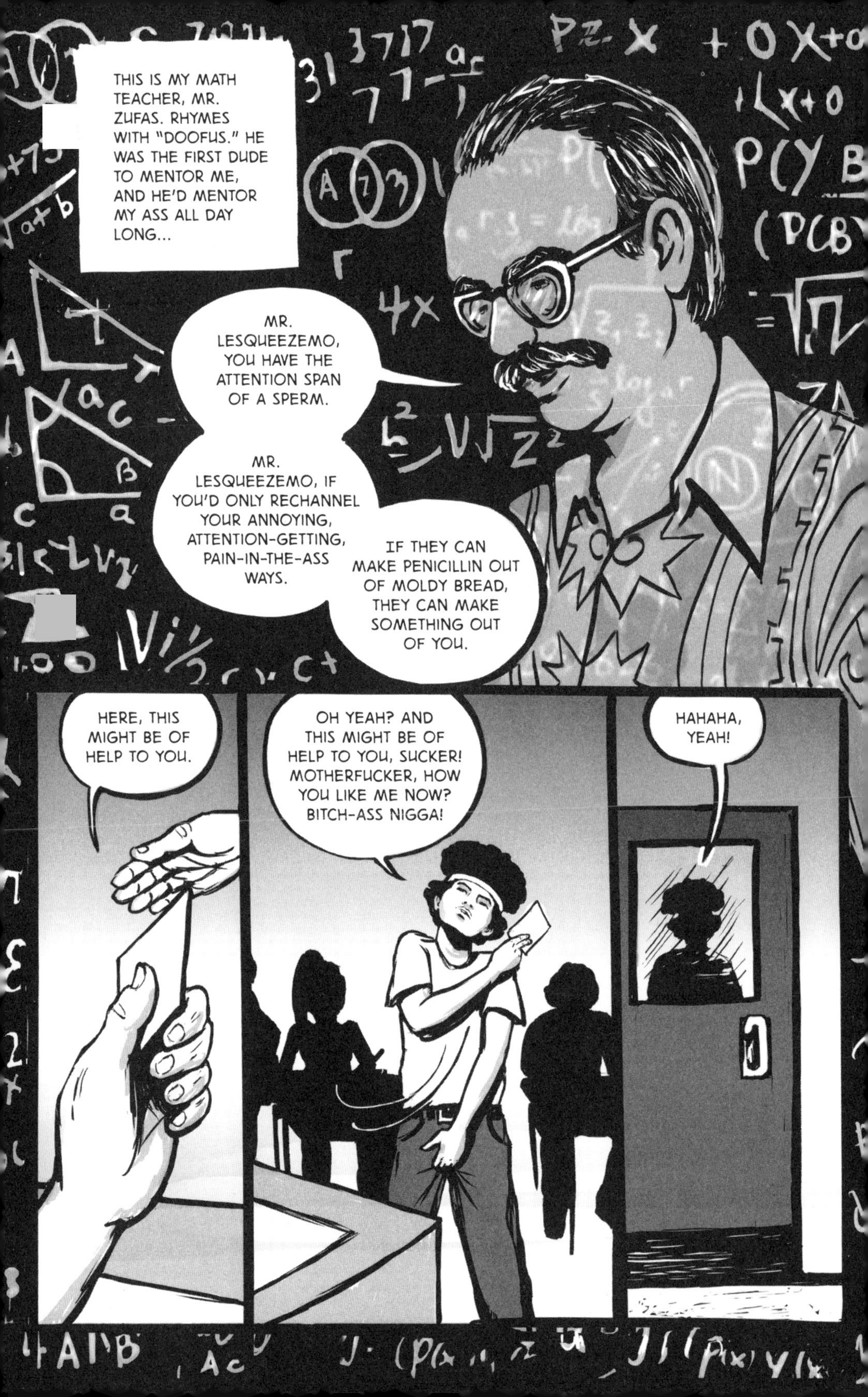
THIS IS MY MATH TEACHER, MR. ZUFAS. RHYMES WITH "DOOFUS." HE WAS THE FIRST DUDE TO MENTOR ME, AND HE'D MENTOR MY ASS ALL DAY LONG...
MR. LESQUEEZEMO, YOU HAVE THE ATTENTION SPAN OF A SPERM.
MR. LESQUEEZEMO, IF YOU'D ONLY RECHANNEL YOUR ANNOYING, ATTENTION-GETTING, PAIN-IN-THE-ASS WAYS.
IF THEY CAN MAKE PENICILLIN OUT OF MOLDY BREAD, THEY CAN MAKE SOMETHING OUT OF YOU.
HERE, THIS MIGHT BE OF HELP TO YOU.
OH YEAH? AND THIS MIGHT BE OF HELP TO YOU, SUCKER! MOTHERFUCKER, HOW YOU LIKE ME NOW? BITCH-ASS NIGGA!
HAHAHA, YEAH!

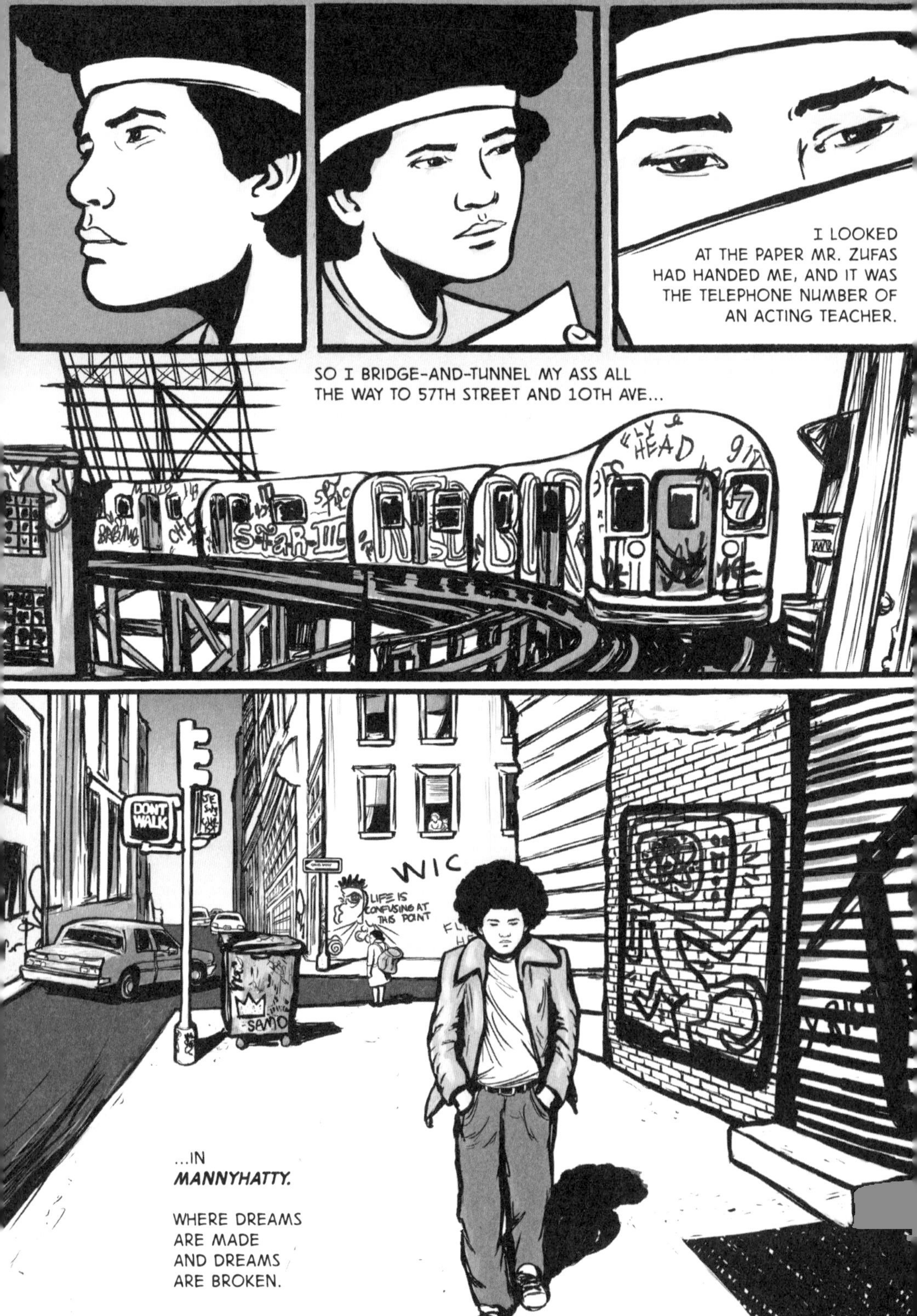
I LOOKED AT THE PAPER MR. ZUFAS HAD HANDED ME, AND IT WAS THE TELEPHONE NUMBER OF AN ACTING TEACHER.
SO I BRIDGE-AND-TUNNEL MY ASS ALL THE WAY TO 57TH STREET AND 10TH AVE...
DONT WALK
WIC
LIFE IS CONFUSING AT THIS POINT
SAMO
...IN *MANNYHATTY.*
WHERE DREAMS ARE MADE AND DREAMS ARE BROKEN.

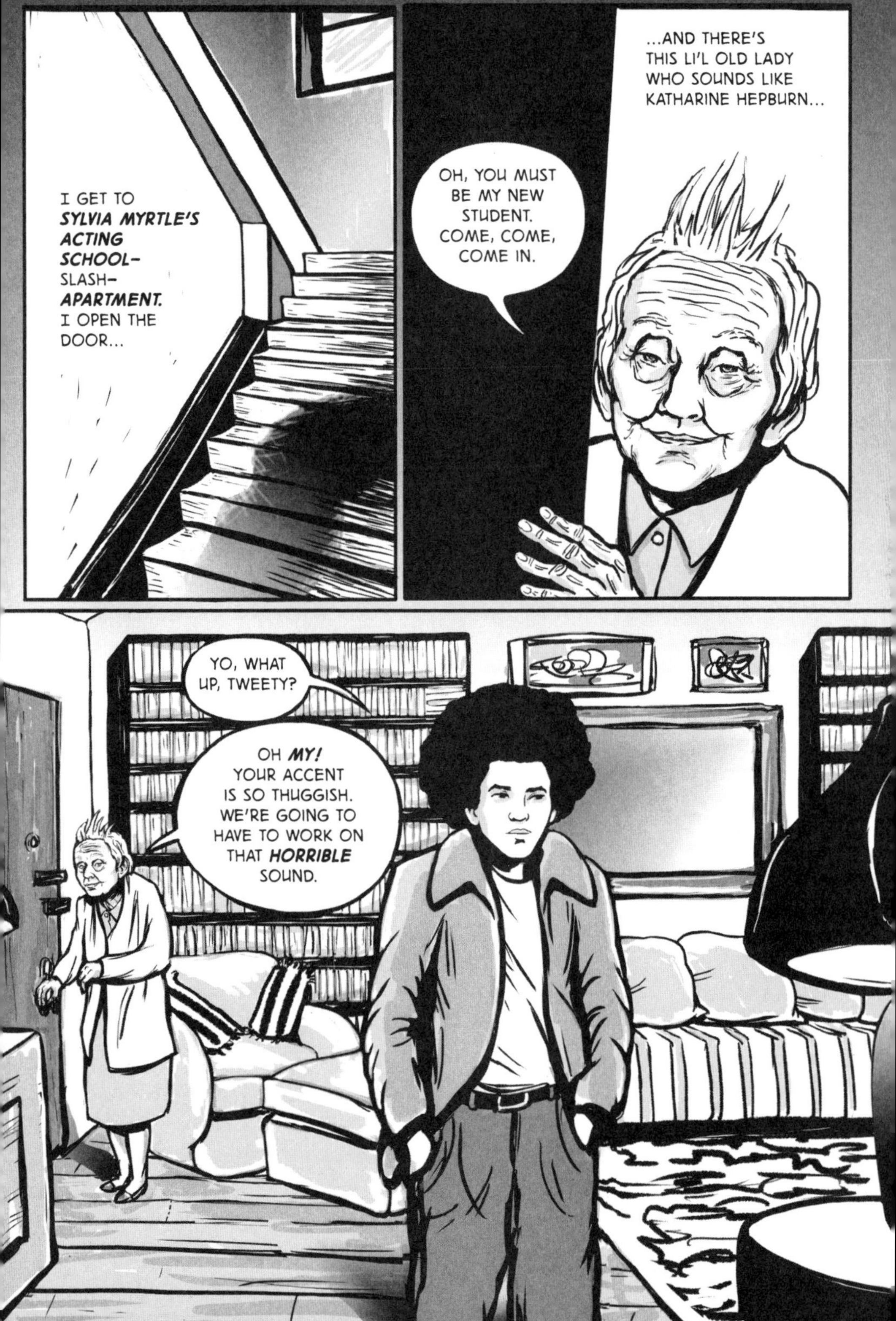
I GET TO SYLVIA MYRTLE'S ACTING SCHOOL-SLASH-APARTMENT. I OPEN THE DOOR...
...AND THERE'S THIS LI'L OLD LADY WHO SOUNDS LIKE KATHARINE HEPBURN...
OH, YOU MUST BE MY NEW STUDENT. COME, COME, COME IN.
YO, WHAT UP, TWEETY?
OH MY! YOUR ACCENT IS SO THUGGISH. WE'RE GOING TO HAVE TO WORK ON THAT HORRIBLE SOUND.

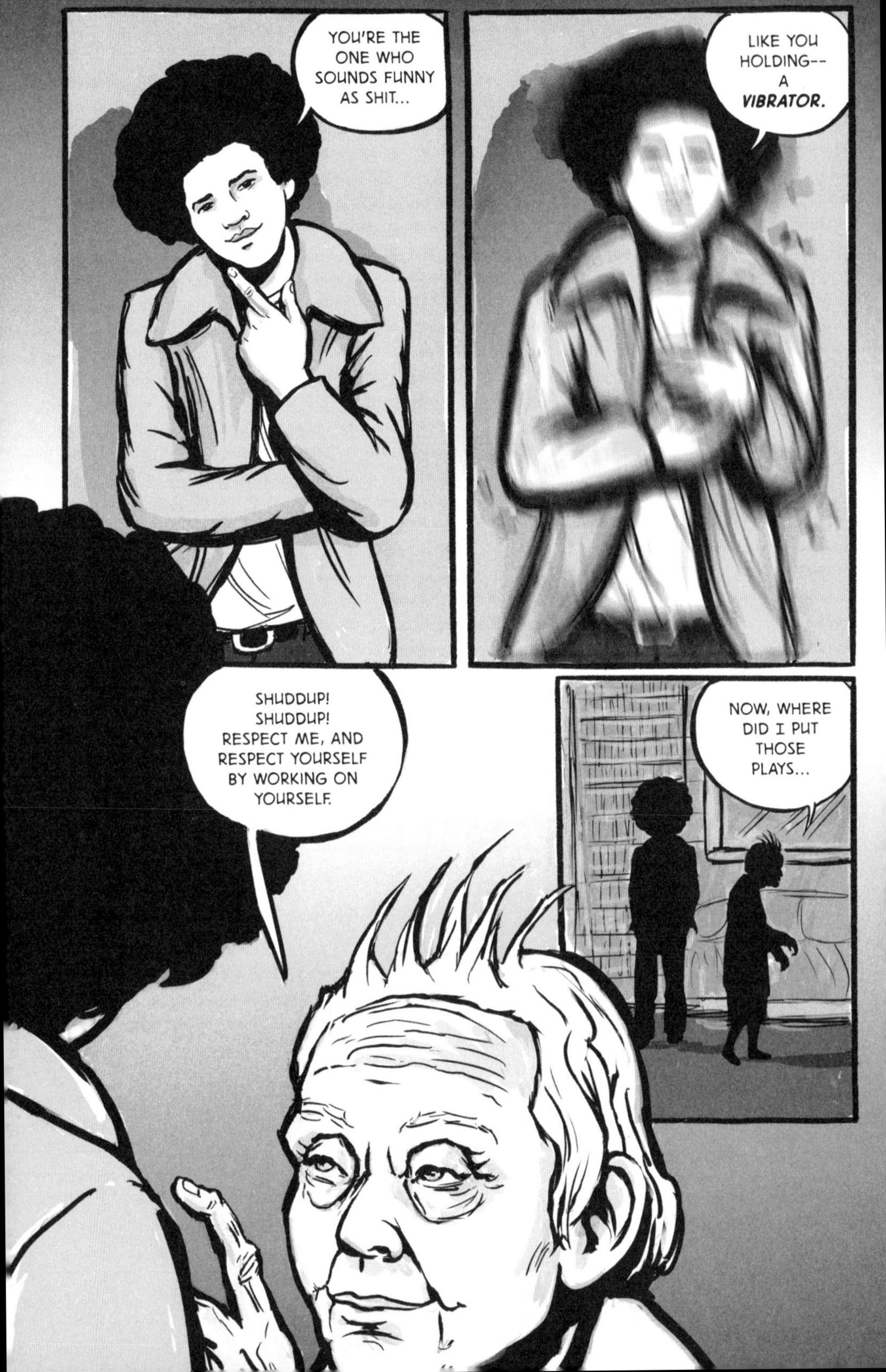
YOU'RE THE ONE WHO SOUNDS FUNNY AS SHIT...
LIKE YOU HOLDING-- A VIBRATOR.
SHUDDUP! SHUDDUP! RESPECT ME, AND RESPECT YOURSELF BY WORKING ON YOURSELF.
NOW, WHERE DID I PUT THOSE PLAYS...

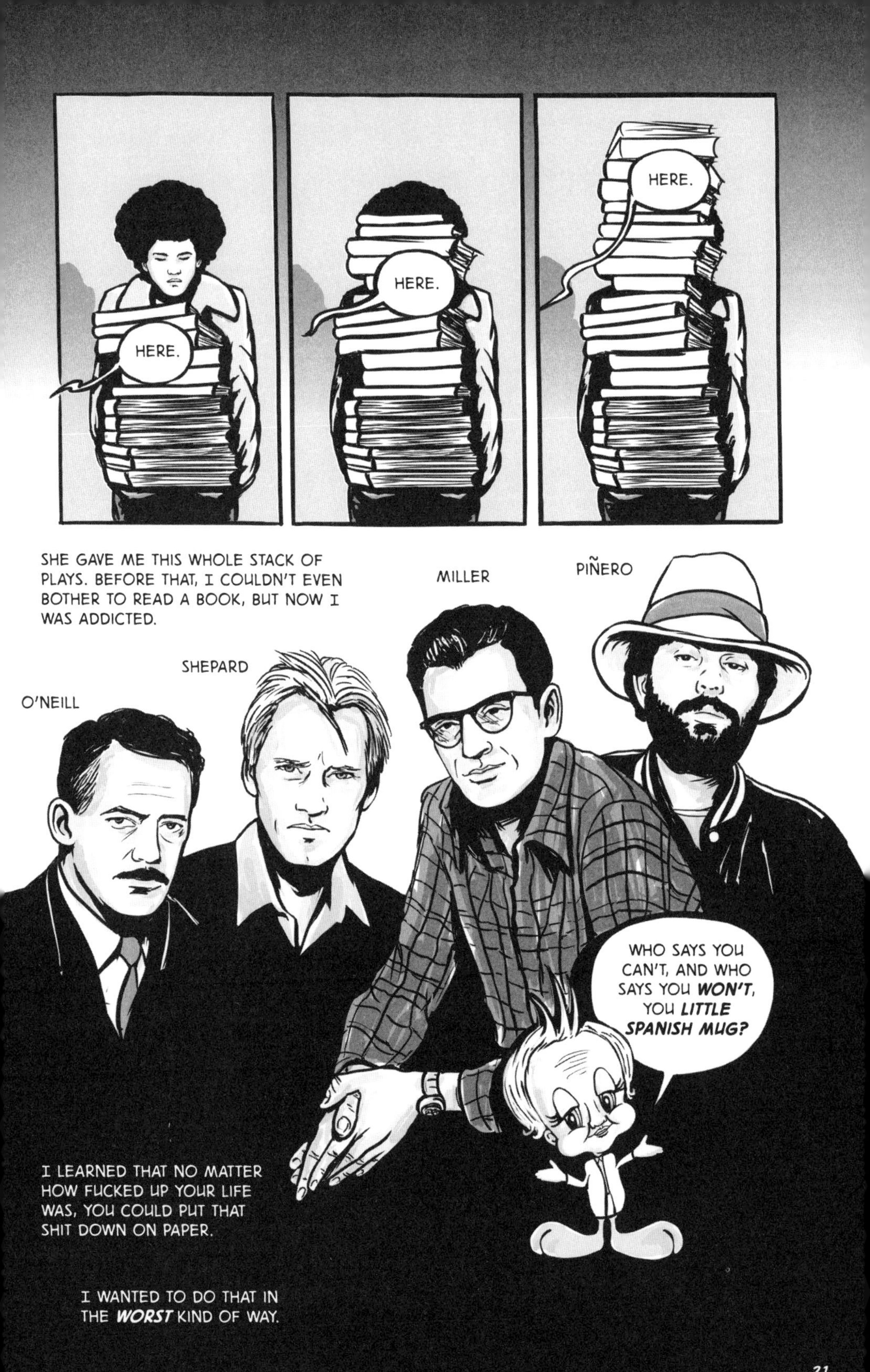
HERE.
HERE.
HERE.
SHE GAVE ME THIS WHOLE STACK OF PLAYS. BEFORE THAT, I COULDN'T EVEN BOTHER TO READ A BOOK, BUT NOW I WAS ADDICTED.
O'NEILL
SHEPARD
MILLER
PIÑERO
WHO SAYS YOU CAN'T, AND WHO SAYS YOU ***WON'T***, YOU ***LITTLE SPANISH MUG?***
I LEARNED THAT NO MATTER HOW FUCKED UP YOUR LIFE WAS, YOU COULD PUT THAT SHIT DOWN ON PAPER.
I WANTED TO DO THAT IN THE ***WORST*** KIND OF WAY.

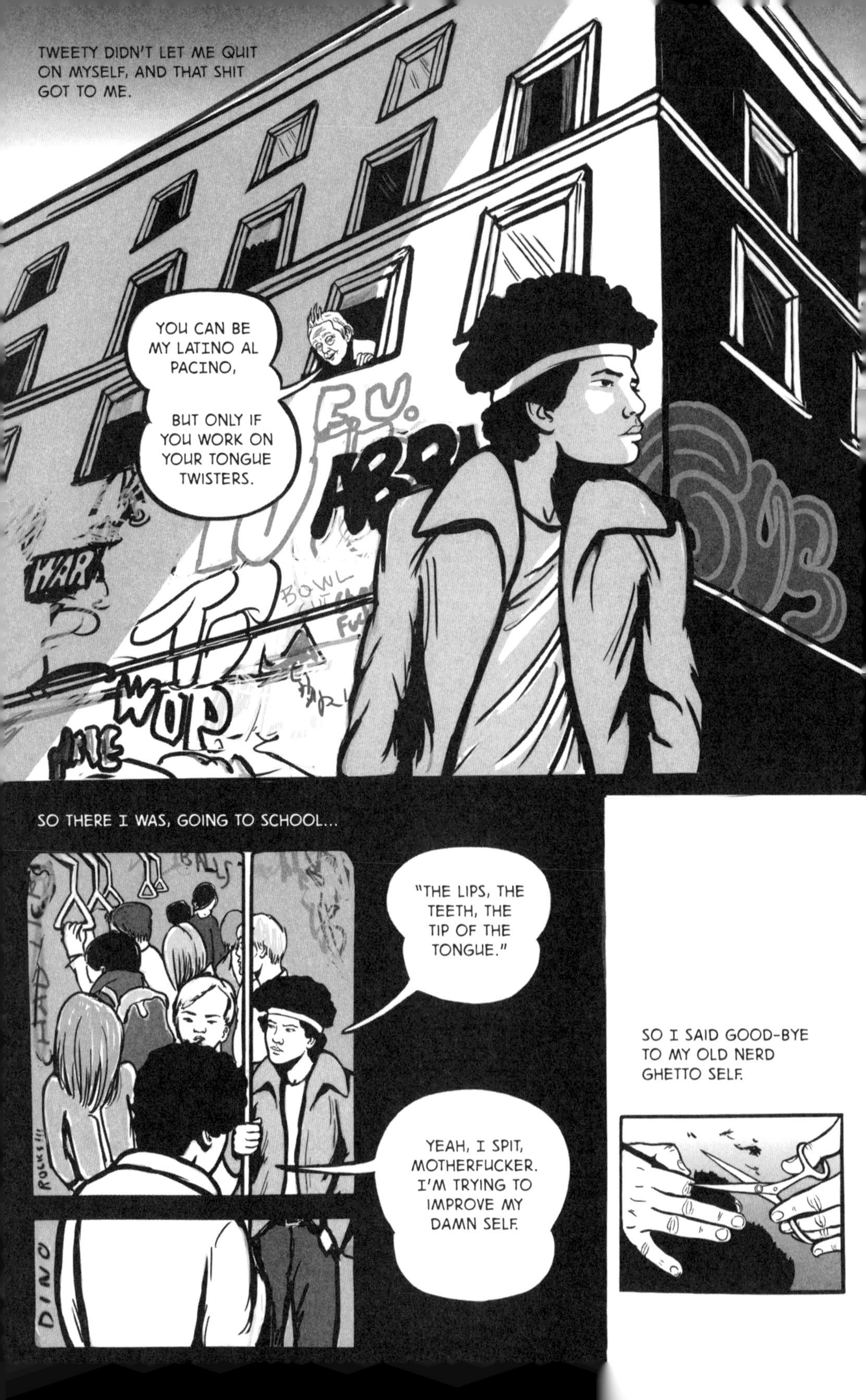
TWEETY DIDN'T LET ME QUIT ON MYSELF, AND THAT SHIT GOT TO ME.
YOU CAN BE MY LATINO AL PACINO,
BUT ONLY IF YOU WORK ON YOUR TONGUE TWISTERS.
SO THERE I WAS, GOING TO SCHOOL...
"THE LIPS, THE TEETH, THE TIP OF THE TONGUE."
YEAH, I SPIT, MOTHERFUCKER. I'M TRYING TO IMPROVE MY DAMN SELF.
SO I SAID GOOD-BYE TO MY OLD NERD GHETTO SELF.

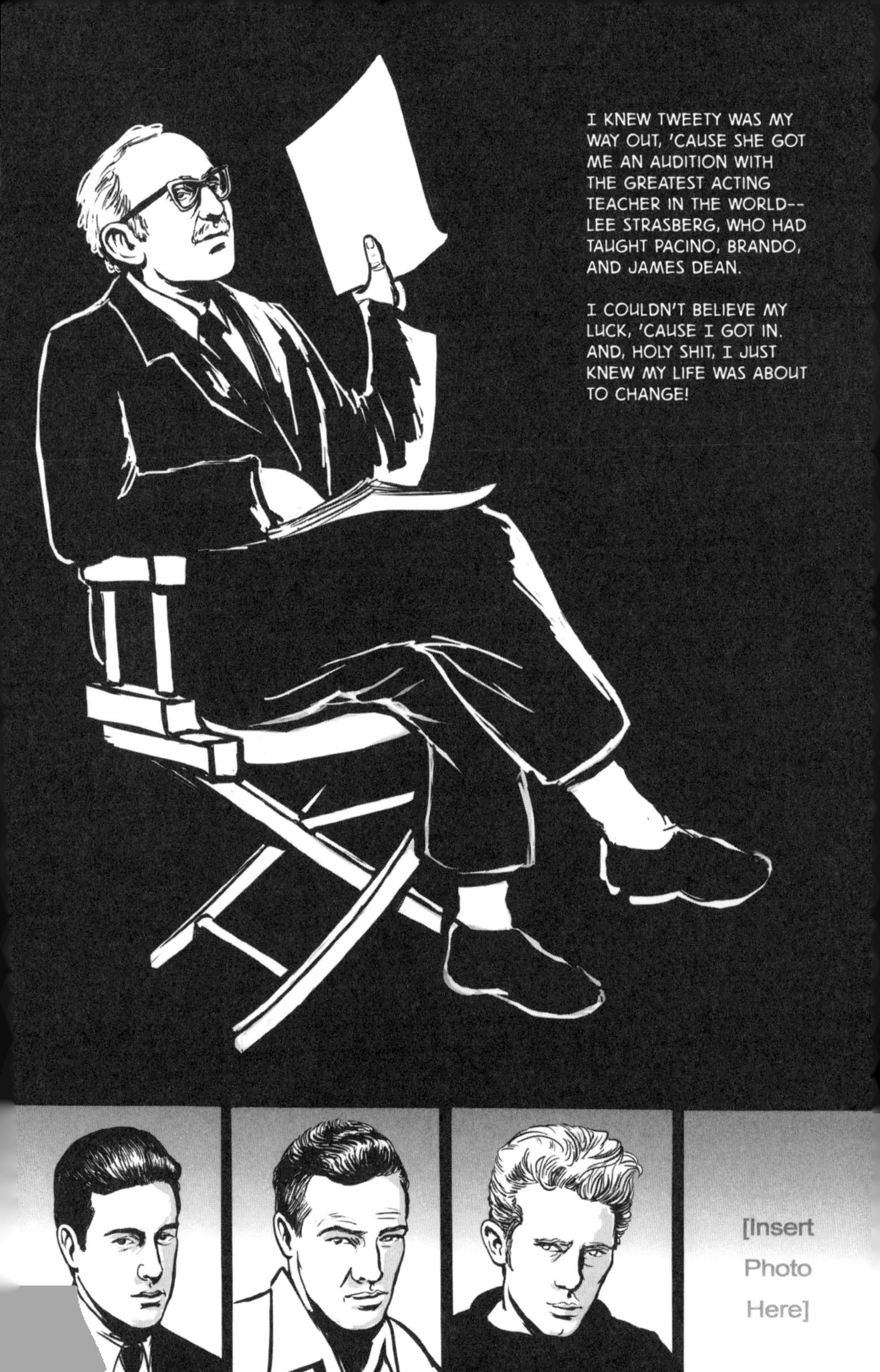
I KNEW TWEETY WAS MY WAY OUT, 'CAUSE SHE GOT ME AN AUDITION WITH THE GREATEST ACTING TEACHER IN THE WORLD-- LEE STRASBERG, WHO HAD TAUGHT PACINO, BRANDO, AND JAMES DEAN.
I COULDN'T BELIEVE MY LUCK, 'CAUSE I GOT IN. AND, HOLY SHIT, I JUST KNEW MY LIFE WAS ABOUT TO CHANGE!
[Insert Photo Here]

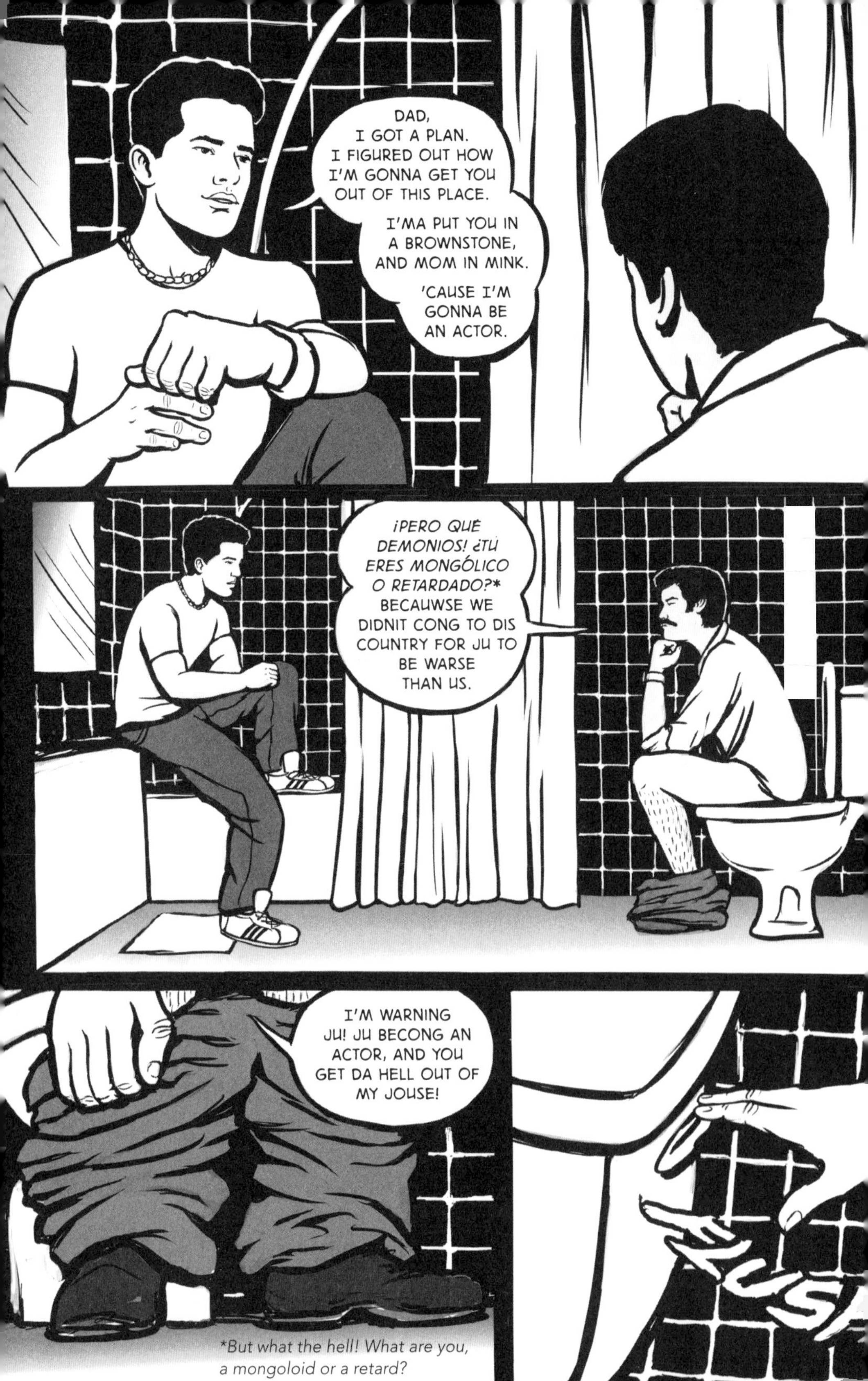
DAD, I GOT A PLAN. I FIGURED OUT HOW I'M GONNA GET YOU OUT OF THIS PLACE.
I'MA PUT YOU IN A BROWNSTONE, AND MOM IN MINK.
'CAUSE I'M GONNA BE AN ACTOR.
¡PERO QUÉ DEMONIOS! ¿TÚ ERES MONGÓLICO O RETARDADO?* BECAUWSE WE DIDNIT CONG TO DIS COUNTRY FOR JU TO BE WARSE THAN US.
I'M WARNING JU! JU BECONG AN ACTOR, AND YOU GET DA HELL OUT OF MY JOUSE!

*But what the hell! What are you, a mongoloid or a retard?

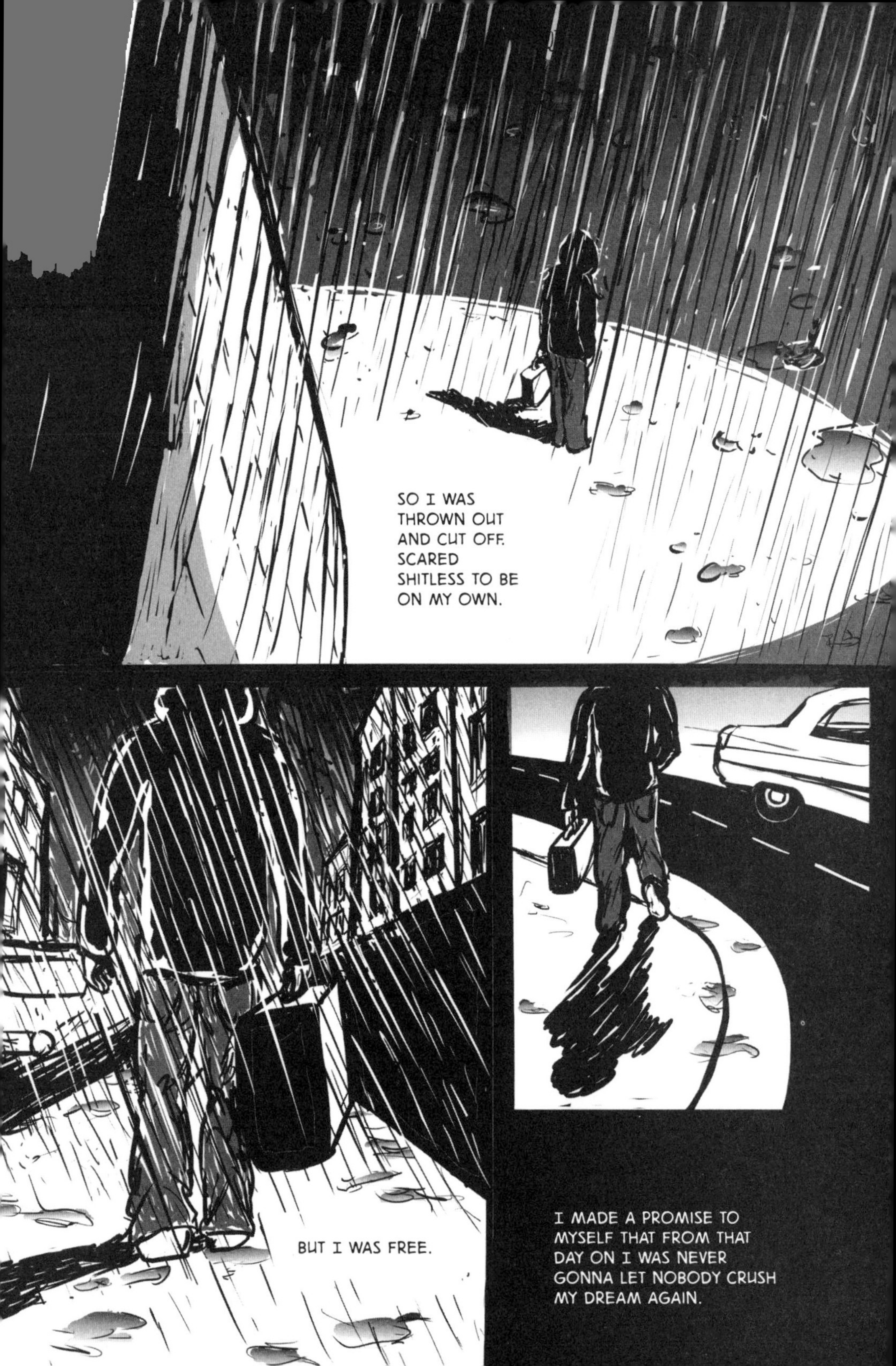
SO I WAS THROWN OUT AND CUT OFF. SCARED SHITLESS TO BE ON MY OWN.
BUT I WAS FREE.
I MADE A PROMISE TO MYSELF THAT FROM THAT DAY ON I WAS NEVER GONNA LET NOBODY CRUSH MY DREAM AGAIN.

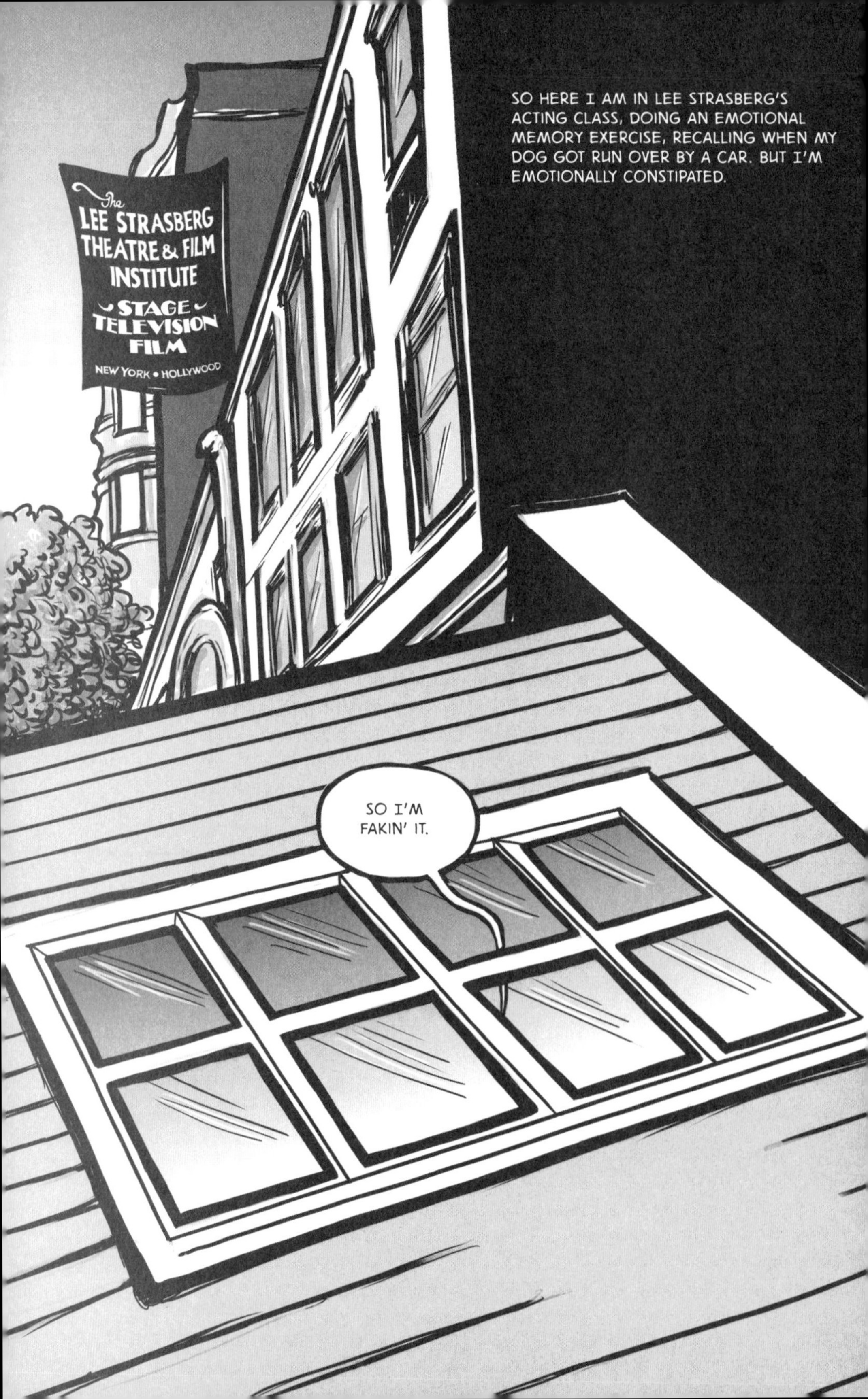
The
LEE STRASBERG
THEATRE & FILM
INSTITUTE
STAGE
TELEVISION
FILM
NEW YORK • HOLLYWOOD
SO HERE I AM IN LEE STRASBERG'S ACTING CLASS, DOING AN EMOTIONAL MEMORY EXERCISE, RECALLING WHEN MY DOG GOT RUN OVER BY A CAR. BUT I'M EMOTIONALLY CONSTIPATED.
SO I'M FAKIN' IT.

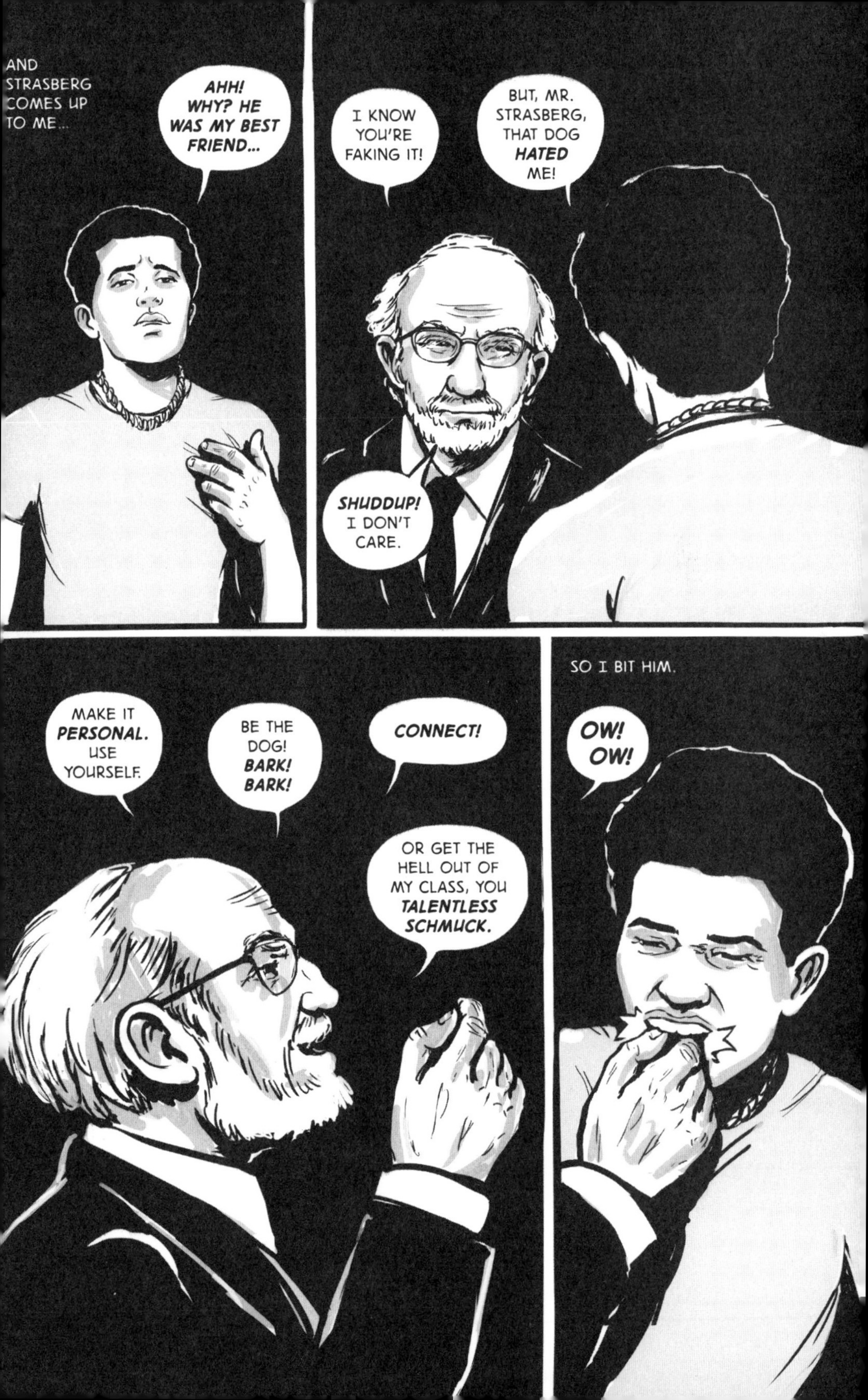
AND STRASBERG COMES UP TO ME...
AHH! WHY? HE WAS MY BEST FRIEND...
I KNOW YOU'RE FAKING IT!
BUT, MR. STRASBERG, THAT DOG HATED ME!
SHUDDUP! I DON'T CARE.
MAKE IT PERSONAL. USE YOURSELF.
BE THE DOG! BARK! BARK!
CONNECT!
OR GET THE HELL OUT OF MY CLASS, YOU TALENTLESS SCHMUCK.
SO I BIT HIM.
OW! OW!

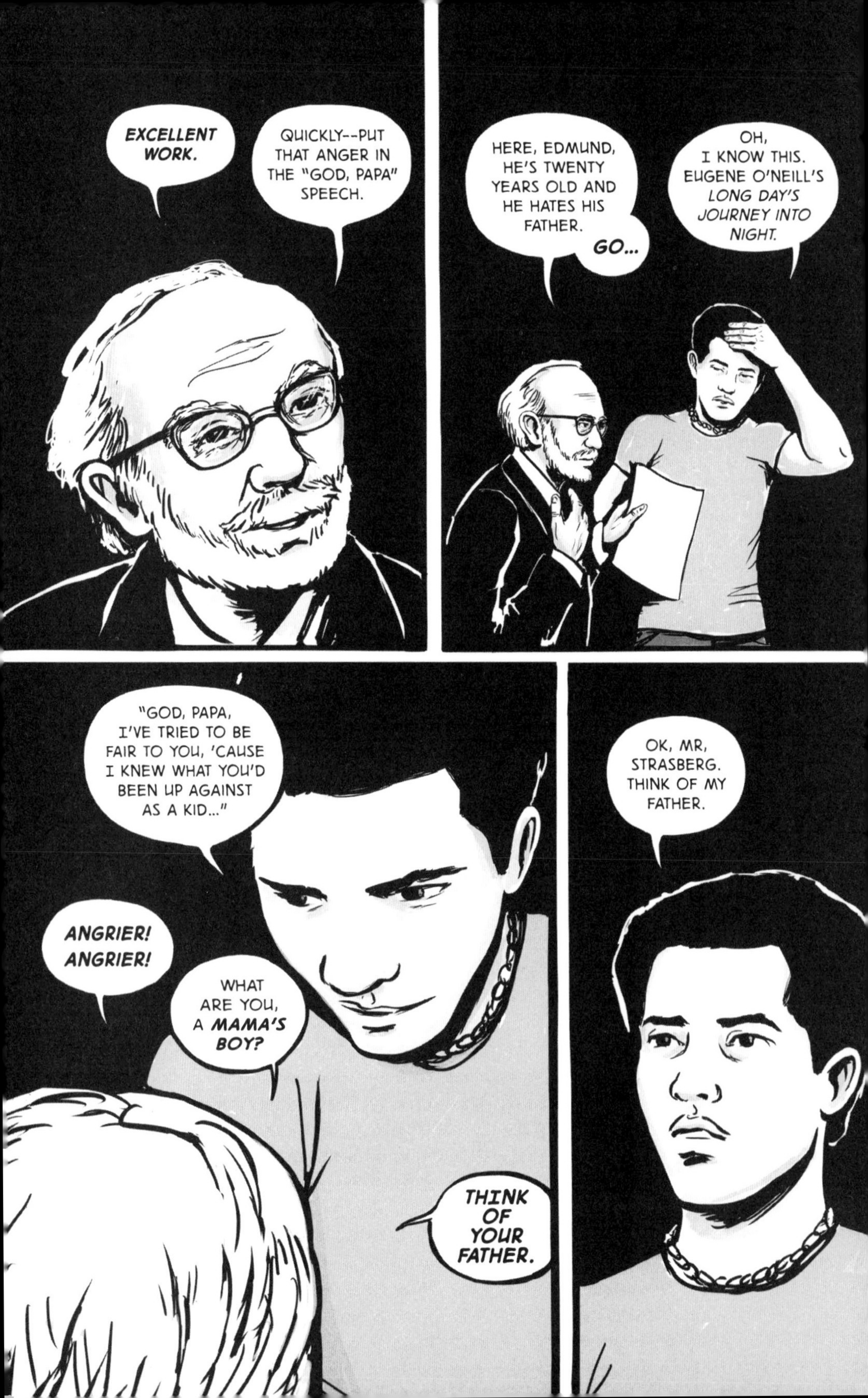
EXCELLENT WORK.
QUICKLY--PUT THAT ANGER IN THE "GOD, PAPA" SPEECH.
HERE, EDMUND, HE'S TWENTY YEARS OLD AND HE HATES HIS FATHER.
GO...
OH, I KNOW THIS. EUGENE O'NEILL'S LONG DAY'S JOURNEY INTO NIGHT.
"GOD, PAPA, I'VE TRIED TO BE FAIR TO YOU, 'CAUSE I KNEW WHAT YOU'D BEEN UP AGAINST AS A KID..."
ANGRIER! ANGRIER!
WHAT ARE YOU, A MAMA'S BOY?
THINK OF YOUR FATHER.
OK, MR. STRASBERG. THINK OF MY FATHER.

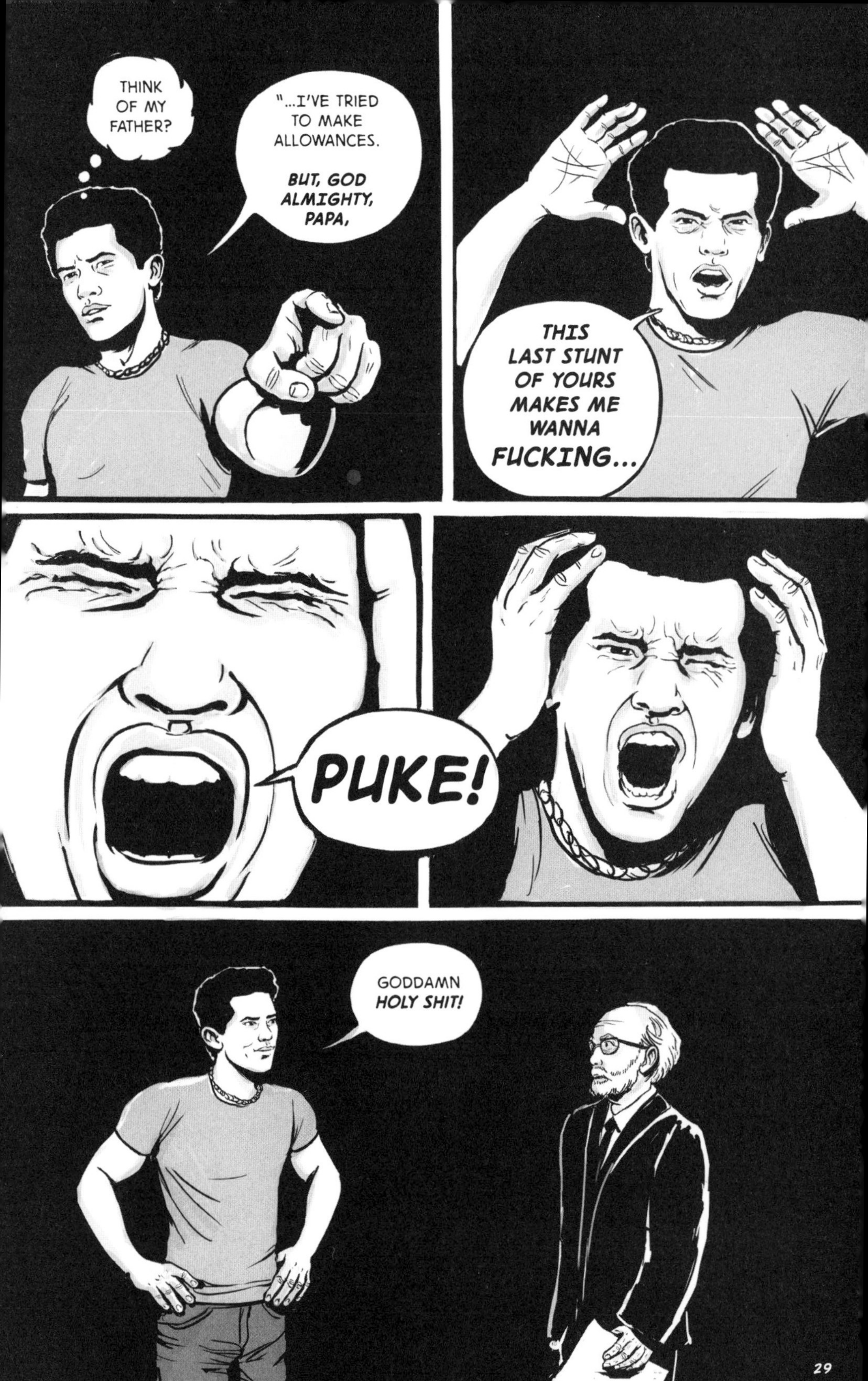
THINK OF MY FATHER?
"...I'VE TRIED TO MAKE ALLOWANCES.
BUT, GOD ALMIGHTY, PAPA,
THIS LAST STUNT OF YOURS MAKES ME WANNA FUCKING...
PUKE!
GODDAMN HOLY SHIT!

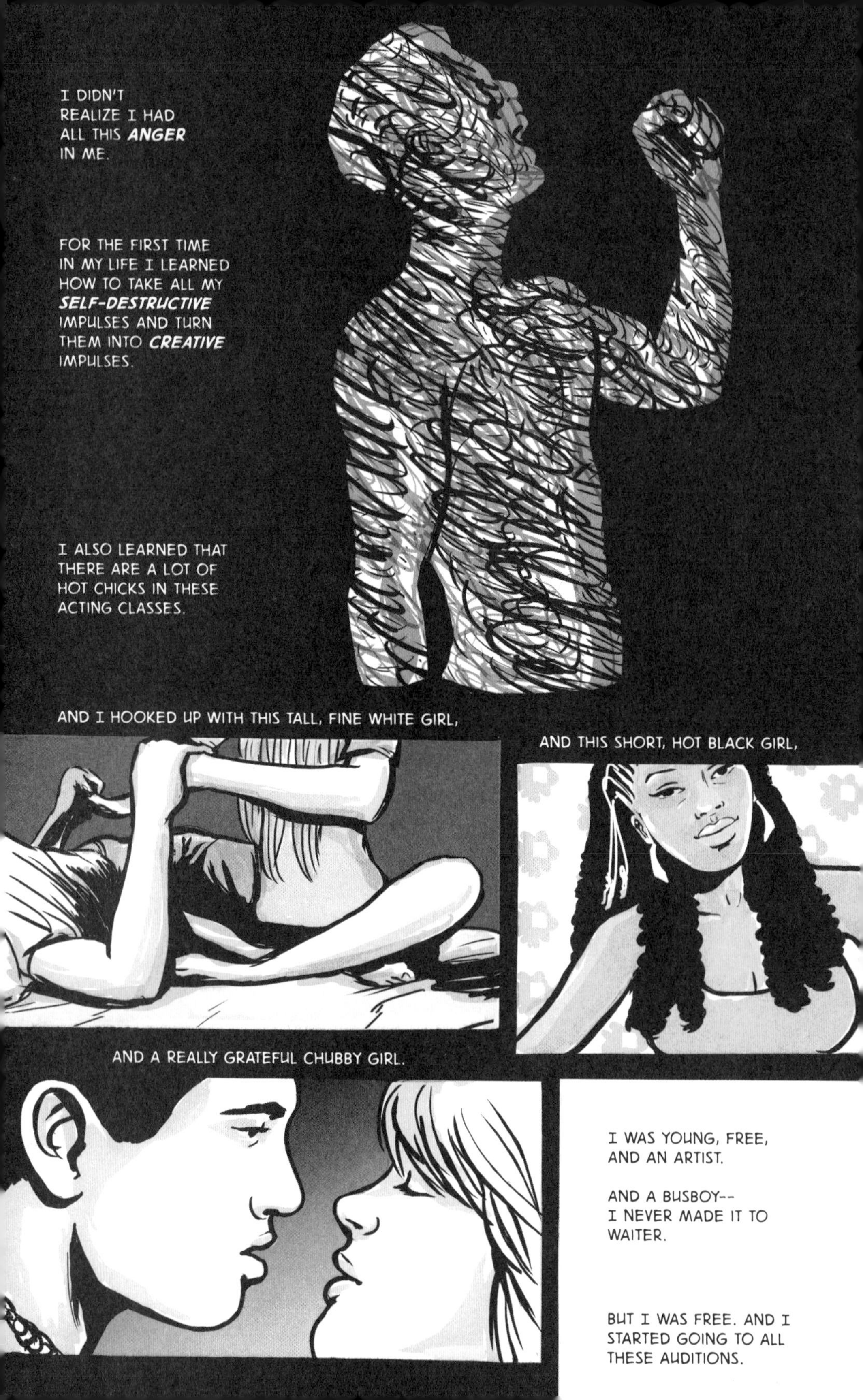
I DIDN'T REALIZE I HAD ALL THIS ANGER IN ME.
FOR THE FIRST TIME IN MY LIFE I LEARNED HOW TO TAKE ALL MY SELF-DESTRUCTIVE IMPULSES AND TURN THEM INTO CREATIVE IMPULSES.
I ALSO LEARNED THAT THERE ARE A LOT OF HOT CHICKS IN THESE ACTING CLASSES.
AND I HOOKED UP WITH THIS TALL, FINE WHITE GIRL,
AND THIS SHORT, HOT BLACK GIRL,
AND A REALLY GRATEFUL CHUBBY GIRL.
I WAS YOUNG, FREE, AND AN ARTIST.
AND A BUSBOY-- I NEVER MADE IT TO WAITER.
BUT I WAS FREE. AND I STARTED GOING TO ALL THESE AUDITIONS.

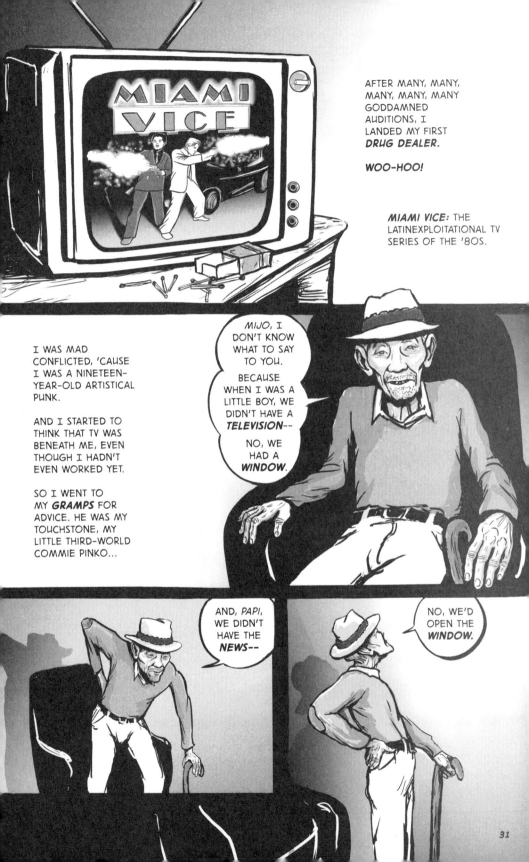

AFTER MANY, MANY, MANY, MANY, MANY GODDAMNED AUDITIONS, I LANDED MY FIRST **DRUG DEALER.**

WOO-HOO!

MIAMI VICE: THE LATINEXPLOITATIONAL TV SERIES OF THE '80S.

I WAS MAD CONFLICTED, 'CAUSE I WAS A NINETEEN-YEAR-OLD ARTISTICAL PUNK.

AND I STARTED TO THINK THAT TV WAS BENEATH ME, EVEN THOUGH I HADN'T EVEN WORKED YET.

SO I WENT TO MY **GRAMPS** FOR ADVICE. HE WAS MY TOUCHSTONE, MY LITTLE THIRD-WORLD COMMIE PINKO...

MIJO, I DON'T KNOW WHAT TO SAY TO YOU.

BECAUSE WHEN I WAS A LITTLE BOY, WE DIDN'T HAVE A *TELEVISION*--

NO, WE HAD A *WINDOW.*

AND, *PAPI,* WE DIDN'T HAVE THE *NEWS*--

NO, WE'D OPEN THE *WINDOW.*

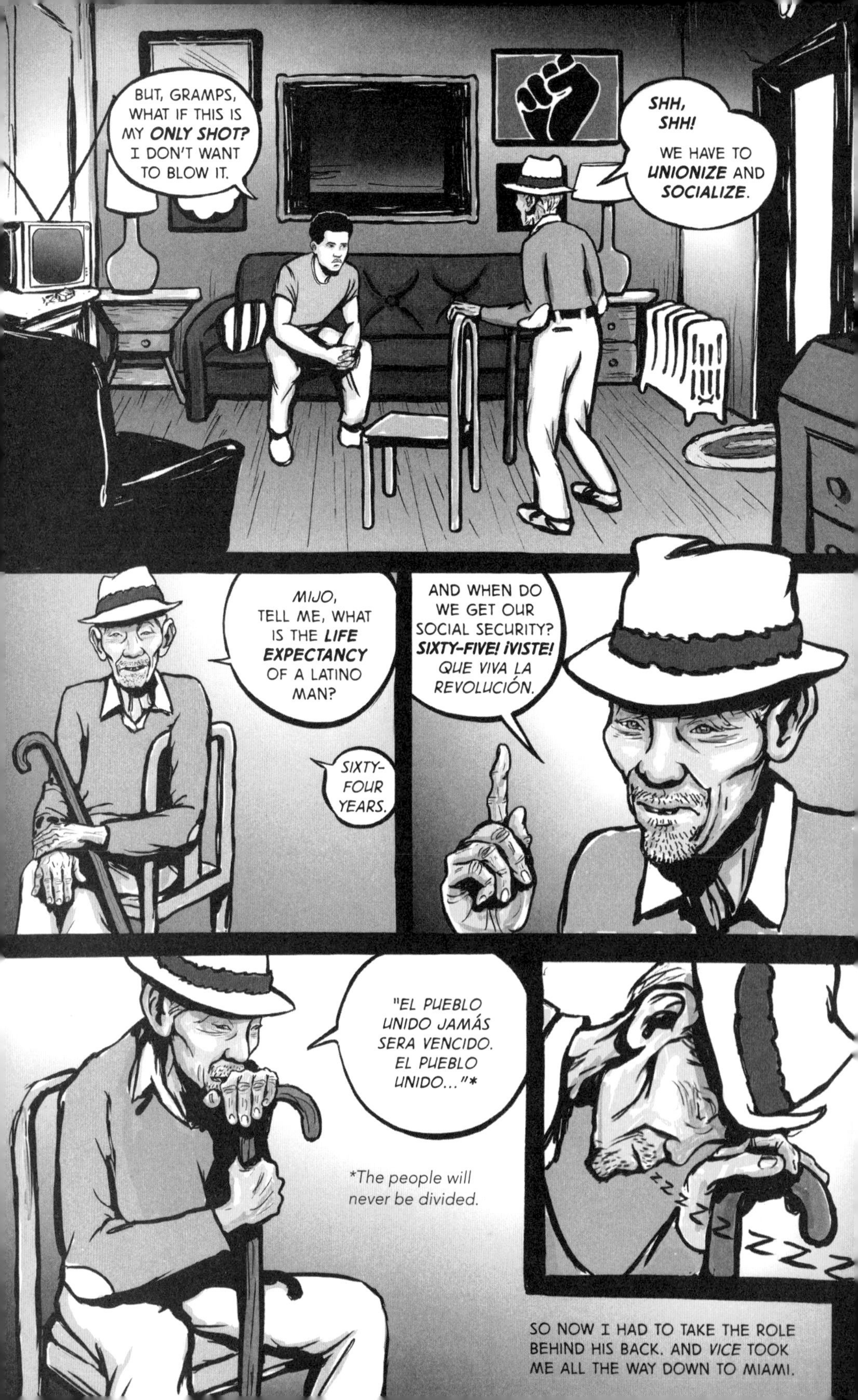
BUT, GRAMPS, WHAT IF THIS IS MY ONLY SHOT? I DON'T WANT TO BLOW IT.
SHH, SHH!
WE HAVE TO UNIONIZE AND SOCIALIZE.
MIJO, TELL ME, WHAT IS THE LIFE EXPECTANCY OF A LATINO MAN?
SIXTY-FOUR YEARS.
AND WHEN DO WE GET OUR SOCIAL SECURITY? SIXTY-FIVE! ¡VISTE! QUE VIVA LA REVOLUCIÓN.
"EL PUEBLO UNIDO JAMÁS SERA VENCIDO. EL PUEBLO UNIDO..."*
*The people will never be divided.
ZZZ
SO NOW I HAD TO TAKE THE ROLE BEHIND HIS BACK. AND VICE TOOK ME ALL THE WAY DOWN TO MIAMI.

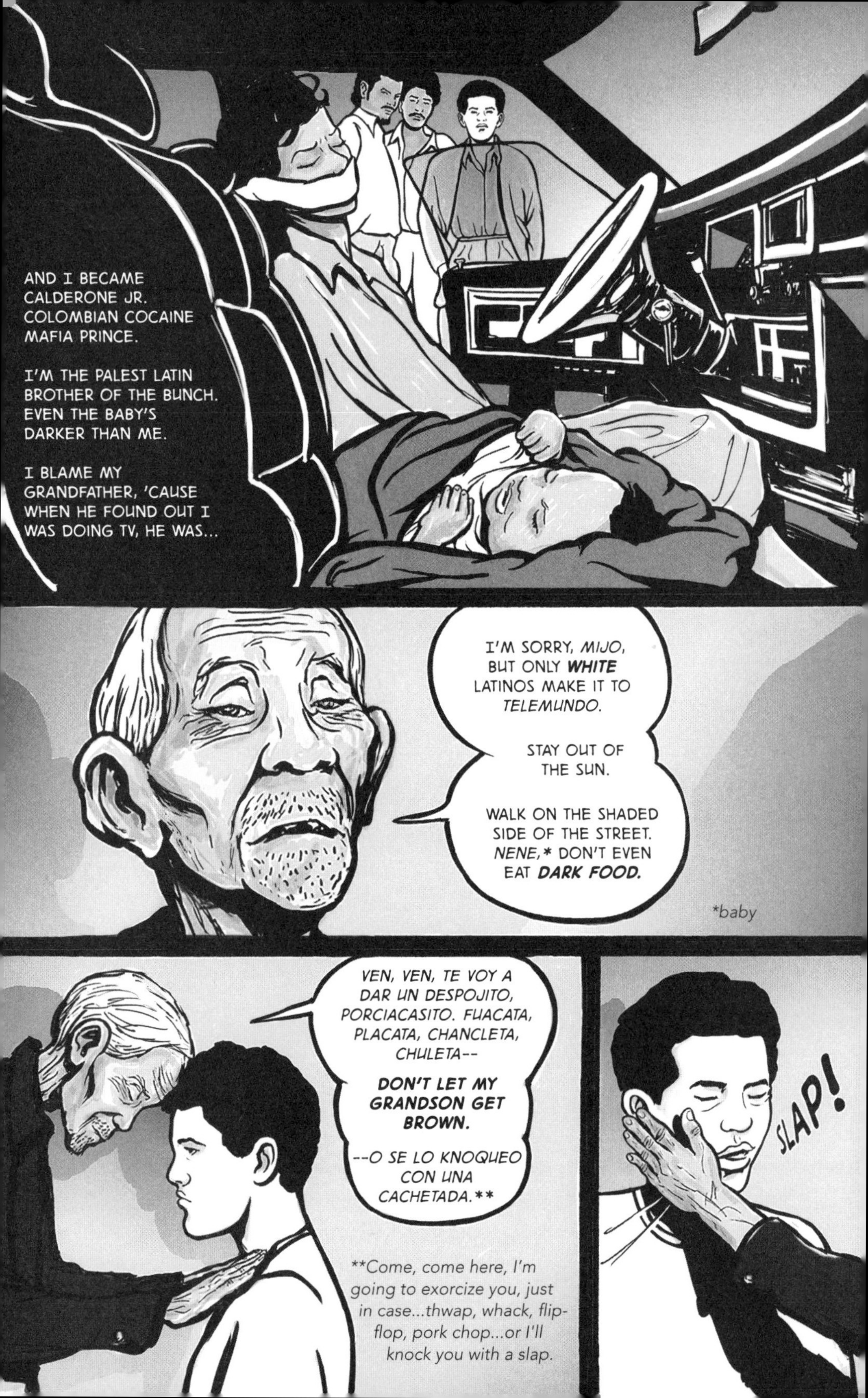
AND I BECAME CALDERONE JR. COLOMBIAN COCAINE MAFIA PRINCE.
I'M THE PALEST LATIN BROTHER OF THE BUNCH. EVEN THE BABY'S DARKER THAN ME.
I BLAME MY GRANDFATHER, 'CAUSE WHEN HE FOUND OUT I WAS DOING TV, HE WAS...
I'M SORRY, *MIJO*, BUT ONLY **WHITE** LATINOS MAKE IT TO *TELEMUNDO*.
STAY OUT OF THE SUN.
WALK ON THE SHADED SIDE OF THE STREET. *NENE,** DON'T EVEN EAT **DARK FOOD.**
*baby
VEN, VEN, TE VOY A DAR UN DESPOJITO, PORCIACASITO. FUACATA, PLACATA, CHANCLETA, CHULETA--
DON'T LET MY GRANDSON GET BROWN.
*--O SE LO KNOQUEO CON UNA CACHETADA.***
**Come, come here, I'm going to exorcize you, just in case...thwap, whack, flip-flop, pork chop...or I'll knock you with a slap.
SLAP!

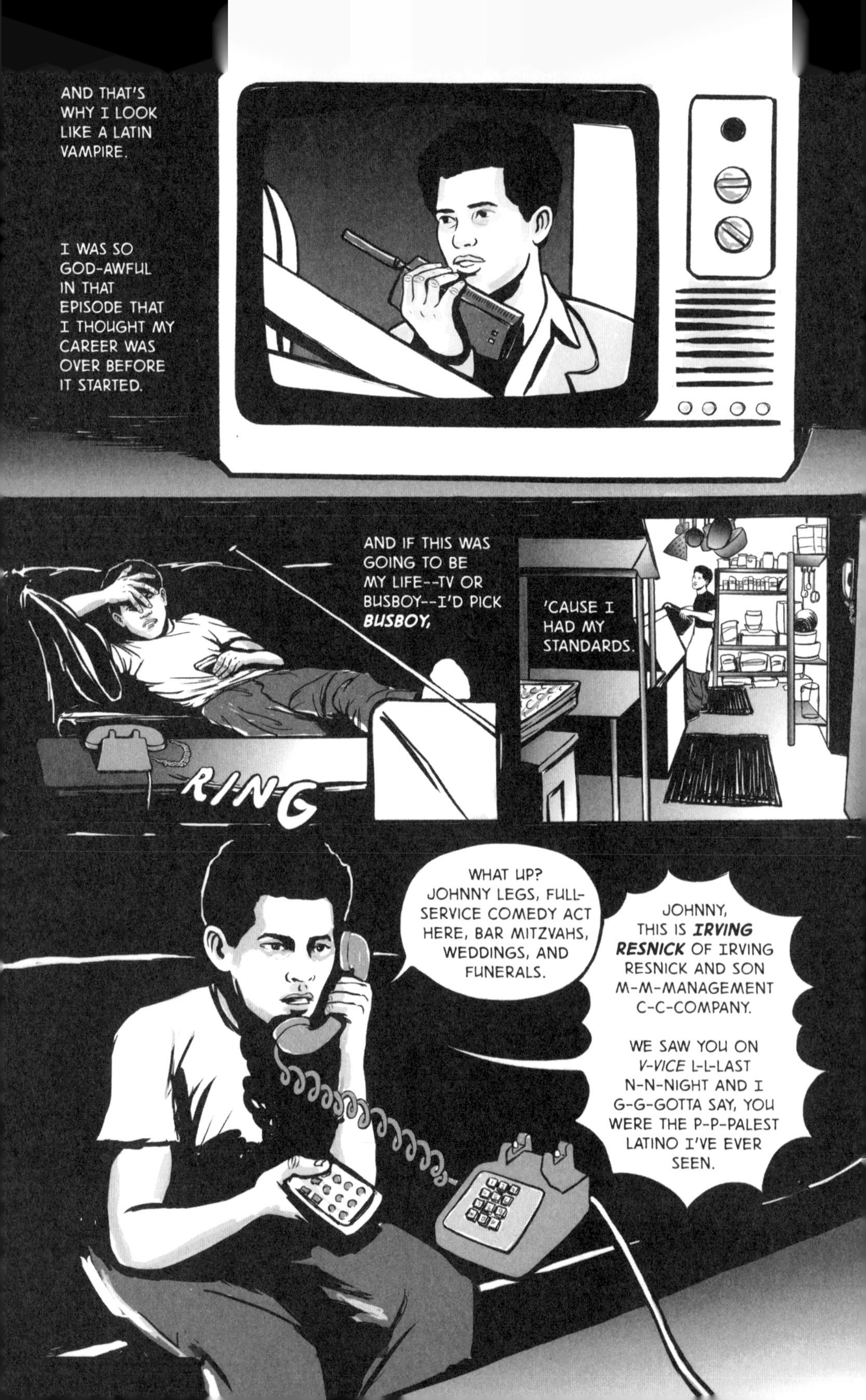
AND THAT'S WHY I LOOK LIKE A LATIN VAMPIRE.
I WAS SO GOD-AWFUL IN THAT EPISODE THAT I THOUGHT MY CAREER WAS OVER BEFORE IT STARTED.
AND IF THIS WAS GOING TO BE MY LIFE--TV OR BUSBOY--I'D PICK ***BUSBOY,***
'CAUSE I HAD MY STANDARDS.
RING
WHAT UP? JOHNNY LEGS, FULL-SERVICE COMEDY ACT HERE, BAR MITZVAHS, WEDDINGS, AND FUNERALS.
JOHNNY, THIS IS ***IRVING RESNICK*** OF IRVING RESNICK AND SON M-M-MANAGEMENT C-C-COMPANY.
WE SAW YOU ON *V-VICE* L-L-LAST N-N-NIGHT AND I G-G-GOTTA SAY, YOU WERE THE P-P-PALEST LATINO I'VE EVER SEEN.

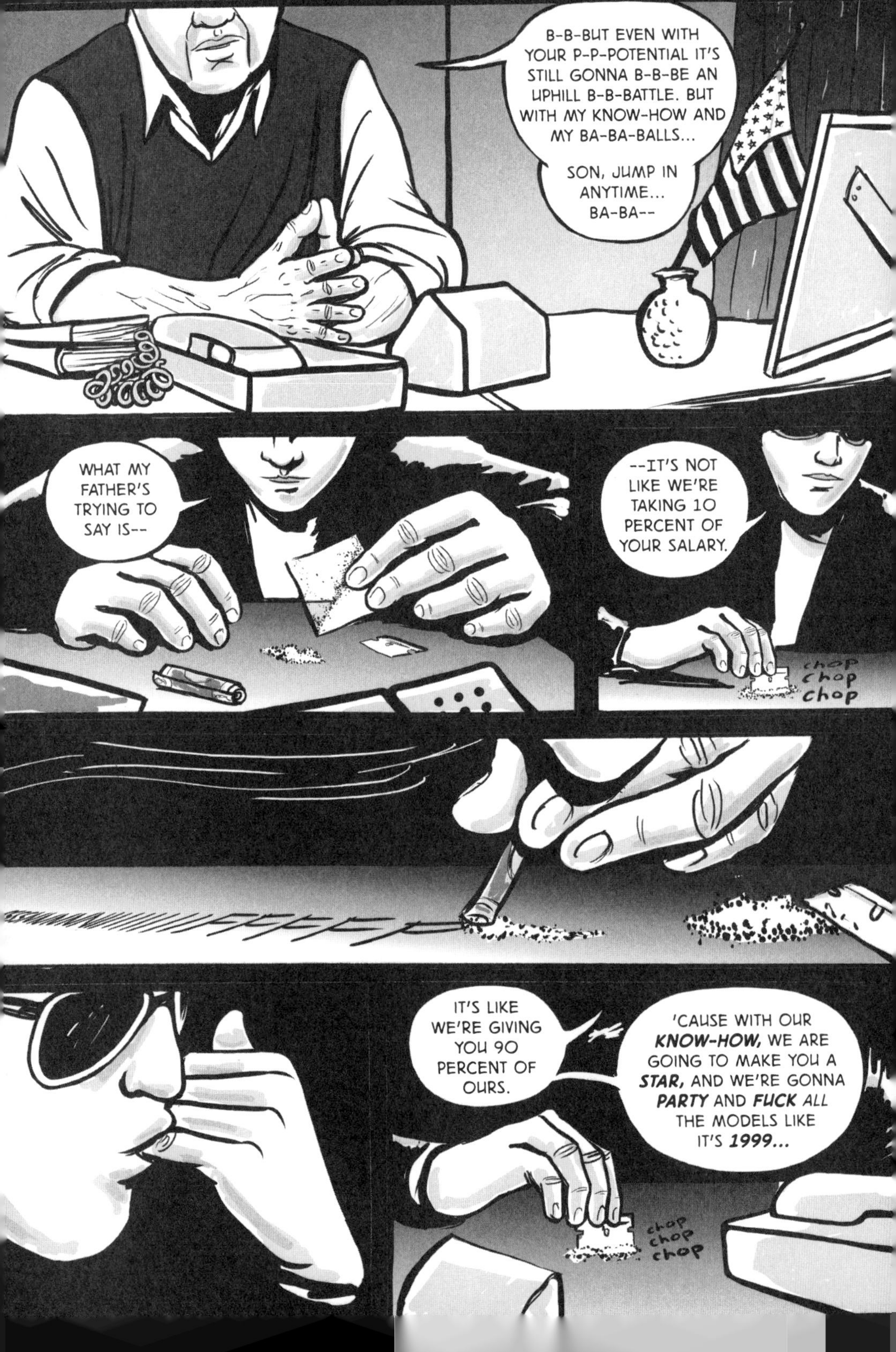
B-B-BUT EVEN WITH YOUR P-P-POTENTIAL IT'S STILL GONNA B-B-BE AN UPHILL B-B-BATTLE. BUT WITH MY KNOW-HOW AND MY BA-BA-BALLS...
SON, JUMP IN ANYTIME... BA-BA--
WHAT MY FATHER'S TRYING TO SAY IS--
--IT'S NOT LIKE WE'RE TAKING 10 PERCENT OF YOUR SALARY.
chop chop chop
SSSNNNNIIIIFFFFFFF
IT'S LIKE WE'RE GIVING YOU 90 PERCENT OF OURS.
'CAUSE WITH OUR **KNOW-HOW,** WE ARE GOING TO MAKE YOU A **STAR,** AND WE'RE GONNA **PARTY** AND **FUCK** *ALL* THE MODELS LIKE IT'S **1999...**
chop chop chop

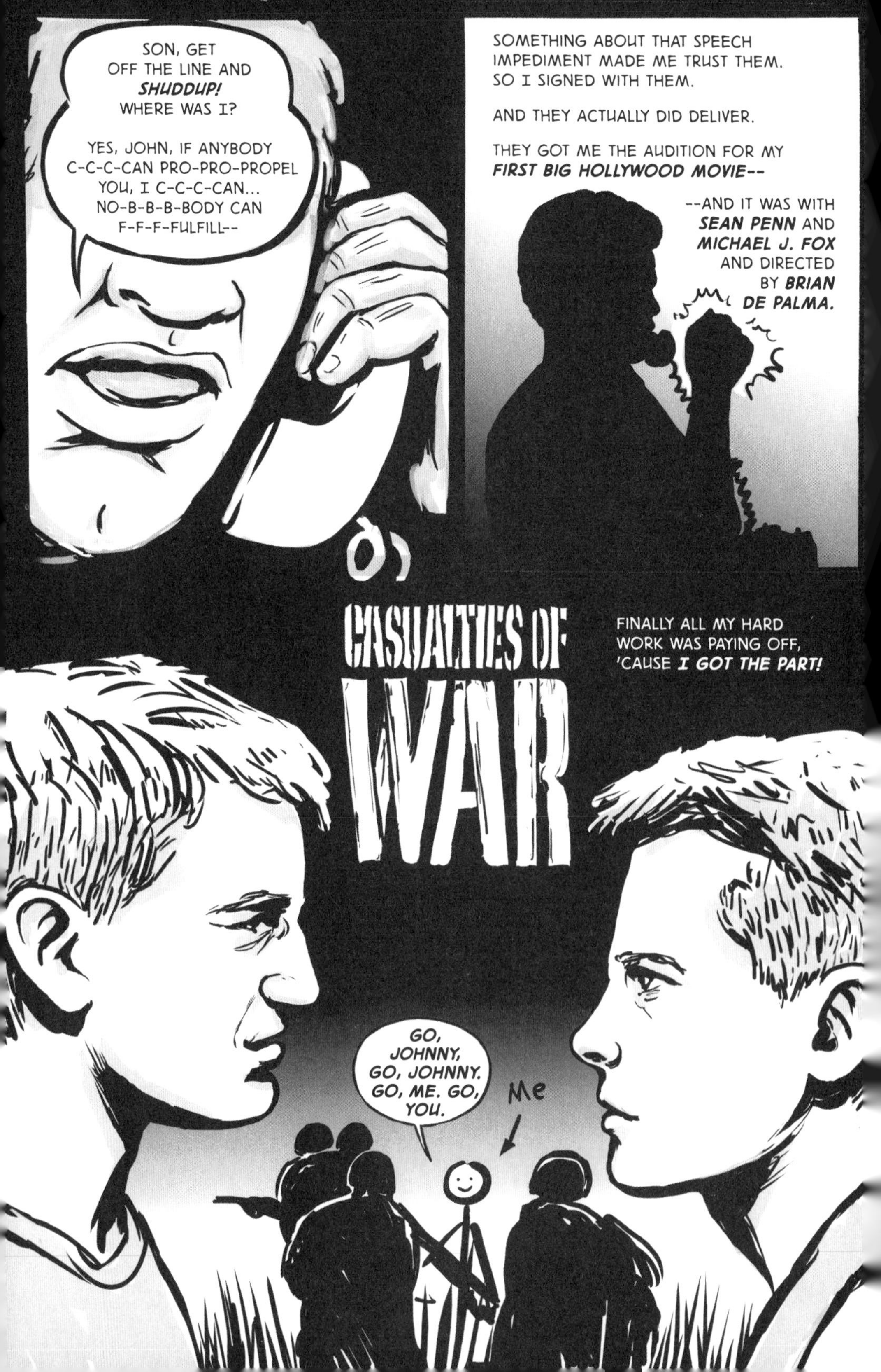
SON, GET OFF THE LINE AND SHUDDUP! WHERE WAS I?
YES, JOHN, IF ANYBODY C-C-C-CAN PRO-PRO-PROPEL YOU, I C-C-C-CAN... NO-B-B-B-BODY CAN F-F-F-FULFILL--
SOMETHING ABOUT THAT SPEECH IMPEDIMENT MADE ME TRUST THEM. SO I SIGNED WITH THEM.
AND THEY ACTUALLY DID DELIVER.
THEY GOT ME THE AUDITION FOR MY FIRST BIG HOLLYWOOD MOVIE--
--AND IT WAS WITH SEAN PENN AND MICHAEL J. FOX AND DIRECTED BY BRIAN DE PALMA.
CASUALTIES OF WAR
FINALLY ALL MY HARD WORK WAS PAYING OFF, 'CAUSE I GOT THE PART!
GO, JOHNNY, GO, JOHNNY. GO, ME. GO, YOU.
Me

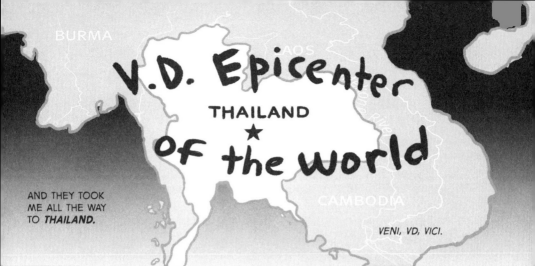

V.D. Epicenter

THAILAND
★

of the world

BURMA

AND THEY TOOK
ME ALL THE WAY
TO **THAILAND.**

VENI, VD, VICI.

CAMBODIA

WHEN I GOT THERE I MADE THE STUPID
MISTAKE OF NOT LISTENING TO MY
GRAMPS, AND I LAID OUT IN THE
SUN, AND I BECAME
A NICE SHADE OF
DOMINICAN...

...AND I
GOT **DEMOTED**
FROM CORPORAL
NASH TO GRUNT
DIAZ,

AND THEY WANTED
ME TO TALK LIKE
CHEECH & CHONG...

ÓRALE,* YOU TELL
ME TO WATCH OUT
FOR **FRIENDLY FIRE?**
THE ONLY FRIENDLY
FIRE I WANT IS
THIS ONE!

*all right

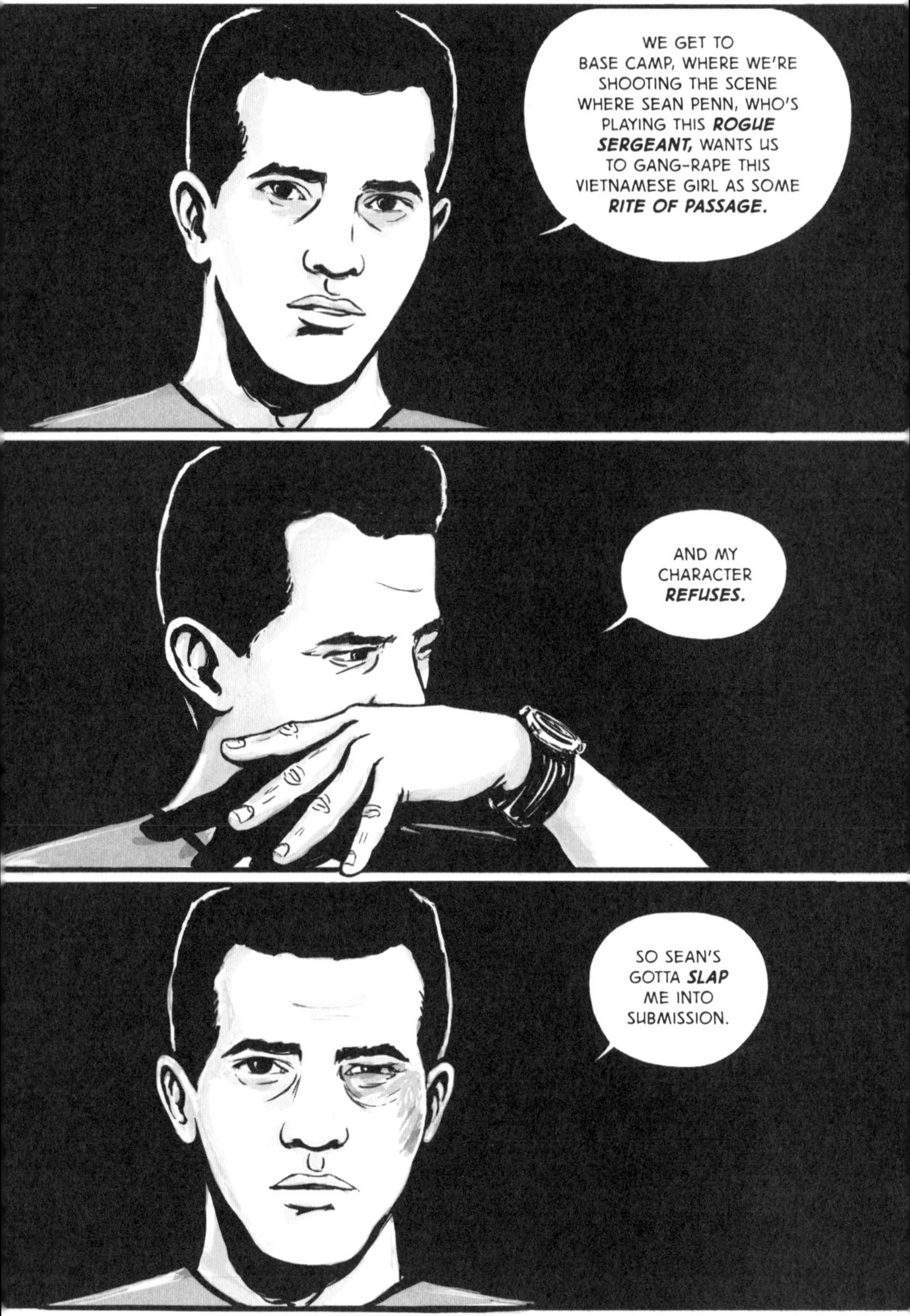
WE GET TO BASE CAMP, WHERE WE'RE SHOOTING THE SCENE WHERE SEAN PENN, WHO'S PLAYING THIS ***ROGUE SERGEANT,*** WANTS US TO GANG-RAPE THIS VIETNAMESE GIRL AS SOME ***RITE OF PASSAGE.***
AND MY CHARACTER ***REFUSES.***
SO SEAN'S GOTTA ***SLAP*** ME INTO SUBMISSION.

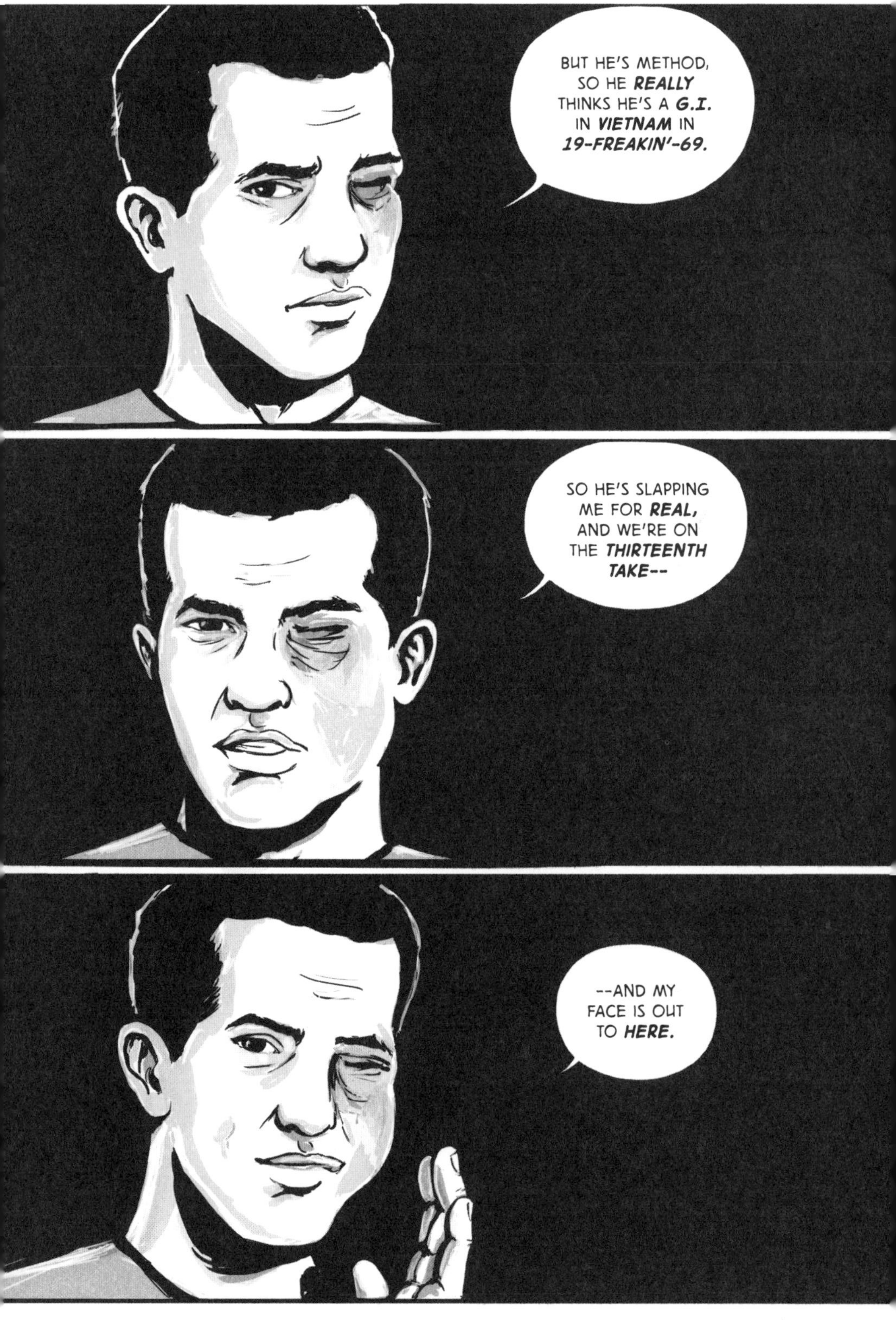
BUT HE'S METHOD, SO HE REALLY THINKS HE'S A G.I. IN VIETNAM IN 19-FREAKIN'-69.
SO HE'S SLAPPING ME FOR REAL, AND WE'RE ON THE THIRTEENTH TAKE--
--AND MY FACE IS OUT TO HERE.

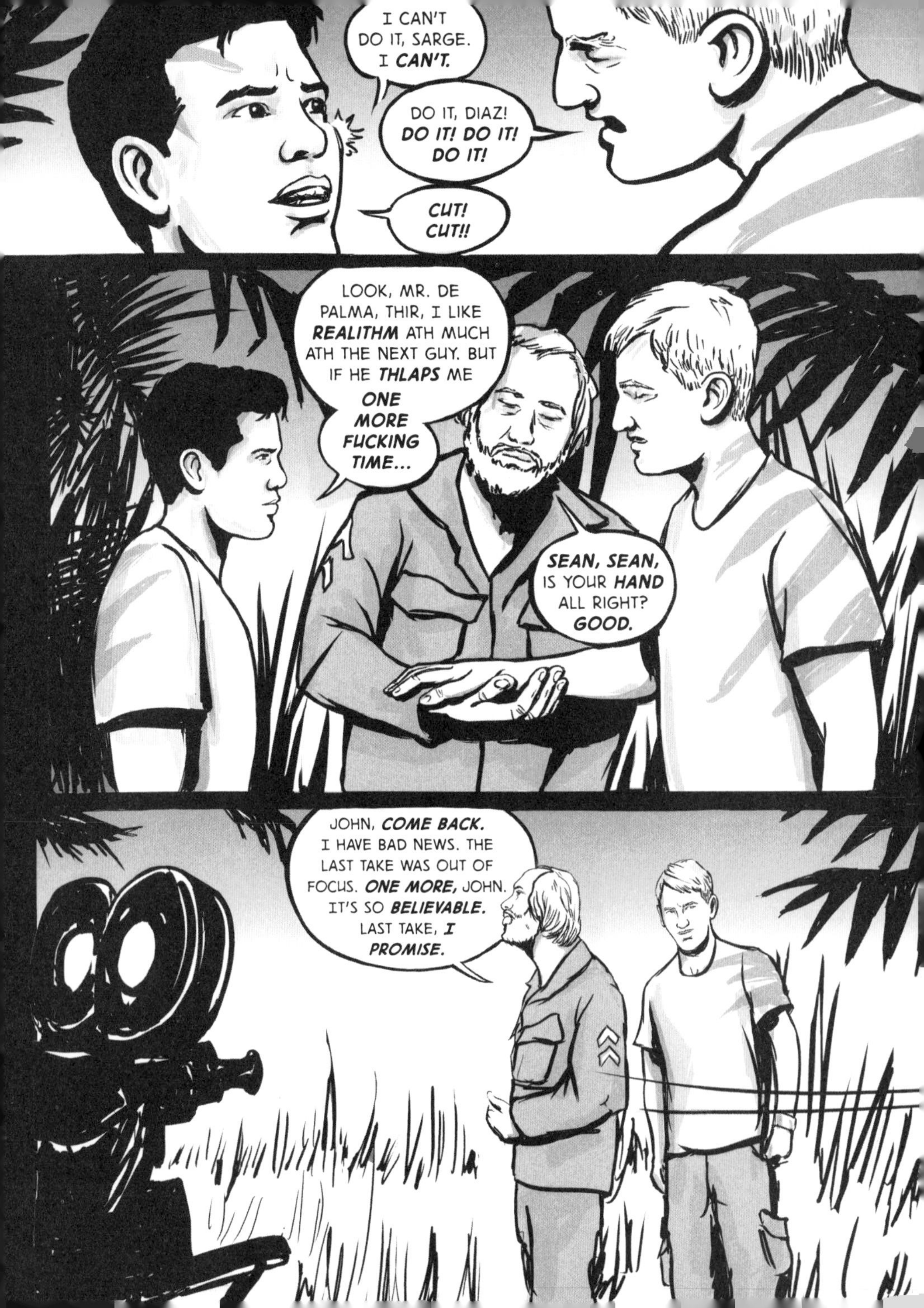
I CAN'T DO IT, SARGE. I **CAN'T.**
DO IT, DIAZ! ***DO IT! DO IT! DO IT!***
CUT! CUT!!
LOOK, MR. DE PALMA, THIR, I LIKE ***REALITHM*** ATH MUCH ATH THE NEXT GUY. BUT IF HE ***THLAPS*** ME ***ONE MORE FUCKING TIME...***
SEAN, SEAN, IS YOUR ***HAND*** ALL RIGHT? ***GOOD.***
JOHN, ***COME BACK.*** I HAVE BAD NEWS. THE LAST TAKE WAS OUT OF FOCUS. ***ONE MORE,*** JOHN. IT'S SO ***BELIEVABLE.*** LAST TAKE, ***I PROMISE.***

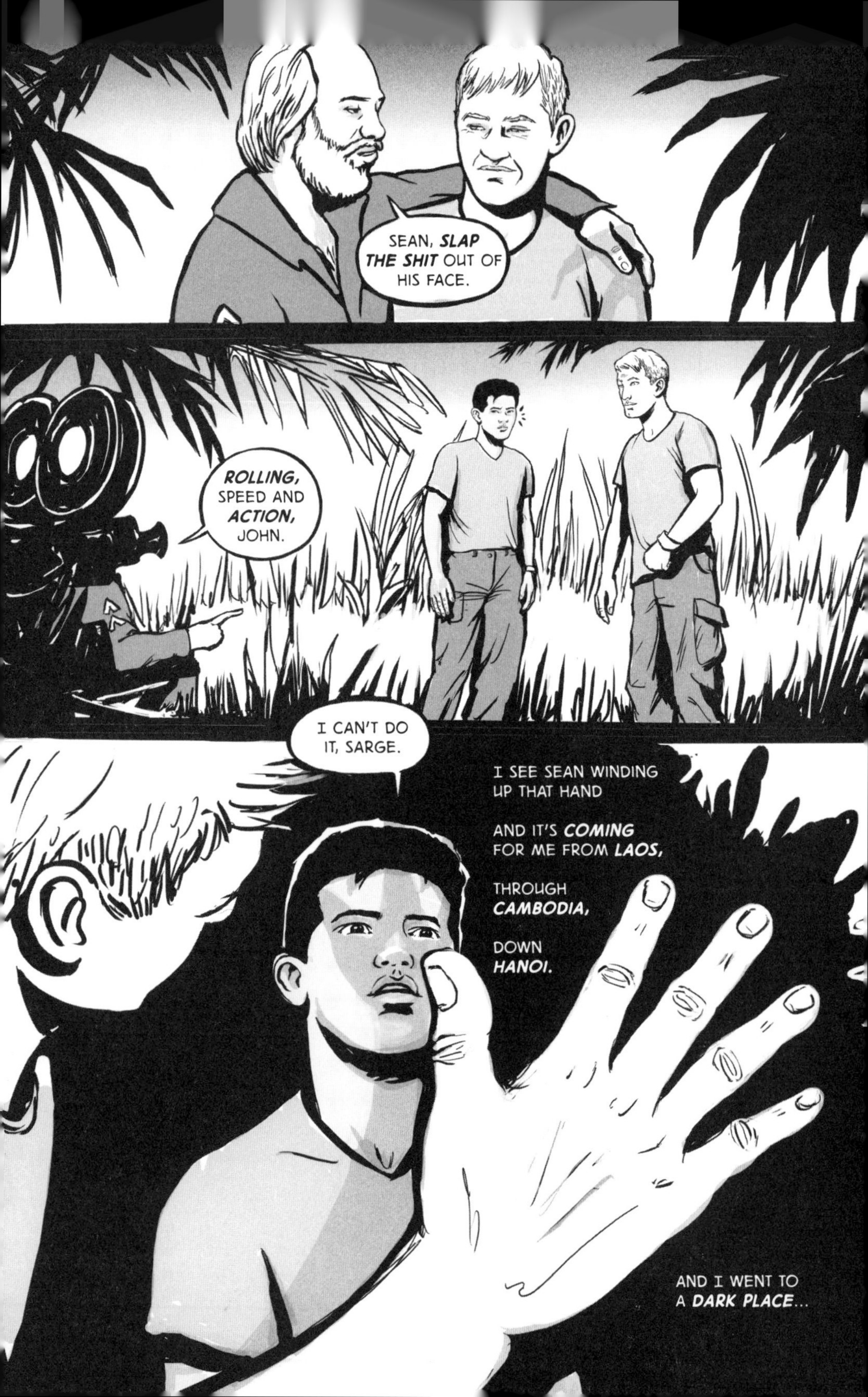
SEAN, SLAP THE SHIT OUT OF HIS FACE.
ROLLING, SPEED AND ACTION, JOHN.
I CAN'T DO IT, SARGE.
I SEE SEAN WINDING UP THAT HAND
AND IT'S COMING FOR ME FROM LAOS,
THROUGH CAMBODIA,
DOWN HANOI.
AND I WENT TO A DARK PLACE...

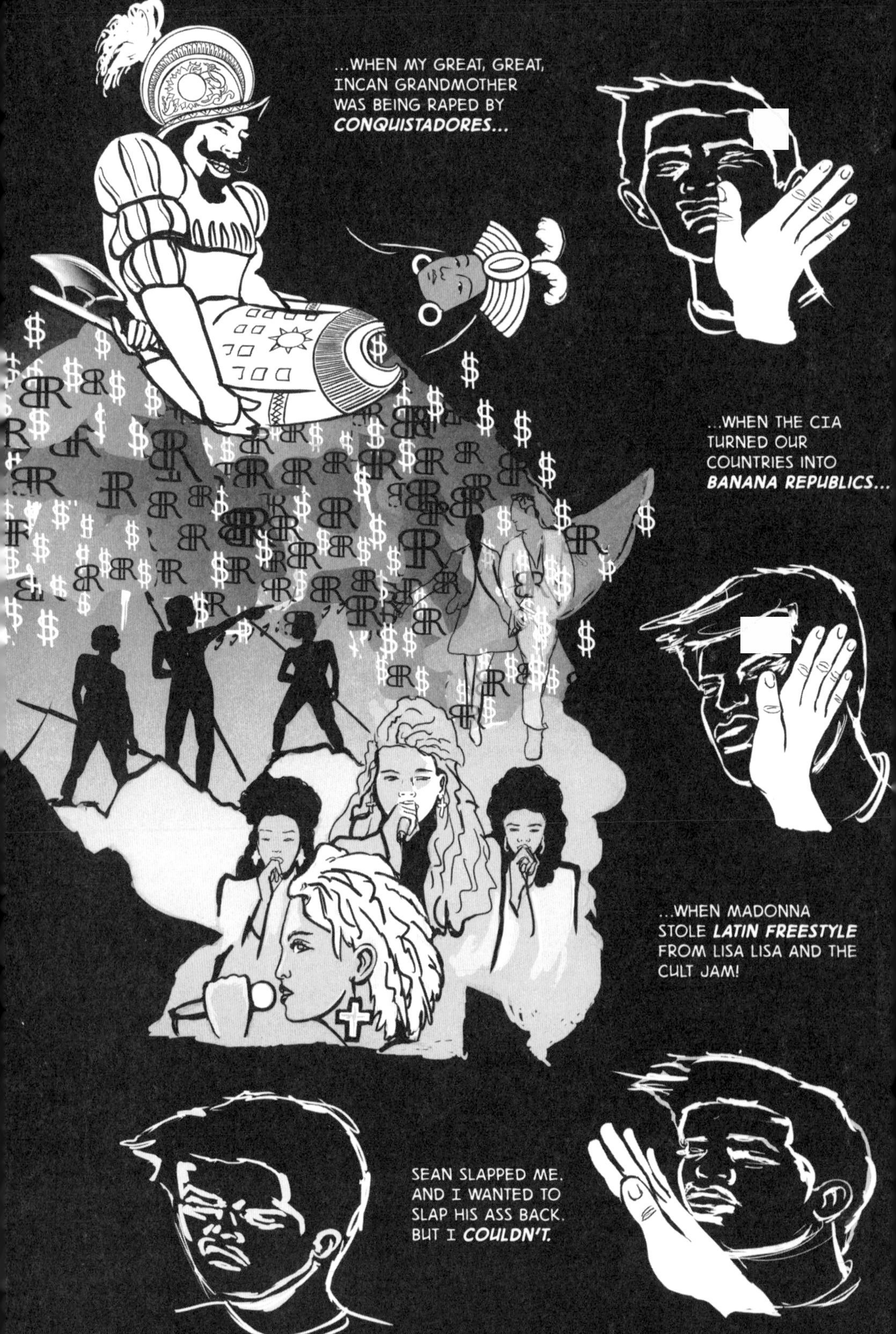
...WHEN MY GREAT, GREAT, INCAN GRANDMOTHER WAS BEING RAPED BY **CONQUISTADORES...**
...WHEN THE CIA TURNED OUR COUNTRIES INTO **BANANA REPUBLICS...**
...WHEN MADONNA STOLE **LATIN FREESTYLE** FROM LISA LISA AND THE CULT JAM!
SEAN SLAPPED ME. AND I WANTED TO SLAP HIS ASS BACK. BUT I **COULDN'T.**

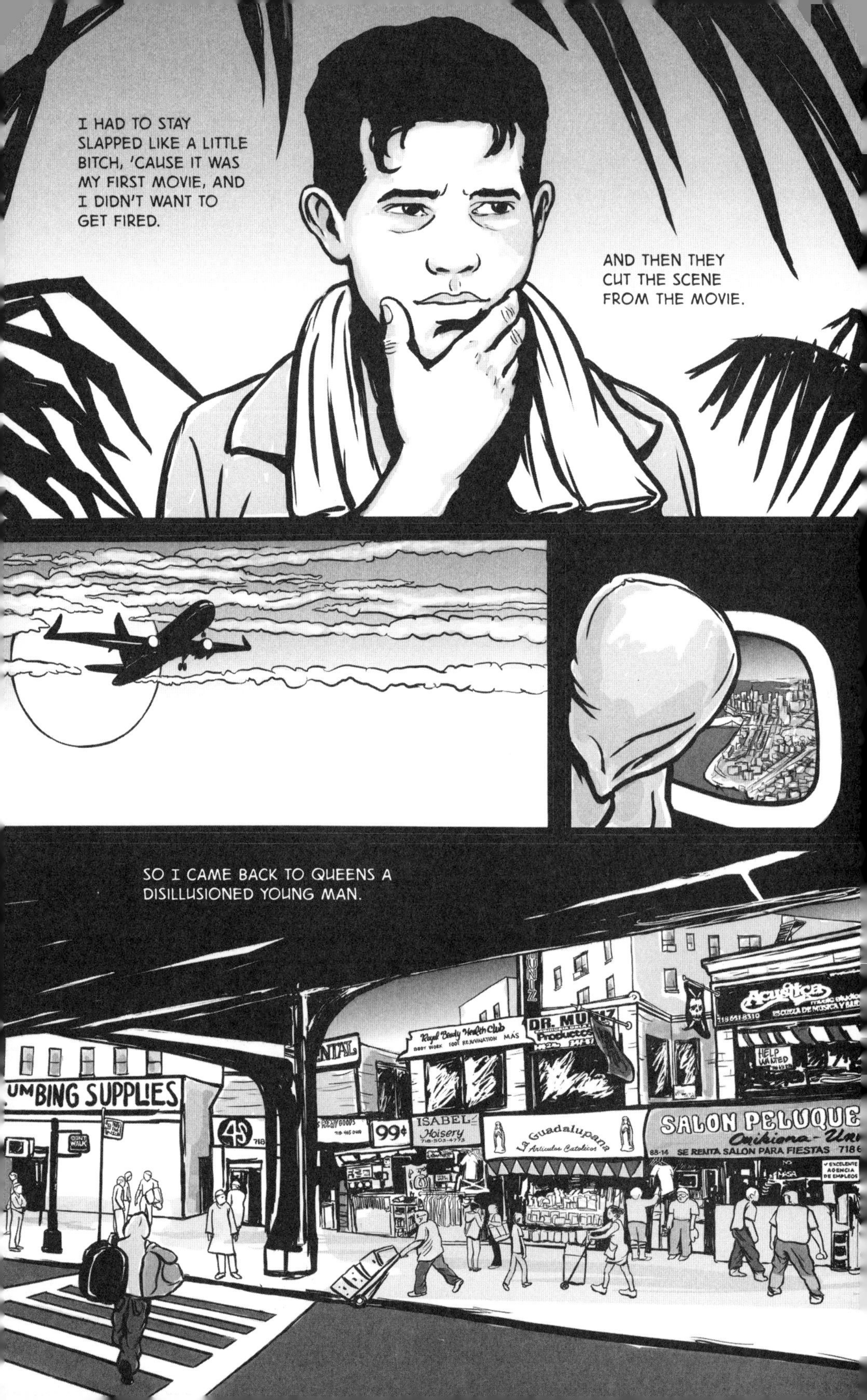
I HAD TO STAY SLAPPED LIKE A LITTLE BITCH, 'CAUSE IT WAS MY FIRST MOVIE, AND I DIDN'T WANT TO GET FIRED.
AND THEN THEY CUT THE SCENE FROM THE MOVIE.
SO I CAME BACK TO QUEENS A DISILLUSIONED YOUNG MAN.
UMBING SUPPLIES
DON'T WALK
Royal Beauty Health Club
ISABEL Hoisery
99¢
La Guadalupana
Articulos Catolicos
SALON PELUQUE
SE RENTA SALON PARA FIESTAS
HELP WANTED

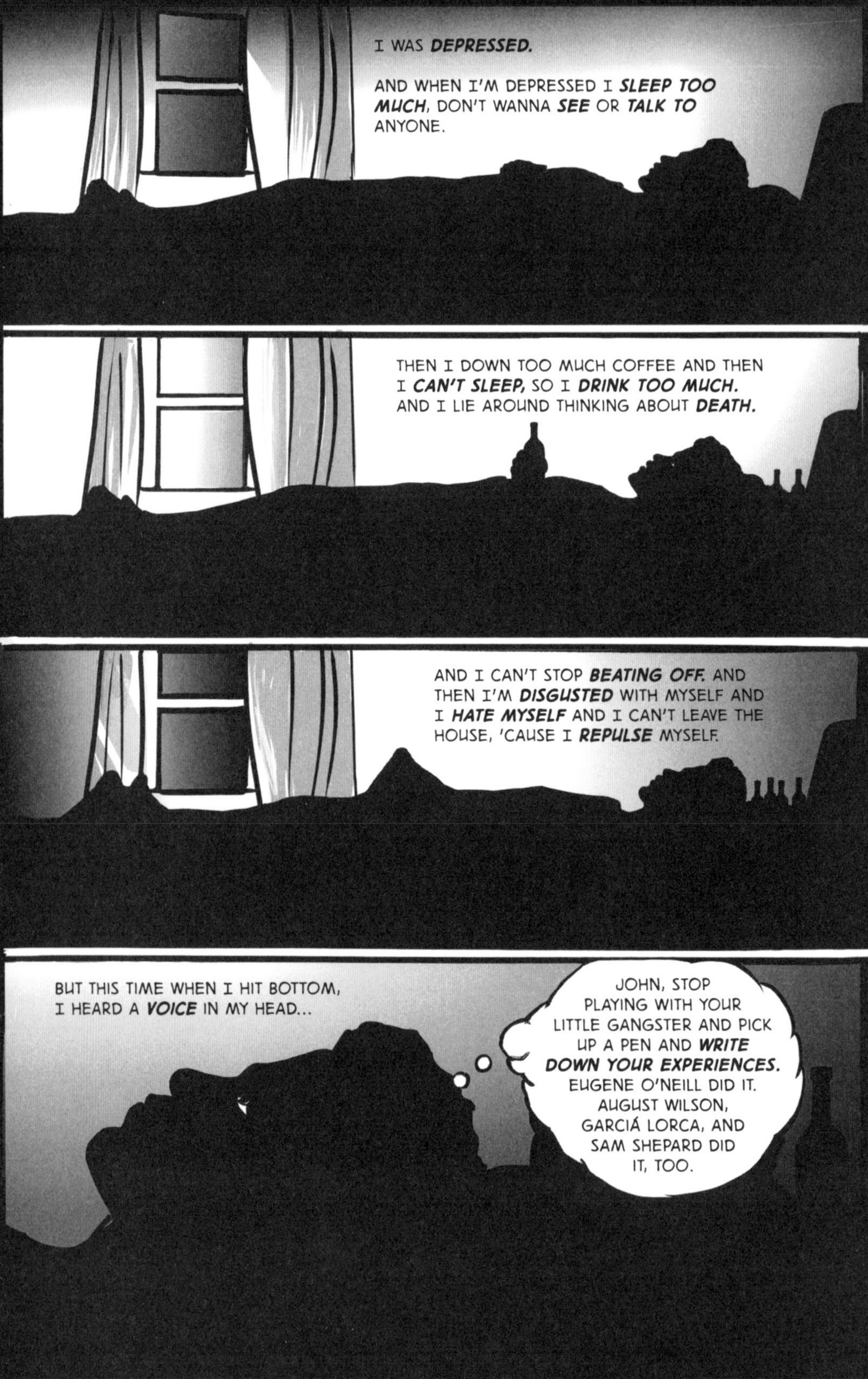
I WAS DEPRESSED.
AND WHEN I'M DEPRESSED I SLEEP TOO MUCH, DON'T WANNA SEE OR TALK TO ANYONE.
THEN I DOWN TOO MUCH COFFEE AND THEN I CAN'T SLEEP, SO I DRINK TOO MUCH. AND I LIE AROUND THINKING ABOUT DEATH.
AND I CAN'T STOP BEATING OFF. AND THEN I'M DISGUSTED WITH MYSELF AND I HATE MYSELF AND I CAN'T LEAVE THE HOUSE, 'CAUSE I REPULSE MYSELF.
BUT THIS TIME WHEN I HIT BOTTOM, I HEARD A VOICE IN MY HEAD...
JOHN, STOP PLAYING WITH YOUR LITTLE GANGSTER AND PICK UP A PEN AND WRITE DOWN YOUR EXPERIENCES. EUGENE O'NEILL DID IT. AUGUST WILSON, GARCIÁ LORCA, AND SAM SHEPARD DID IT, TOO.

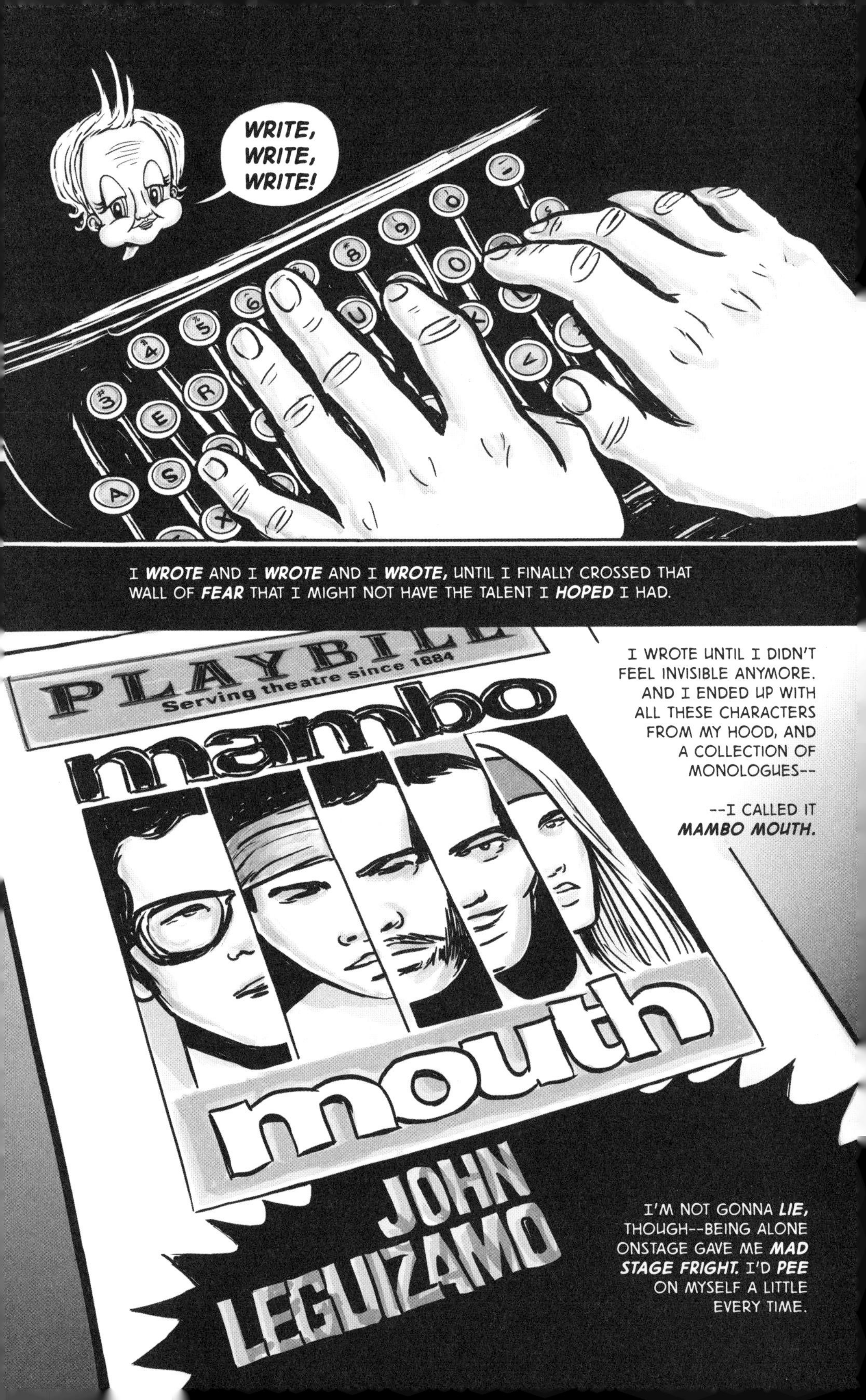
WRITE, WRITE, WRITE!
I WROTE AND I WROTE AND I WROTE, UNTIL I FINALLY CROSSED THAT WALL OF FEAR THAT I MIGHT NOT HAVE THE TALENT I HOPED I HAD.
I WROTE UNTIL I DIDN'T FEEL INVISIBLE ANYMORE. AND I ENDED UP WITH ALL THESE CHARACTERS FROM MY HOOD, AND A COLLECTION OF MONOLOGUES--
--I CALLED IT MAMBO MOUTH.
PLAYBILL
Serving theatre since 1884
mambo mouth
JOHN LEGUIZAMO
I'M NOT GONNA LIE, THOUGH--BEING ALONE ONSTAGE GAVE ME MAD STAGE FRIGHT. I'D PEE ON MYSELF A LITTLE EVERY TIME.

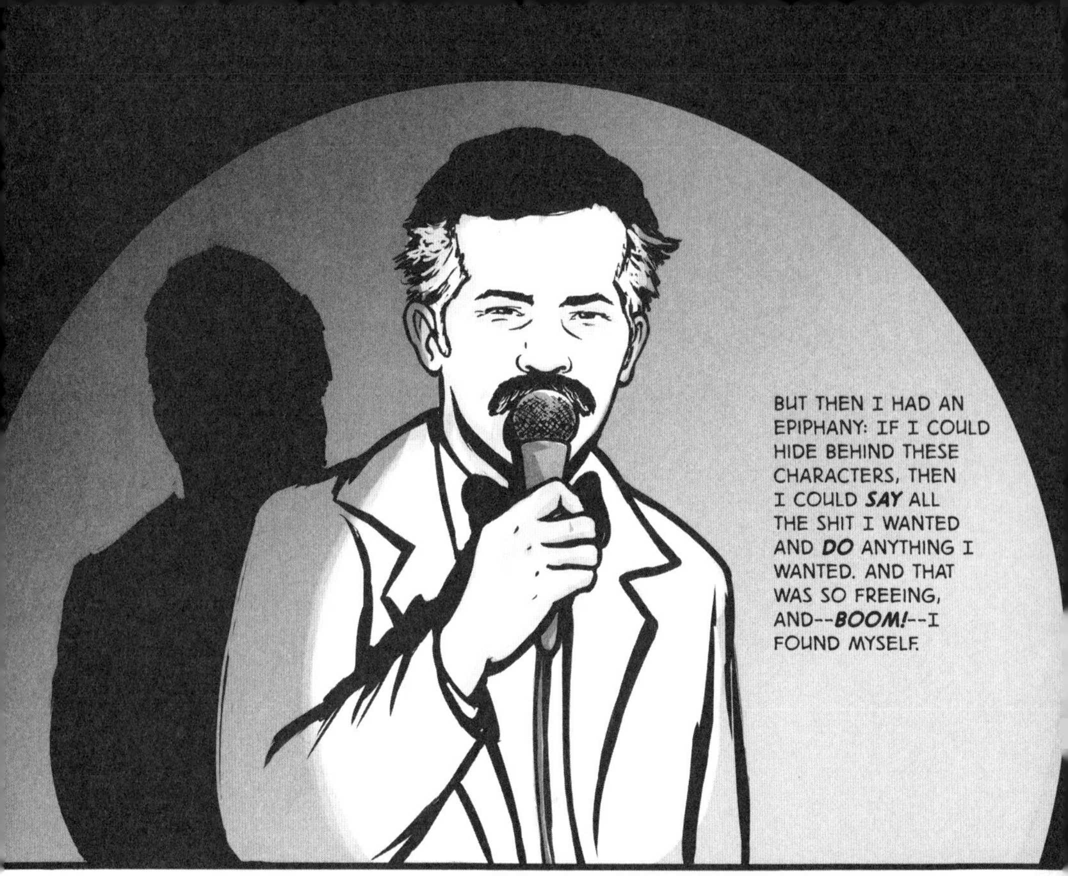
BUT THEN I HAD AN EPIPHANY: IF I COULD HIDE BEHIND THESE CHARACTERS, THEN I COULD **SAY** ALL THE SHIT I WANTED AND **DO** ANYTHING I WANTED. AND THAT WAS SO FREEING, AND--**BOOM!**--I FOUND MYSELF.

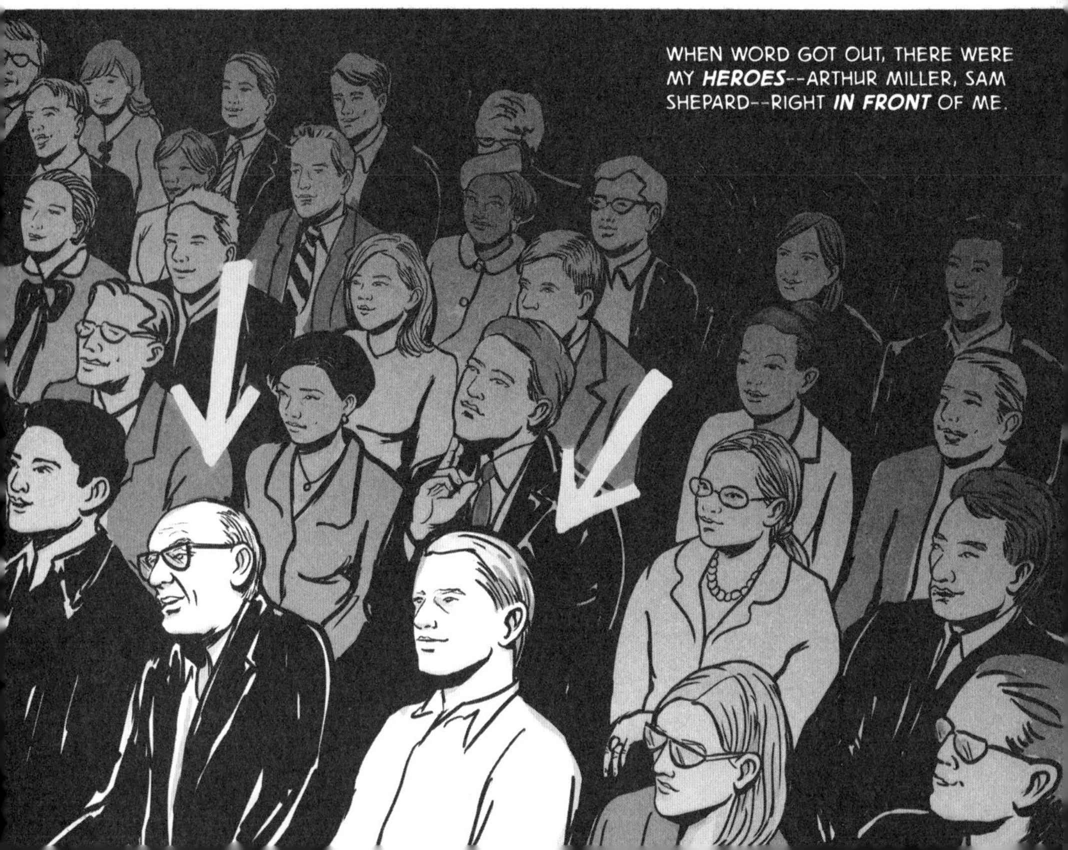
WHEN WORD GOT OUT, THERE WERE MY **HEROES**--ARTHUR MILLER, SAM SHEPARD--RIGHT **IN FRONT** OF ME.

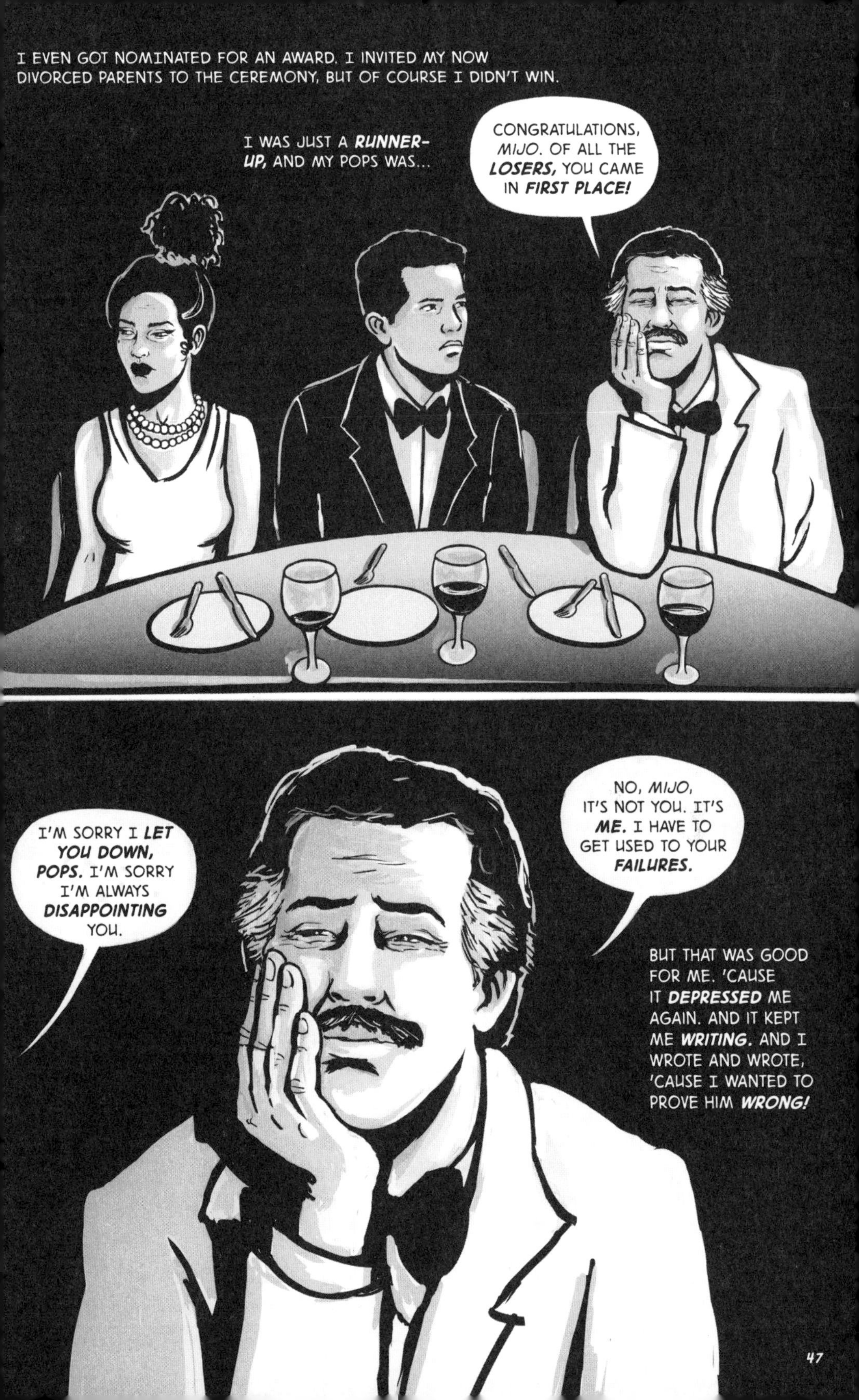
I EVEN GOT NOMINATED FOR AN AWARD. I INVITED MY NOW DIVORCED PARENTS TO THE CEREMONY, BUT OF COURSE I DIDN'T WIN.
I WAS JUST A ***RUNNER-UP,*** AND MY POPS WAS...
CONGRATULATIONS, *MIJO*. OF ALL THE ***LOSERS,*** YOU CAME IN ***FIRST PLACE!***
I'M SORRY I ***LET YOU DOWN, POPS.*** I'M SORRY I'M ALWAYS ***DISAPPOINTING*** YOU.
NO, *MIJO*, IT'S NOT YOU. IT'S ***ME.*** I HAVE TO GET USED TO YOUR ***FAILURES.***
BUT THAT WAS GOOD FOR ME. 'CAUSE IT ***DEPRESSED*** ME AGAIN. AND IT KEPT ME ***WRITING.*** AND I WROTE AND WROTE, 'CAUSE I WANTED TO PROVE HIM ***WRONG!***

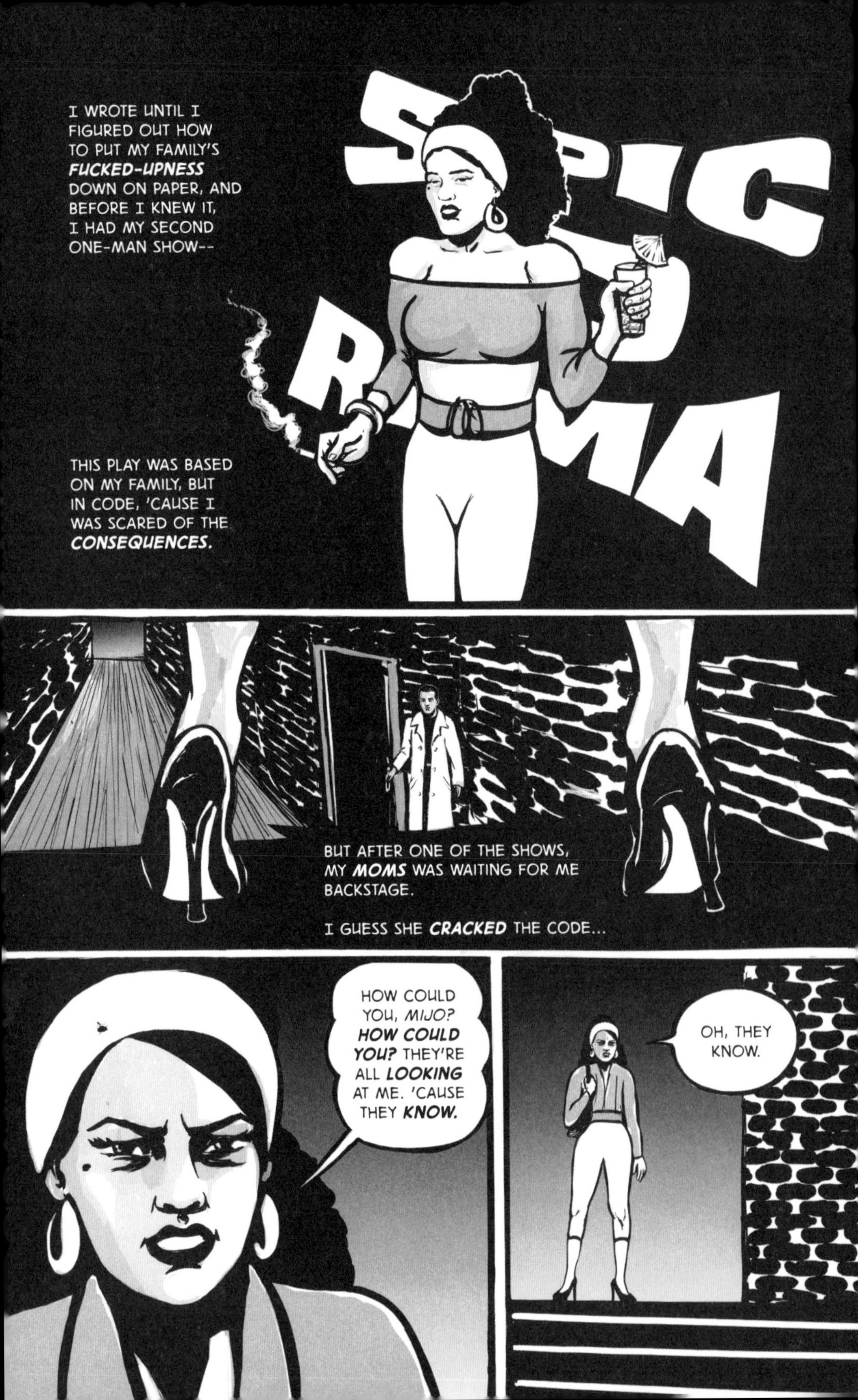
I WROTE UNTIL I FIGURED OUT HOW TO PUT MY FAMILY'S ***FUCKED-UPNESS*** DOWN ON PAPER, AND BEFORE I KNEW IT, I HAD MY SECOND ONE-MAN SHOW--
THIS PLAY WAS BASED ON MY FAMILY, BUT IN CODE, 'CAUSE I WAS SCARED OF THE ***CONSEQUENCES.***
BUT AFTER ONE OF THE SHOWS, MY ***MOMS*** WAS WAITING FOR ME BACKSTAGE.
I GUESS SHE ***CRACKED*** THE CODE...
HOW COULD YOU, *MIJO?* ***HOW COULD YOU?*** THEY'RE ALL ***LOOKING*** AT ME. 'CAUSE THEY ***KNOW.***
OH, THEY KNOW.

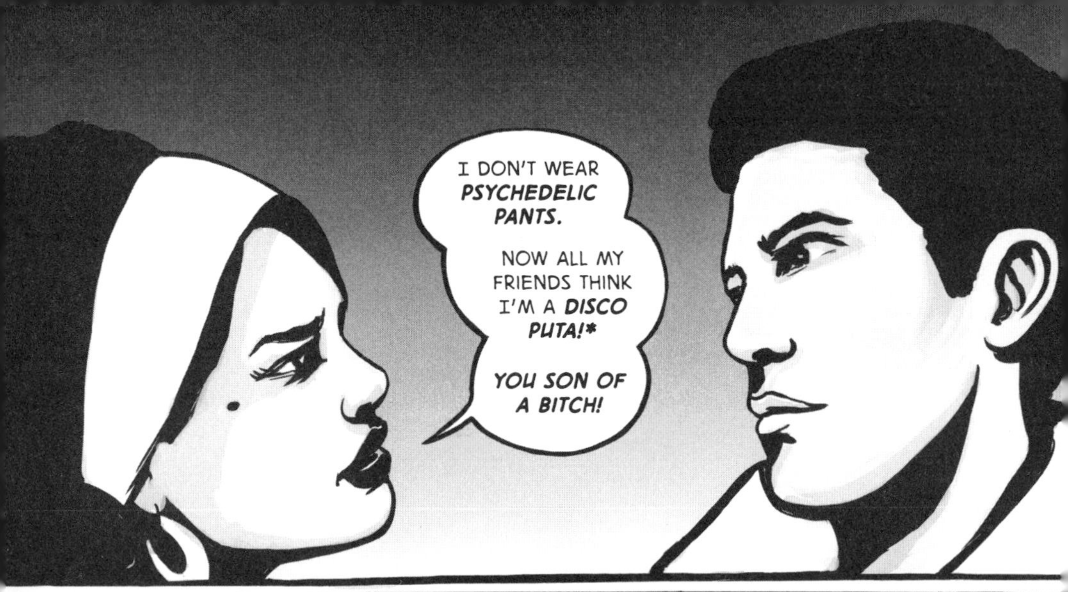
I DON'T WEAR PSYCHEDELIC PANTS.
NOW ALL MY FRIENDS THINK I'M A DISCO PUTA!*
YOU SON OF A BITCH!

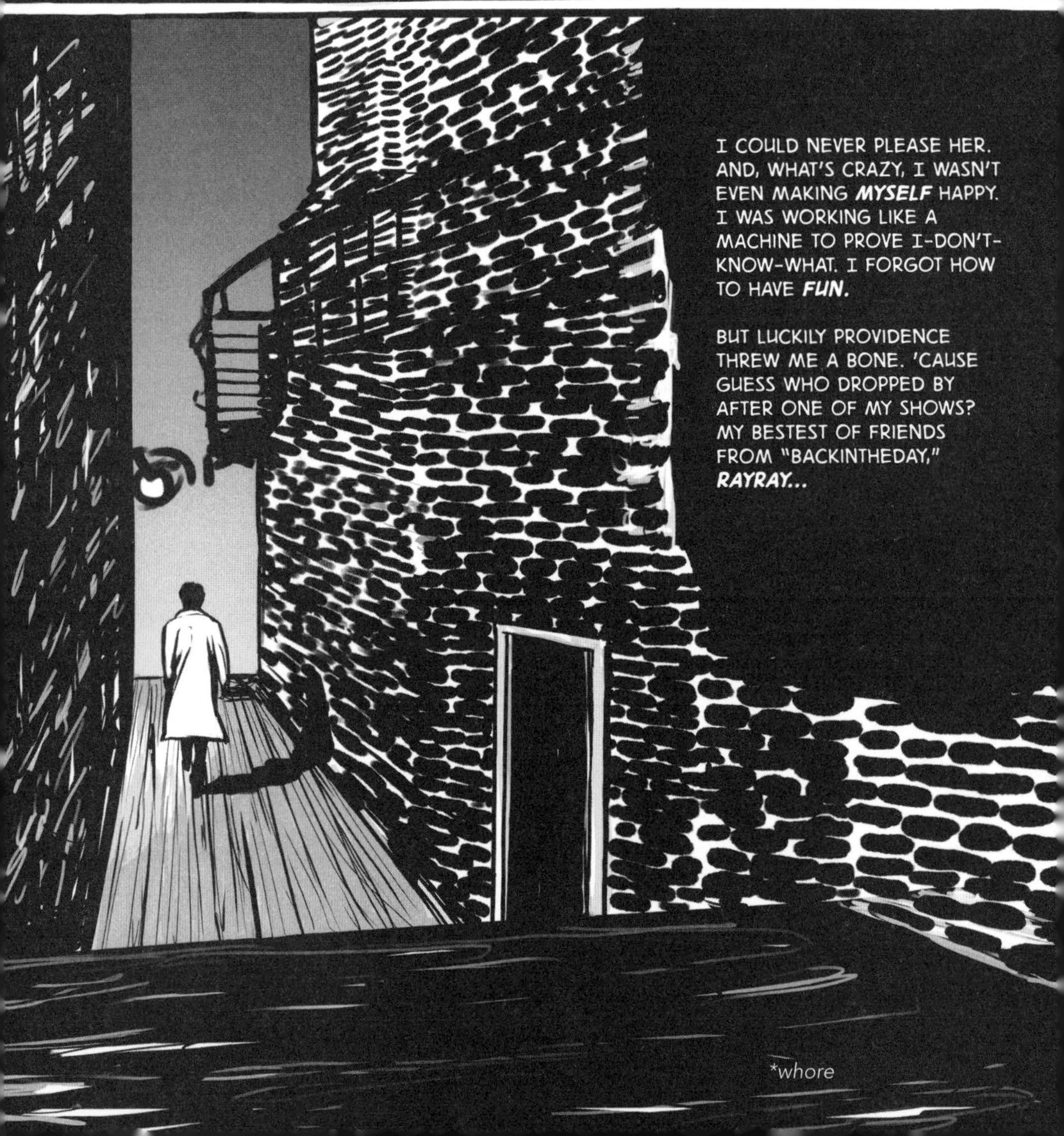
I COULD NEVER PLEASE HER. AND, WHAT'S CRAZY, I WASN'T EVEN MAKING MYSELF HAPPY. I WAS WORKING LIKE A MACHINE TO PROVE I-DON'T-KNOW-WHAT. I FORGOT HOW TO HAVE FUN.
BUT LUCKILY PROVIDENCE THREW ME A BONE. 'CAUSE GUESS WHO DROPPED BY AFTER ONE OF MY SHOWS? MY BESTEST OF FRIENDS FROM "BACKINTHEDAY," RAYRAY...
*whore

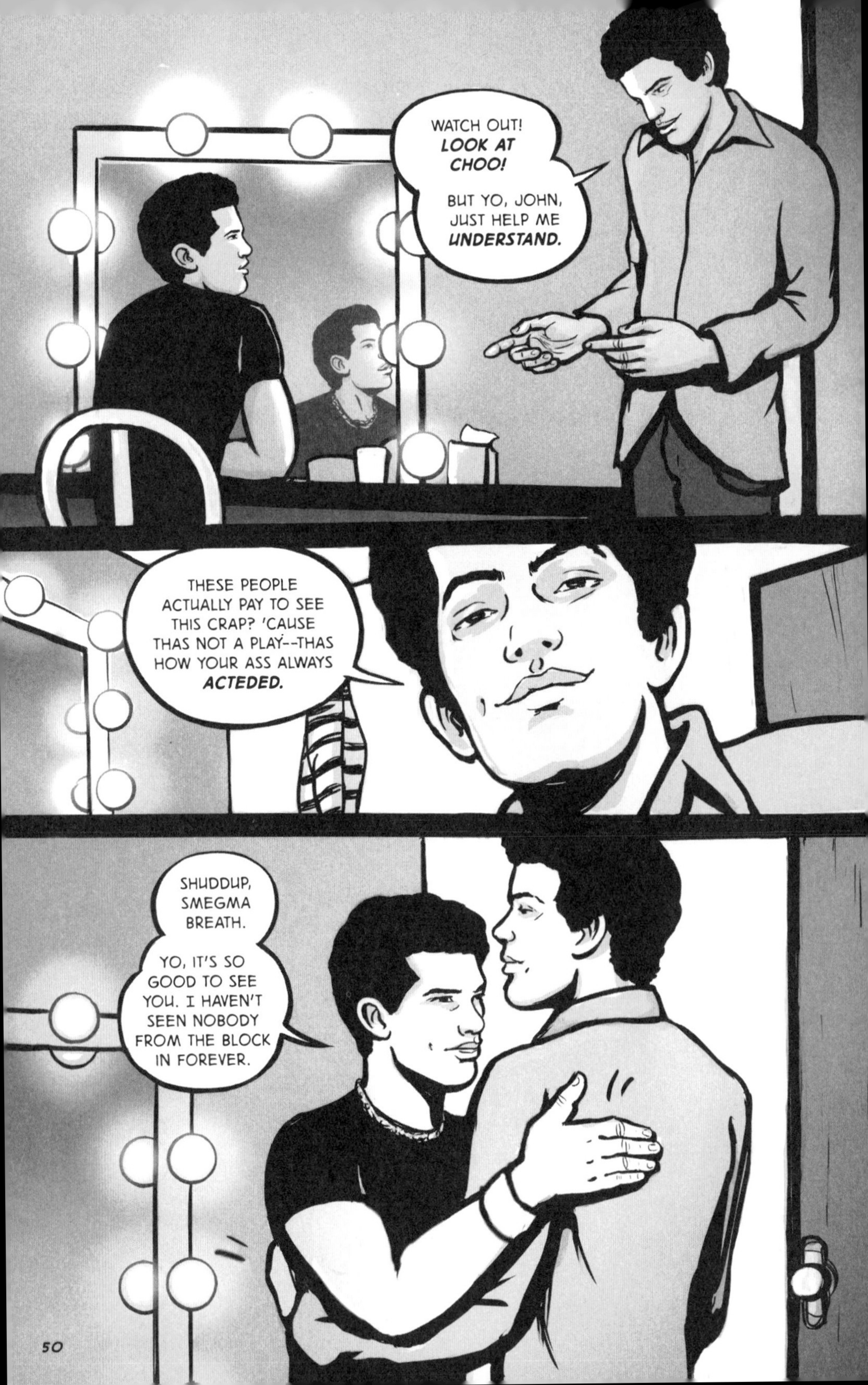
WATCH OUT! LOOK AT CHOO!
BUT YO, JOHN, JUST HELP ME UNDERSTAND.
THESE PEOPLE ACTUALLY PAY TO SEE THIS CRAP? 'CAUSE THAS NOT A PLAY--THAS HOW YOUR ASS ALWAYS ACTEDED.
SHUDDUP, SMEGMA BREATH.
YO, IT'S SO GOOD TO SEE YOU. I HAVEN'T SEEN NOBODY FROM THE BLOCK IN FOREVER.

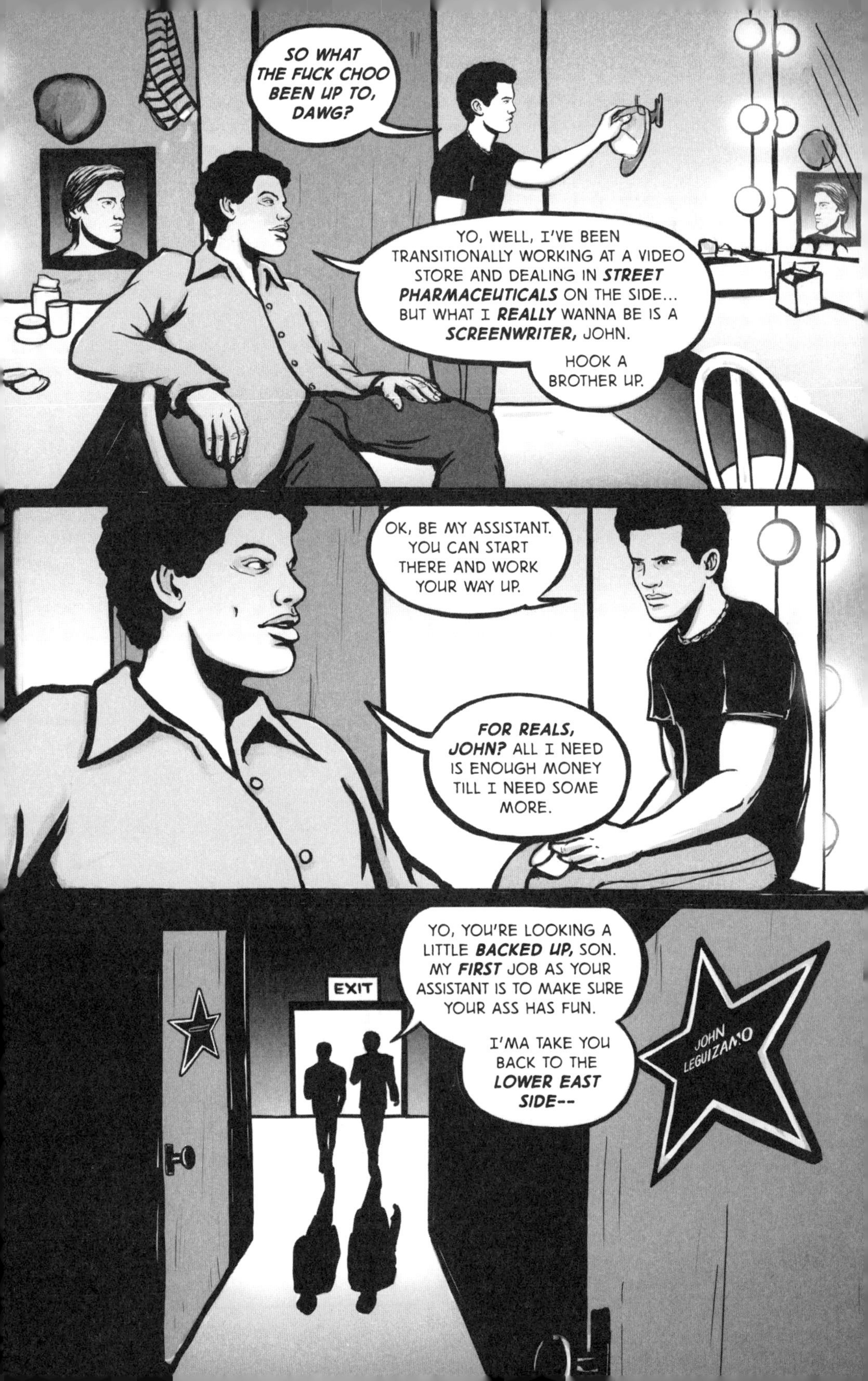
SO WHAT THE FUCK CHOO BEEN UP TO, DAWG?
YO, WELL, I'VE BEEN TRANSITIONALLY WORKING AT A VIDEO STORE AND DEALING IN STREET PHARMACEUTICALS ON THE SIDE... BUT WHAT I REALLY WANNA BE IS A SCREENWRITER, JOHN.
HOOK A BROTHER UP.
OK, BE MY ASSISTANT. YOU CAN START THERE AND WORK YOUR WAY UP.
FOR REALS, JOHN? ALL I NEED IS ENOUGH MONEY TILL I NEED SOME MORE.
YO, YOU'RE LOOKING A LITTLE BACKED UP, SON. MY FIRST JOB AS YOUR ASSISTANT IS TO MAKE SURE YOUR ASS HAS FUN.
I'MA TAKE YOU BACK TO THE LOWER EAST SIDE--
EXIT
JOHN LEGUIZAMO

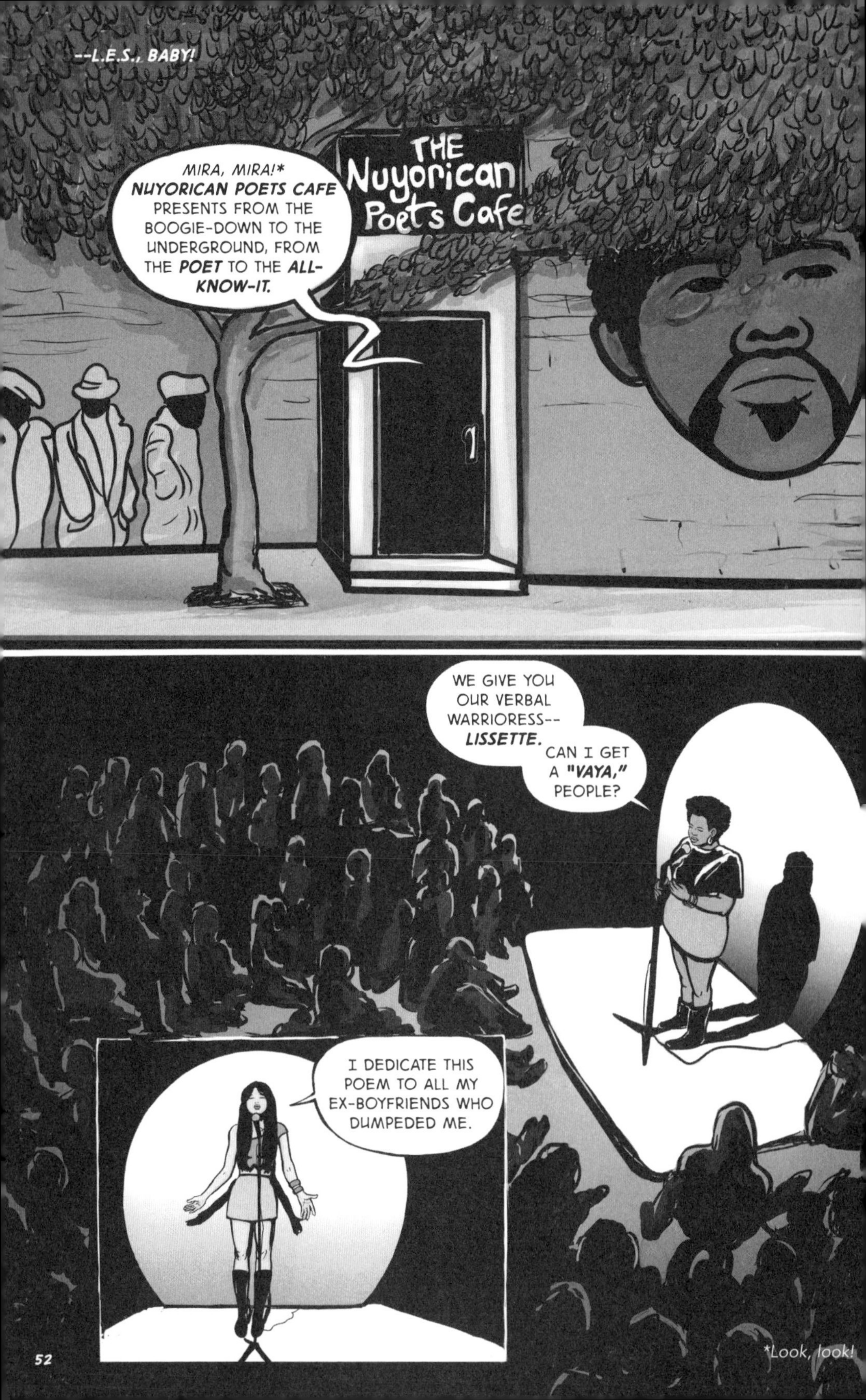

--L.E.S., BABY!
MIRA, MIRA!* NUYORICAN POETS CAFE PRESENTS FROM THE BOOGIE-DOWN TO THE UNDERGROUND, FROM THE POET TO THE ALL-KNOW-IT.
THE Nuyorican Poet's Cafe
WE GIVE YOU OUR VERBAL WARRIORESS-- LISSETTE.
CAN I GET A "VAYA," PEOPLE?
I DEDICATE THIS POEM TO ALL MY EX-BOYFRIENDS WHO DUMPEDED ME.

*Look, look!

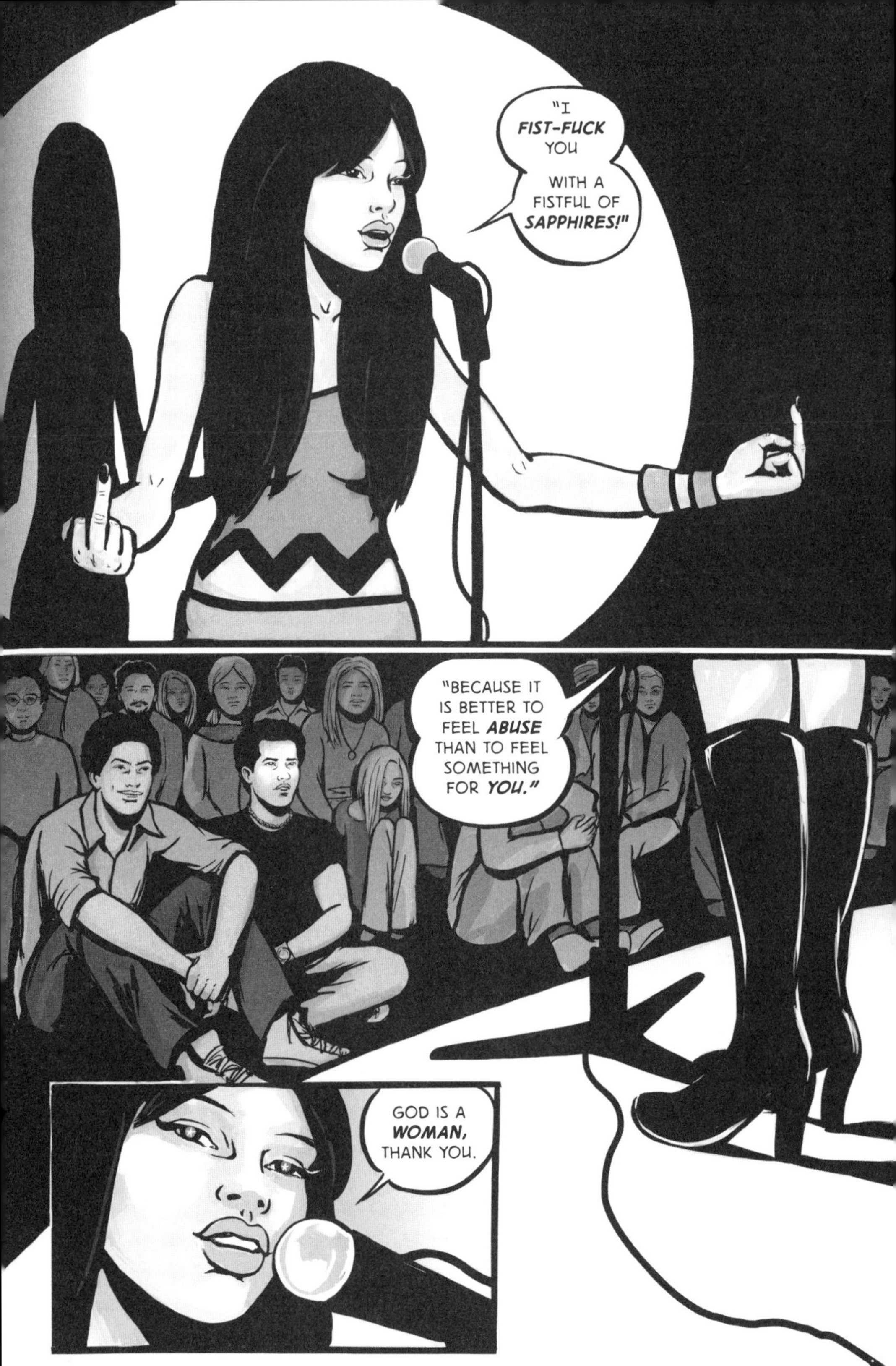
"I FIST-FUCK YOU WITH A FISTFUL OF SAPPHIRES!"
"BECAUSE IT IS BETTER TO FEEL ABUSE THAN TO FEEL SOMETHING FOR YOU."
GOD IS A WOMAN, THANK YOU.

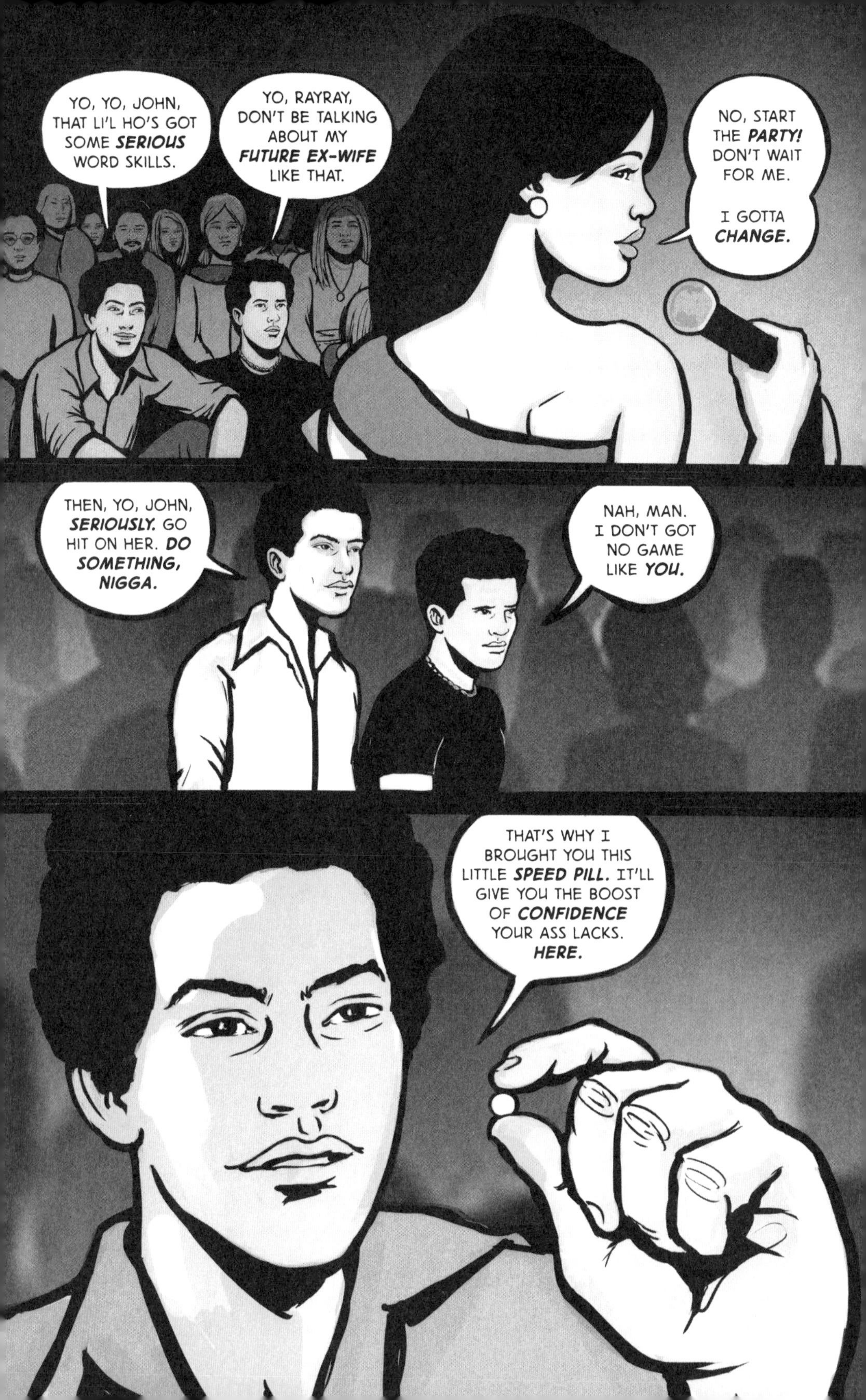
YO, YO, JOHN, THAT LI'L HO'S GOT SOME **SERIOUS** WORD SKILLS.
YO, RAYRAY, DON'T BE TALKING ABOUT MY **FUTURE EX-WIFE** LIKE THAT.
NO, START THE **PARTY!** DON'T WAIT FOR ME.
I GOTTA **CHANGE.**
THEN, YO, JOHN, **SERIOUSLY.** GO HIT ON HER. **DO SOMETHING, NIGGA.**
NAH, MAN. I DON'T GOT NO GAME LIKE **YOU.**
THAT'S WHY I BROUGHT YOU THIS LITTLE **SPEED PILL.** IT'LL GIVE YOU THE BOOST OF **CONFIDENCE** YOUR ASS LACKS. **HERE.**

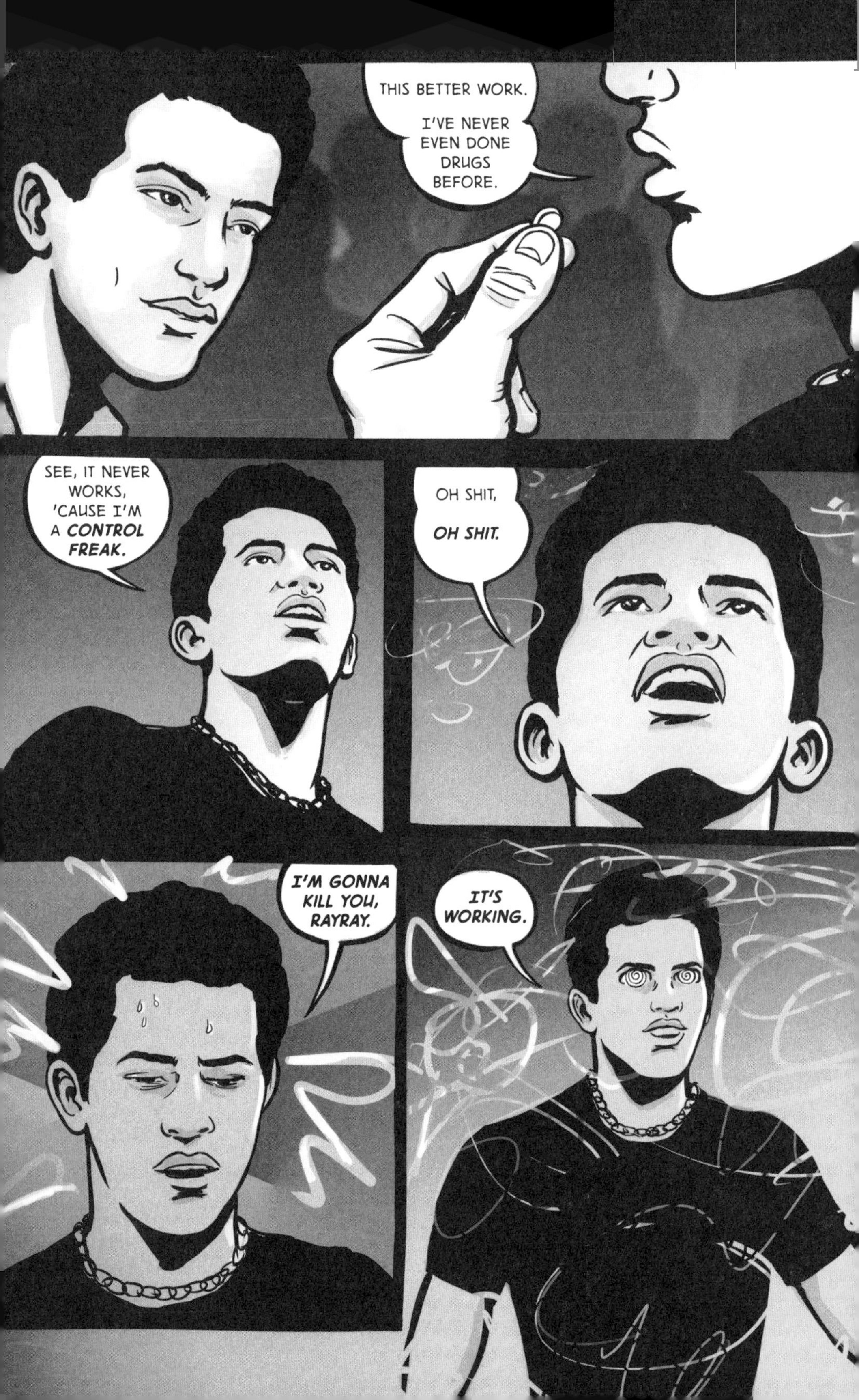
THIS BETTER WORK.
I'VE NEVER EVEN DONE DRUGS BEFORE.
SEE, IT NEVER WORKS, 'CAUSE I'M A CONTROL FREAK.
OH SHIT,
OH SHIT.
I'M GONNA KILL YOU, RAYRAY.
IT'S WORKING.

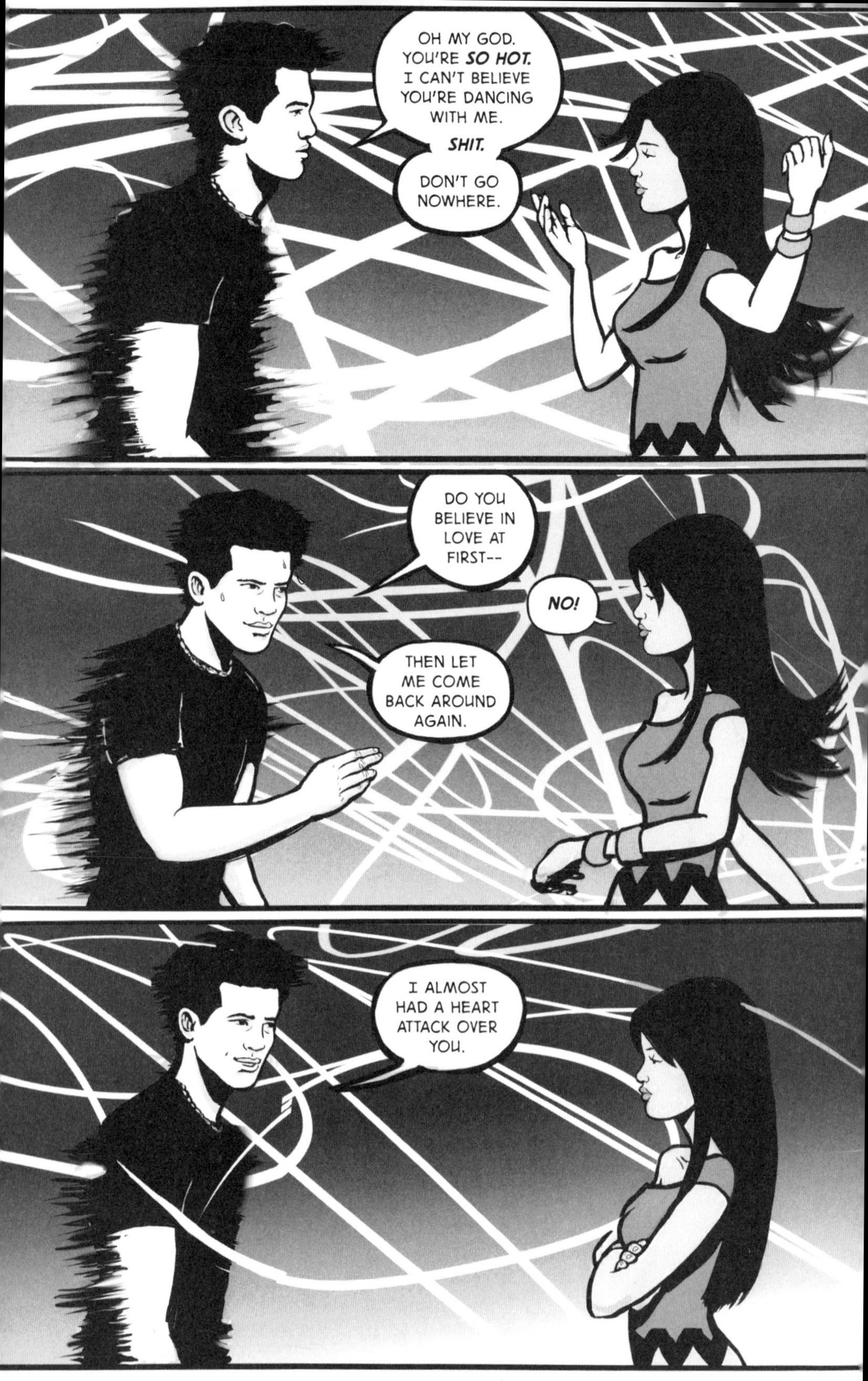
OH MY GOD. YOU'RE **SO HOT.** I CAN'T BELIEVE YOU'RE DANCING WITH ME.
SHIT.
DON'T GO NOWHERE.
DO YOU BELIEVE IN LOVE AT FIRST--
NO!
THEN LET ME COME BACK AROUND AGAIN.
I ALMOST HAD A HEART ATTACK OVER YOU.

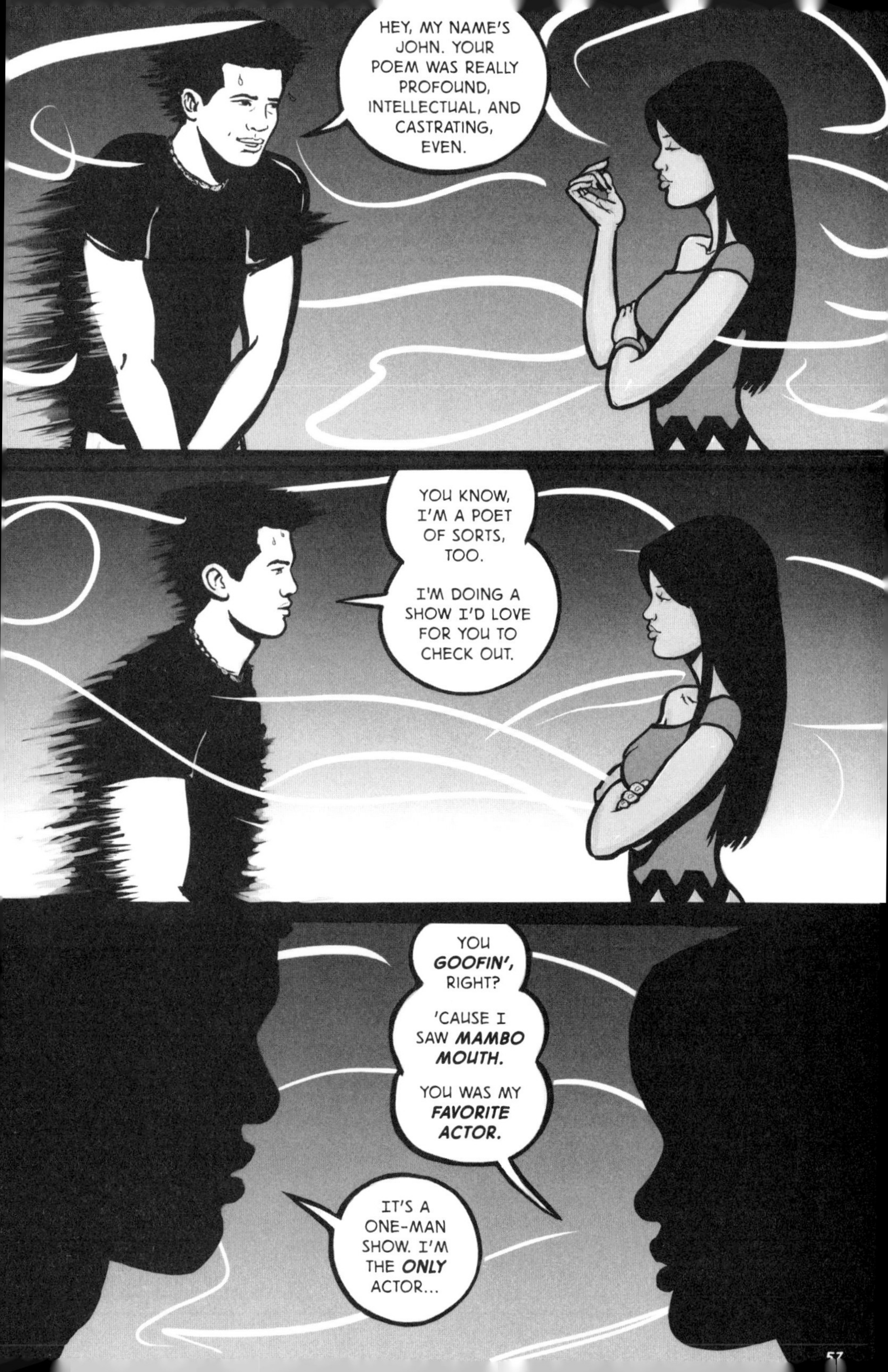
HEY, MY NAME'S JOHN. YOUR POEM WAS REALLY PROFOUND, INTELLECTUAL, AND CASTRATING, EVEN.
YOU KNOW, I'M A POET OF SORTS, TOO.
I'M DOING A SHOW I'D LOVE FOR YOU TO CHECK OUT.
YOU *GOOFIN'*, RIGHT?
'CAUSE I SAW *MAMBO MOUTH.*
YOU WAS MY *FAVORITE ACTOR.*
IT'S A ONE-MAN SHOW. I'M THE *ONLY* ACTOR...

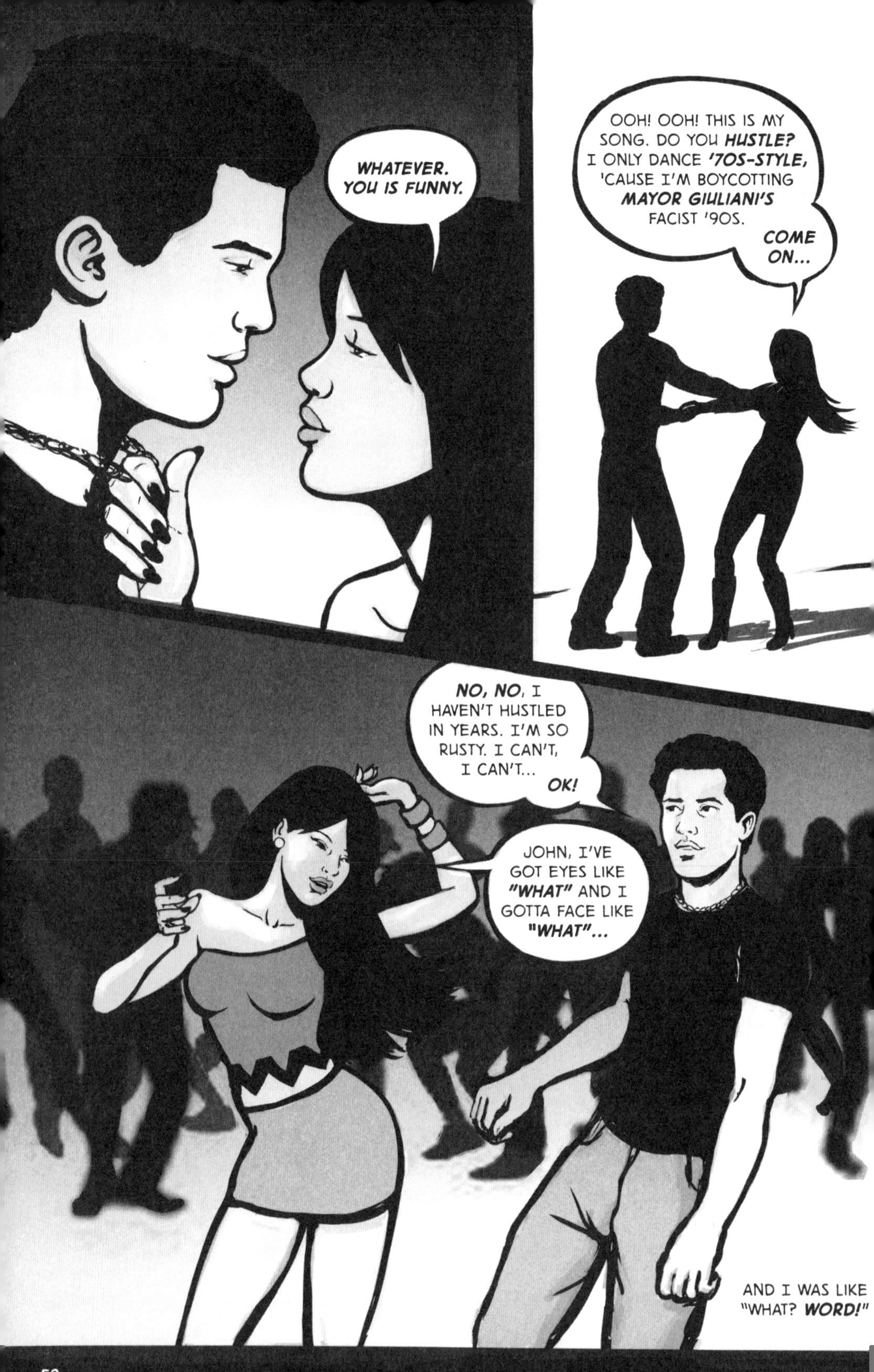
WHATEVER. YOU IS FUNNY.
OOH! OOH! THIS IS MY SONG. DO YOU HUSTLE? I ONLY DANCE '70S-STYLE, 'CAUSE I'M BOYCOTTING MAYOR GIULIANI'S FACIST '90S.
COME ON...
NO, NO, I HAVEN'T HUSTLED IN YEARS. I'M SO RUSTY. I CAN'T, I CAN'T...
OK!
JOHN, I'VE GOT EYES LIKE "WHAT" AND I GOTTA FACE LIKE "WHAT"...
AND I WAS LIKE "WHAT? WORD!"

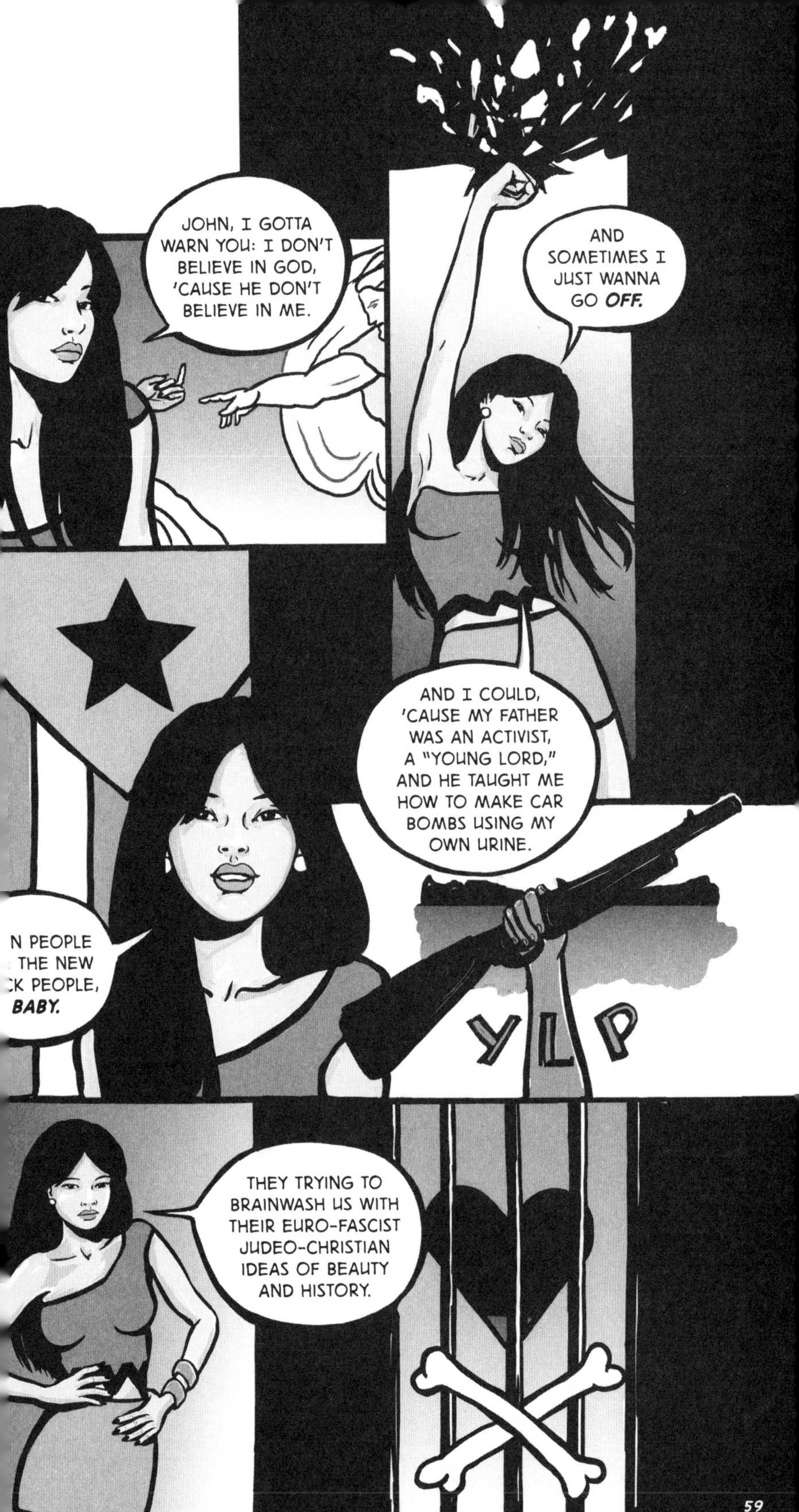

JOHN, I GOTTA WARN YOU: I DON'T BELIEVE IN GOD, 'CAUSE HE DON'T BELIEVE IN ME.
AND SOMETIMES I JUST WANNA GO ***OFF.***
AND I COULD, 'CAUSE MY FATHER WAS AN ACTIVIST, A "YOUNG LORD," AND HE TAUGHT ME HOW TO MAKE CAR BOMBS USING MY OWN URINE.
N PEOPLE
THE NEW
K PEOPLE,
BABY.
YLP
THEY TRYING TO BRAINWASH US WITH THEIR EURO-FASCIST JUDEO-CHRISTIAN IDEAS OF BEAUTY AND HISTORY.

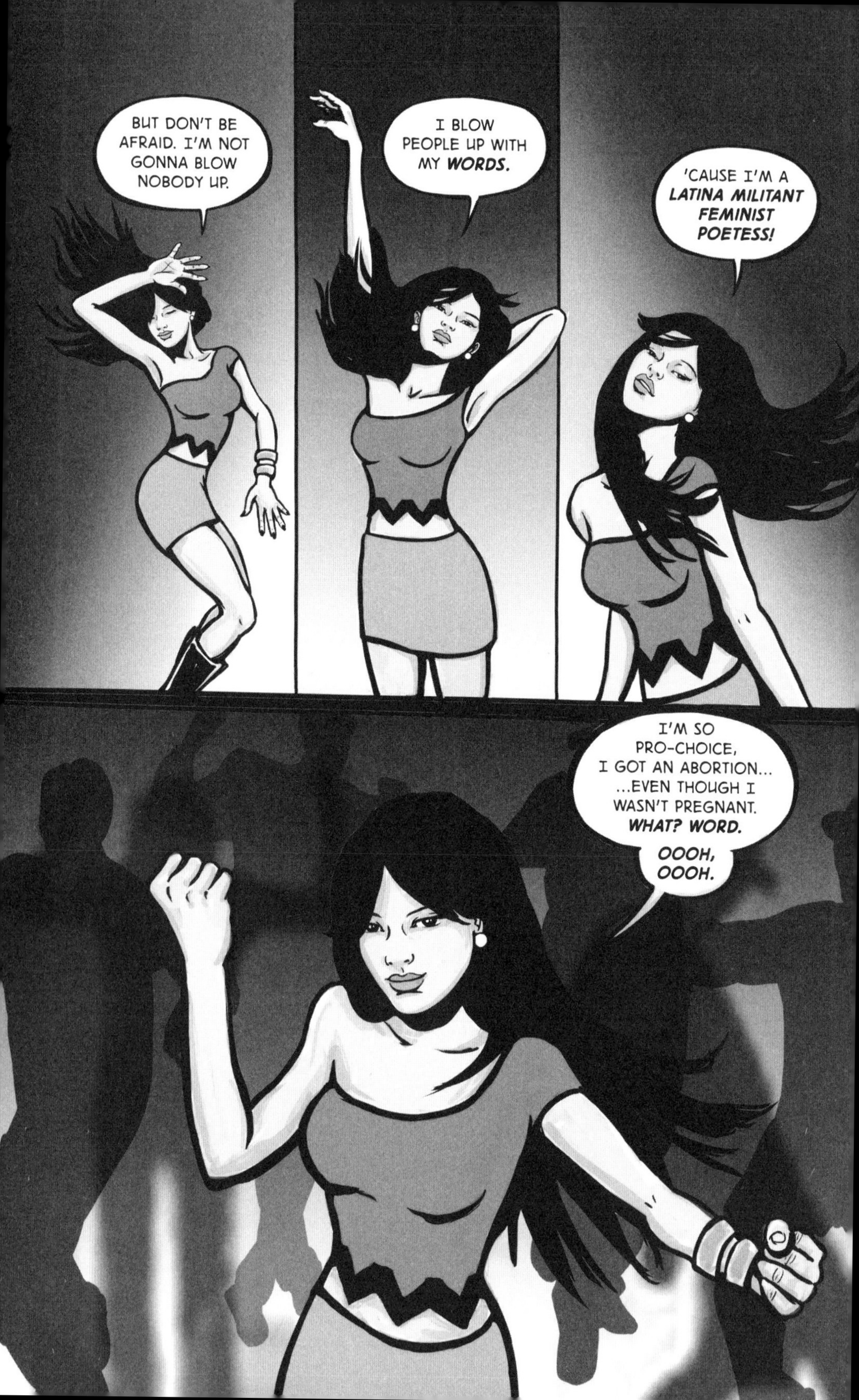
BUT DON'T BE AFRAID. I'M NOT GONNA BLOW NOBODY UP.
I BLOW PEOPLE UP WITH MY **WORDS.**
'CAUSE I'M A **LATINA MILITANT FEMINIST POETESS!**
I'M SO PRO-CHOICE, I GOT AN ABORTION... ...EVEN THOUGH I WASN'T PREGNANT. **WHAT? WORD.**
OOOH, OOOH.

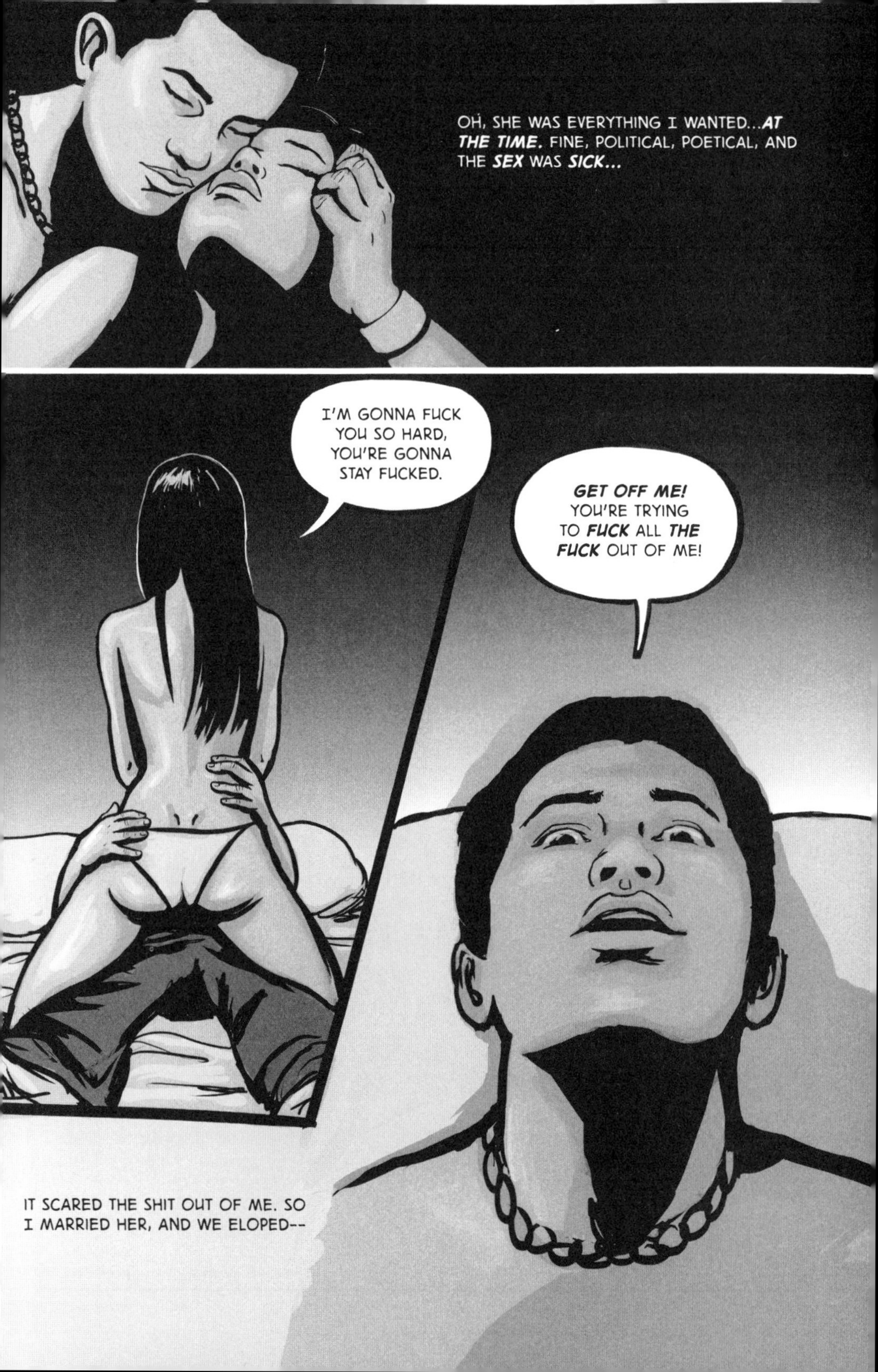
OH, SHE WAS EVERYTHING I WANTED...**AT THE TIME.** FINE, POLITICAL, POETICAL, AND THE **SEX** WAS **SICK...**
I'M GONNA FUCK YOU SO HARD, YOU'RE GONNA STAY FUCKED.
GET OFF ME! YOU'RE TRYING TO **FUCK** ALL **THE FUCK** OUT OF ME!
IT SCARED THE SHIT OUT OF ME. SO I MARRIED HER, AND WE ELOPED--

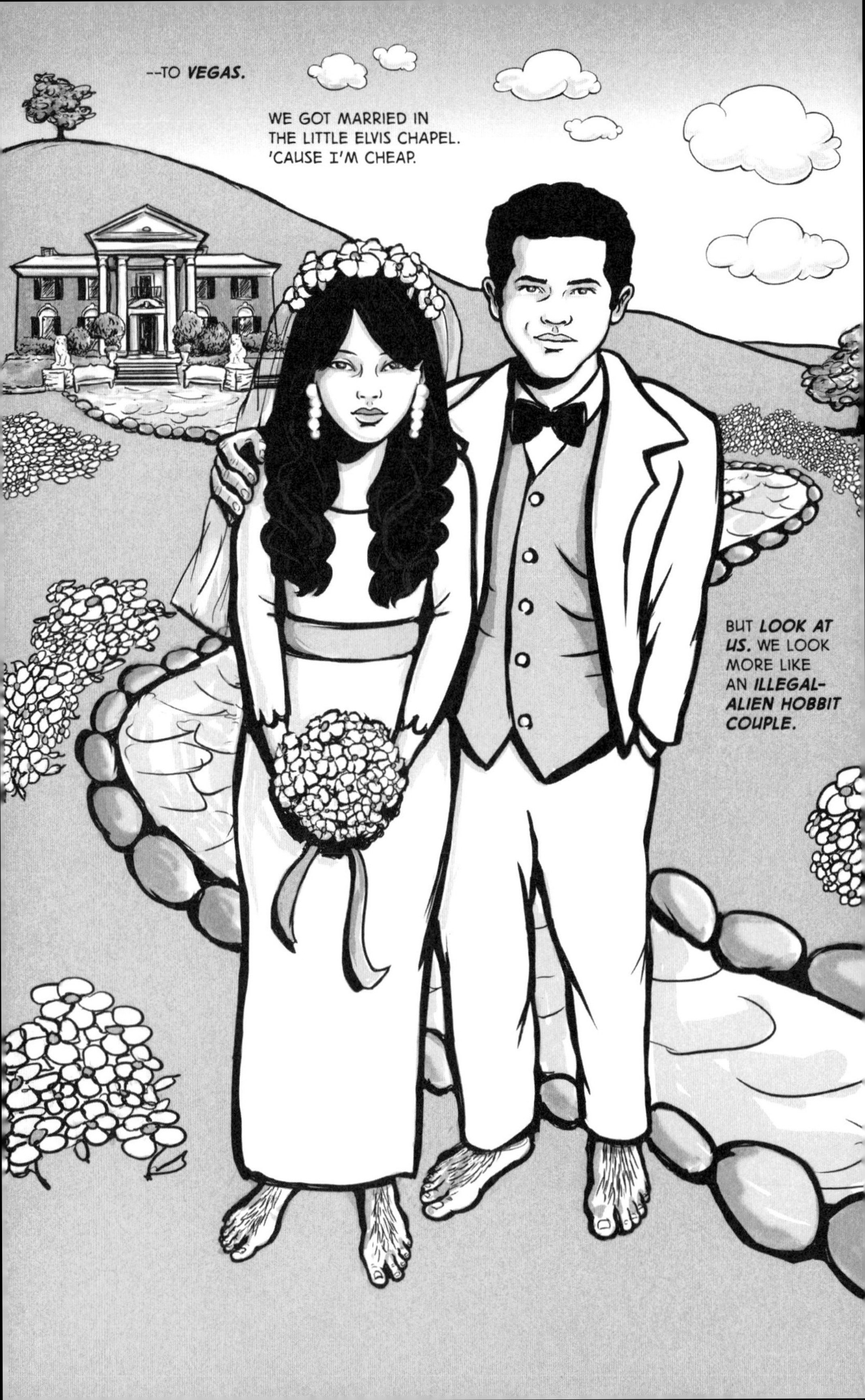
--TO VEGAS.
WE GOT MARRIED IN THE LITTLE ELVIS CHAPEL. 'CAUSE I'M CHEAP.
BUT LOOK AT US. WE LOOK MORE LIKE AN ILLEGAL-ALIEN HOBBIT COUPLE.

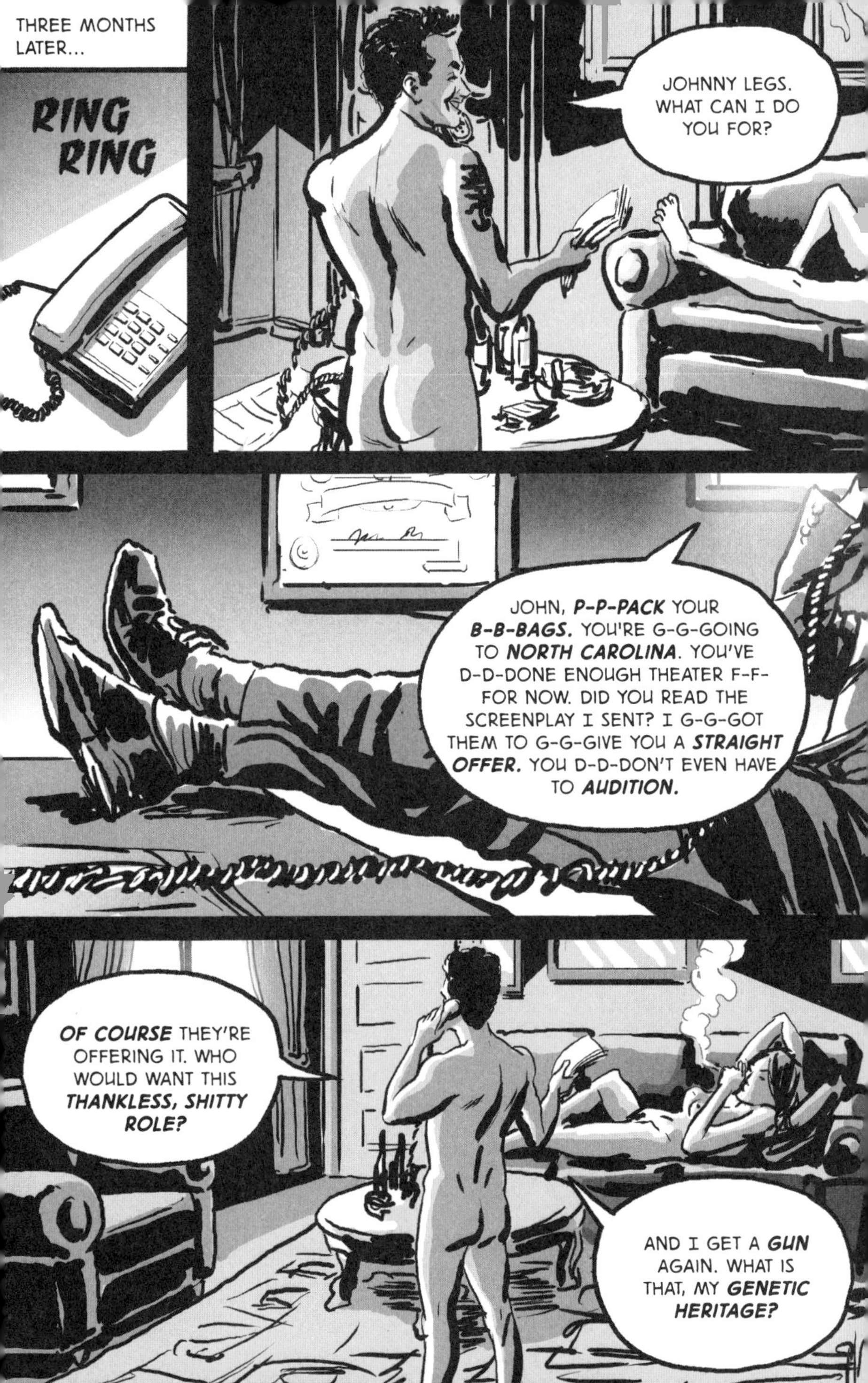
THREE MONTHS LATER...
RING RING
JOHNNY LEGS. WHAT CAN I DO YOU FOR?
JOHN, P-P-PACK YOUR B-B-BAGS. YOU'RE G-G-GOING TO NORTH CAROLINA. YOU'VE D-D-DONE ENOUGH THEATER F-F-FOR NOW. DID YOU READ THE SCREENPLAY I SENT? I G-G-GOT THEM TO G-G-GIVE YOU A STRAIGHT OFFER. YOU D-D-DON'T EVEN HAVE TO AUDITION.
OF COURSE THEY'RE OFFERING IT. WHO WOULD WANT THIS THANKLESS, SHITTY ROLE?
AND I GET A GUN AGAIN. WHAT IS THAT, MY GENETIC HERITAGE?

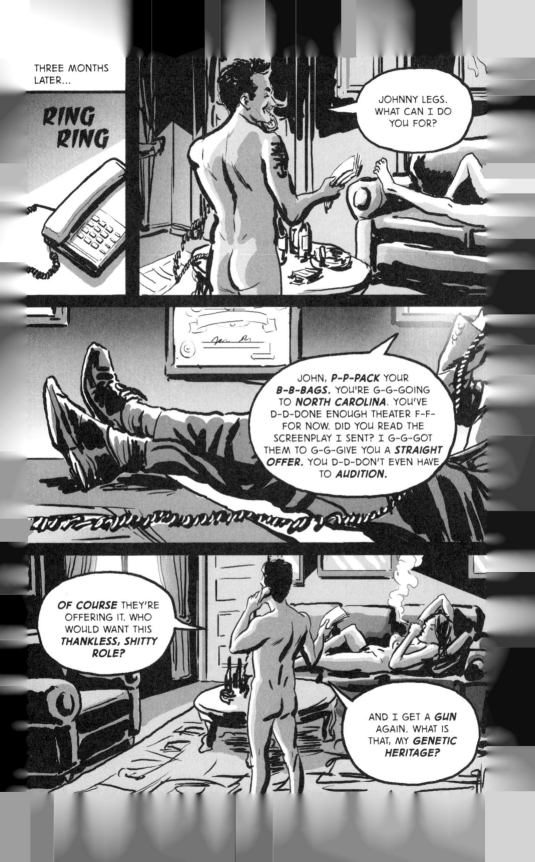

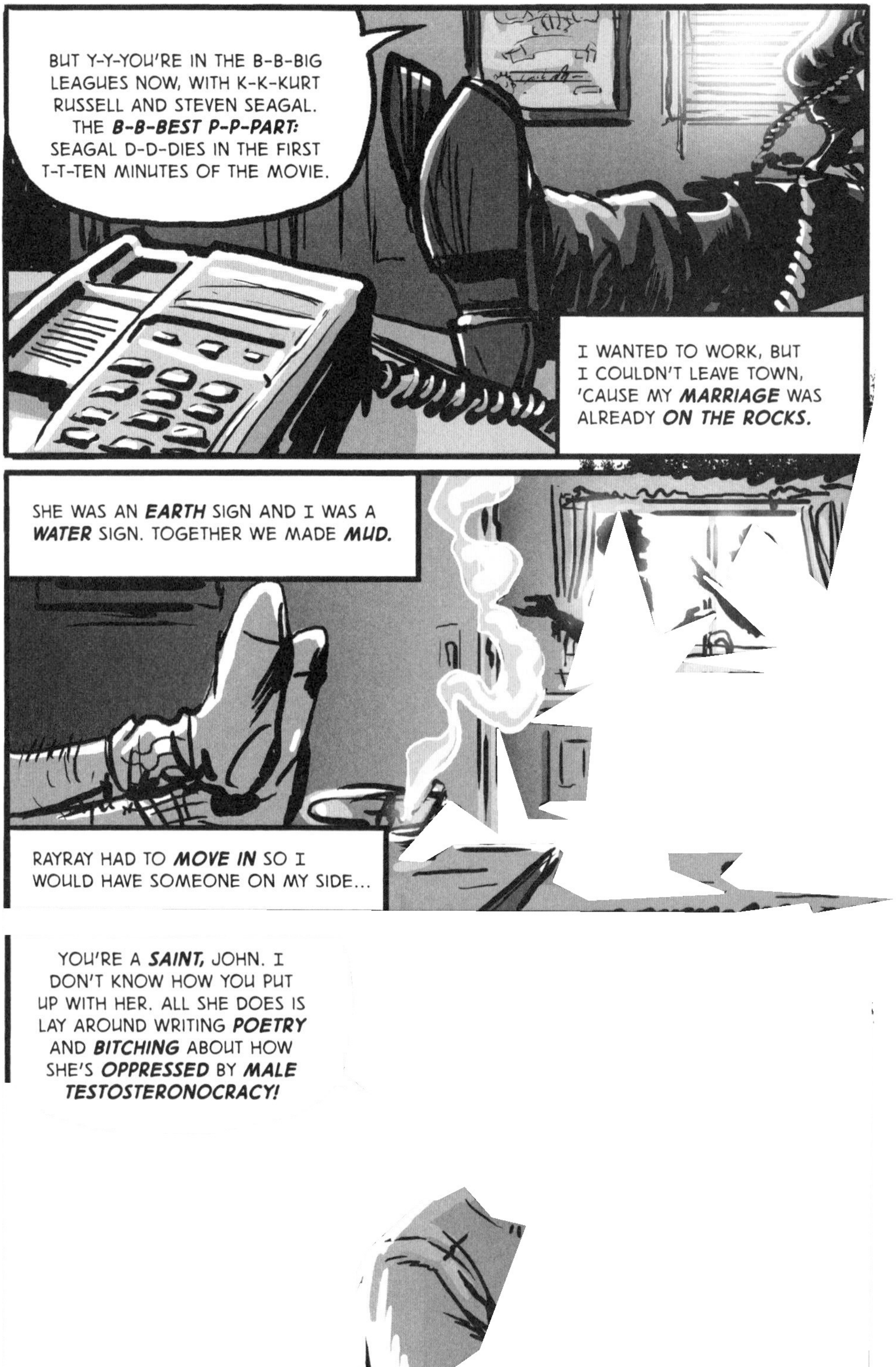
BUT Y-Y-YOU'RE IN THE B-B-BIG LEAGUES NOW, WITH K-K-KURT RUSSELL AND STEVEN SEAGAL. THE B-B-BEST P-P-PART: SEAGAL D-D-DIES IN THE FIRST T-T-TEN MINUTES OF THE MOVIE.
I WANTED TO WORK, BUT I COULDN'T LEAVE TOWN, 'CAUSE MY MARRIAGE WAS ALREADY ON THE ROCKS.
SHE WAS AN EARTH SIGN AND I WAS A WATER SIGN. TOGETHER WE MADE MUD.
RAYRAY HAD TO MOVE IN SO I WOULD HAVE SOMEONE ON MY SIDE...
YOU'RE A SAINT, JOHN. I DON'T KNOW HOW YOU PUT UP WITH HER. ALL SHE DOES IS LAY AROUND WRITING POETRY AND BITCHING ABOUT HOW SHE'S OPPRESSED BY MALE TESTOSTERONOCRACY!

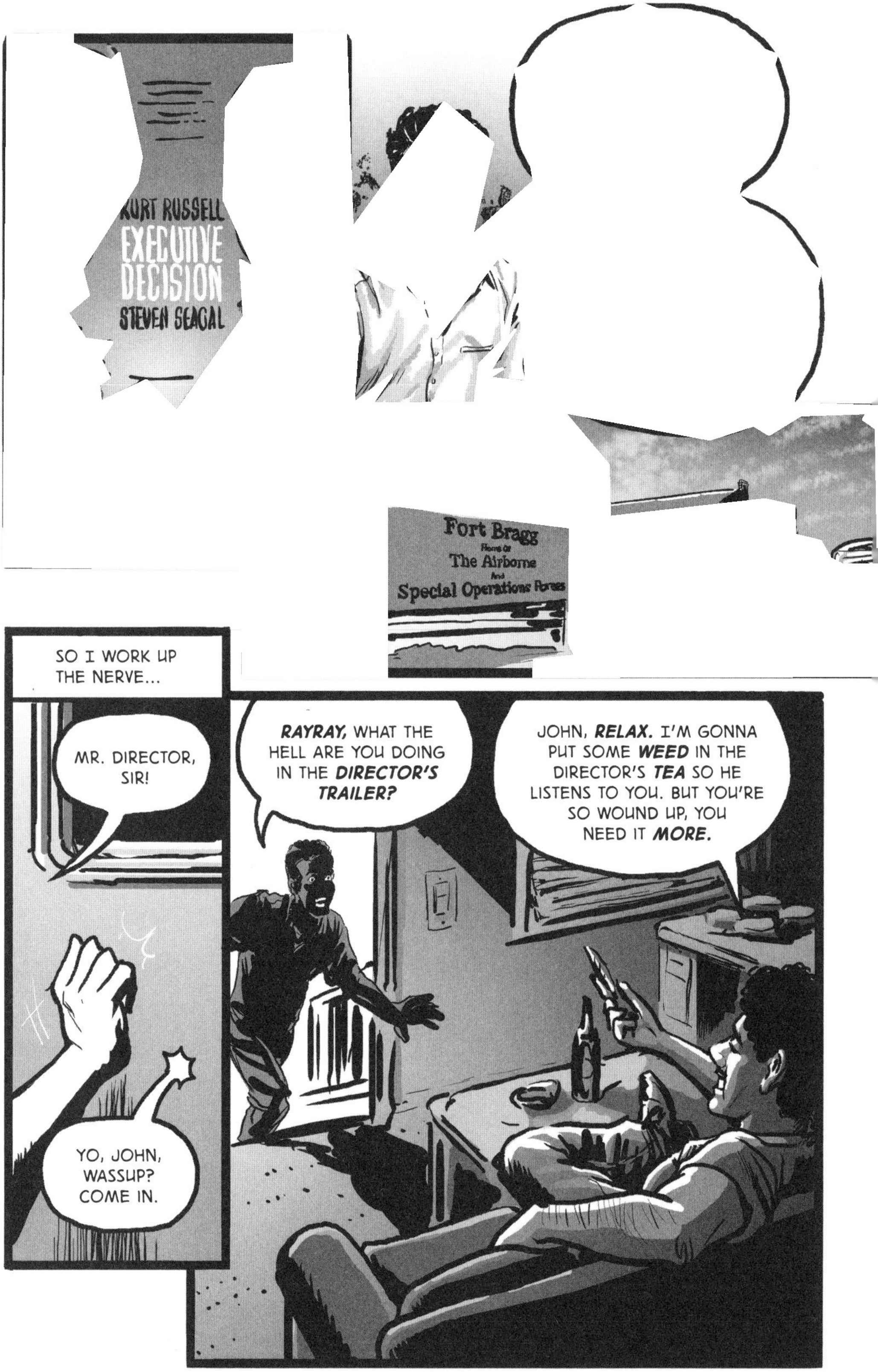
KURT RUSSELL
EXECUTIVE DECISION
STEVEN SEAGAL
Fort Bragg
Home of
The Airborne
And
Special Operations Forces
SO I WORK UP THE NERVE...
MR. DIRECTOR, SIR!
YO, JOHN, WASSUP? COME IN.
RAYRAY, WHAT THE HELL ARE YOU DOING IN THE DIRECTOR'S TRAILER?
JOHN, RELAX. I'M GONNA PUT SOME WEED IN THE DIRECTOR'S TEA SO HE LISTENS TO YOU. BUT YOU'RE SO WOUND UP, YOU NEED IT MORE.

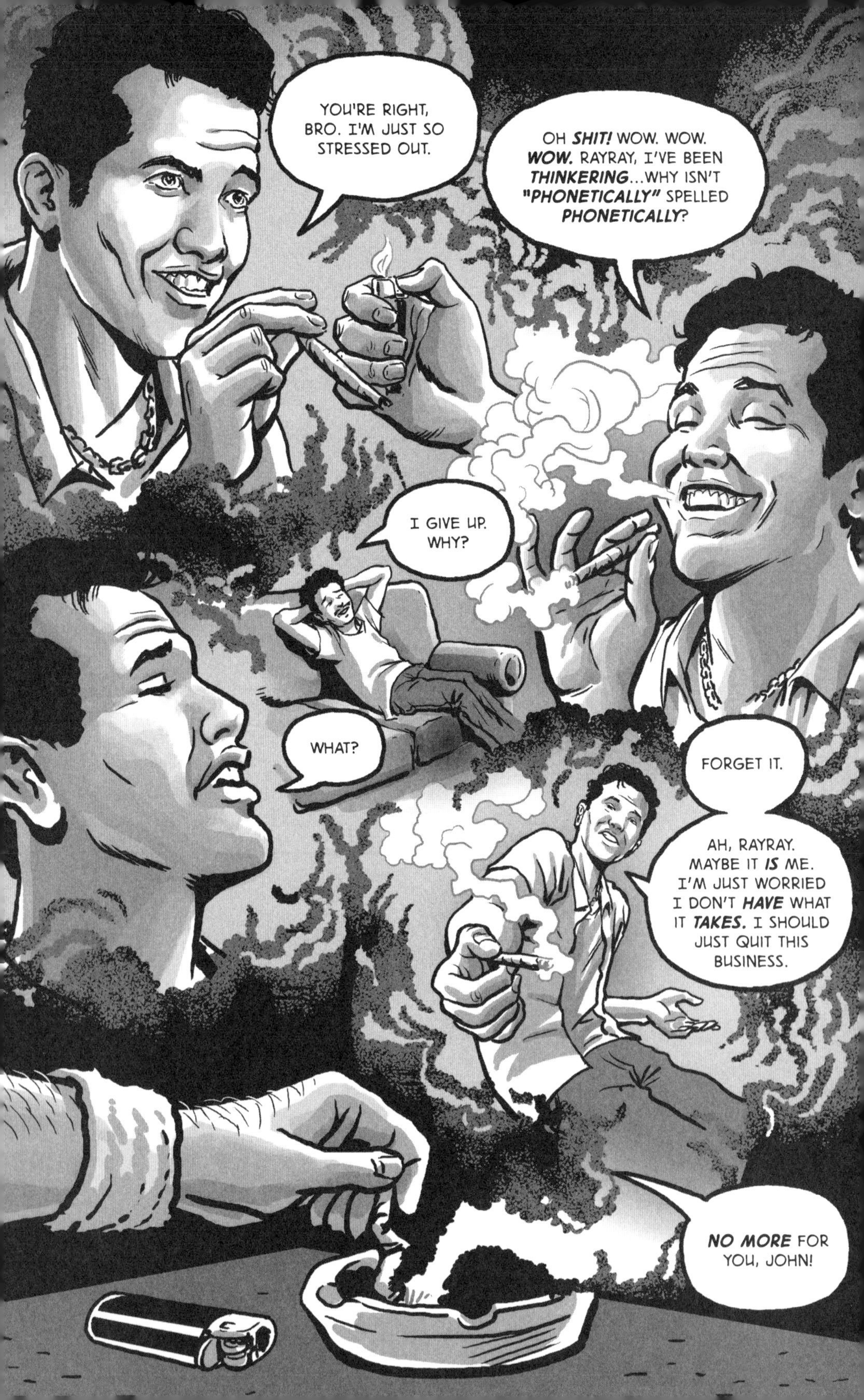
YOU'RE RIGHT, BRO. I'M JUST SO STRESSED OUT.
OH SHIT! WOW. WOW. WOW. RAYRAY, I'VE BEEN THINKERING...WHY ISN'T "PHONETICALLY" SPELLED PHONETICALLY?
I GIVE UP. WHY?
WHAT?
FORGET IT.
AH, RAYRAY. MAYBE IT IS ME. I'M JUST WORRIED I DON'T HAVE WHAT IT TAKES. I SHOULD JUST QUIT THIS BUSINESS.
NO MORE FOR YOU, JOHN!

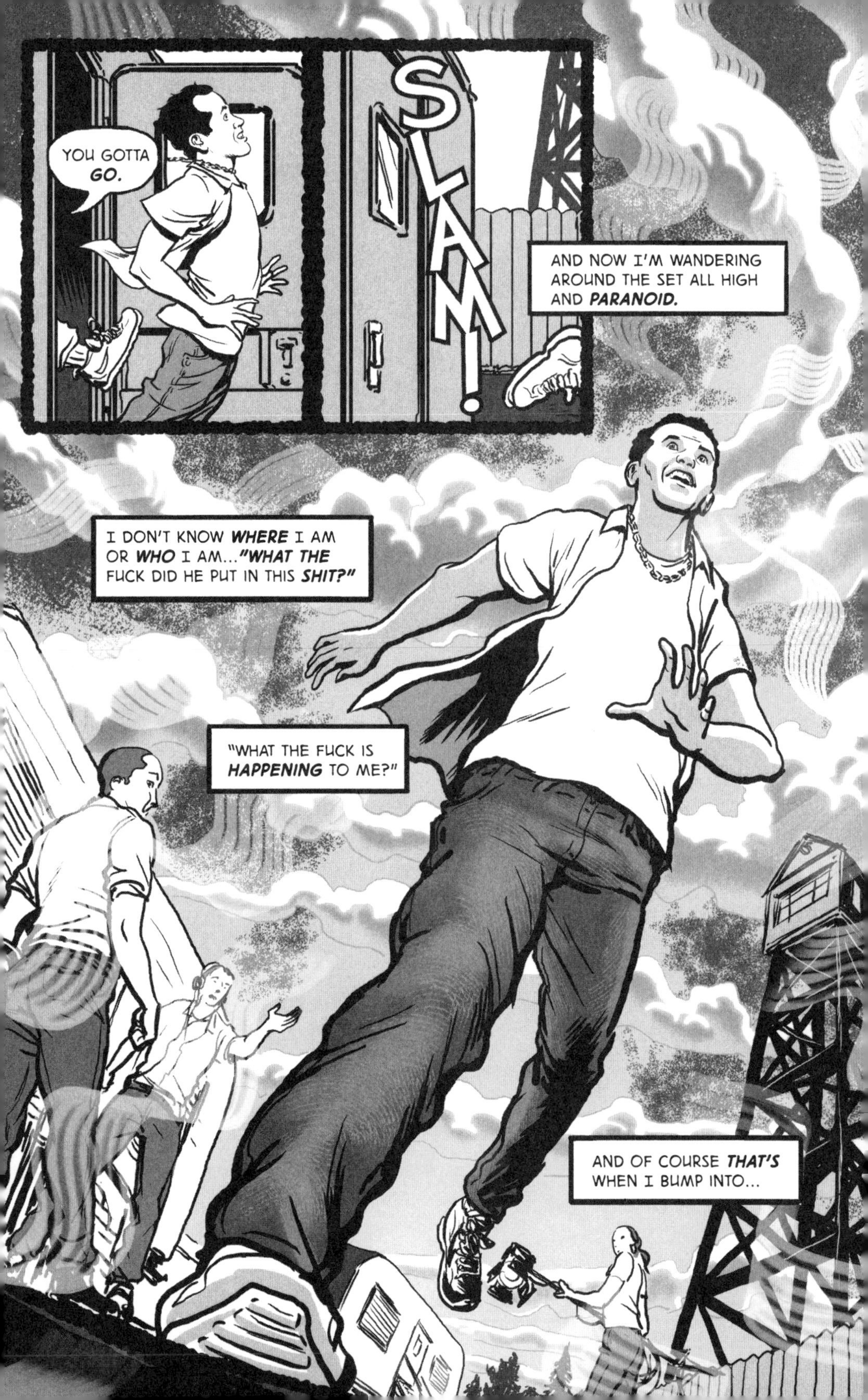

YOU GOTTA GO.
SLAM!
AND NOW I'M WANDERING AROUND THE SET ALL HIGH AND PARANOID.
I DON'T KNOW WHERE I AM OR WHO I AM..."WHAT THE FUCK DID HE PUT IN THIS SHIT?"
"WHAT THE FUCK IS HAPPENING TO ME?"
AND OF COURSE THAT'S WHEN I BUMP INTO...

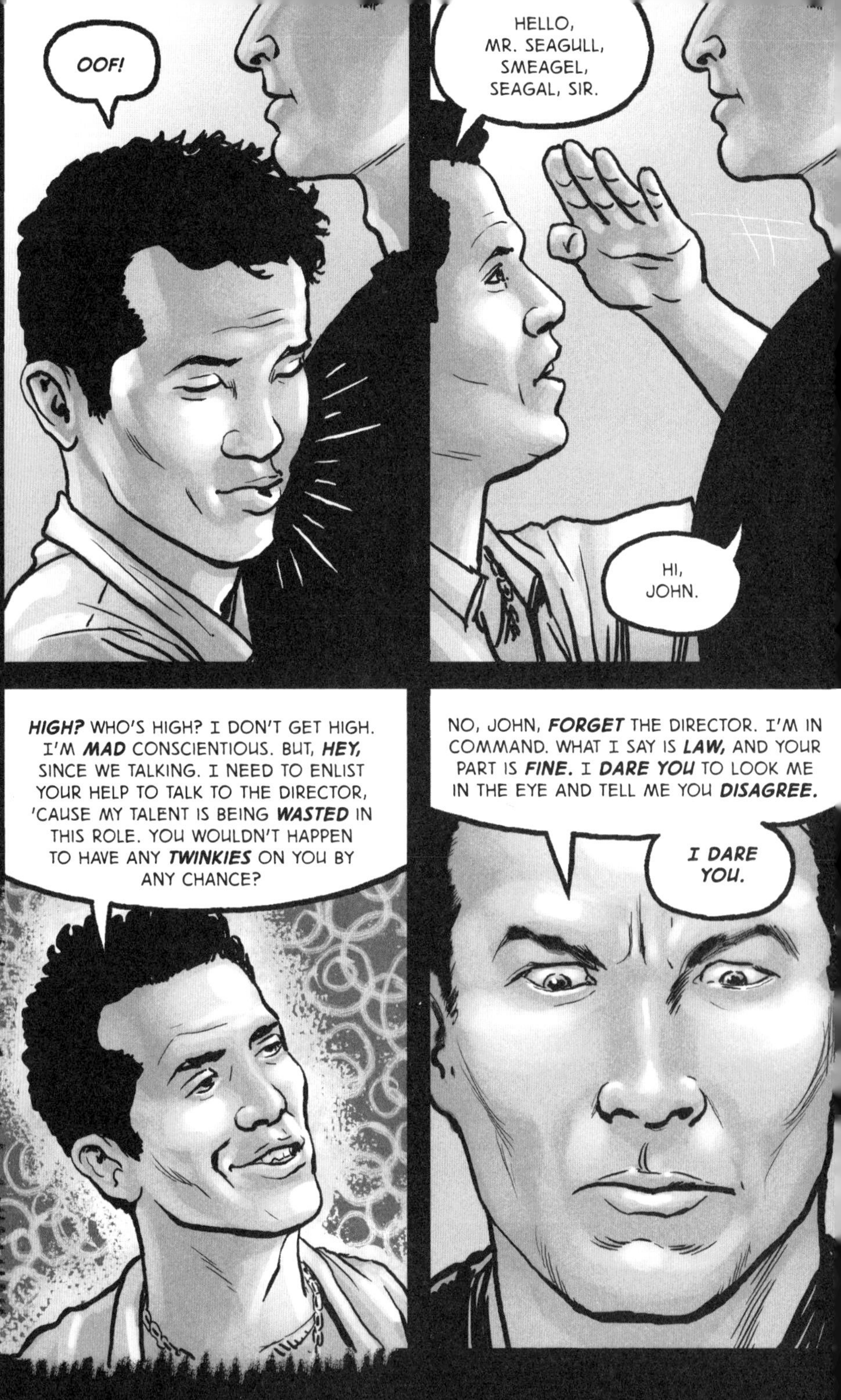
OOF!
HELLO, MR. SEAGULL, SMEAGEL, SEAGAL, SIR.
HI, JOHN.
HIGH? WHO'S HIGH? I DON'T GET HIGH. I'M MAD CONSCIENTIOUS. BUT, HEY, SINCE WE TALKING. I NEED TO ENLIST YOUR HELP TO TALK TO THE DIRECTOR, 'CAUSE MY TALENT IS BEING WASTED IN THIS ROLE. YOU WOULDN'T HAPPEN TO HAVE ANY TWINKIES ON YOU BY ANY CHANCE?
NO, JOHN, FORGET THE DIRECTOR. I'M IN COMMAND. WHAT I SAY IS LAW, AND YOUR PART IS FINE. I DARE YOU TO LOOK ME IN THE EYE AND TELL ME YOU DISAGREE.
I DARE YOU.

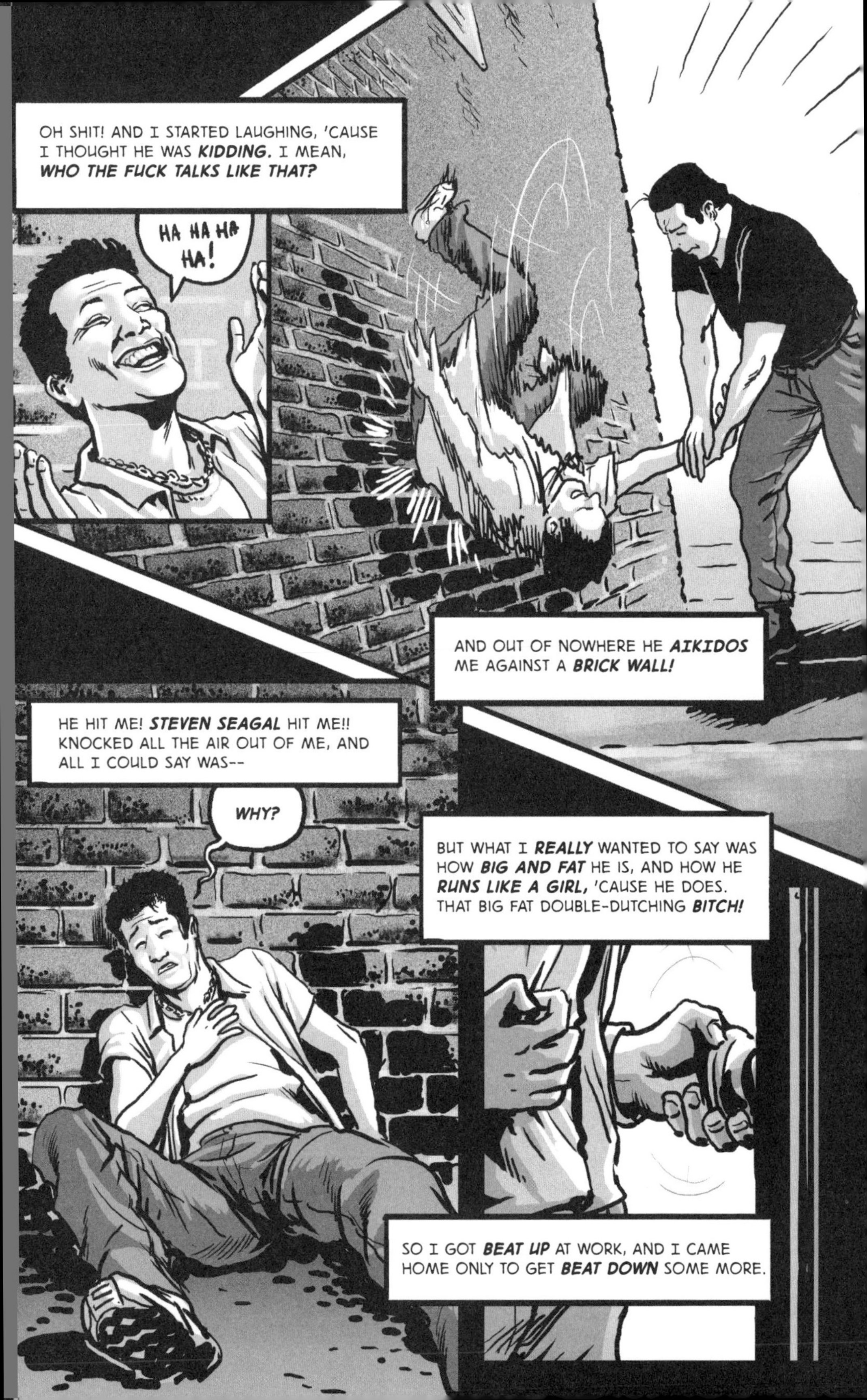
OH SHIT! AND I STARTED LAUGHING, 'CAUSE I THOUGHT HE WAS KIDDING. I MEAN, WHO THE FUCK TALKS LIKE THAT?
HA HA HA HA!
AND OUT OF NOWHERE HE AIKIDOS ME AGAINST A BRICK WALL!
HE HIT ME! STEVEN SEAGAL HIT ME!! KNOCKED ALL THE AIR OUT OF ME, AND ALL I COULD SAY WAS--
WHY?
BUT WHAT I REALLY WANTED TO SAY WAS HOW BIG AND FAT HE IS, AND HOW HE RUNS LIKE A GIRL, 'CAUSE HE DOES. THAT BIG FAT DOUBLE-DUTCHING BITCH!
SO I GOT BEAT UP AT WORK, AND I CAME HOME ONLY TO GET BEAT DOWN SOME MORE.

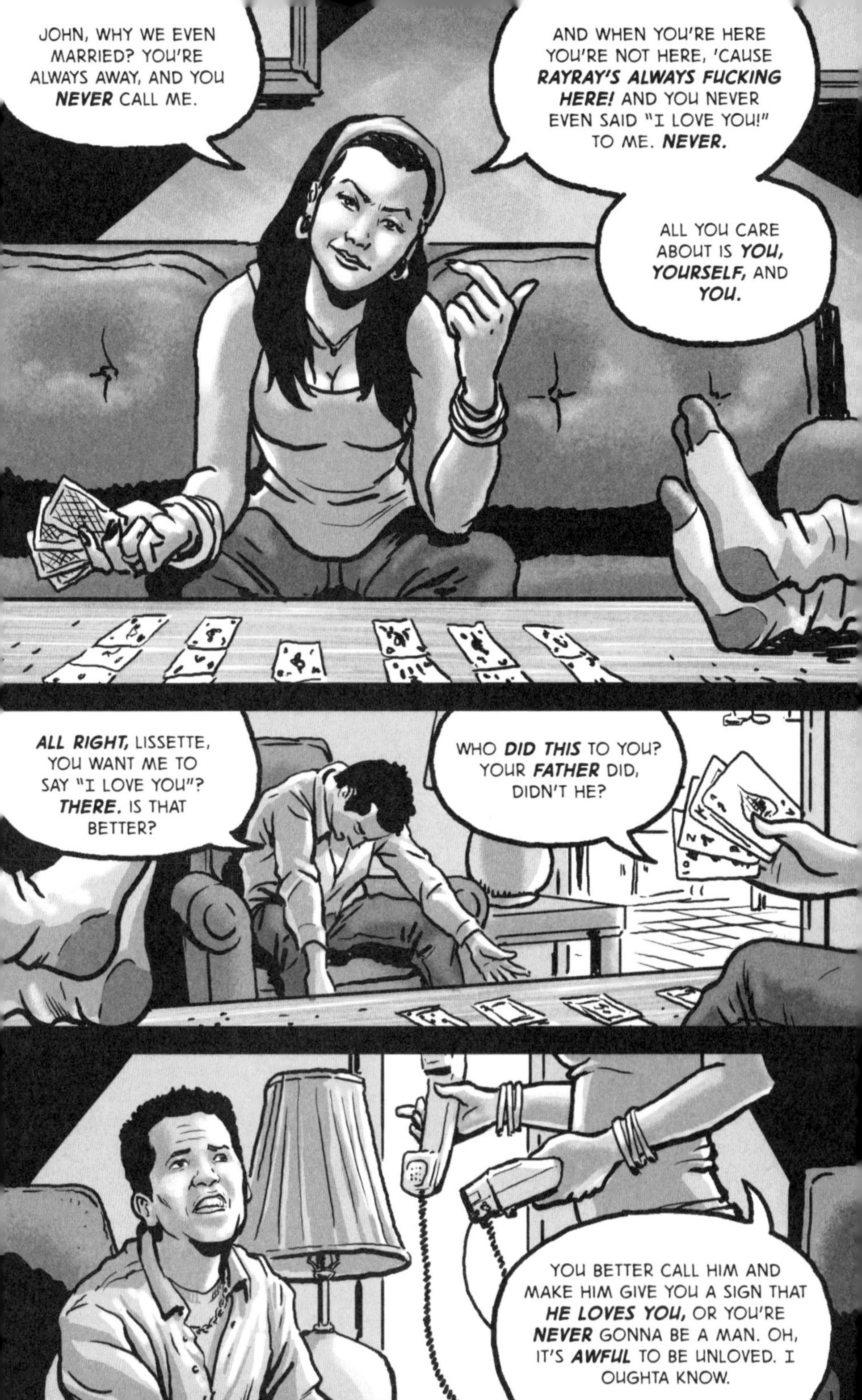
JOHN, WHY WE EVEN MARRIED? YOU'RE ALWAYS AWAY, AND YOU NEVER CALL ME.
AND WHEN YOU'RE HERE YOU'RE NOT HERE, 'CAUSE RAYRAY'S ALWAYS FUCKING HERE! AND YOU NEVER EVEN SAID "I LOVE YOU!" TO ME. NEVER.
ALL YOU CARE ABOUT IS YOU, YOURSELF, AND YOU.
ALL RIGHT, LISSETTE, YOU WANT ME TO SAY "I LOVE YOU"? THERE. IS THAT BETTER?
WHO DID THIS TO YOU? YOUR FATHER DID, DIDN'T HE?
YOU BETTER CALL HIM AND MAKE HIM GIVE YOU A SIGN THAT HE LOVES YOU, OR YOU'RE NEVER GONNA BE A MAN. OH, IT'S AWFUL TO BE UNLOVED. I OUGHTA KNOW.

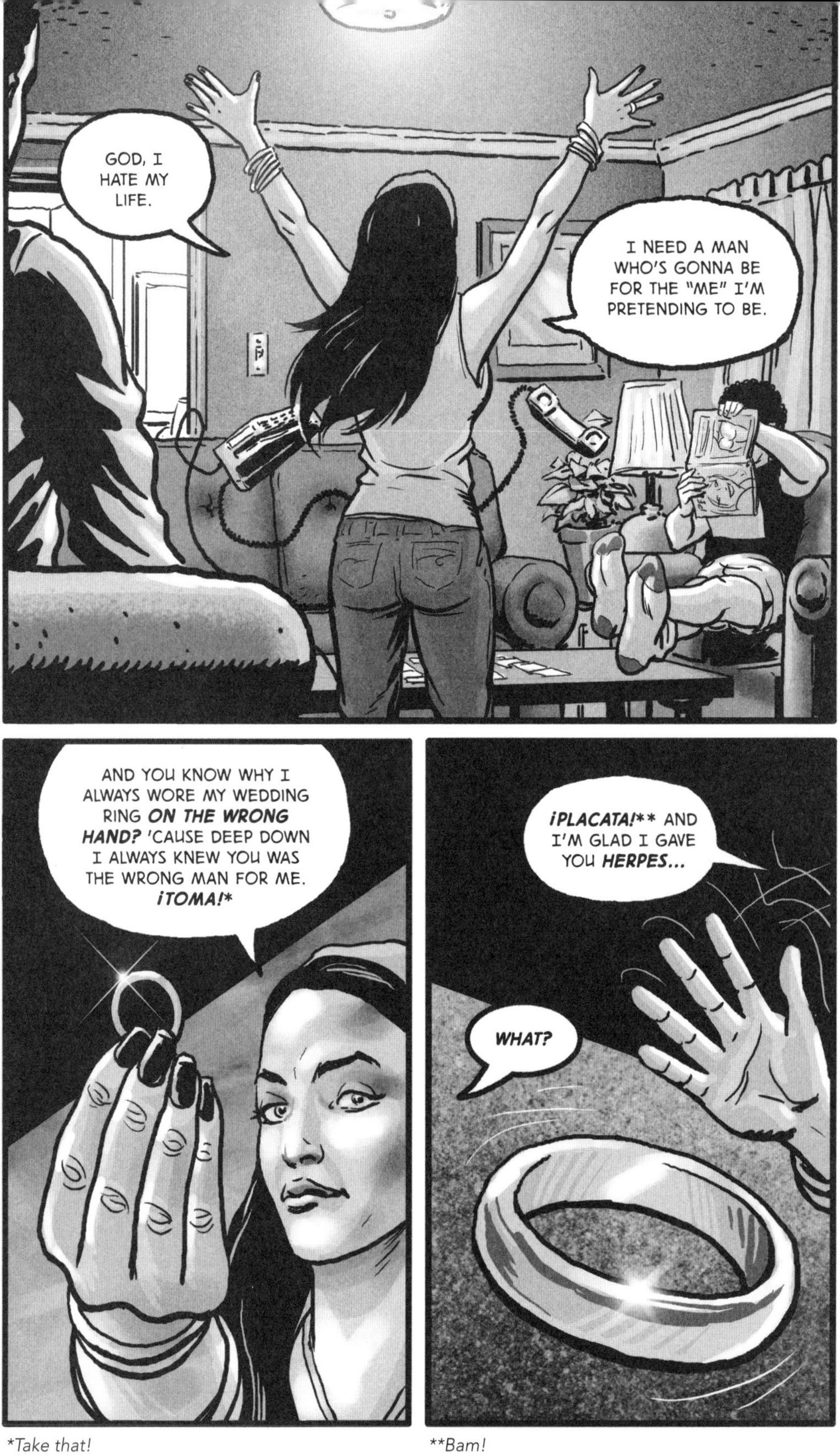
GOD, I HATE MY LIFE.
I NEED A MAN WHO'S GONNA BE FOR THE "ME" I'M PRETENDING TO BE.
AND YOU KNOW WHY I ALWAYS WORE MY WEDDING RING ***ON THE WRONG HAND?*** 'CAUSE DEEP DOWN I ALWAYS KNEW YOU WAS THE WRONG MAN FOR ME. ***¡TOMA!****
¡PLACATA!** AND I'M GLAD I GAVE YOU ***HERPES...***
WHAT?

*Take that!

**Bam!

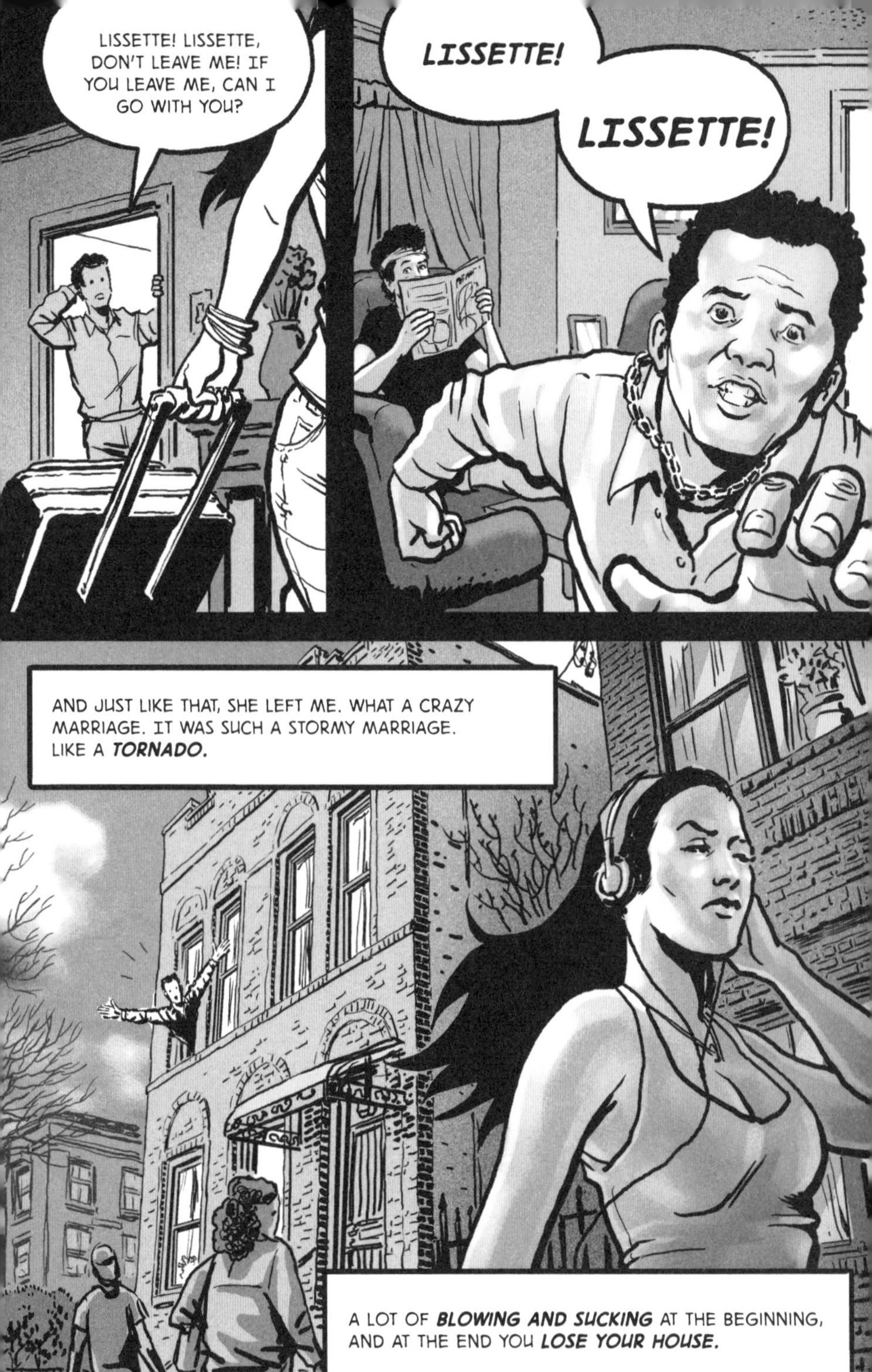
LISSETTE! LISSETTE, DON'T LEAVE ME! IF YOU LEAVE ME, CAN I GO WITH YOU?
LISSETTE!
LISSETTE!
AND JUST LIKE THAT, SHE LEFT ME. WHAT A CRAZY MARRIAGE. IT WAS SUCH A STORMY MARRIAGE. LIKE A TORNADO.
A LOT OF BLOWING AND SUCKING AT THE BEGINNING, AND AT THE END YOU LOSE YOUR HOUSE.

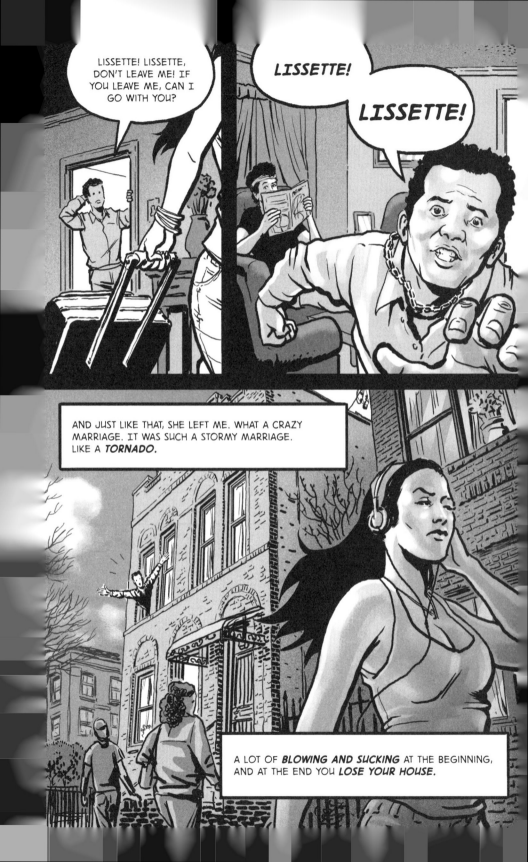

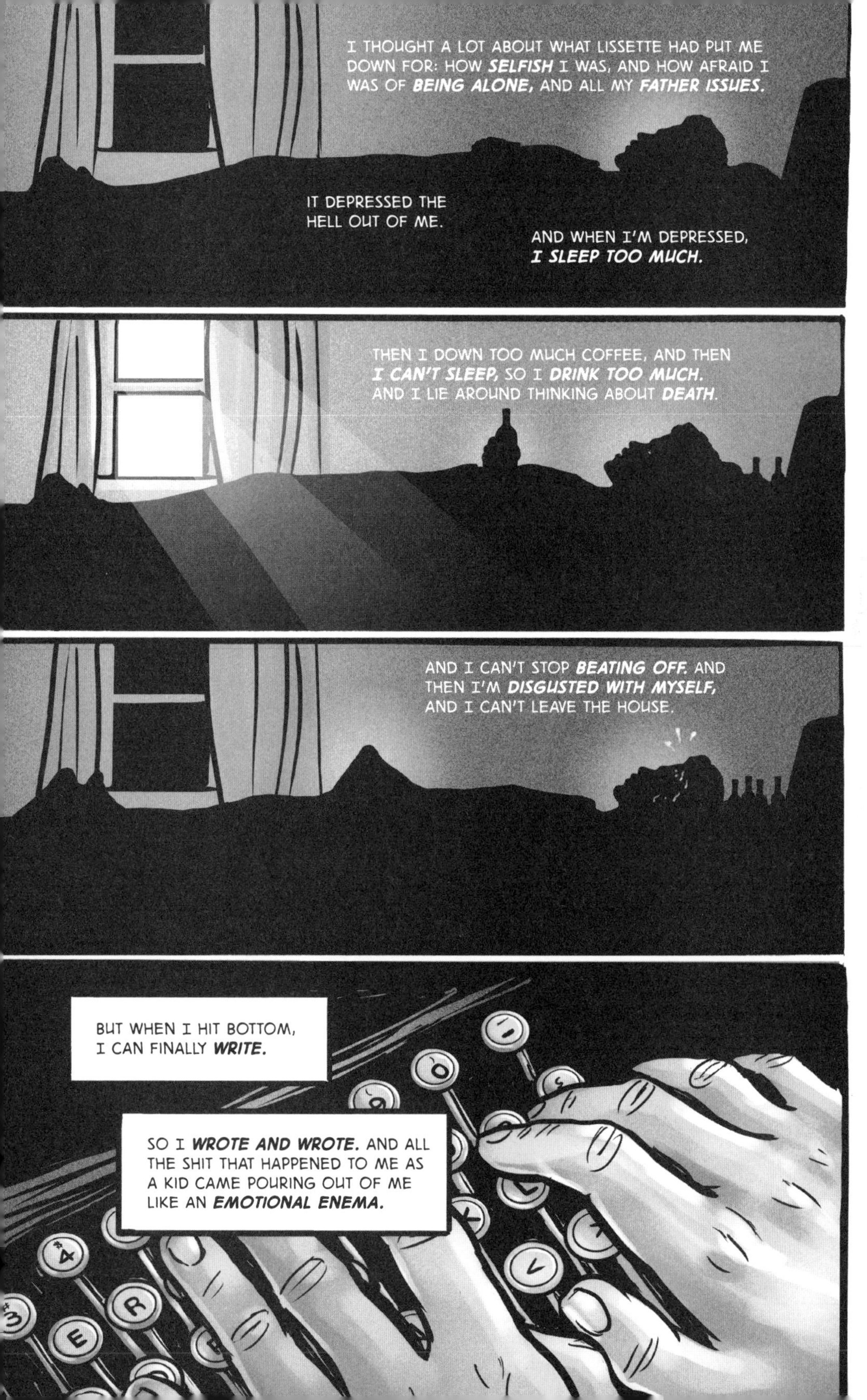

I THOUGHT A LOT ABOUT WHAT LISSETTE HAD PUT ME DOWN FOR: HOW SELFISH I WAS, AND HOW AFRAID I WAS OF BEING ALONE, AND ALL MY FATHER ISSUES.
IT DEPRESSED THE HELL OUT OF ME.
AND WHEN I'M DEPRESSED, I SLEEP TOO MUCH.
THEN I DOWN TOO MUCH COFFEE, AND THEN I CAN'T SLEEP, SO I DRINK TOO MUCH. AND I LIE AROUND THINKING ABOUT DEATH.
AND I CAN'T STOP BEATING OFF. AND THEN I'M DISGUSTED WITH MYSELF, AND I CAN'T LEAVE THE HOUSE.
BUT WHEN I HIT BOTTOM, I CAN FINALLY WRITE.
SO I WROTE AND WROTE. AND ALL THE SHIT THAT HAPPENED TO ME AS A KID CAME POURING OUT OF ME LIKE AN EMOTIONAL ENEMA.

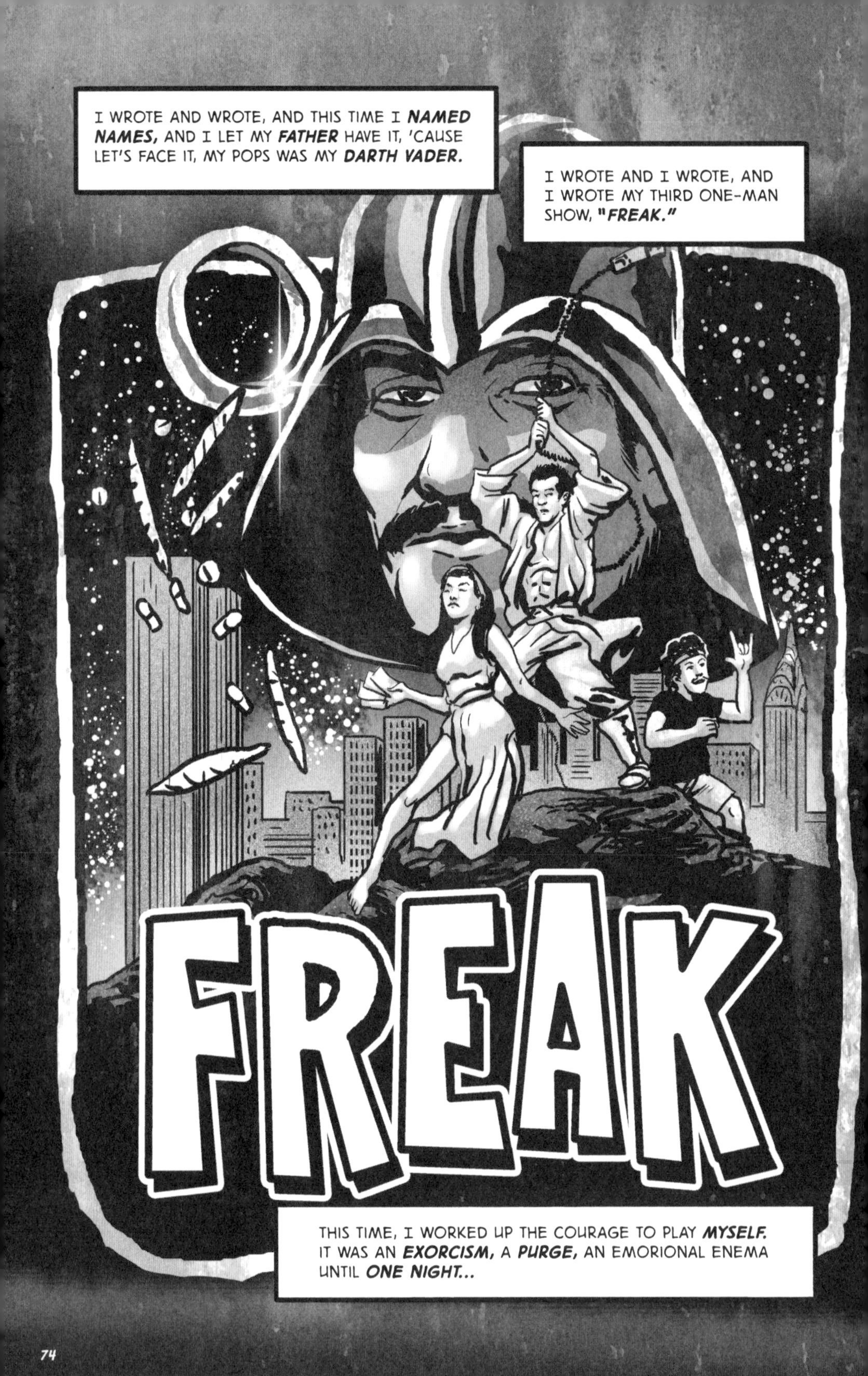
I WROTE AND WROTE, AND THIS TIME I NAMED NAMES, AND I LET MY FATHER HAVE IT, 'CAUSE LET'S FACE IT, MY POPS WAS MY DARTH VADER.
I WROTE AND I WROTE, AND I WROTE MY THIRD ONE-MAN SHOW, "FREAK."
FREAK
THIS TIME, I WORKED UP THE COURAGE TO PLAY MYSELF. IT WAS AN EXORCISM, A PURGE, AN EMORIONAL ENEMA UNTIL ONE NIGHT...

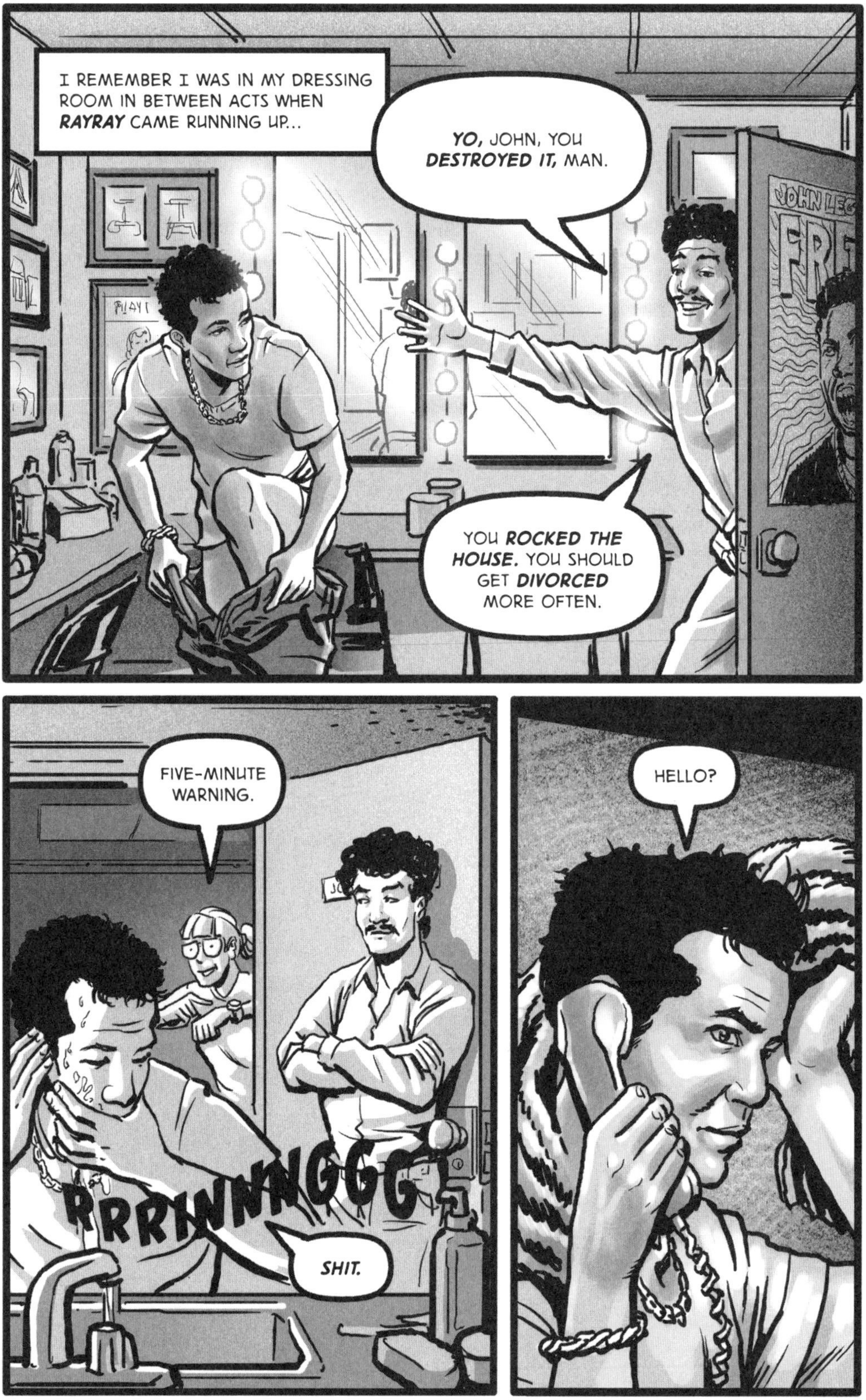
I REMEMBER I WAS IN MY DRESSING ROOM IN BETWEEN ACTS WHEN RAYRAY CAME RUNNING UP...
YO, JOHN, YOU DESTROYED IT, MAN.
YOU ROCKED THE HOUSE. YOU SHOULD GET DIVORCED MORE OFTEN.
FIVE-MINUTE WARNING.
RRRINNNGGG
SHIT.
HELLO?

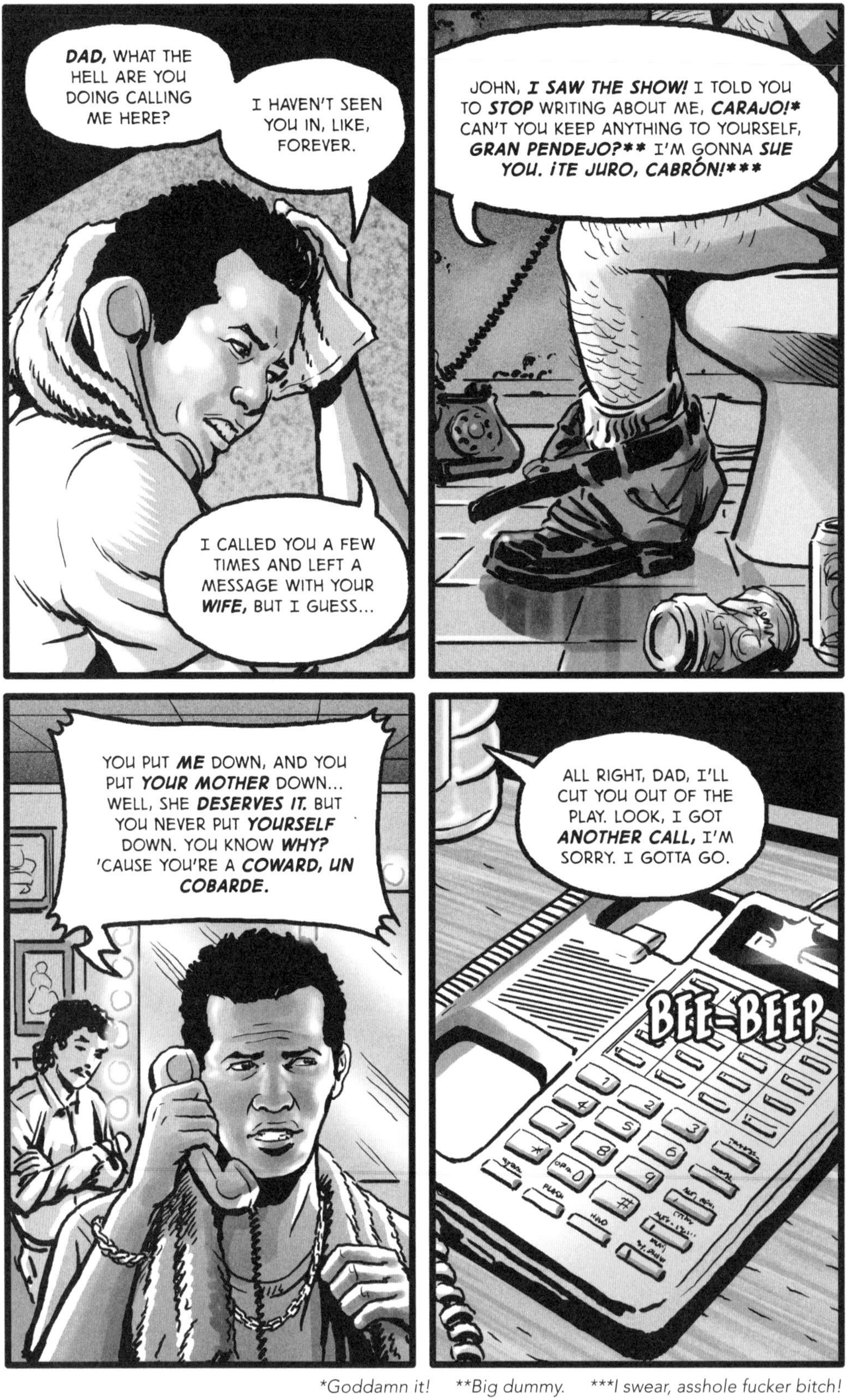
DAD, WHAT THE HELL ARE YOU DOING CALLING ME HERE?
I HAVEN'T SEEN YOU IN, LIKE, FOREVER.
I CALLED YOU A FEW TIMES AND LEFT A MESSAGE WITH YOUR WIFE, BUT I GUESS...
JOHN, I SAW THE SHOW! I TOLD YOU TO STOP WRITING ABOUT ME, CARAJO!* CAN'T YOU KEEP ANYTHING TO YOURSELF, GRAN PENDEJO?** I'M GONNA SUE YOU. ¡TE JURO, CABRÓN!***
YOU PUT ME DOWN, AND YOU PUT YOUR MOTHER DOWN... WELL, SHE DESERVES IT. BUT YOU NEVER PUT YOURSELF DOWN. YOU KNOW WHY? 'CAUSE YOU'RE A COWARD, UN COBARDE.
ALL RIGHT, DAD, I'LL CUT YOU OUT OF THE PLAY. LOOK, I GOT ANOTHER CALL, I'M SORRY. I GOTTA GO.
BEE-BEEP

*Goddamn it! **Big dummy. ***I swear, asshole fucker bitch!

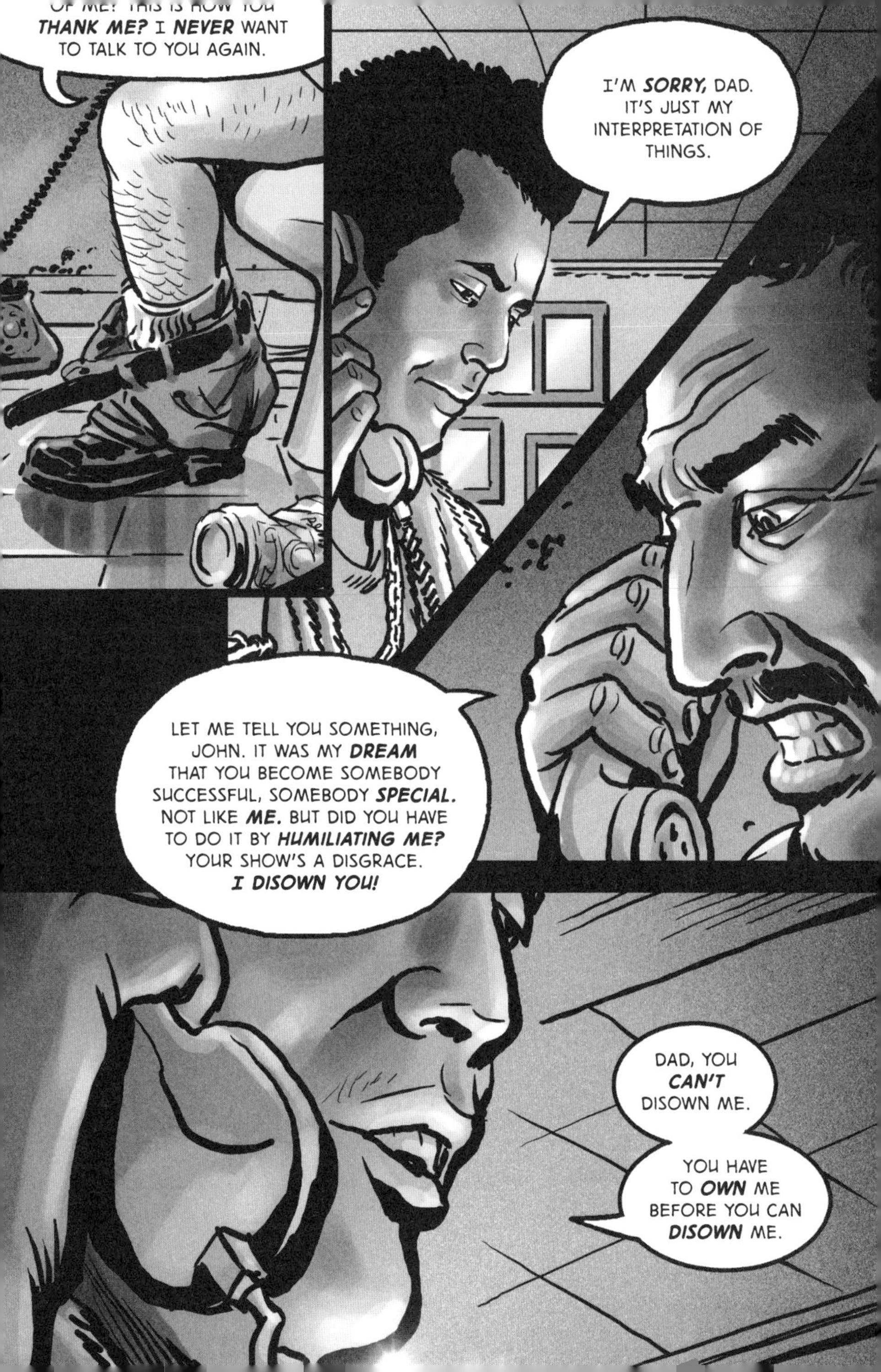
THANK ME? I NEVER WANT TO TALK TO YOU AGAIN.
I'M SORRY, DAD. IT'S JUST MY INTERPRETATION OF THINGS.
LET ME TELL YOU SOMETHING, JOHN. IT WAS MY DREAM THAT YOU BECOME SOMEBODY SUCCESSFUL, SOMEBODY SPECIAL. NOT LIKE ME. BUT DID YOU HAVE TO DO IT BY HUMILIATING ME? YOUR SHOW'S A DISGRACE. I DISOWN YOU!
DAD, YOU CAN'T DISOWN ME.
YOU HAVE TO OWN ME BEFORE YOU CAN DISOWN ME.

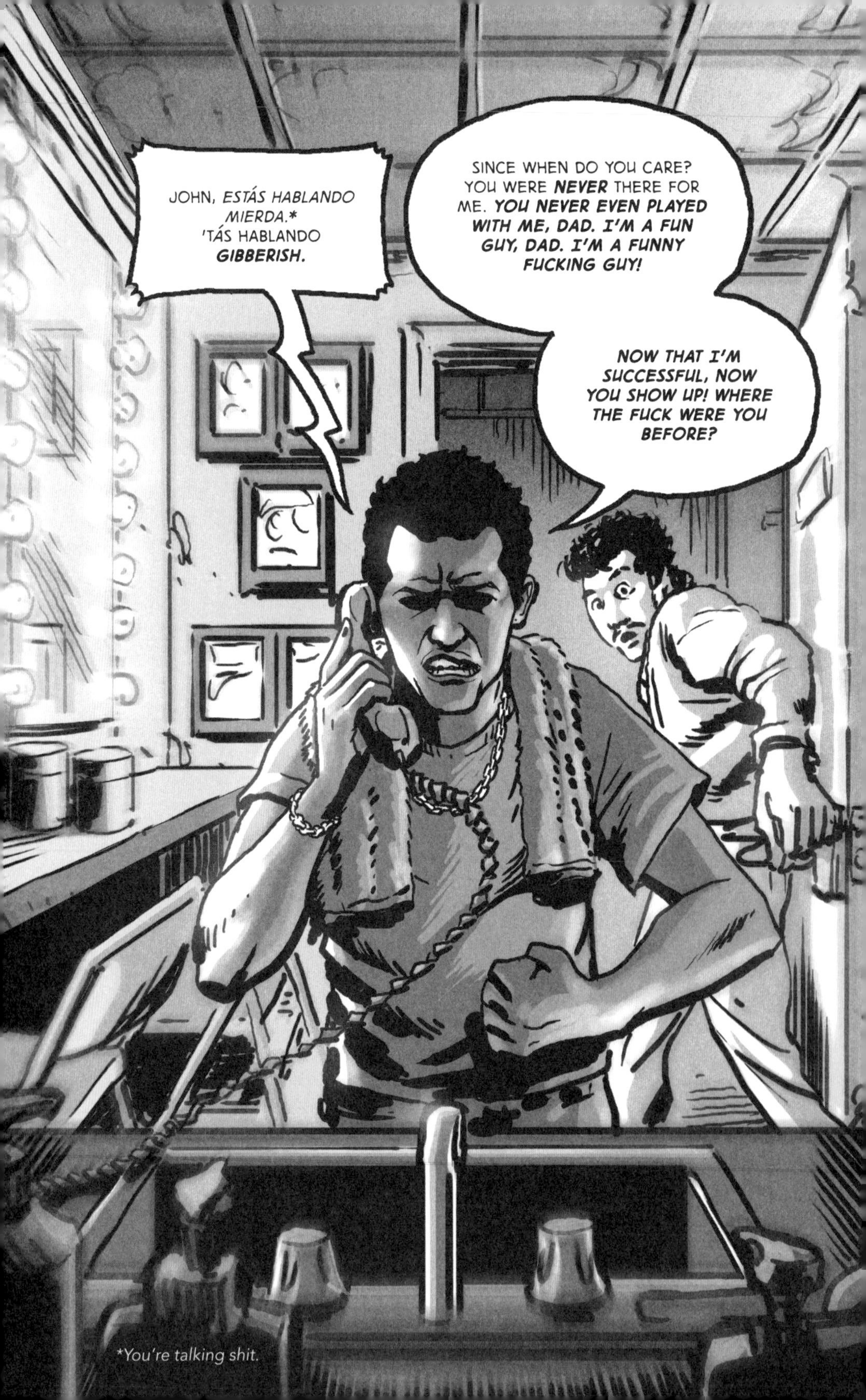
JOHN, *ESTÁS HABLANDO MIERDA.** 'TÁS HABLANDO **GIBBERISH.**
SINCE WHEN DO YOU CARE? YOU WERE **NEVER** THERE FOR ME. ***YOU NEVER EVEN PLAYED WITH ME, DAD. I'M A FUN GUY, DAD. I'M A FUNNY FUCKING GUY!***
NOW THAT I'M SUCCESSFUL, NOW YOU SHOW UP! WHERE THE FUCK WERE YOU BEFORE?

**You're talking shit.*

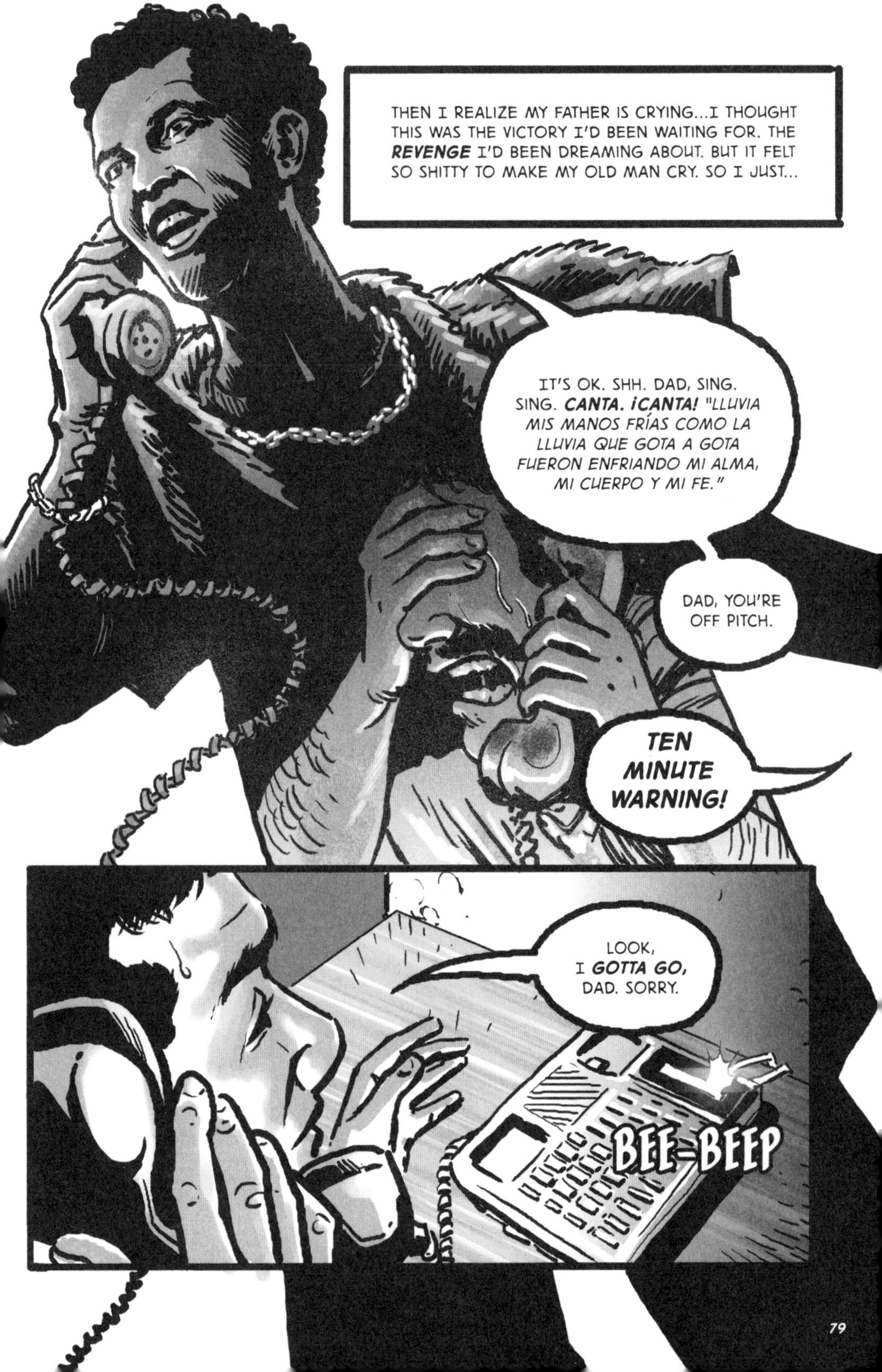

THEN I REALIZE MY FATHER IS CRYING...I THOUGHT THIS WAS THE VICTORY I'D BEEN WAITING FOR. THE ***REVENGE*** I'D BEEN DREAMING ABOUT. BUT IT FELT SO SHITTY TO MAKE MY OLD MAN CRY. SO I JUST...
IT'S OK. SHH. DAD, SING. SING. ***CANTA. ¡CANTA!*** *"LLUVIA MIS MANOS FRÍAS COMO LA LLUVIA QUE GOTA A GOTA FUERON ENFRIANDO MI ALMA, MI CUERPO Y MI FE."*
DAD, YOU'RE OFF PITCH.
TEN MINUTE WARNING!
LOOK, I ***GOTTA GO,*** DAD. SORRY.
BEE-BEEP

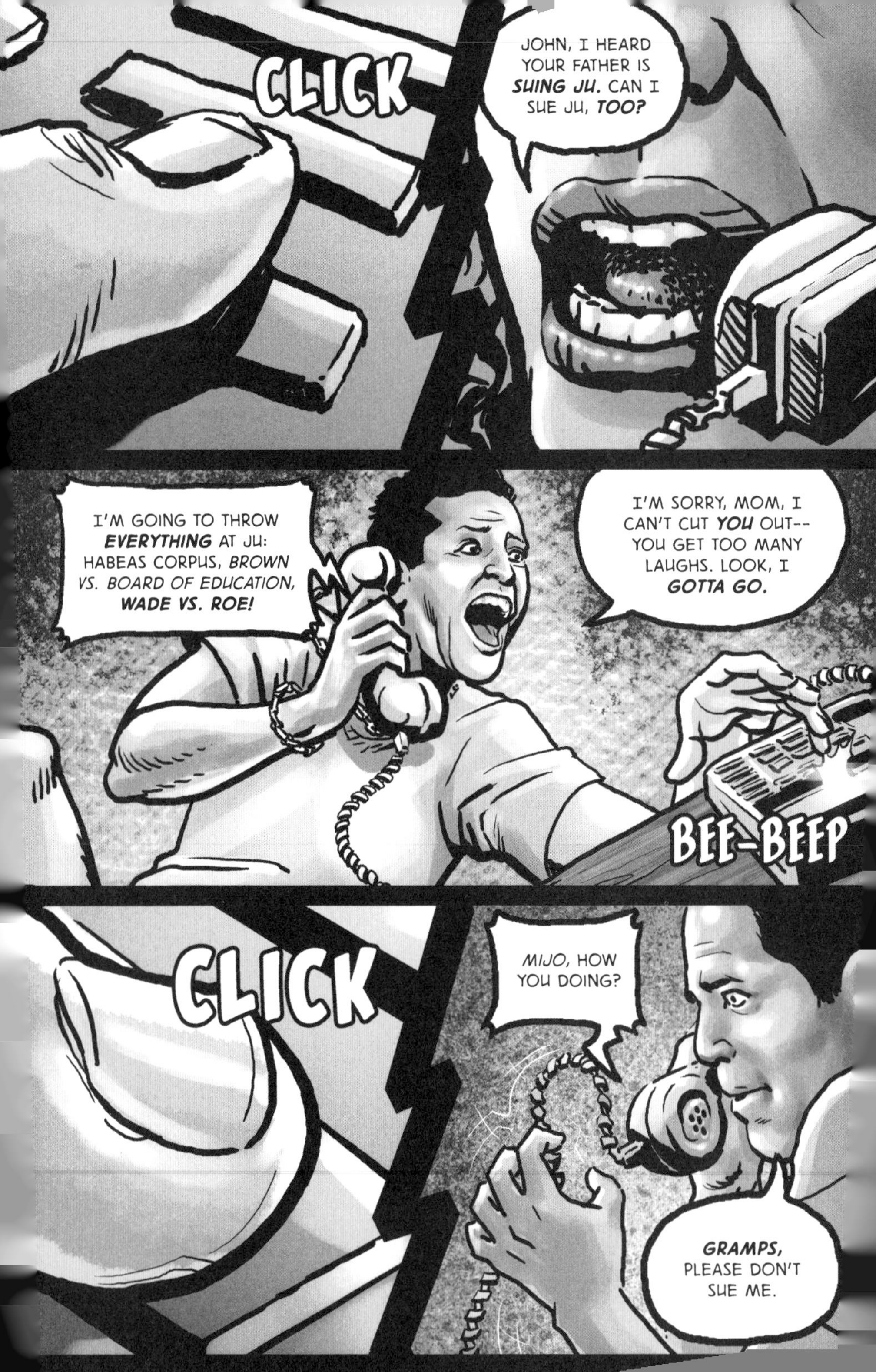
CLICK
JOHN, I HEARD YOUR FATHER IS **SUING JU.** CAN I SUE JU, ***TOO?***
I'M GOING TO THROW ***EVERYTHING*** AT JU: HABEAS CORPUS, *BROWN VS. BOARD OF EDUCATION*, ***WADE VS. ROE!***
I'M SORRY, MOM, I CAN'T CUT ***YOU*** OUT-- YOU GET TOO MANY LAUGHS. LOOK, I ***GOTTA GO.***
BEE-BEEP
CLICK
MIJO, HOW YOU DOING?
GRAMPS, PLEASE DON'T SUE ME.

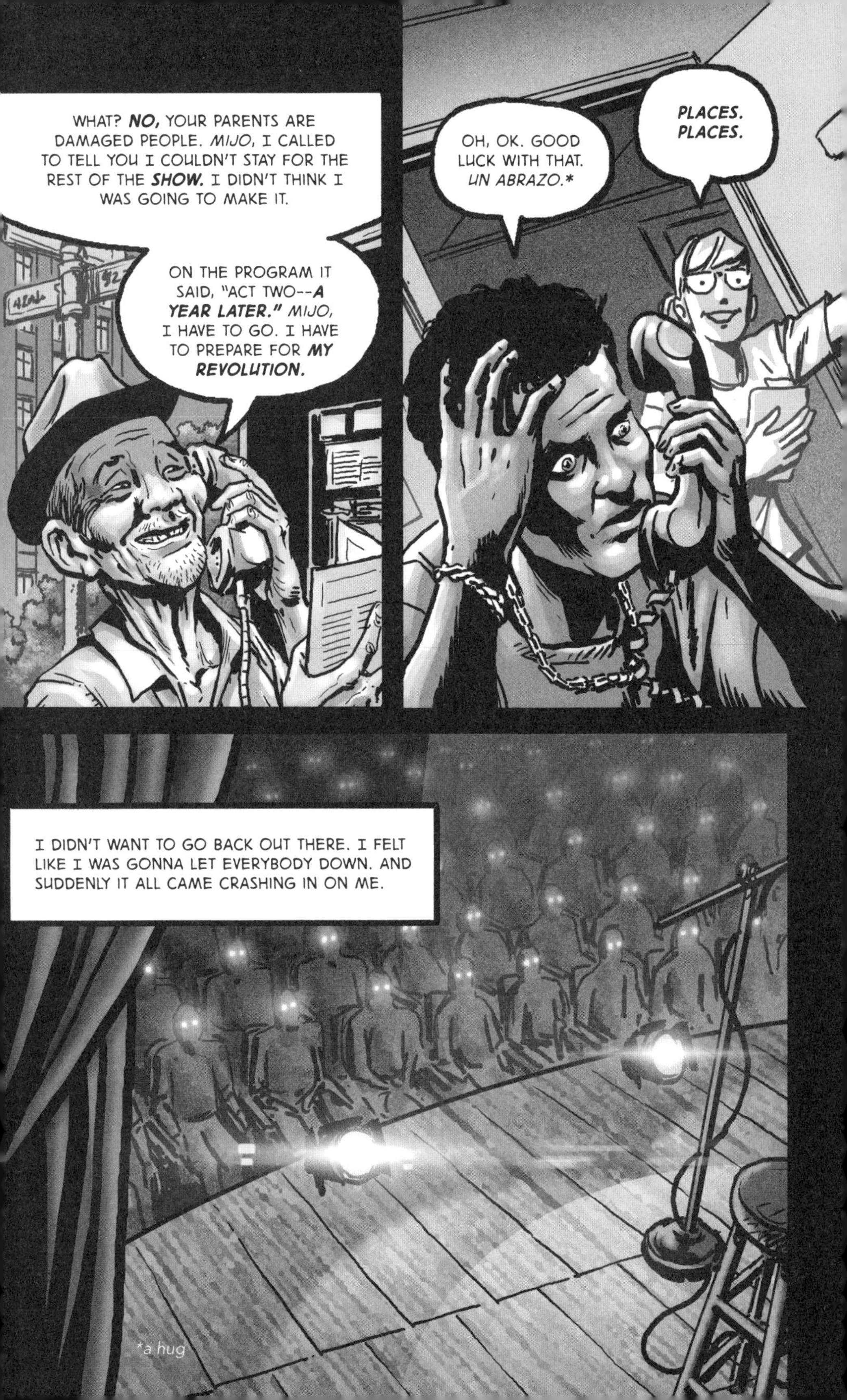

WHAT? **NO,** YOUR PARENTS ARE DAMAGED PEOPLE. *MIJO,* I CALLED TO TELL YOU I COULDN'T STAY FOR THE REST OF THE **SHOW.** I DIDN'T THINK I WAS GOING TO MAKE IT.
ON THE PROGRAM IT SAID, "ACT TWO--**A YEAR LATER.**" *MIJO,* I HAVE TO GO. I HAVE TO PREPARE FOR **MY REVOLUTION.**
OH, OK. GOOD LUCK WITH THAT. *UN ABRAZO.**
PLACES. PLACES.
I DIDN'T WANT TO GO BACK OUT THERE. I FELT LIKE I WAS GONNA LET EVERYBODY DOWN. AND SUDDENLY IT ALL CAME CRASHING IN ON ME.

*a hug

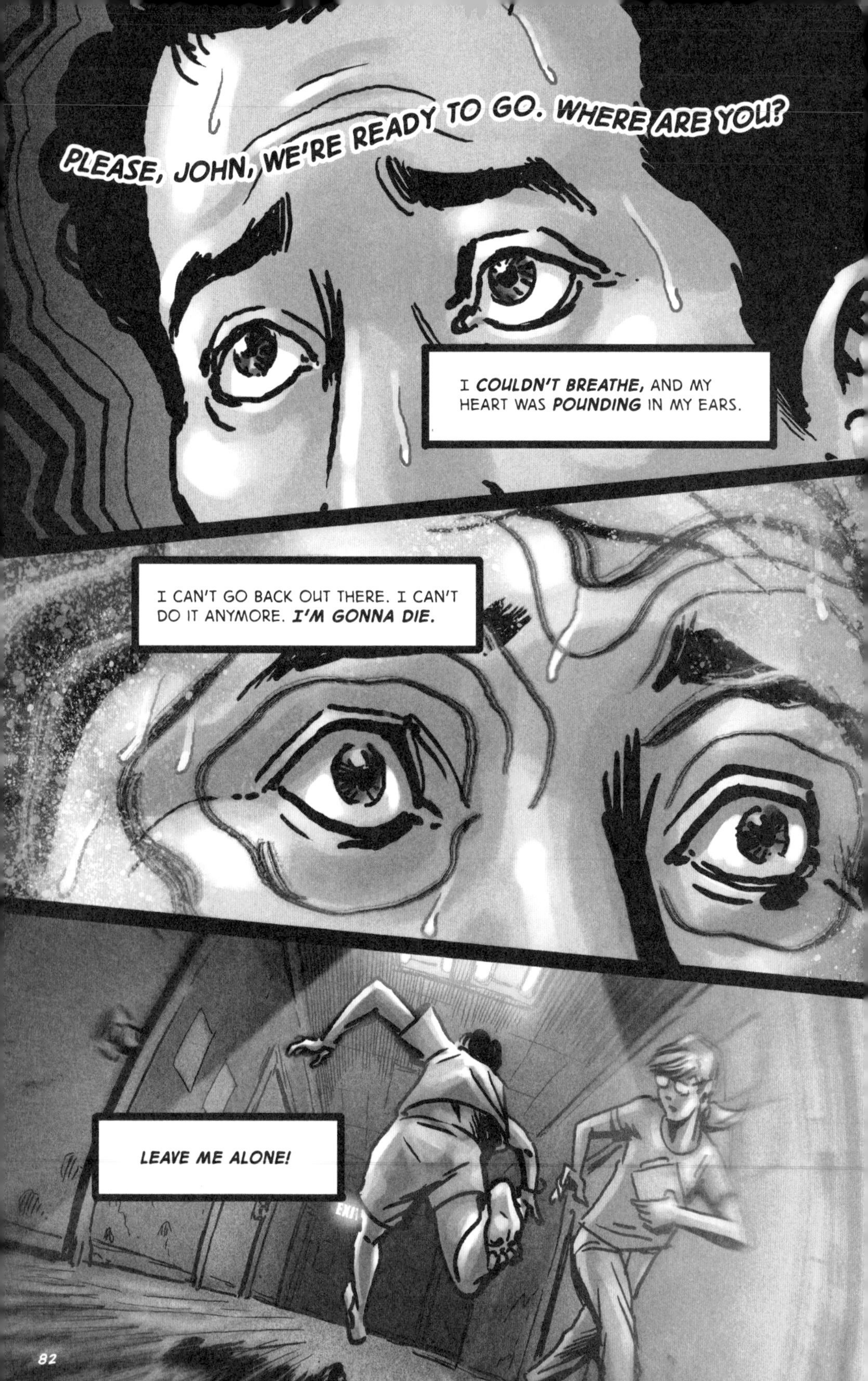
PLEASE, JOHN, WE'RE READY TO GO. WHERE ARE YOU?
I COULDN'T BREATHE, AND MY HEART WAS POUNDING IN MY EARS.
I CAN'T GO BACK OUT THERE. I CAN'T DO IT ANYMORE. I'M GONNA DIE.
LEAVE ME ALONE!
EXIT

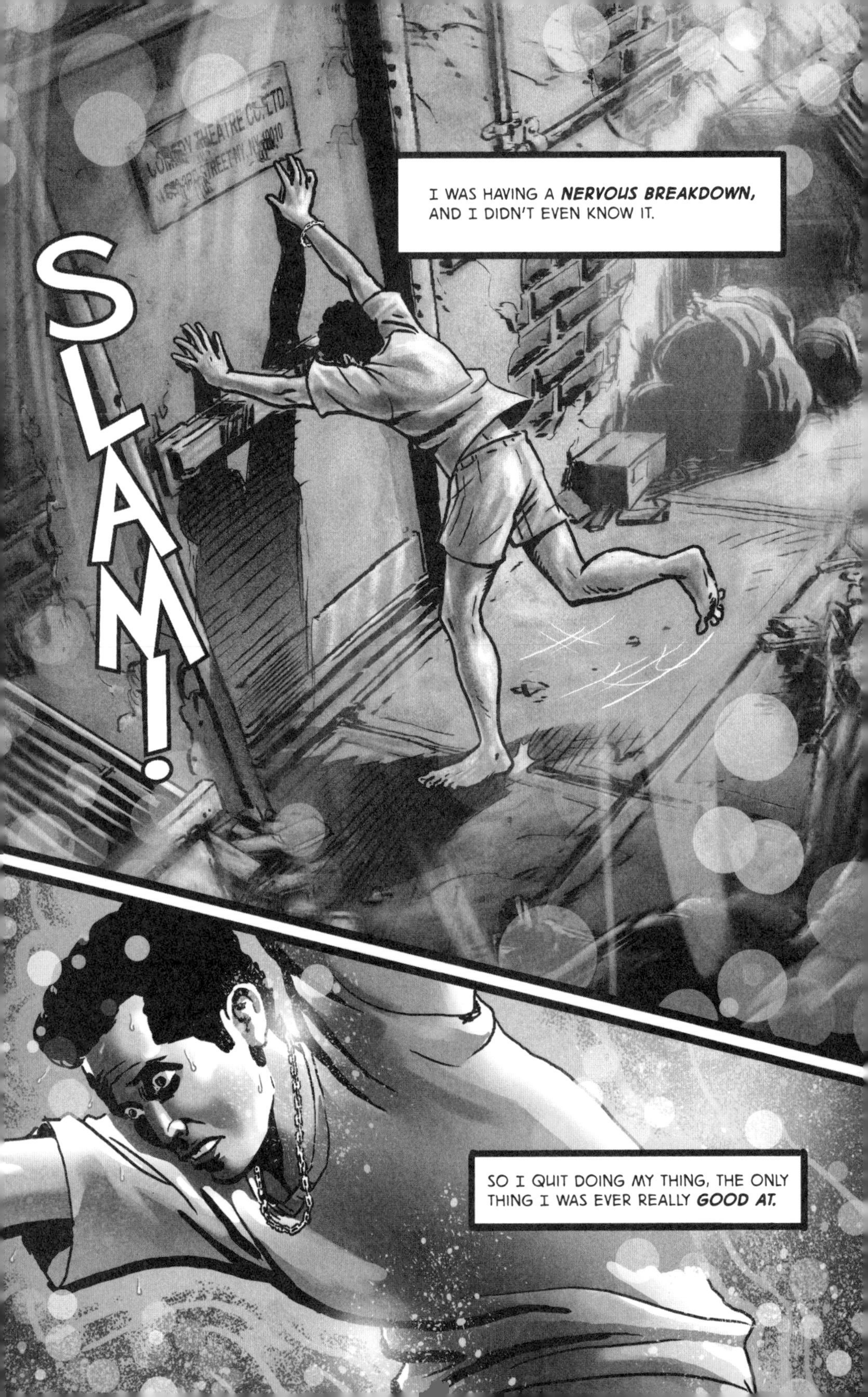
I WAS HAVING A ***NERVOUS BREAKDOWN,*** AND I DIDN'T EVEN KNOW IT.
SLAM!
SO I QUIT DOING MY THING, THE ONLY THING I WAS EVER REALLY ***GOOD AT.***

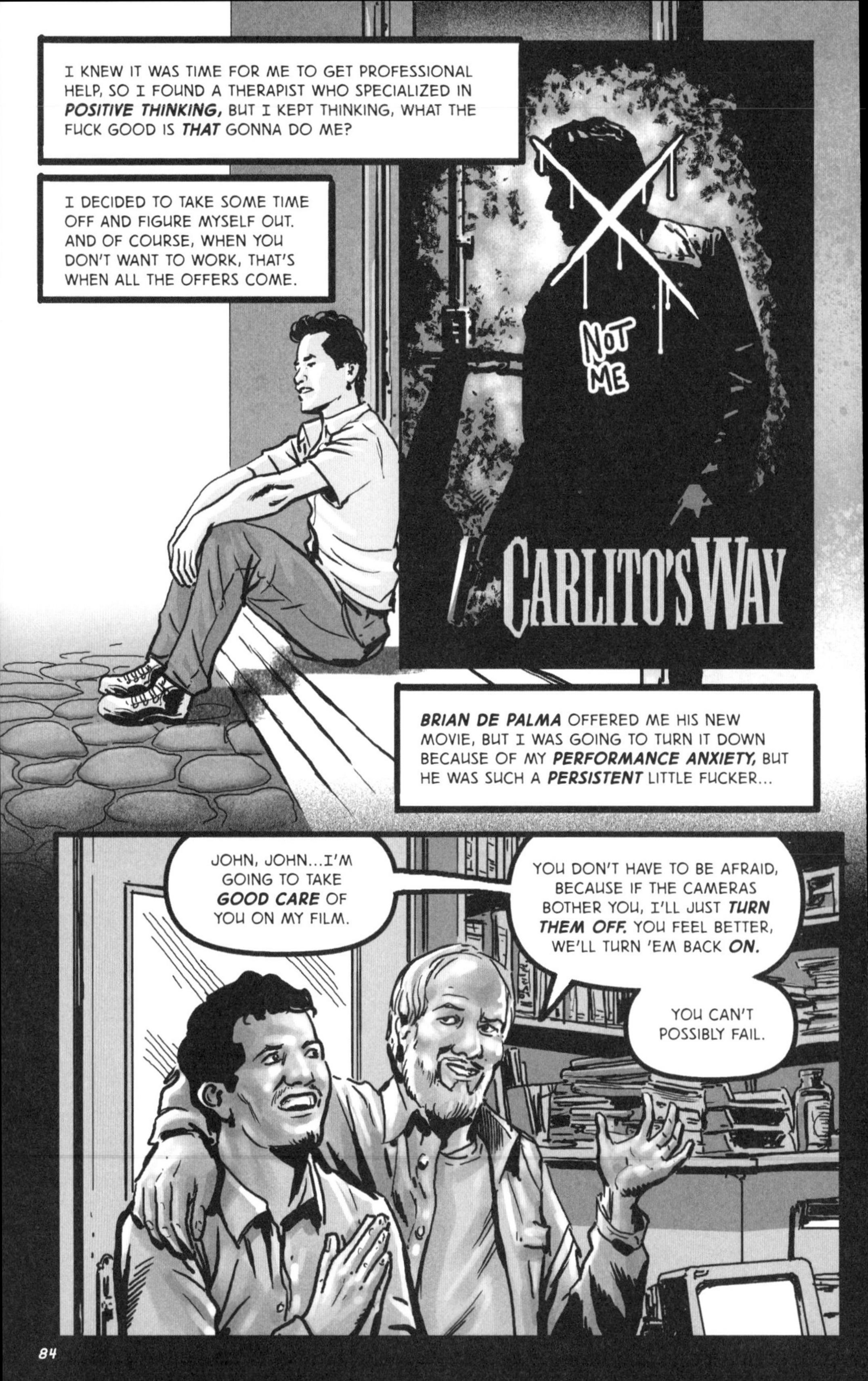
I KNEW IT WAS TIME FOR ME TO GET PROFESSIONAL HELP, SO I FOUND A THERAPIST WHO SPECIALIZED IN ***POSITIVE THINKING,*** BUT I KEPT THINKING, WHAT THE FUCK GOOD IS ***THAT*** GONNA DO ME?
I DECIDED TO TAKE SOME TIME OFF AND FIGURE MYSELF OUT. AND OF COURSE, WHEN YOU DON'T WANT TO WORK, THAT'S WHEN ALL THE OFFERS COME.
NOT ME
CARLITO'S WAY
BRIAN DE PALMA OFFERED ME HIS NEW MOVIE, BUT I WAS GOING TO TURN IT DOWN BECAUSE OF MY ***PERFORMANCE ANXIETY,*** BUT HE WAS SUCH A ***PERSISTENT*** LITTLE FUCKER...
JOHN, JOHN...I'M GOING TO TAKE ***GOOD CARE*** OF YOU ON MY FILM.
YOU DON'T HAVE TO BE AFRAID, BECAUSE IF THE CAMERAS BOTHER YOU, I'LL JUST ***TURN THEM OFF.*** YOU FEEL BETTER, WE'LL TURN 'EM BACK ***ON.***
YOU CAN'T POSSIBLY FAIL.

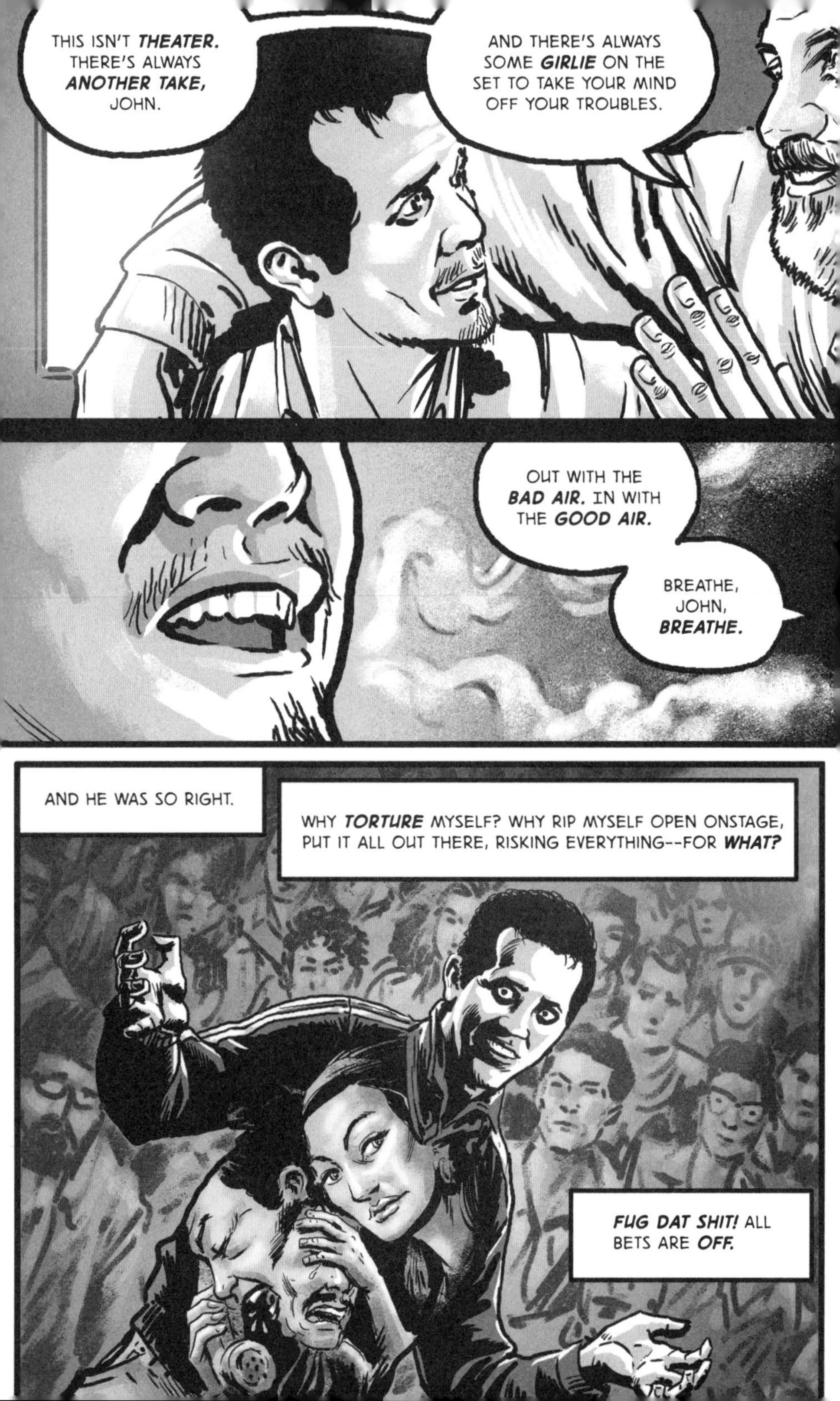
THIS ISN'T THEATER. THERE'S ALWAYS ANOTHER TAKE, JOHN.
AND THERE'S ALWAYS SOME GIRLIE ON THE SET TO TAKE YOUR MIND OFF YOUR TROUBLES.
OUT WITH THE BAD AIR. IN WITH THE GOOD AIR.
BREATHE, JOHN, BREATHE.
AND HE WAS SO RIGHT.
WHY TORTURE MYSELF? WHY RIP MYSELF OPEN ONSTAGE, PUT IT ALL OUT THERE, RISKING EVERYTHING--FOR WHAT?
FUG DAT SHIT! ALL BETS ARE OFF.

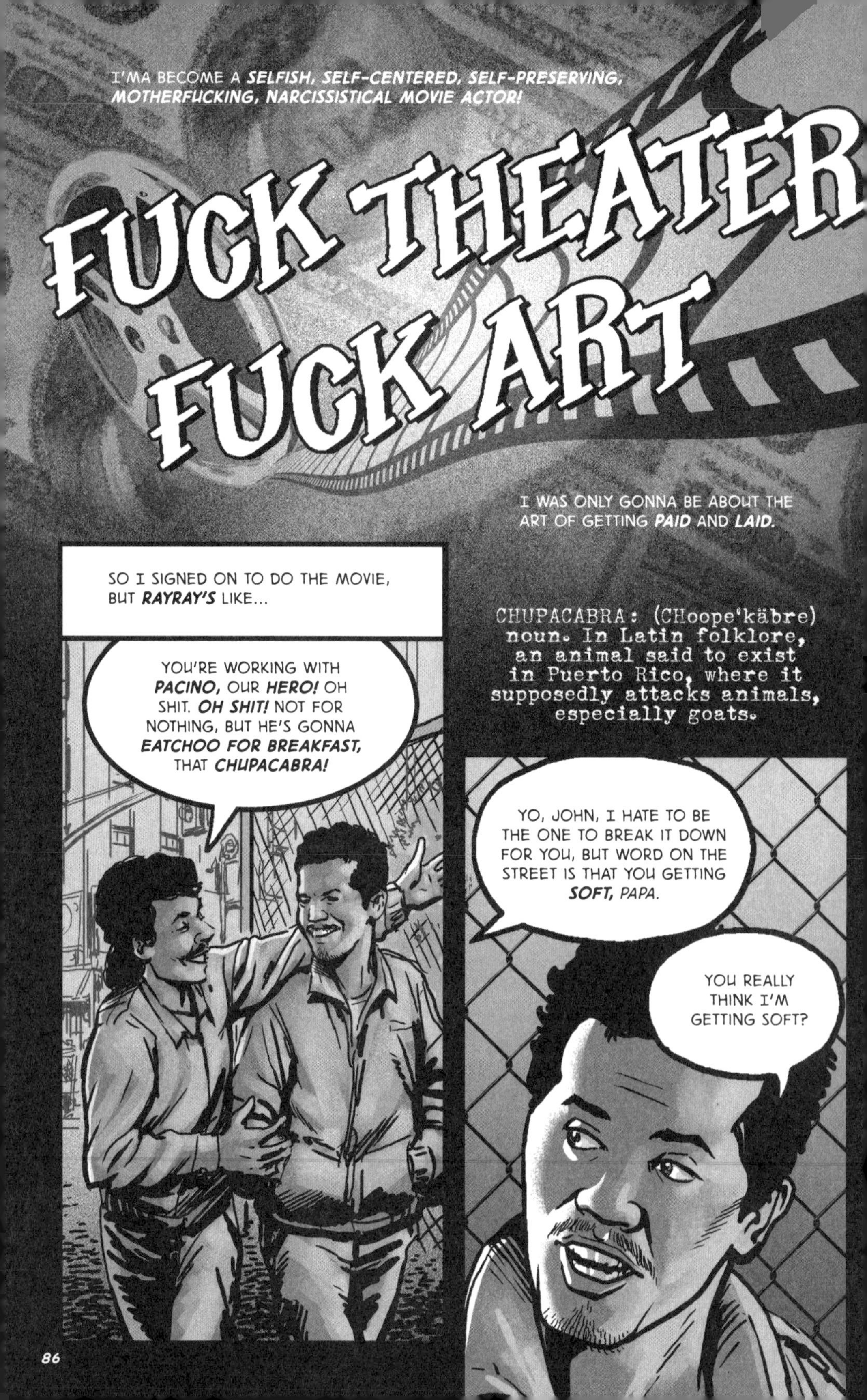
I'MA BECOME A SELFISH, SELF-CENTERED, SELF-PRESERVING, MOTHERFUCKING, NARCISSISTICAL MOVIE ACTOR!
FUCK THEATER
FUCK ART
I WAS ONLY GONNA BE ABOUT THE ART OF GETTING PAID AND LAID.
SO I SIGNED ON TO DO THE MOVIE, BUT RAYRAY'S LIKE...
YOU'RE WORKING WITH PACINO, OUR HERO! OH SHIT. OH SHIT! NOT FOR NOTHING, BUT HE'S GONNA EATCHOO FOR BREAKFAST, THAT CHUPACABRA!
CHUPACABRA: (CHoope'käbre) noun. In Latin folklore, an animal said to exist in Puerto Rico, where it supposedly attacks animals, especially goats.
YO, JOHN, I HATE TO BE THE ONE TO BREAK IT DOWN FOR YOU, BUT WORD ON THE STREET IS THAT YOU GETTING SOFT, PAPA.
YOU REALLY THINK I'M GETTING SOFT?

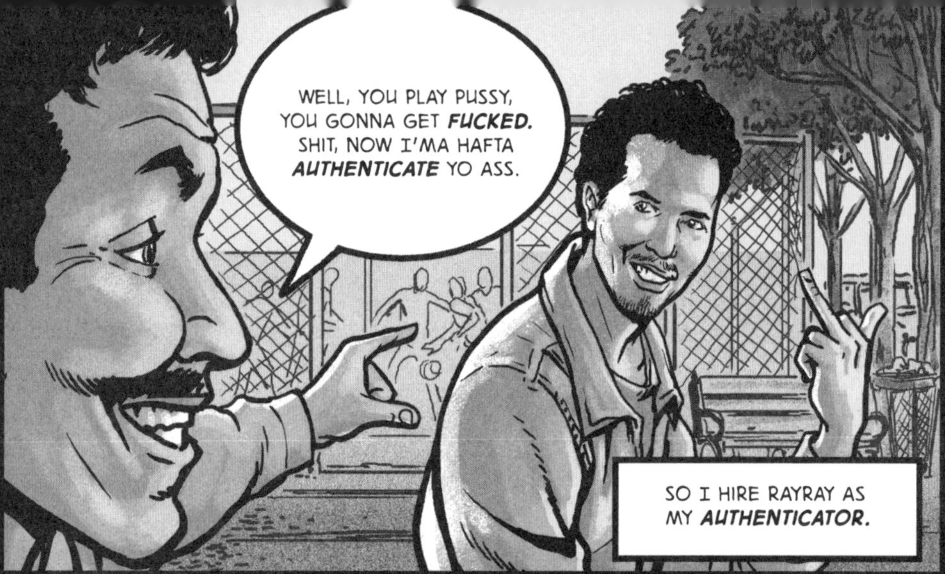
WELL, YOU PLAY PUSSY, YOU GONNA GET FUCKED. SHIT, NOW I'MA HAFTA AUTHENTICATE YO ASS.
SO I HIRE RAYRAY AS MY AUTHENTICATOR.

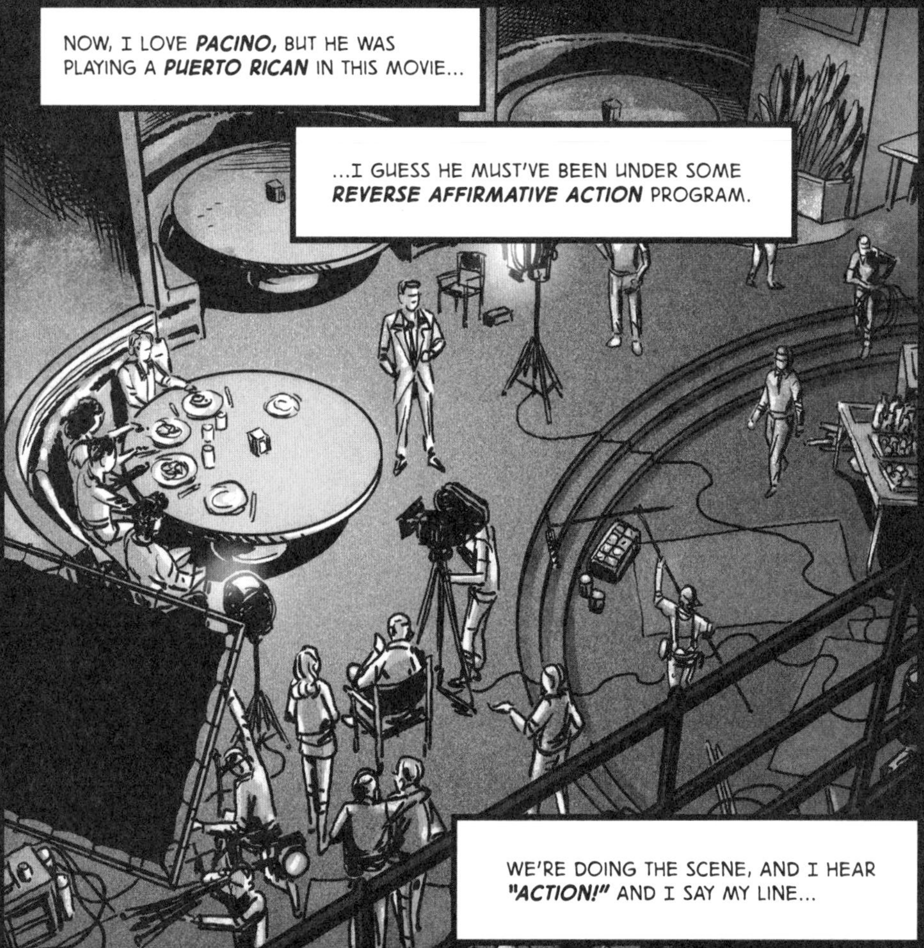
NOW, I LOVE PACINO, BUT HE WAS PLAYING A PUERTO RICAN IN THIS MOVIE...
...I GUESS HE MUST'VE BEEN UNDER SOME REVERSE AFFIRMATIVE ACTION PROGRAM.
WE'RE DOING THE SCENE, AND I HEAR "ACTION!" AND I SAY MY LINE...

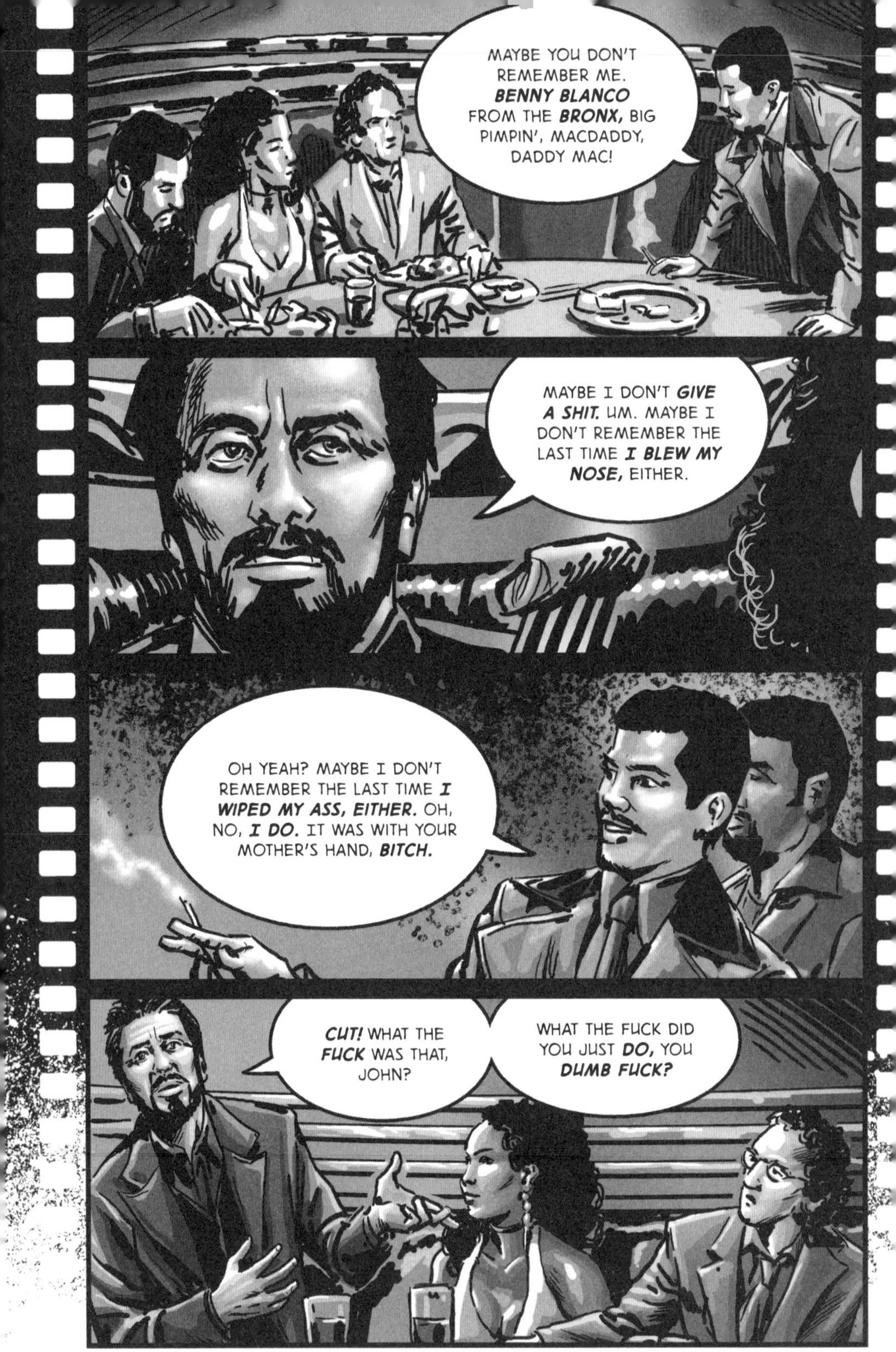
MAYBE YOU DON'T REMEMBER ME. BENNY BLANCO FROM THE BRONX, BIG PIMPIN', MACDADDY, DADDY MAC!
MAYBE I DON'T GIVE A SHIT. UM. MAYBE I DON'T REMEMBER THE LAST TIME I BLEW MY NOSE, EITHER.
OH YEAH? MAYBE I DON'T REMEMBER THE LAST TIME I WIPED MY ASS, EITHER. OH, NO, I DO. IT WAS WITH YOUR MOTHER'S HAND, BITCH.
CUT! WHAT THE FUCK WAS THAT, JOHN?
WHAT THE FUCK DID YOU JUST DO, YOU DUMB FUCK?

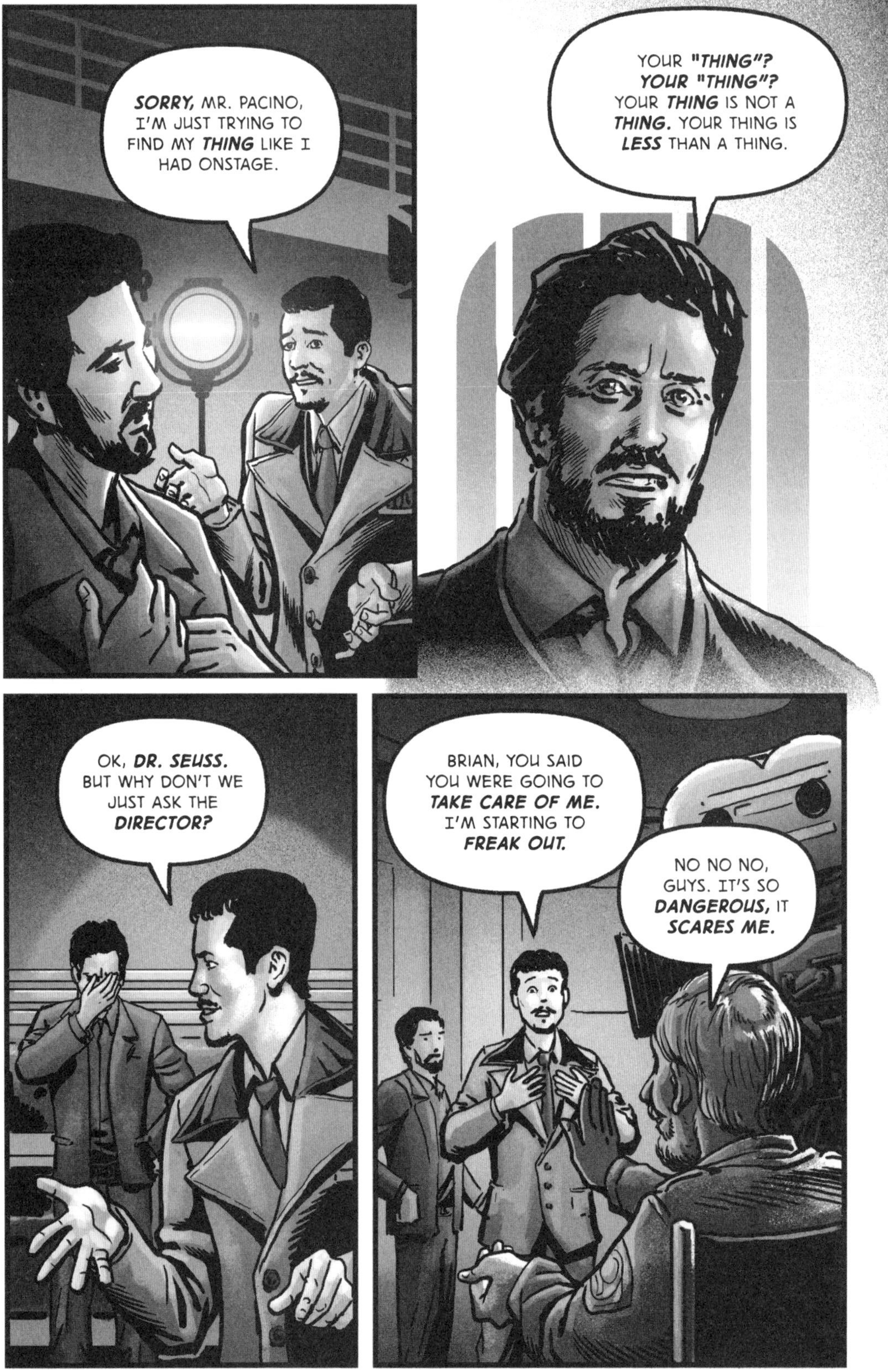
SORRY, MR. PACINO, I'M JUST TRYING TO FIND MY THING LIKE I HAD ONSTAGE.
YOUR "THING"? YOUR "THING"? YOUR THING IS NOT A THING. YOUR THING IS LESS THAN A THING.
OK, DR. SEUSS. BUT WHY DON'T WE JUST ASK THE DIRECTOR?
BRIAN, YOU SAID YOU WERE GOING TO TAKE CARE OF ME. I'M STARTING TO FREAK OUT.
NO NO NO, GUYS. IT'S SO DANGEROUS, IT SCARES ME.

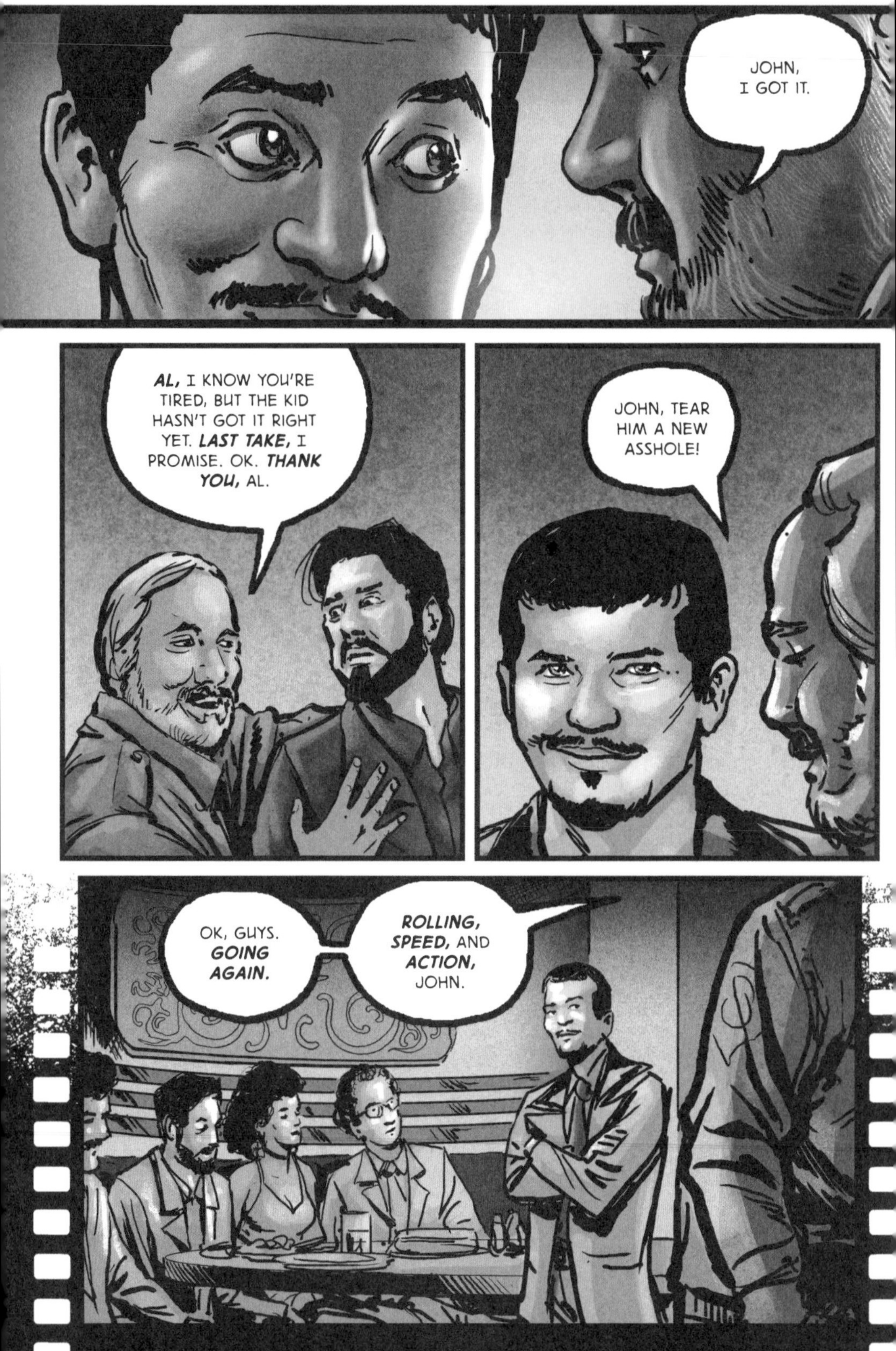
JOHN,
I GOT IT.
AL, I KNOW YOU'RE TIRED, BUT THE KID HASN'T GOT IT RIGHT YET. LAST TAKE, I PROMISE. OK. THANK YOU, AL.
JOHN, TEAR HIM A NEW ASSHOLE!
OK, GUYS. GOING AGAIN.
ROLLING, SPEED, AND ACTION, JOHN.

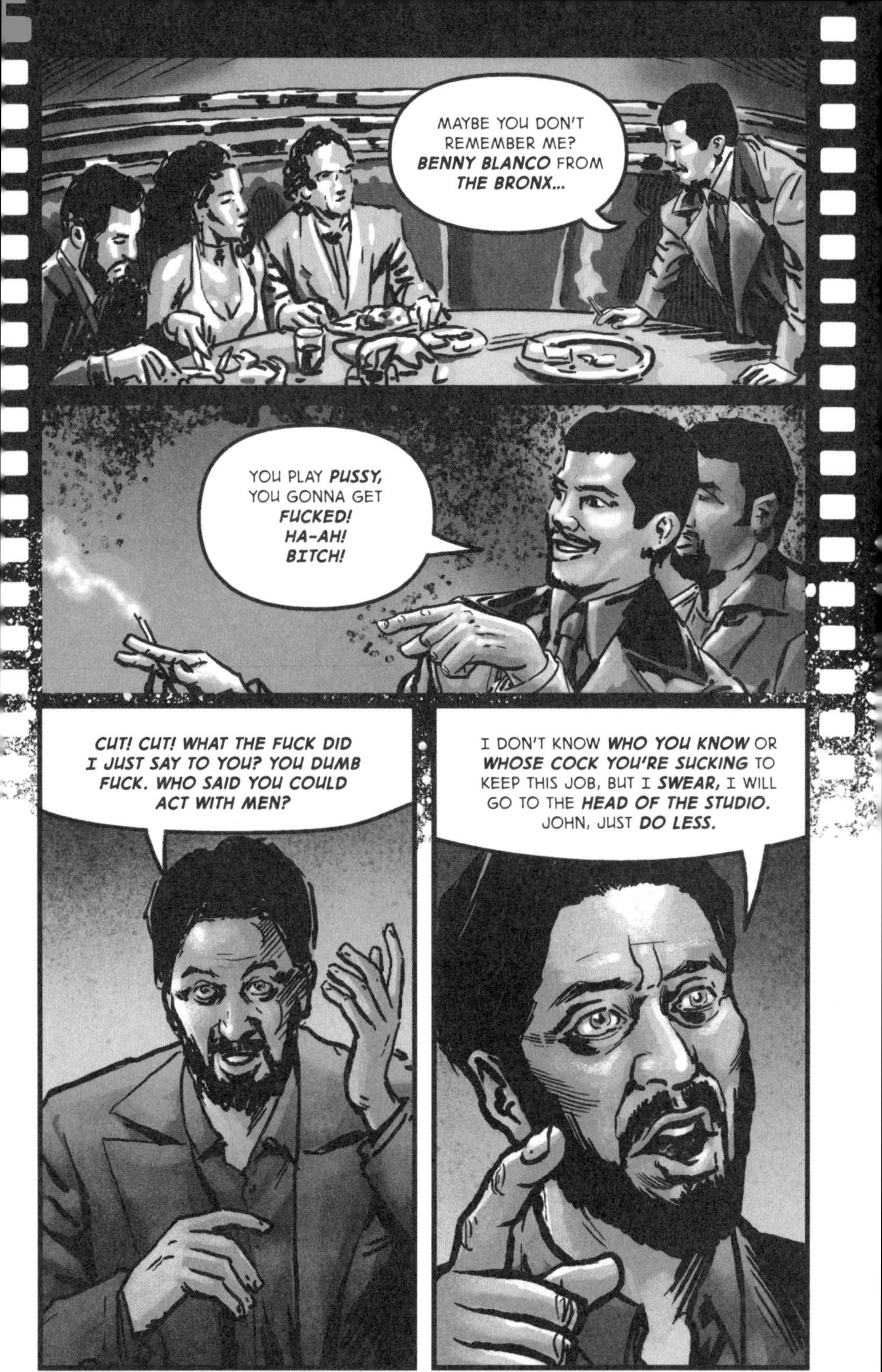
MAYBE YOU DON'T REMEMBER ME? BENNY BLANCO FROM THE BRONX...
YOU PLAY PUSSY, YOU GONNA GET FUCKED! HA-AH! BITCH!
CUT! CUT! WHAT THE FUCK DID I JUST SAY TO YOU? YOU DUMB FUCK. WHO SAID YOU COULD ACT WITH MEN?
I DON'T KNOW WHO YOU KNOW OR WHOSE COCK YOU'RE SUCKING TO KEEP THIS JOB, BUT I SWEAR, I WILL GO TO THE HEAD OF THE STUDIO. JOHN, JUST DO LESS.

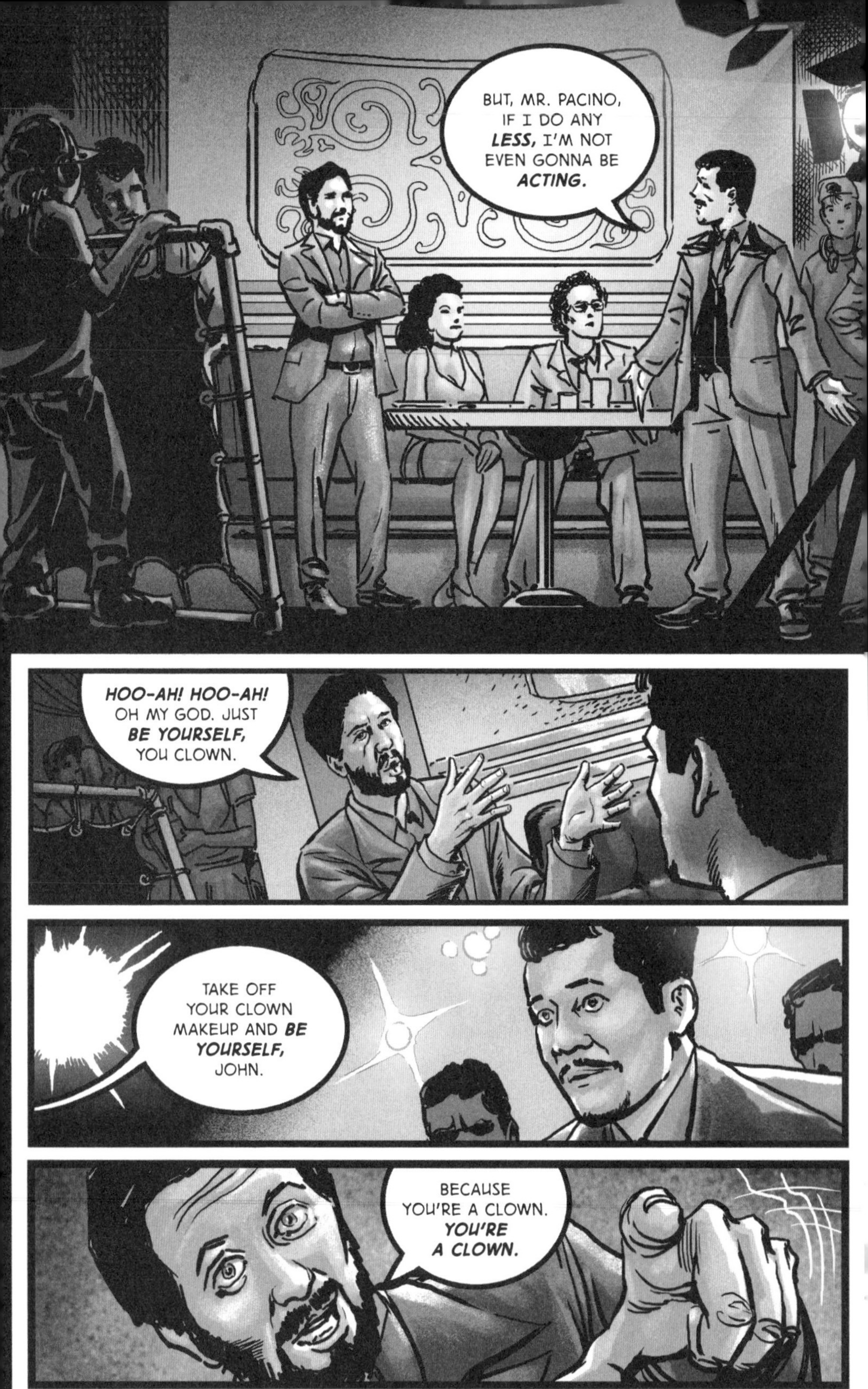
BUT, MR. PACINO, IF I DO ANY LESS, I'M NOT EVEN GONNA BE ACTING.
HOO-AH! HOO-AH! OH MY GOD. JUST BE YOURSELF, YOU CLOWN.
TAKE OFF YOUR CLOWN MAKEUP AND BE YOURSELF, JOHN.
BECAUSE YOU'RE A CLOWN. YOU'RE A CLOWN.

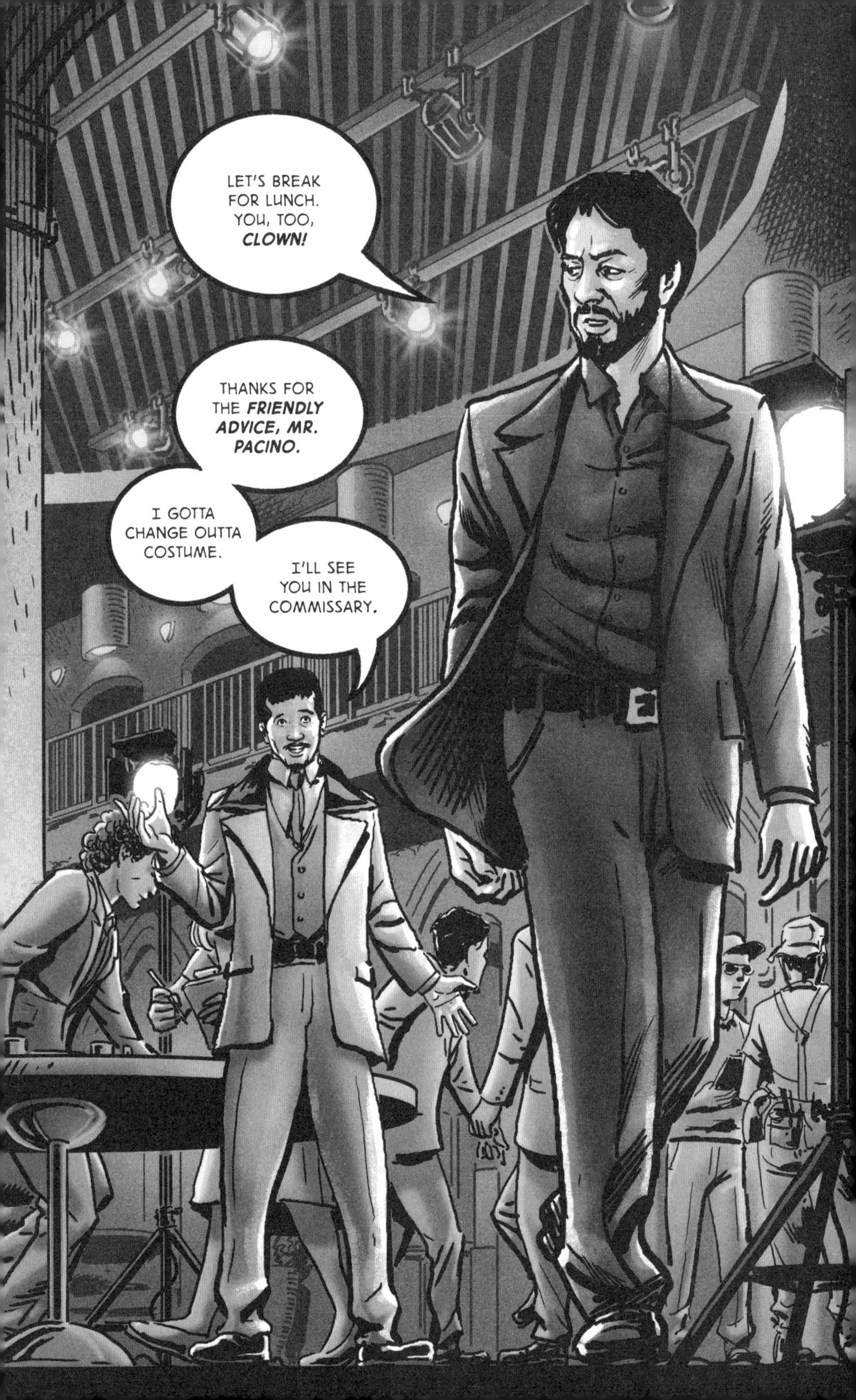
LET'S BREAK FOR LUNCH. YOU, TOO, ***CLOWN!***
THANKS FOR THE ***FRIENDLY ADVICE, MR. PACINO.***
I GOTTA CHANGE OUTTA COSTUME.
I'LL SEE YOU IN THE COMMISSARY.

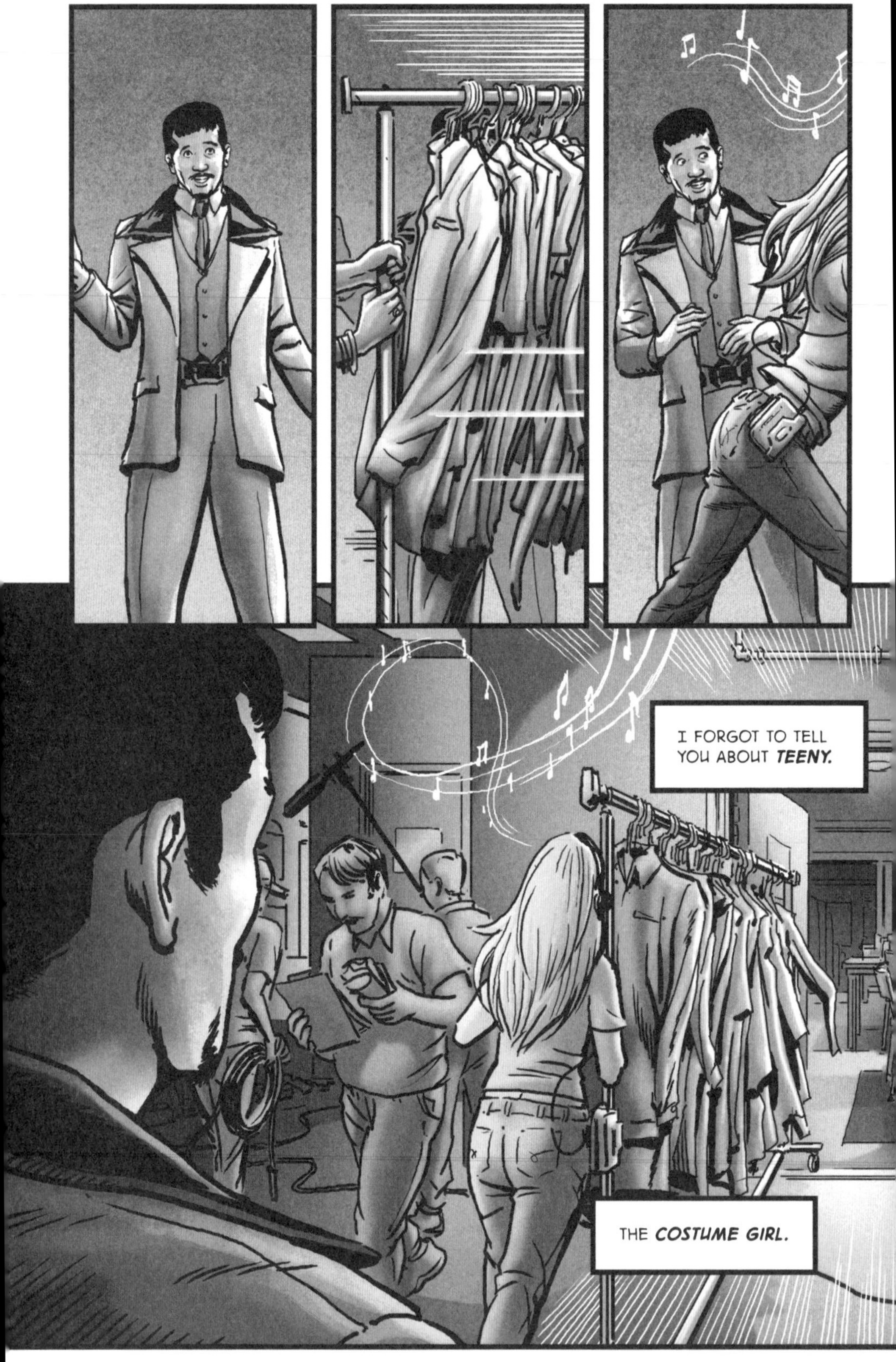
I FORGOT TO TELL YOU ABOUT TEENY.
THE COSTUME GIRL.

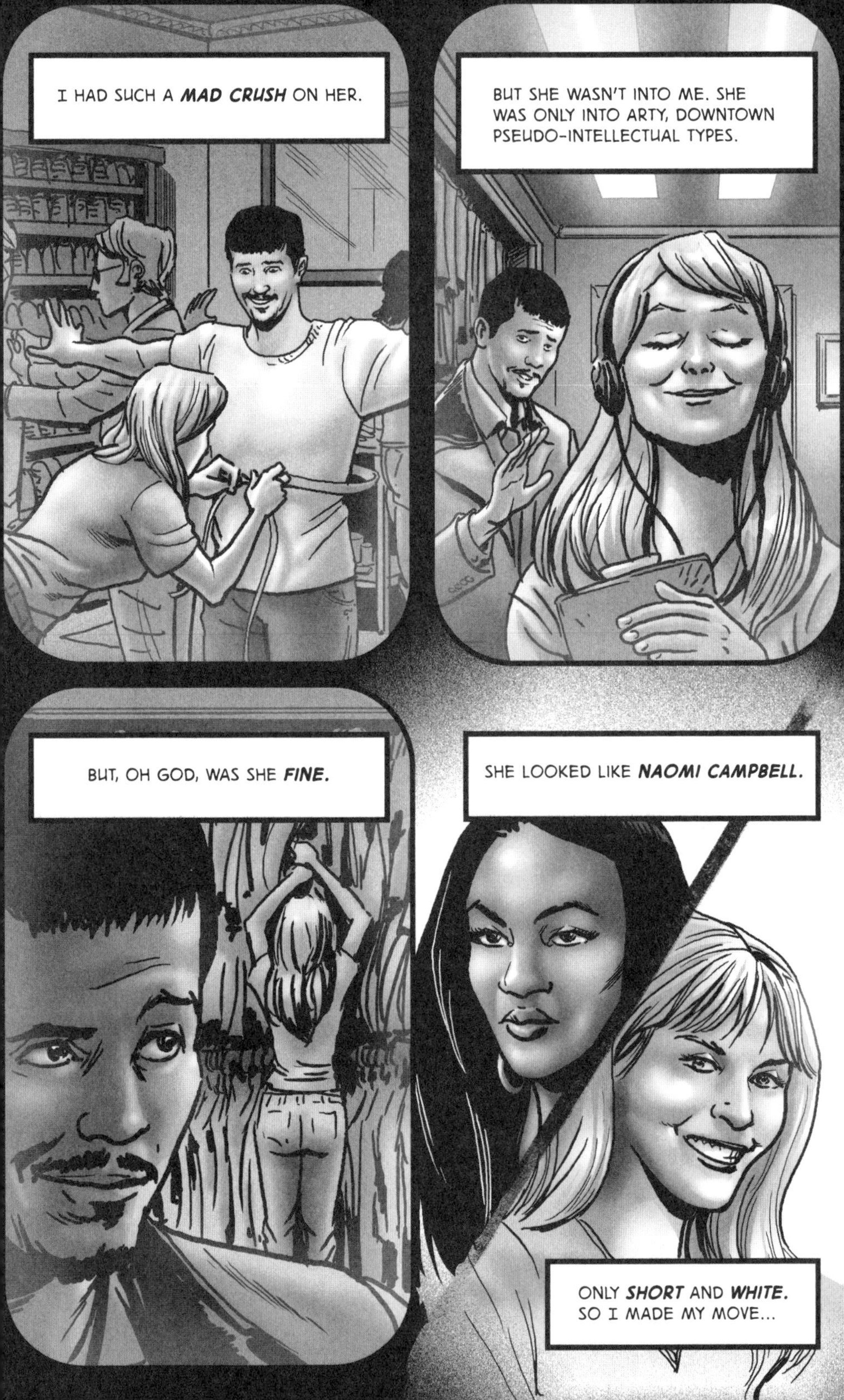
I HAD SUCH A ***MAD CRUSH*** ON HER.
BUT SHE WASN'T INTO ME. SHE WAS ONLY INTO ARTY, DOWNTOWN PSEUDO-INTELLECTUAL TYPES.
BUT, OH GOD, WAS SHE ***FINE.***
SHE LOOKED LIKE ***NAOMI CAMPBELL.***
ONLY ***SHORT*** AND ***WHITE.***
SO I MADE MY MOVE...

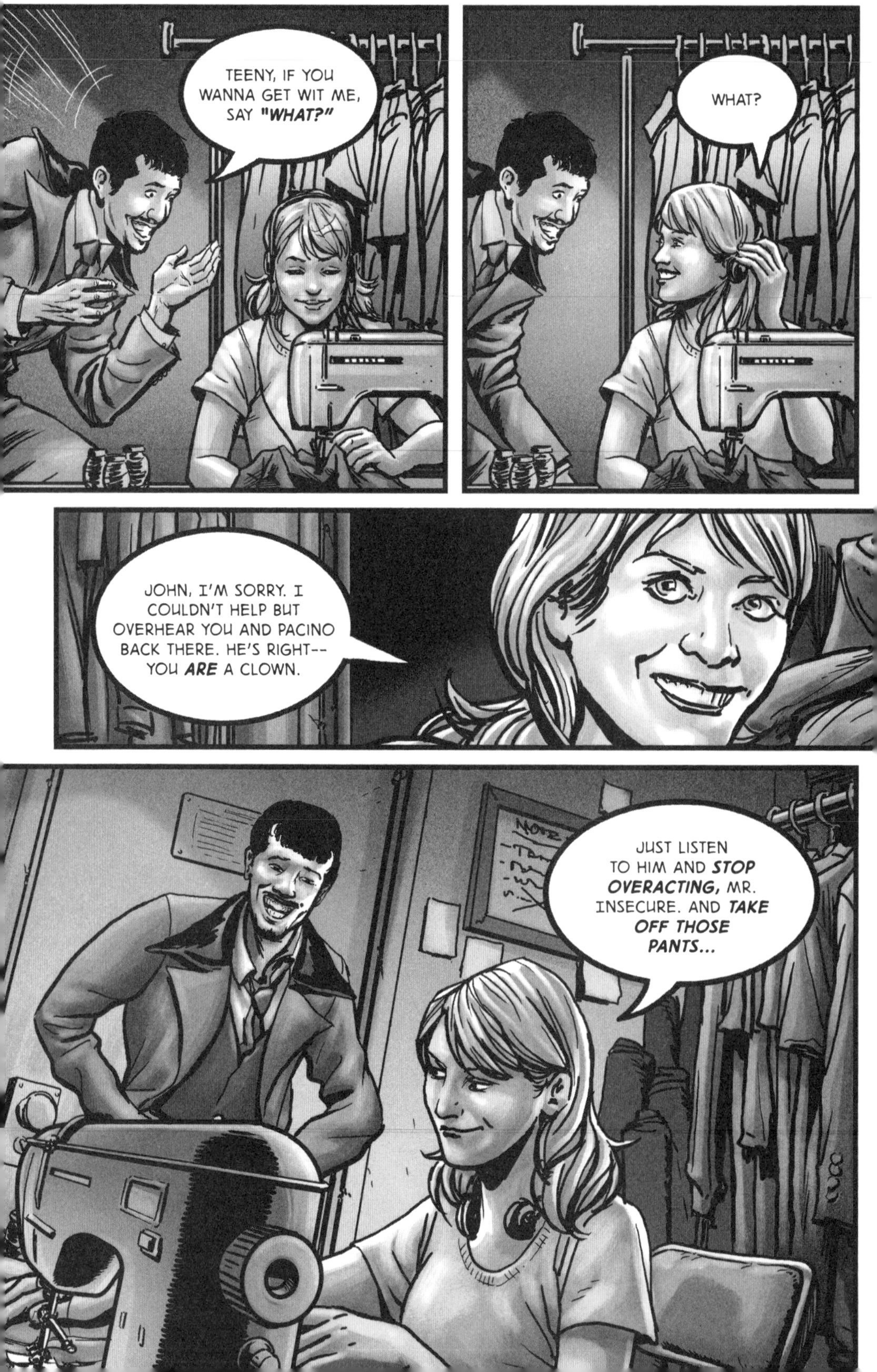
TEENY, IF YOU WANNA GET WIT ME, SAY "WHAT?"
WHAT?
JOHN, I'M SORRY. I COULDN'T HELP BUT OVERHEAR YOU AND PACINO BACK THERE. HE'S RIGHT-- YOU ARE A CLOWN.
JUST LISTEN TO HIM AND STOP OVERACTING, MR. INSECURE. AND TAKE OFF THOSE PANTS...

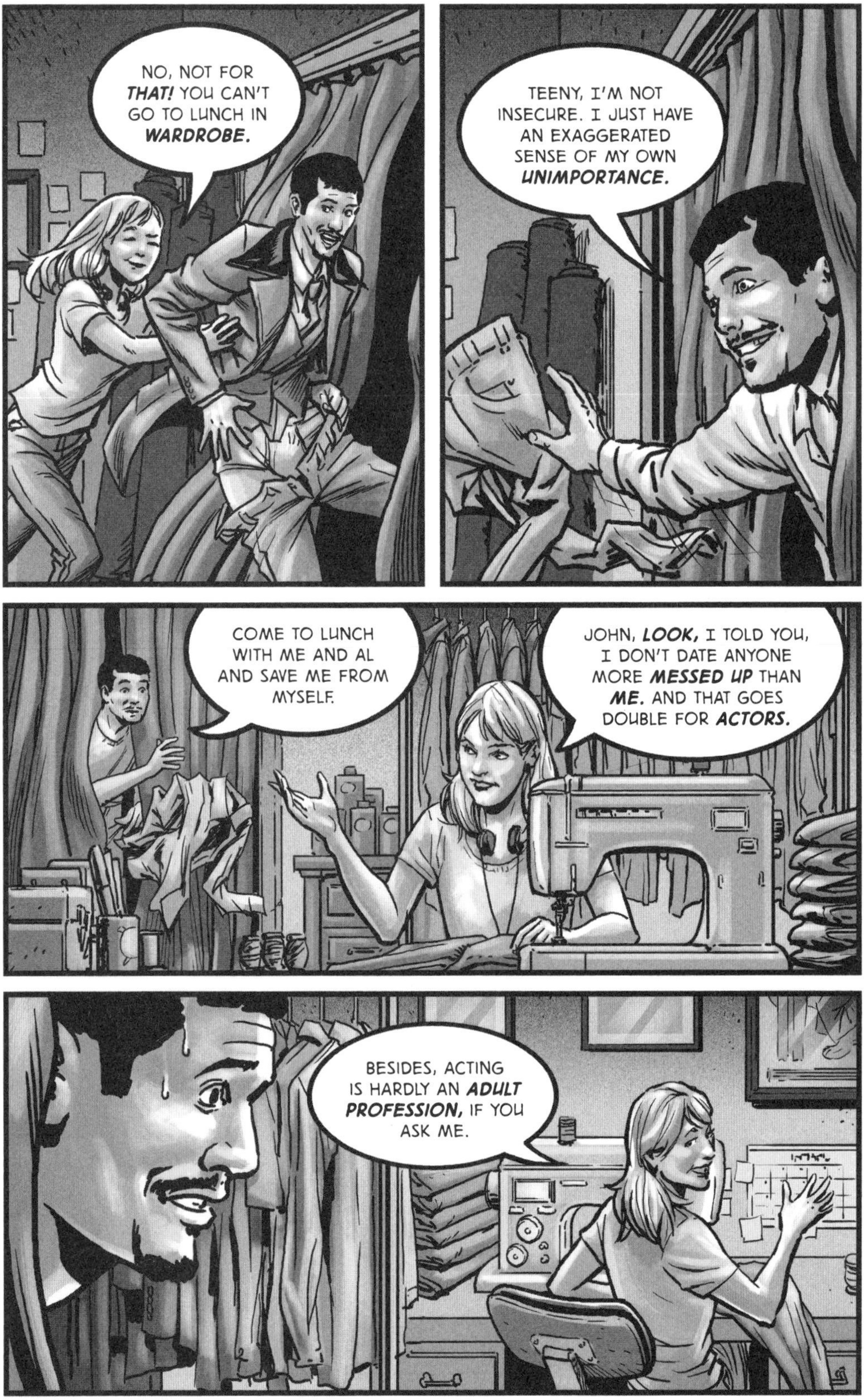
NO, NOT FOR THAT! YOU CAN'T GO TO LUNCH IN WARDROBE.
TEENY, I'M NOT INSECURE. I JUST HAVE AN EXAGGERATED SENSE OF MY OWN UNIMPORTANCE.
COME TO LUNCH WITH ME AND AL AND SAVE ME FROM MYSELF.
JOHN, LOOK, I TOLD YOU, I DON'T DATE ANYONE MORE MESSED UP THAN ME. AND THAT GOES DOUBLE FOR ACTORS.
BESIDES, ACTING IS HARDLY AN ADULT PROFESSION, IF YOU ASK ME.

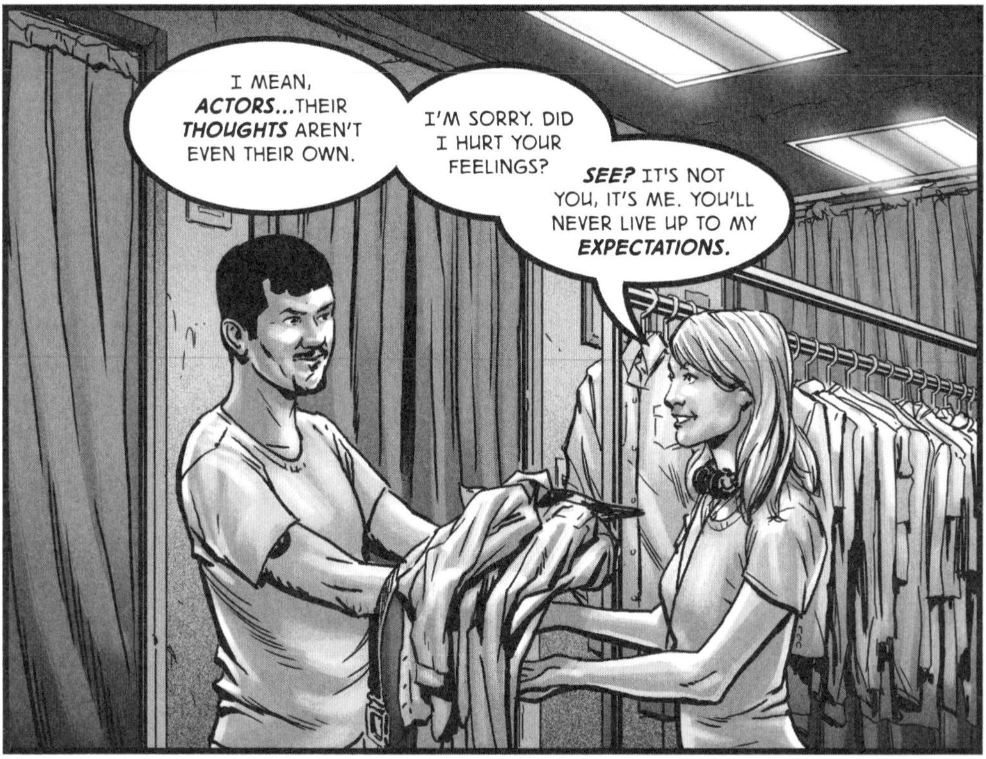
I MEAN, ACTORS...THEIR THOUGHTS AREN'T EVEN THEIR OWN.
I'M SORRY. DID I HURT YOUR FEELINGS?
SEE? IT'S NOT YOU, IT'S ME. YOU'LL NEVER LIVE UP TO MY EXPECTATIONS.

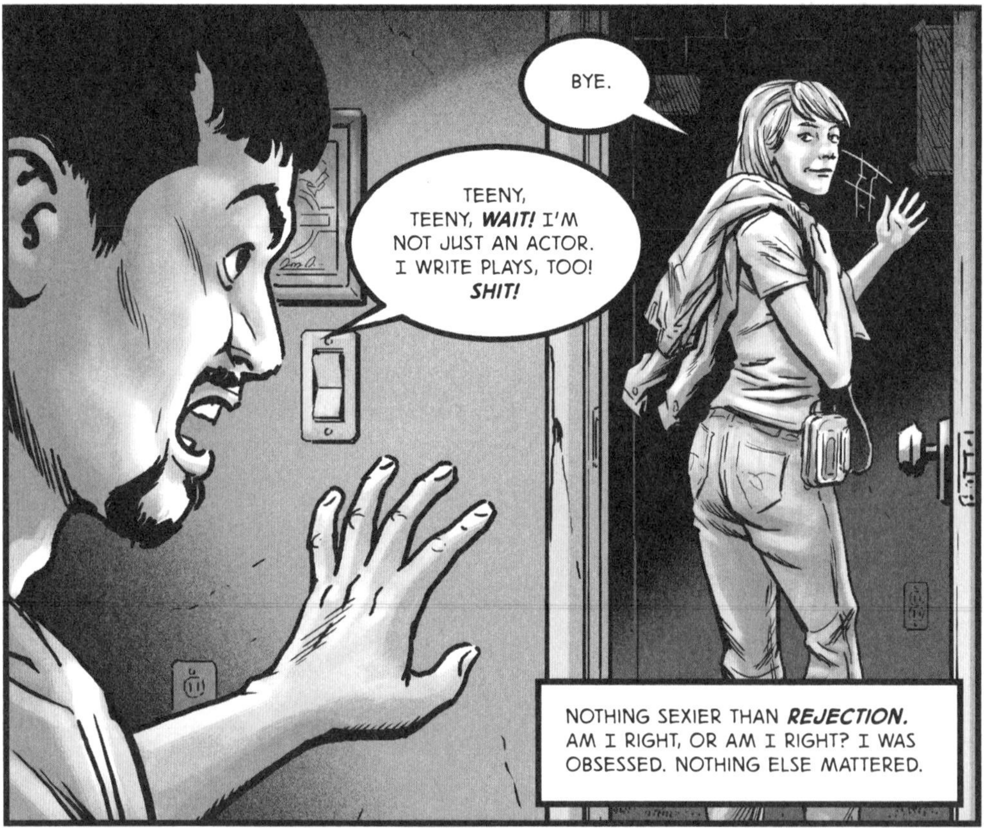
BYE.
TEENY, TEENY, WAIT! I'M NOT JUST AN ACTOR. I WRITE PLAYS, TOO! SHIT!
NOTHING SEXIER THAN REJECTION. AM I RIGHT, OR AM I RIGHT? I WAS OBSESSED. NOTHING ELSE MATTERED.

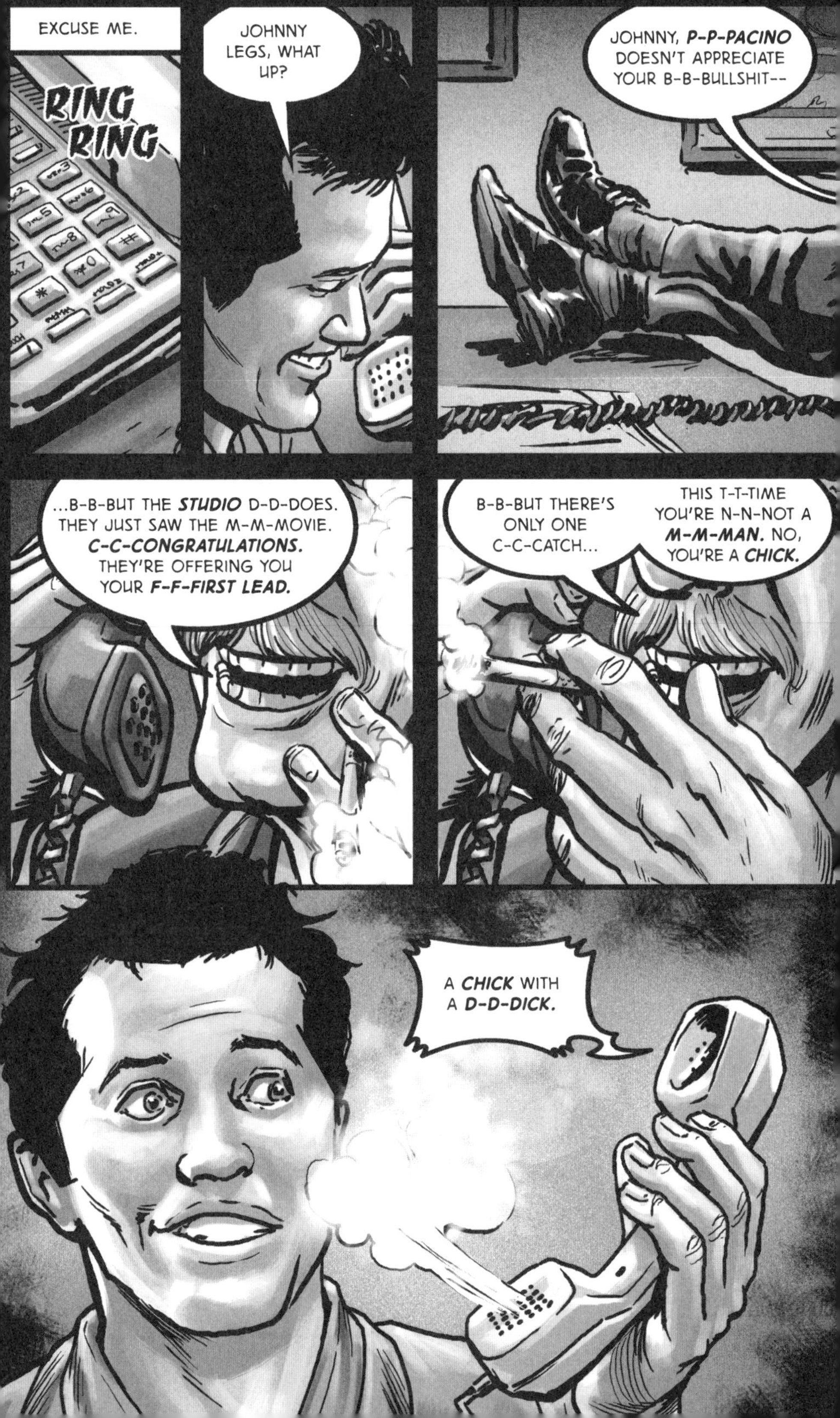
EXCUSE ME.
RING RING
JOHNNY LEGS, WHAT UP?
JOHNNY, P-P-PACINO DOESN'T APPRECIATE YOUR B-B-BULLSHIT--
...B-B-BUT THE STUDIO D-D-DOES. THEY JUST SAW THE M-M-MOVIE. C-C-CONGRATULATIONS. THEY'RE OFFERING YOU YOUR F-F-FIRST LEAD.
B-B-BUT THERE'S ONLY ONE C-C-CATCH...
THIS T-T-TIME YOU'RE N-N-NOT A M-M-MAN. NO, YOU'RE A CHICK.
A CHICK WITH A D-D-DICK.

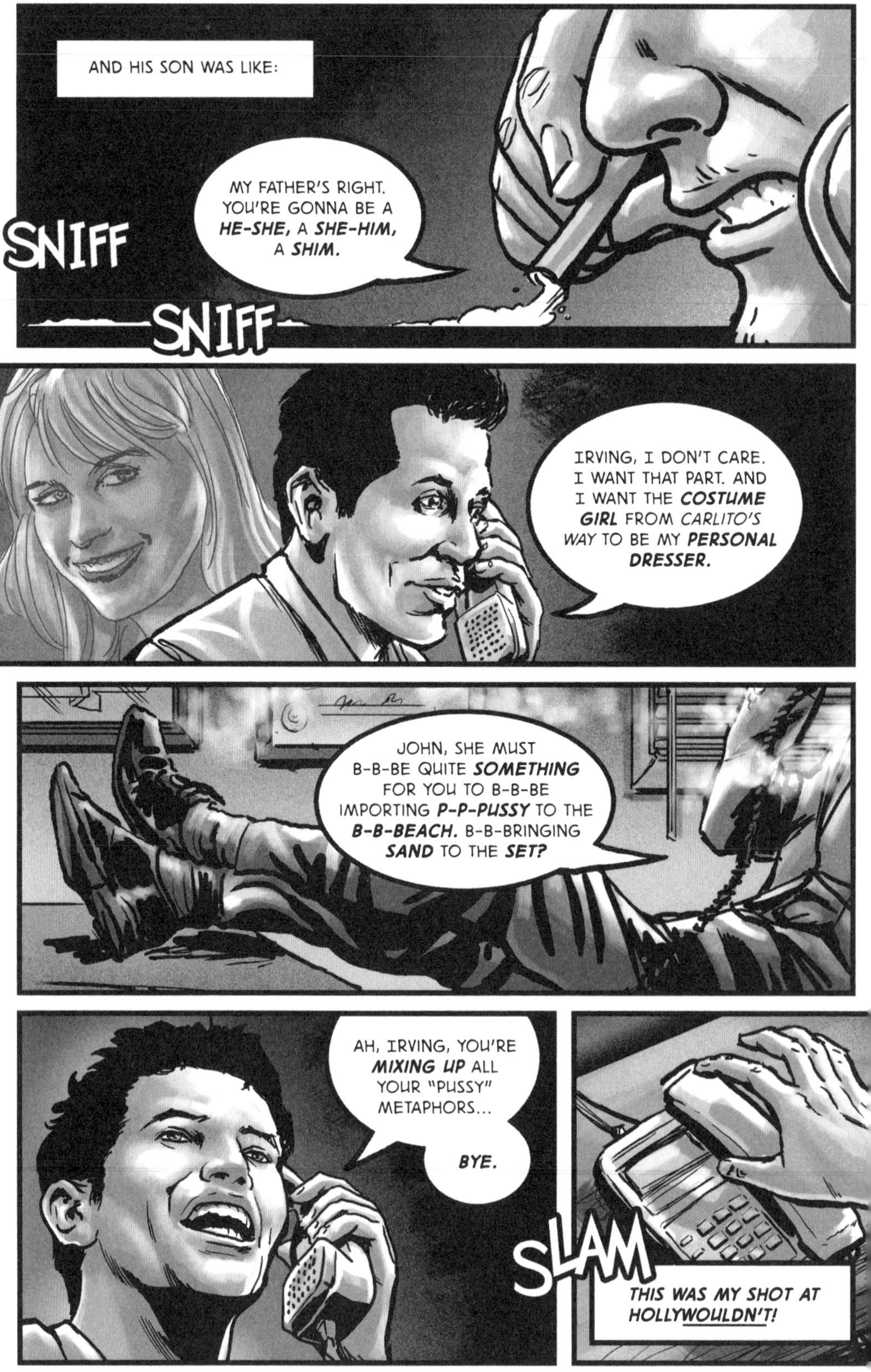
AND HIS SON WAS LIKE:
MY FATHER'S RIGHT. YOU'RE GONNA BE A HE-SHE, A SHE-HIM, A SHIM.
SNIFF
SNIFF
IRVING, I DON'T CARE. I WANT THAT PART. AND I WANT THE COSTUME GIRL FROM CARLITO'S WAY TO BE MY PERSONAL DRESSER.
JOHN, SHE MUST B-B-BE QUITE SOMETHING FOR YOU TO B-B-BE IMPORTING P-P-PUSSY TO THE B-B-BEACH. B-B-BRINGING SAND TO THE SET?
AH, IRVING, YOU'RE MIXING UP ALL YOUR "PUSSY" METAPHORS...
BYE.
SLAM
THIS WAS MY SHOT AT HOLLYWOULDN'T!

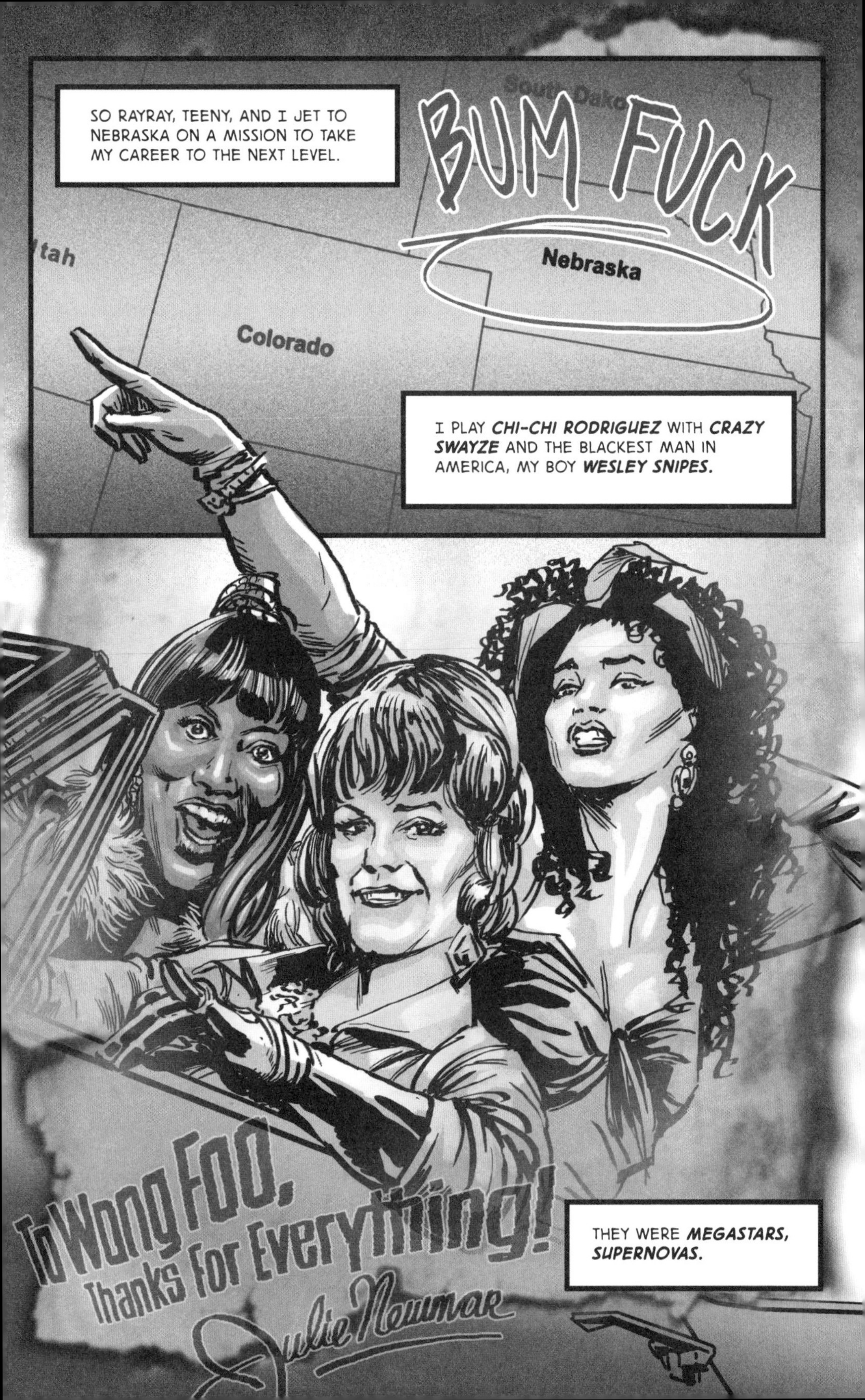

SO RAYRAY, TEENY, AND I JET TO NEBRASKA ON A MISSION TO TAKE MY CAREER TO THE NEXT LEVEL.
BUM FUCK
Nebraska
Colorado
I PLAY ***CHI-CHI RODRIGUEZ*** WITH ***CRAZY SWAYZE*** AND THE BLACKEST MAN IN AMERICA, MY BOY ***WESLEY SNIPES.***
To Wong Foo, Thanks for Everything! Julie Newmar
THEY WERE ***MEGASTARS, SUPERNOVAS.***

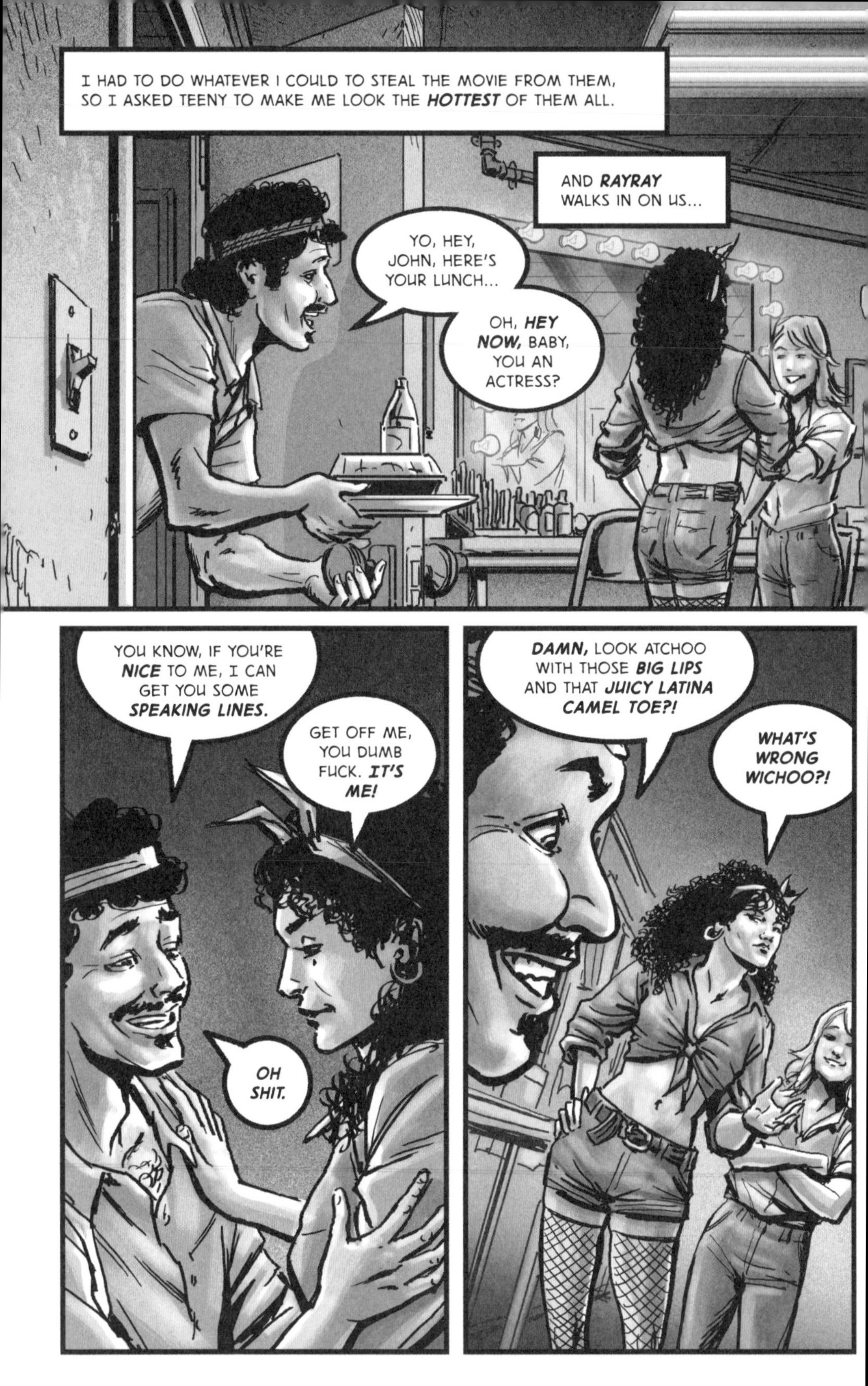
I HAD TO DO WHATEVER I COULD TO STEAL THE MOVIE FROM THEM, SO I ASKED TEENY TO MAKE ME LOOK THE *HOTTEST* OF THEM ALL.
AND *RAYRAY* WALKS IN ON US...
YO, HEY, JOHN, HERE'S YOUR LUNCH...
OH, *HEY NOW,* BABY, YOU AN ACTRESS?
YOU KNOW, IF YOU'RE *NICE* TO ME, I CAN GET YOU SOME *SPEAKING LINES.*
GET OFF ME, YOU DUMB FUCK. *IT'S ME!*
OH SHIT.
DAMN, LOOK ATCHOO WITH THOSE *BIG LIPS* AND THAT *JUICY LATINA CAMEL TOE?!*
WHAT'S WRONG WICHOO?!

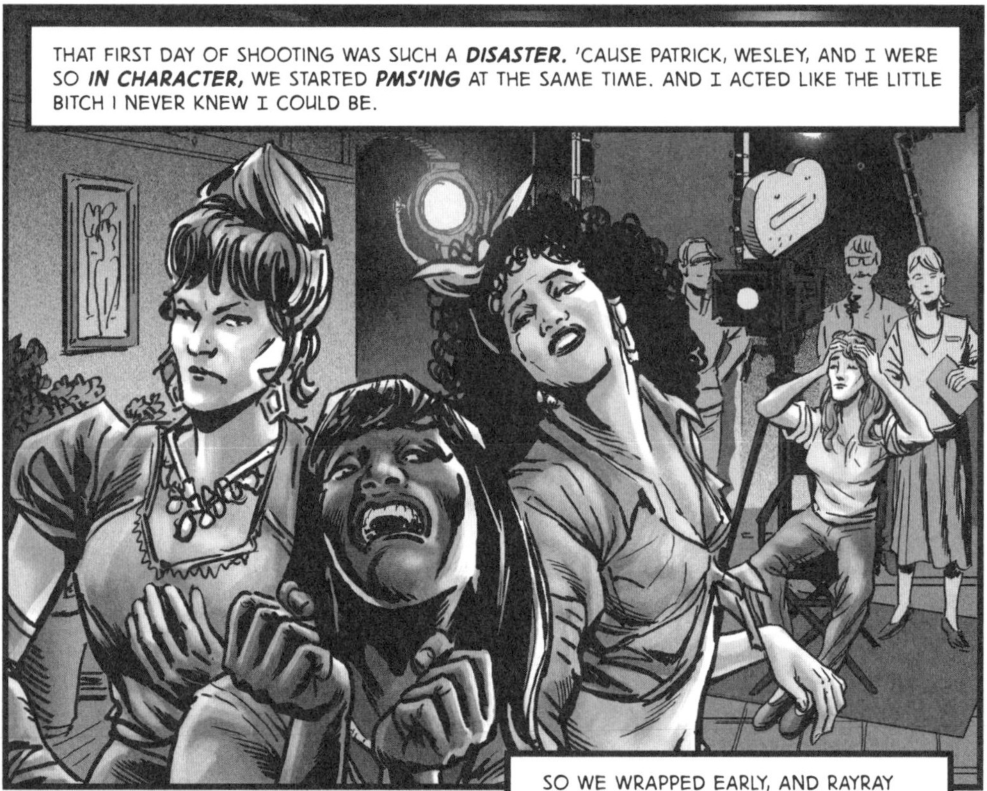
THAT FIRST DAY OF SHOOTING WAS SUCH A **DISASTER.** 'CAUSE PATRICK, WESLEY, AND I WERE SO **IN CHARACTER,** WE STARTED **PMS'ING** AT THE SAME TIME. AND I ACTED LIKE THE LITTLE BITCH I NEVER KNEW I COULD BE.

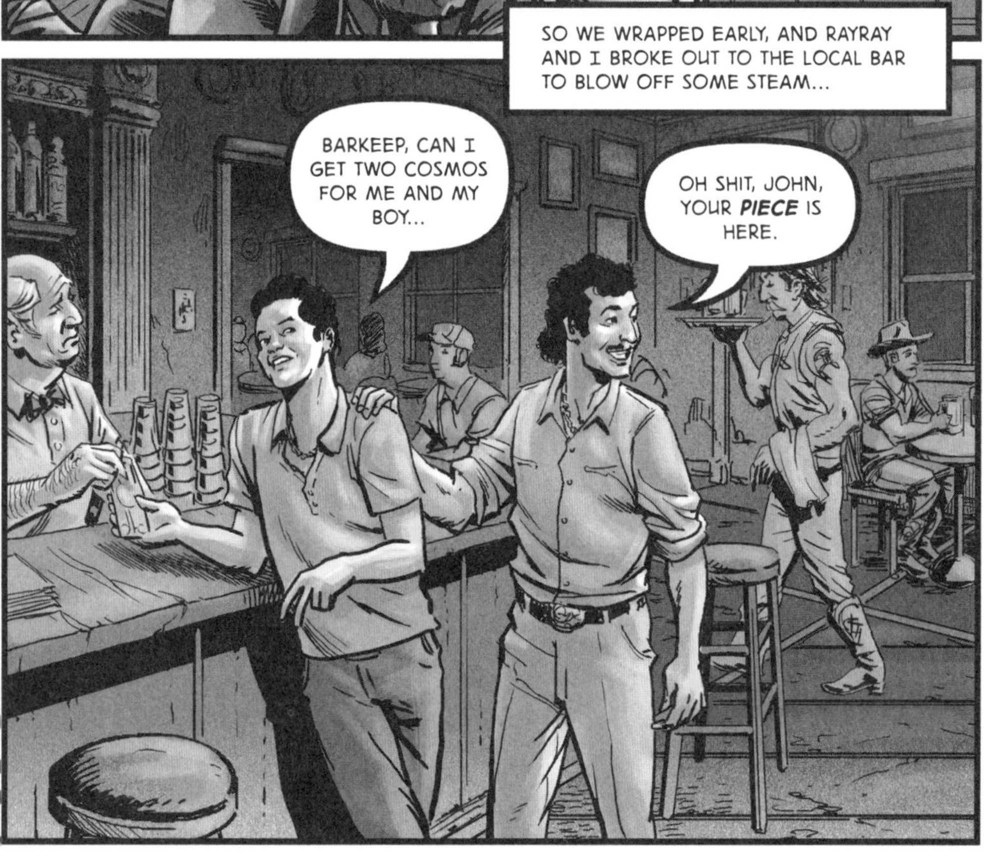
SO WE WRAPPED EARLY, AND RAYRAY AND I BROKE OUT TO THE LOCAL BAR TO BLOW OFF SOME STEAM...
BARKEEP, CAN I GET TWO COSMOS FOR ME AND MY BOY...
OH SHIT, JOHN, YOUR **PIECE** IS HERE.

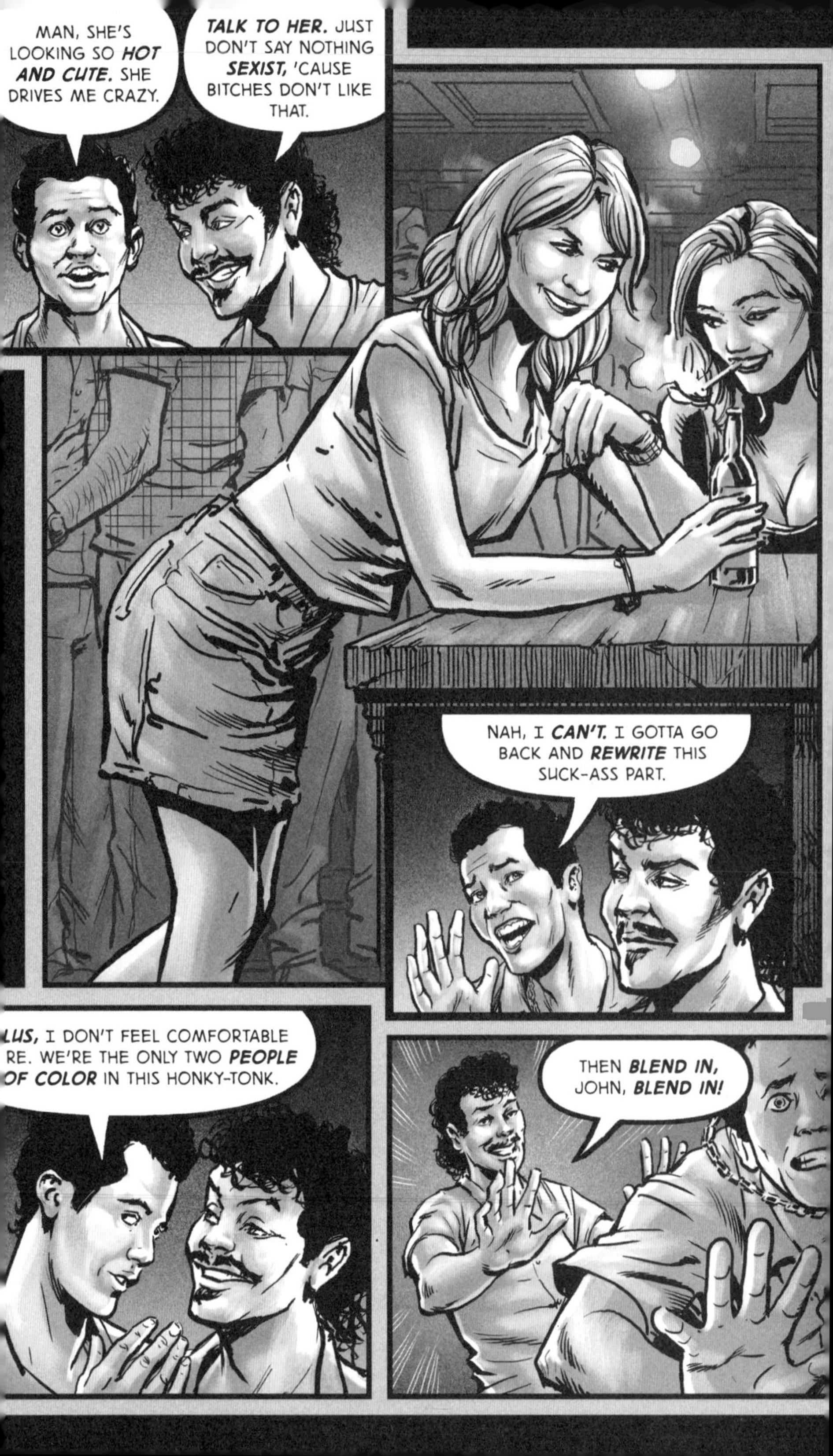
MAN, SHE'S LOOKING SO HOT AND CUTE. SHE DRIVES ME CRAZY.
TALK TO HER. JUST DON'T SAY NOTHING SEXIST, 'CAUSE BITCHES DON'T LIKE THAT.
NAH, I CAN'T. I GOTTA GO BACK AND REWRITE THIS SUCK-ASS PART.
LUS, I DON'T FEEL COMFORTABLE RE. WE'RE THE ONLY TWO PEOPLE OF COLOR IN THIS HONKY-TONK.
THEN BLEND IN, JOHN, BLEND IN!

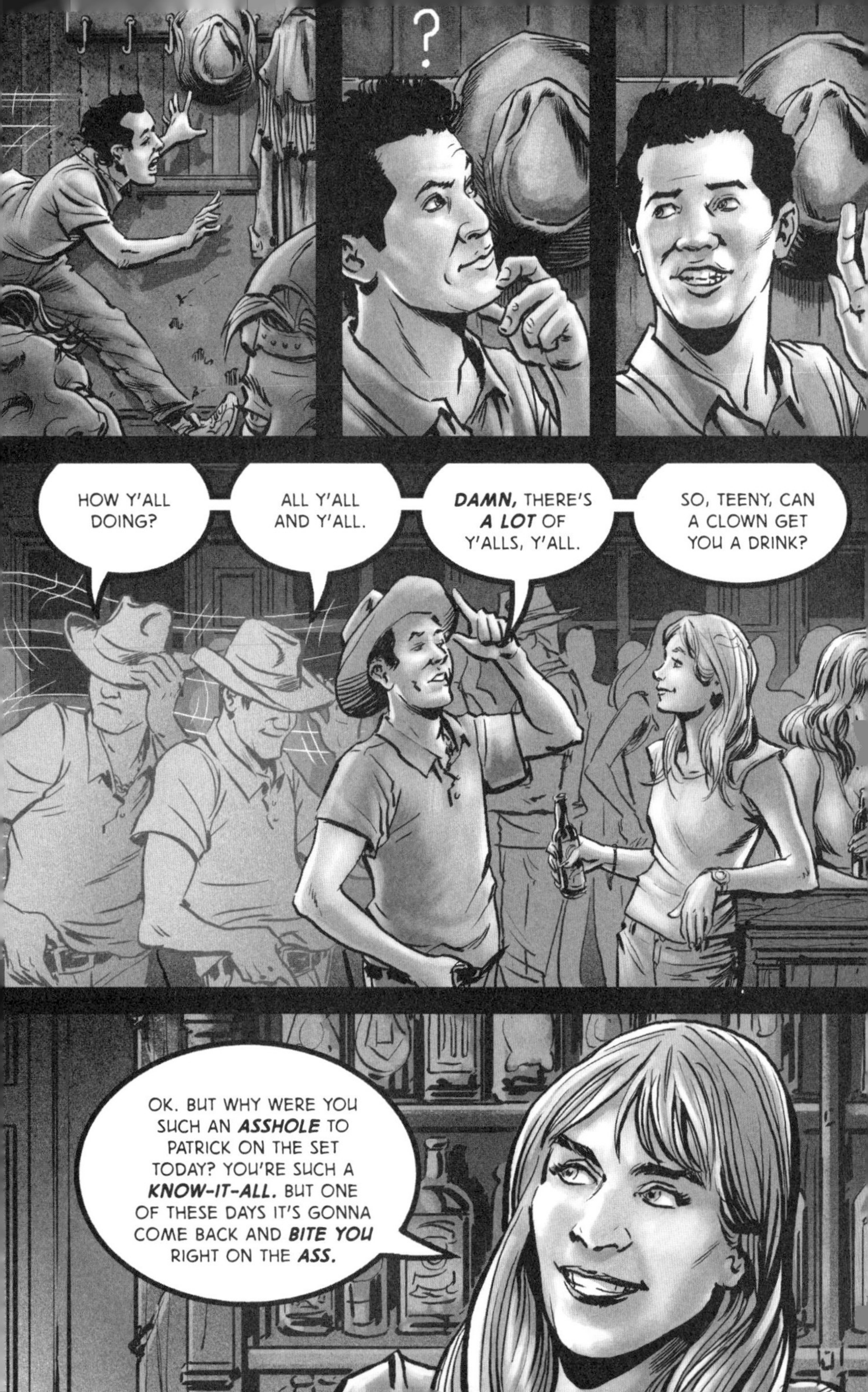
?
HOW Y'ALL DOING?
ALL Y'ALL AND Y'ALL.
DAMN, THERE'S A LOT OF Y'ALLS, Y'ALL.
SO, TEENY, CAN A CLOWN GET YOU A DRINK?
OK. BUT WHY WERE YOU SUCH AN ASSHOLE TO PATRICK ON THE SET TODAY? YOU'RE SUCH A KNOW-IT-ALL. BUT ONE OF THESE DAYS IT'S GONNA COME BACK AND BITE YOU RIGHT ON THE ASS.

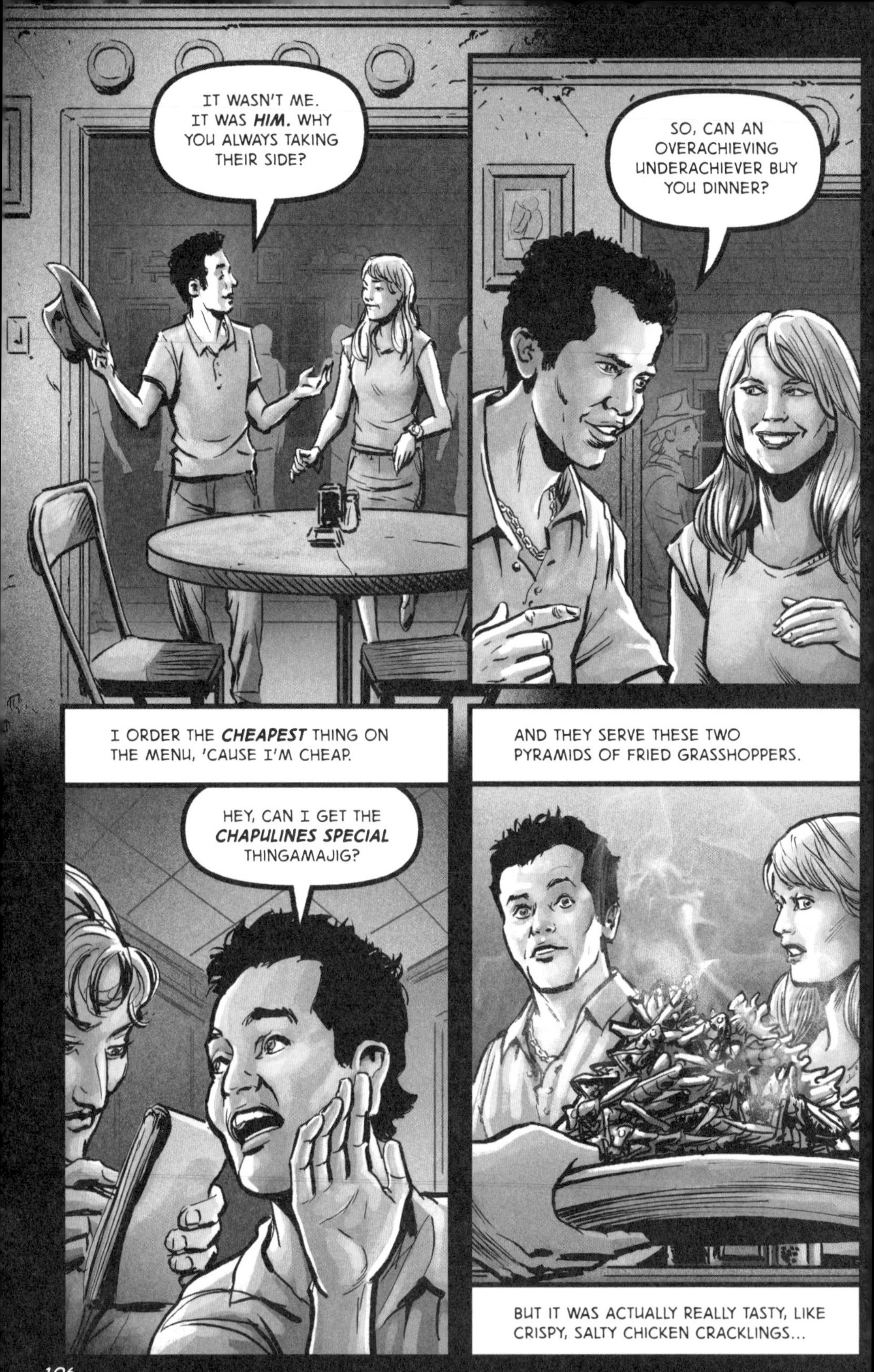
IT WASN'T ME. IT WAS HIM. WHY YOU ALWAYS TAKING THEIR SIDE?
SO, CAN AN OVERACHIEVING UNDERACHIEVER BUY YOU DINNER?
I ORDER THE CHEAPEST THING ON THE MENU, 'CAUSE I'M CHEAP.
HEY, CAN I GET THE CHAPULINES SPECIAL THINGAMAJIG?
AND THEY SERVE THESE TWO PYRAMIDS OF FRIED GRASSHOPPERS.
BUT IT WAS ACTUALLY REALLY TASTY, LIKE CRISPY, SALTY CHICKEN CRACKLINGS...

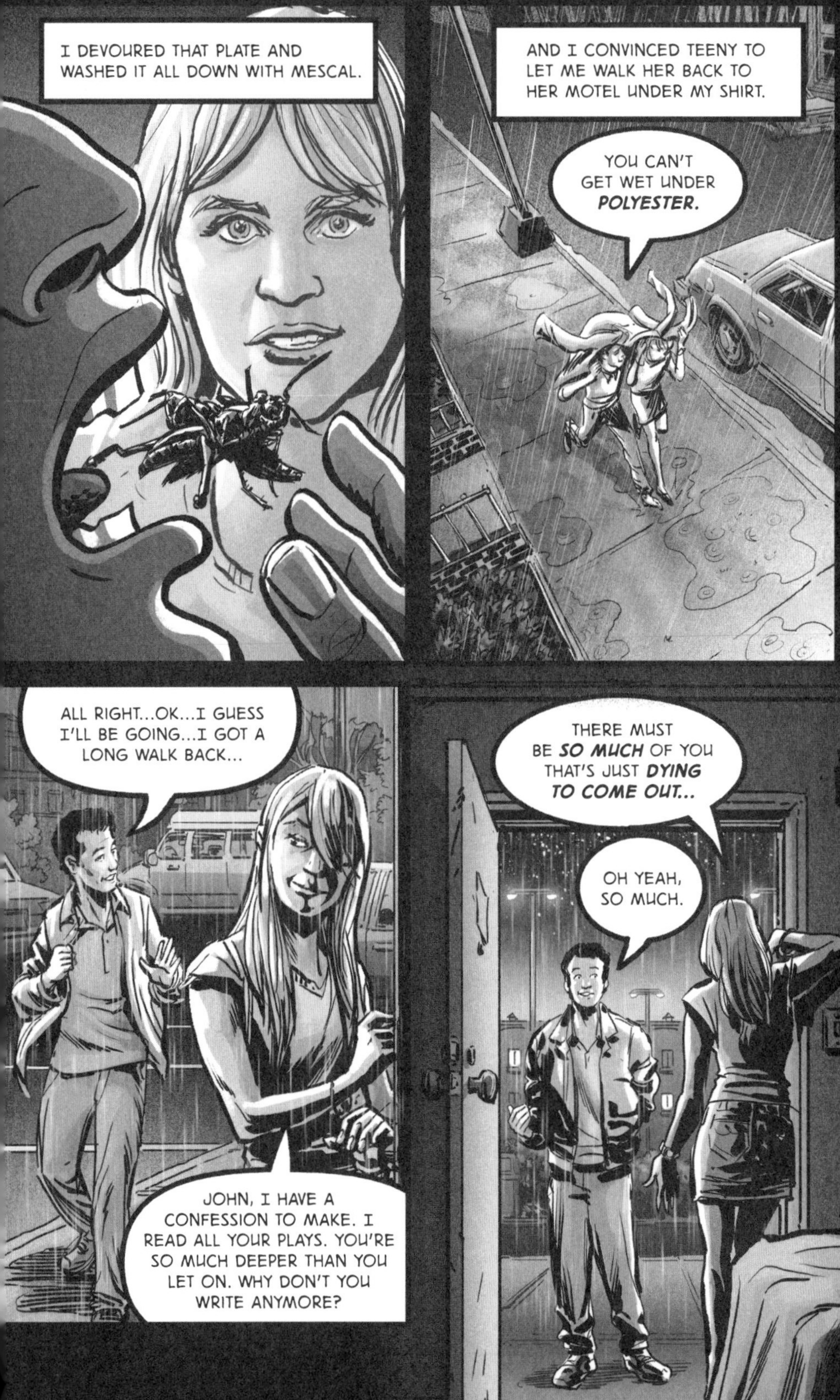

I DEVOURED THAT PLATE AND WASHED IT ALL DOWN WITH MESCAL.
AND I CONVINCED TEENY TO LET ME WALK HER BACK TO HER MOTEL UNDER MY SHIRT.
YOU CAN'T GET WET UNDER **POLYESTER.**
ALL RIGHT...OK...I GUESS I'LL BE GOING...I GOT A LONG WALK BACK...
JOHN, I HAVE A CONFESSION TO MAKE. I READ ALL YOUR PLAYS. YOU'RE SO MUCH DEEPER THAN YOU LET ON. WHY DON'T YOU WRITE ANYMORE?
THERE MUST BE ***SO MUCH*** OF YOU THAT'S JUST ***DYING TO COME OUT...***
OH YEAH, SO MUCH.

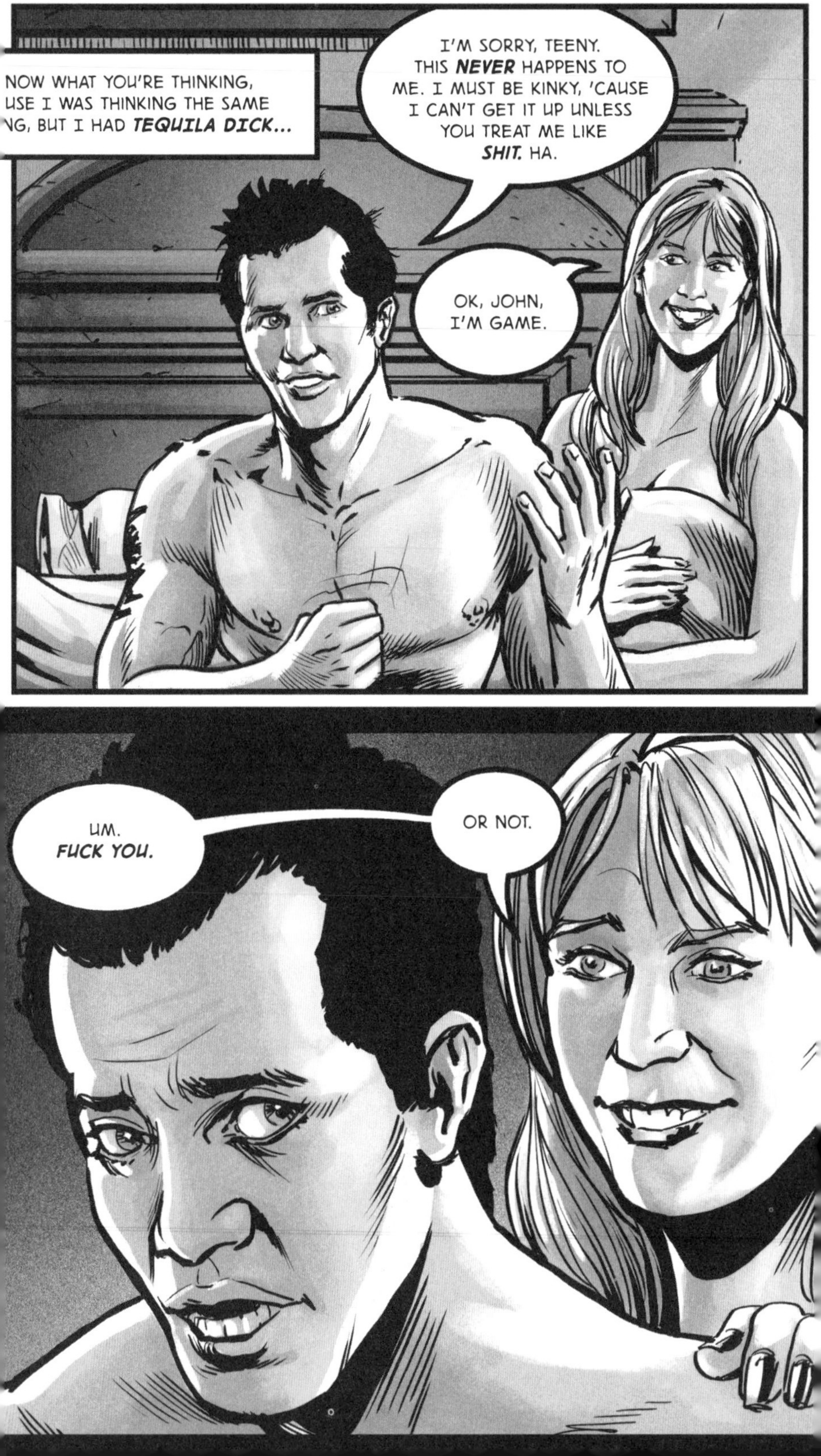
NOW WHAT YOU'RE THINKING, USE I WAS THINKING THE SAME NG, BUT I HAD ***TEQUILA DICK...***
I'M SORRY, TEENY. THIS ***NEVER*** HAPPENS TO ME. I MUST BE KINKY, 'CAUSE I CAN'T GET IT UP UNLESS YOU TREAT ME LIKE ***SHIT.*** HA.
OK, JOHN, I'M GAME.
UM. ***FUCK YOU.***
OR NOT.

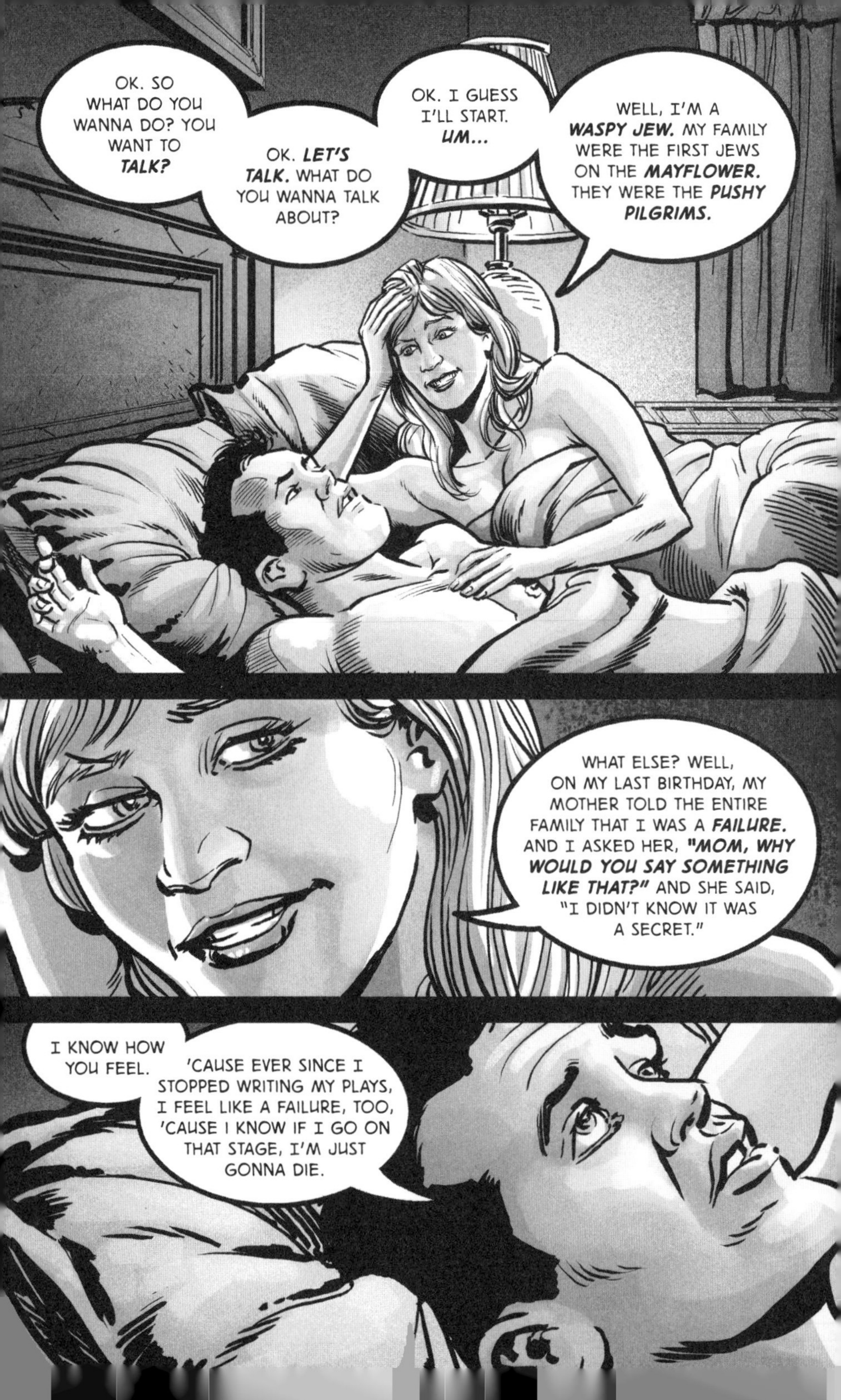
OK. SO WHAT DO YOU WANNA DO? YOU WANT TO **TALK?**
OK. ***LET'S TALK.*** WHAT DO YOU WANNA TALK ABOUT?
OK. I GUESS I'LL START. ***UM...***
WELL, I'M A ***WASPY JEW.*** MY FAMILY WERE THE FIRST JEWS ON THE ***MAYFLOWER.*** THEY WERE THE ***PUSHY PILGRIMS.***
WHAT ELSE? WELL, ON MY LAST BIRTHDAY, MY MOTHER TOLD THE ENTIRE FAMILY THAT I WAS A ***FAILURE.*** AND I ASKED HER, ***"MOM, WHY WOULD YOU SAY SOMETHING LIKE THAT?"*** AND SHE SAID, "I DIDN'T KNOW IT WAS A SECRET."
I KNOW HOW YOU FEEL.
'CAUSE EVER SINCE I STOPPED WRITING MY PLAYS, I FEEL LIKE A FAILURE, TOO, 'CAUSE I KNOW IF I GO ON THAT STAGE, I'M JUST GONNA DIE.

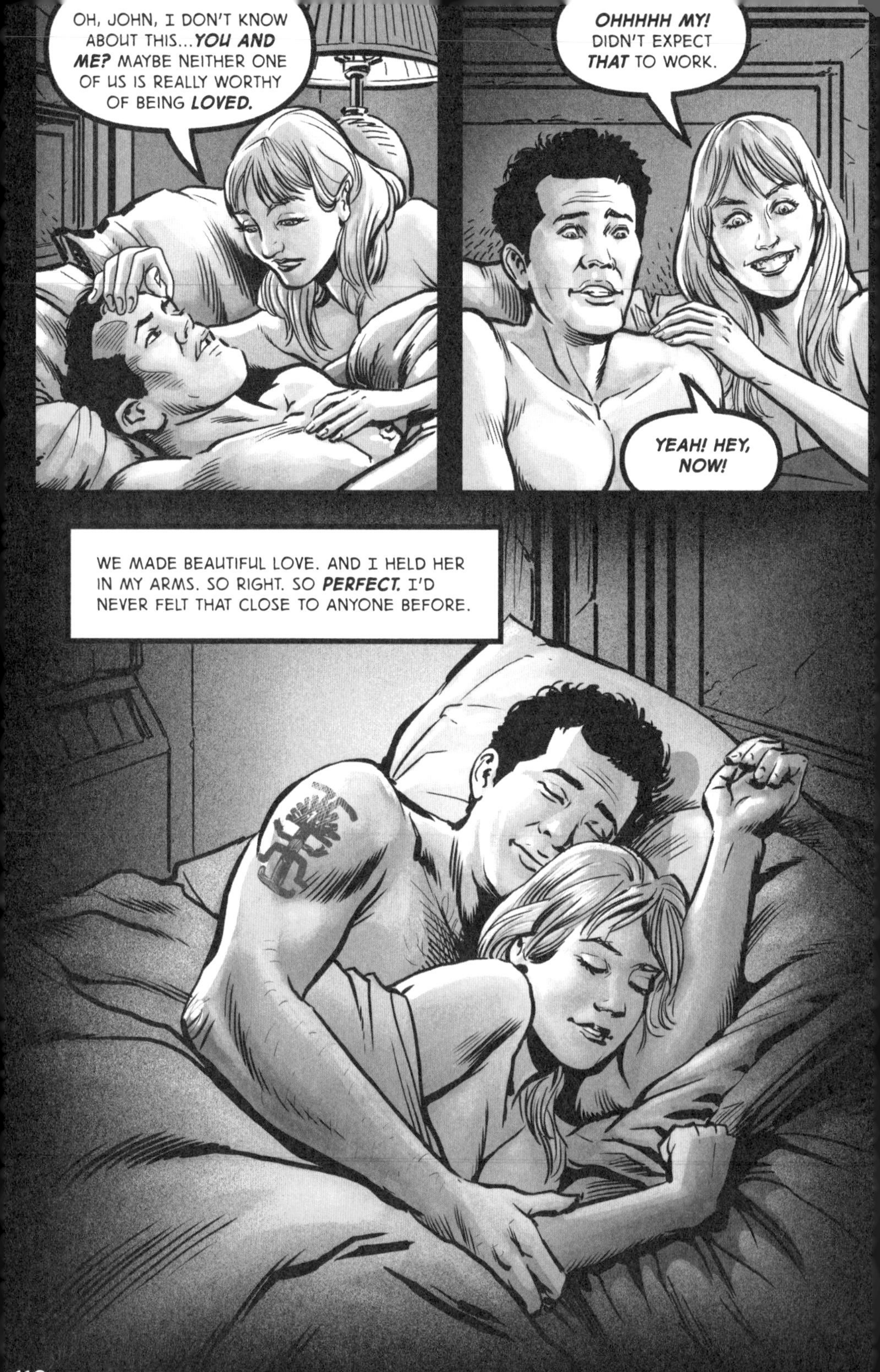
OH, JOHN, I DON'T KNOW ABOUT THIS...YOU AND ME? MAYBE NEITHER ONE OF US IS REALLY WORTHY OF BEING LOVED.
OHHHHH MY! DIDN'T EXPECT THAT TO WORK.
YEAH! HEY, NOW!
WE MADE BEAUTIFUL LOVE. AND I HELD HER IN MY ARMS. SO RIGHT. SO PERFECT. I'D NEVER FELT THAT CLOSE TO ANYONE BEFORE.

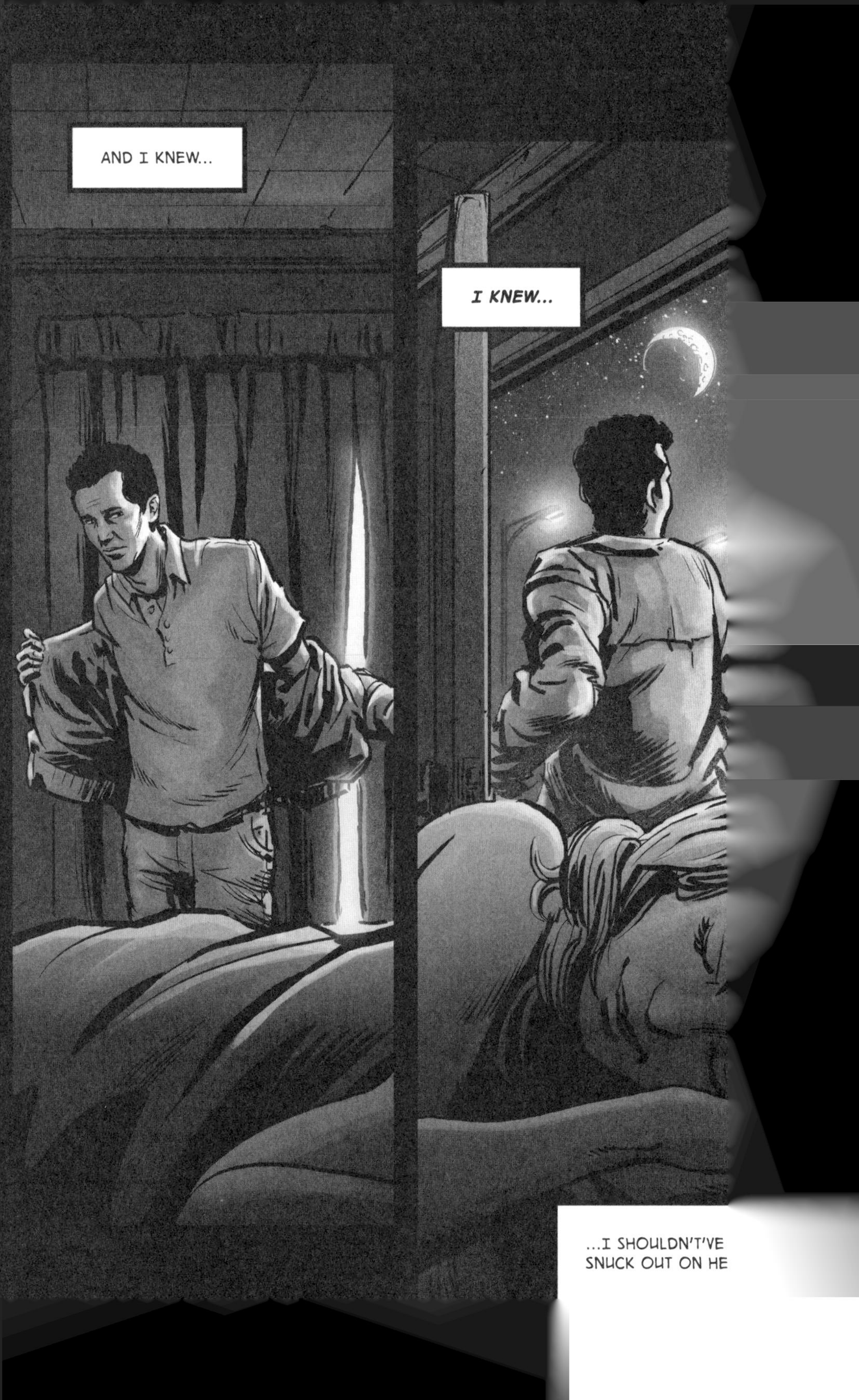
AND I KNEW...
I KNEW...
...I SHOULDN'T'VE
SNUCK OUT ON HE

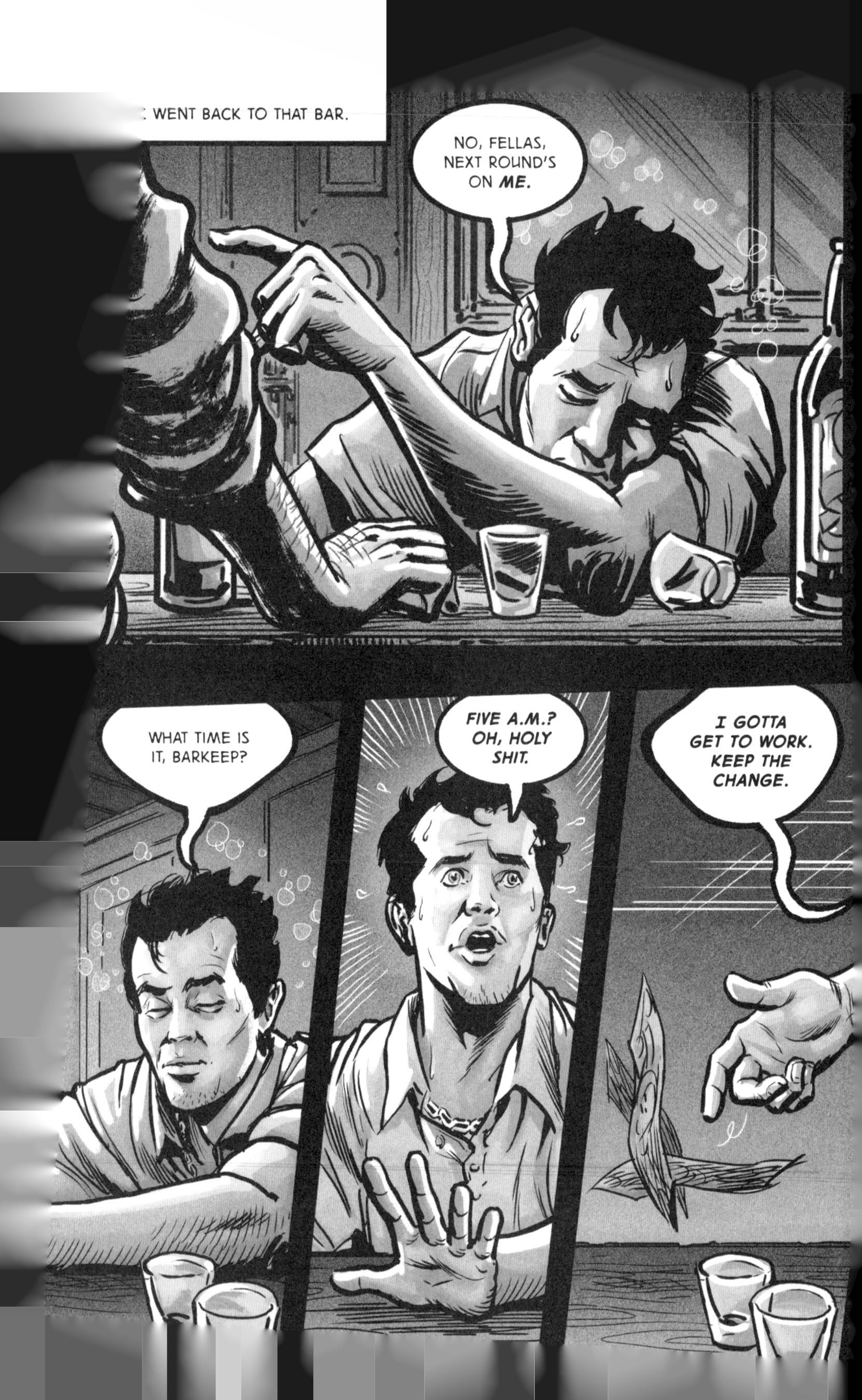
WENT BACK TO THAT BAR.
NO, FELLAS, NEXT ROUND'S ON *ME.*
WHAT TIME IS IT, BARKEEP?
FIVE A.M.? OH, HOLY SHIT.
I GOTTA GET TO WORK. KEEP THE CHANGE.

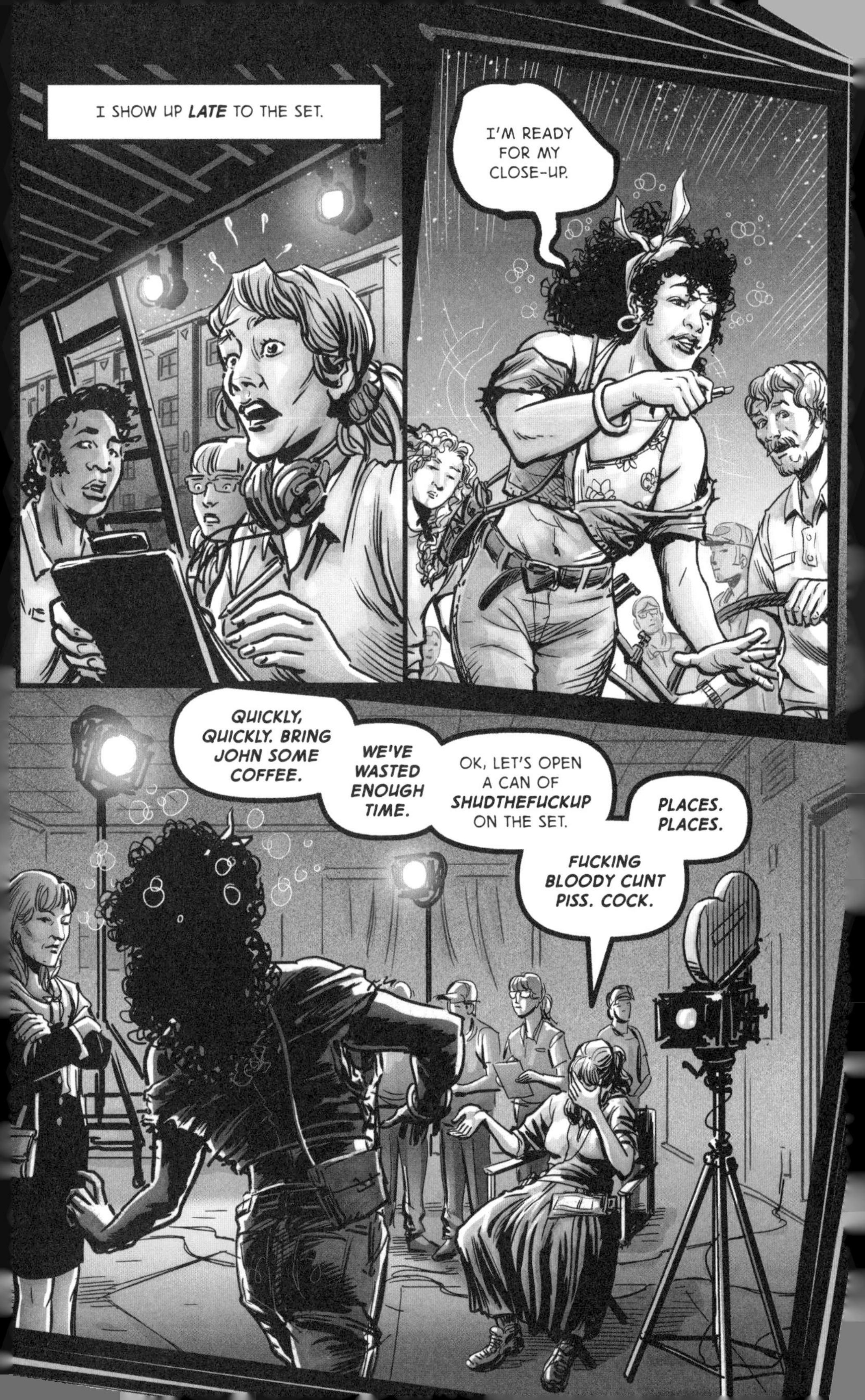
I SHOW UP LATE TO THE SET.
I'M READY FOR MY CLOSE-UP.
QUICKLY, QUICKLY. BRING JOHN SOME COFFEE.
WE'VE WASTED ENOUGH TIME.
OK, LET'S OPEN A CAN OF SHUDTHEFUCKUP ON THE SET.
PLACES. PLACES.
FUCKING BLOODY CUNT PISS. COCK.

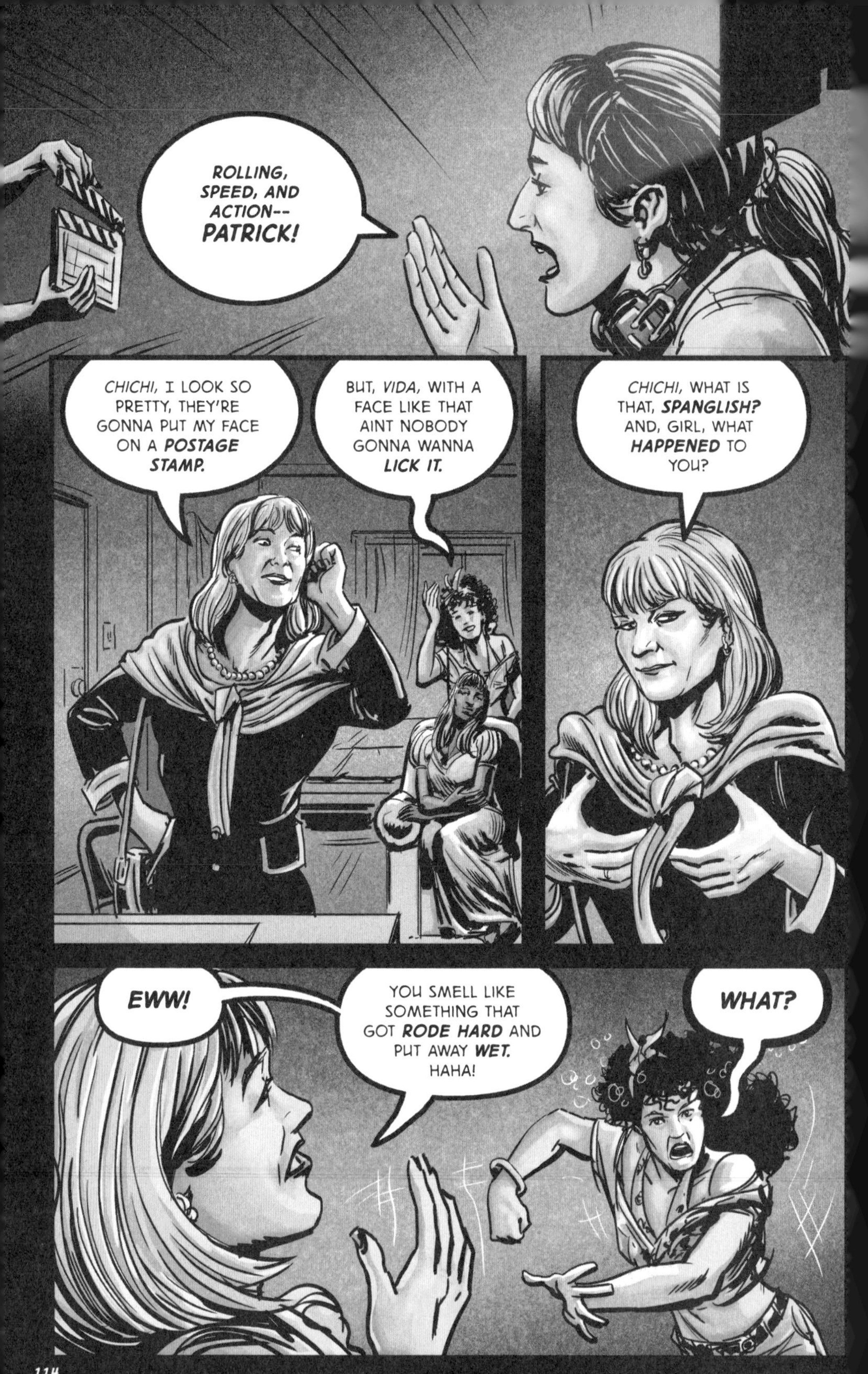
ROLLING, SPEED, AND ACTION-- PATRICK!
CHICHI, I LOOK SO PRETTY, THEY'RE GONNA PUT MY FACE ON A POSTAGE STAMP.
BUT, VIDA, WITH A FACE LIKE THAT AINT NOBODY GONNA WANNA LICK IT.
CHICHI, WHAT IS THAT, SPANGLISH? AND, GIRL, WHAT HAPPENED TO YOU?
EWW!
YOU SMELL LIKE SOMETHING THAT GOT RODE HARD AND PUT AWAY WET. HAHA!
WHAT?

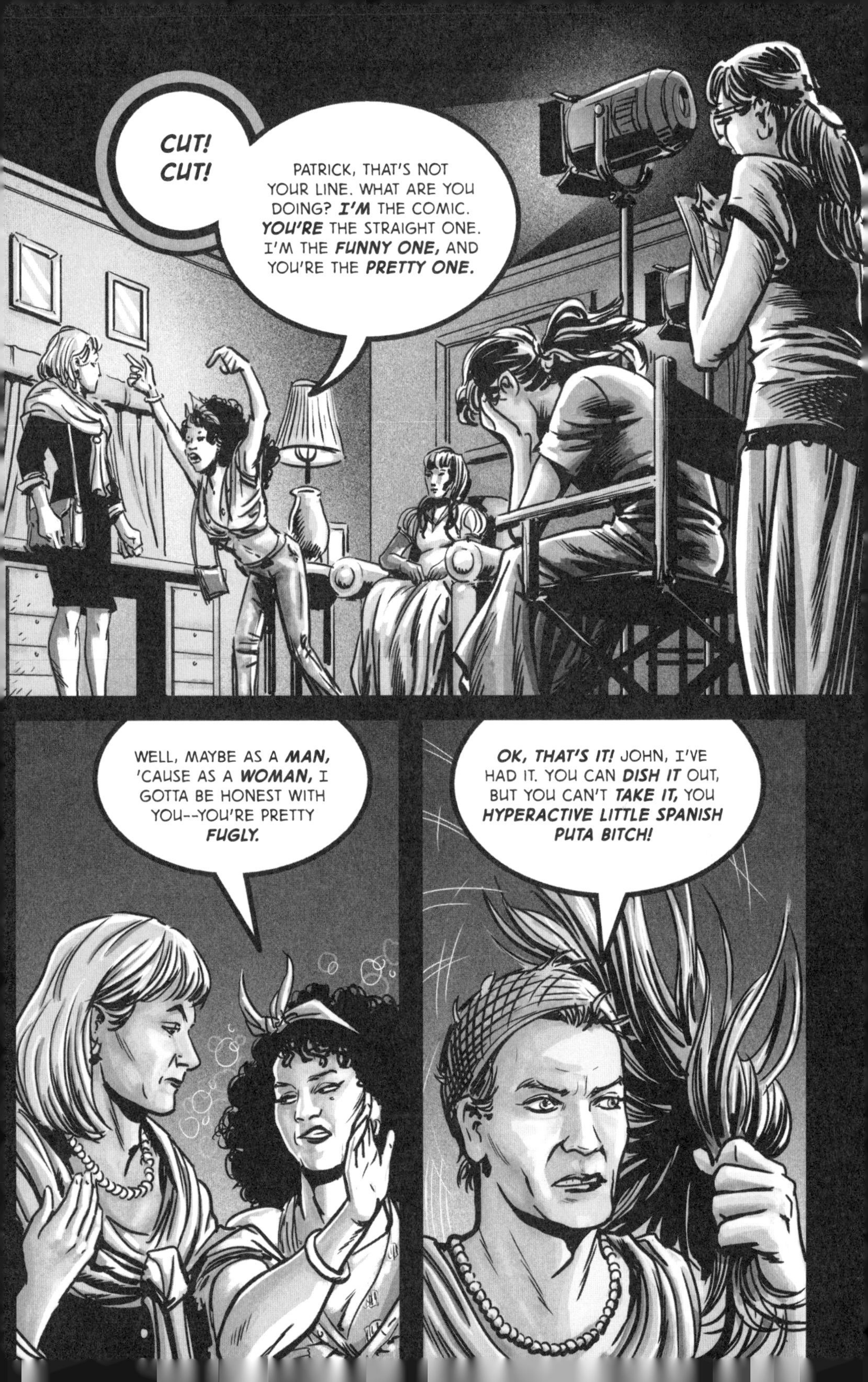
CUT! CUT!
PATRICK, THAT'S NOT YOUR LINE. WHAT ARE YOU DOING? I'M THE COMIC. YOU'RE THE STRAIGHT ONE. I'M THE FUNNY ONE, AND YOU'RE THE PRETTY ONE.
WELL, MAYBE AS A MAN, 'CAUSE AS A WOMAN, I GOTTA BE HONEST WITH YOU--YOU'RE PRETTY FUGLY.
OK, THAT'S IT! JOHN, I'VE HAD IT. YOU CAN DISH IT OUT, BUT YOU CAN'T TAKE IT, YOU HYPERACTIVE LITTLE SPANISH PUTA BITCH!

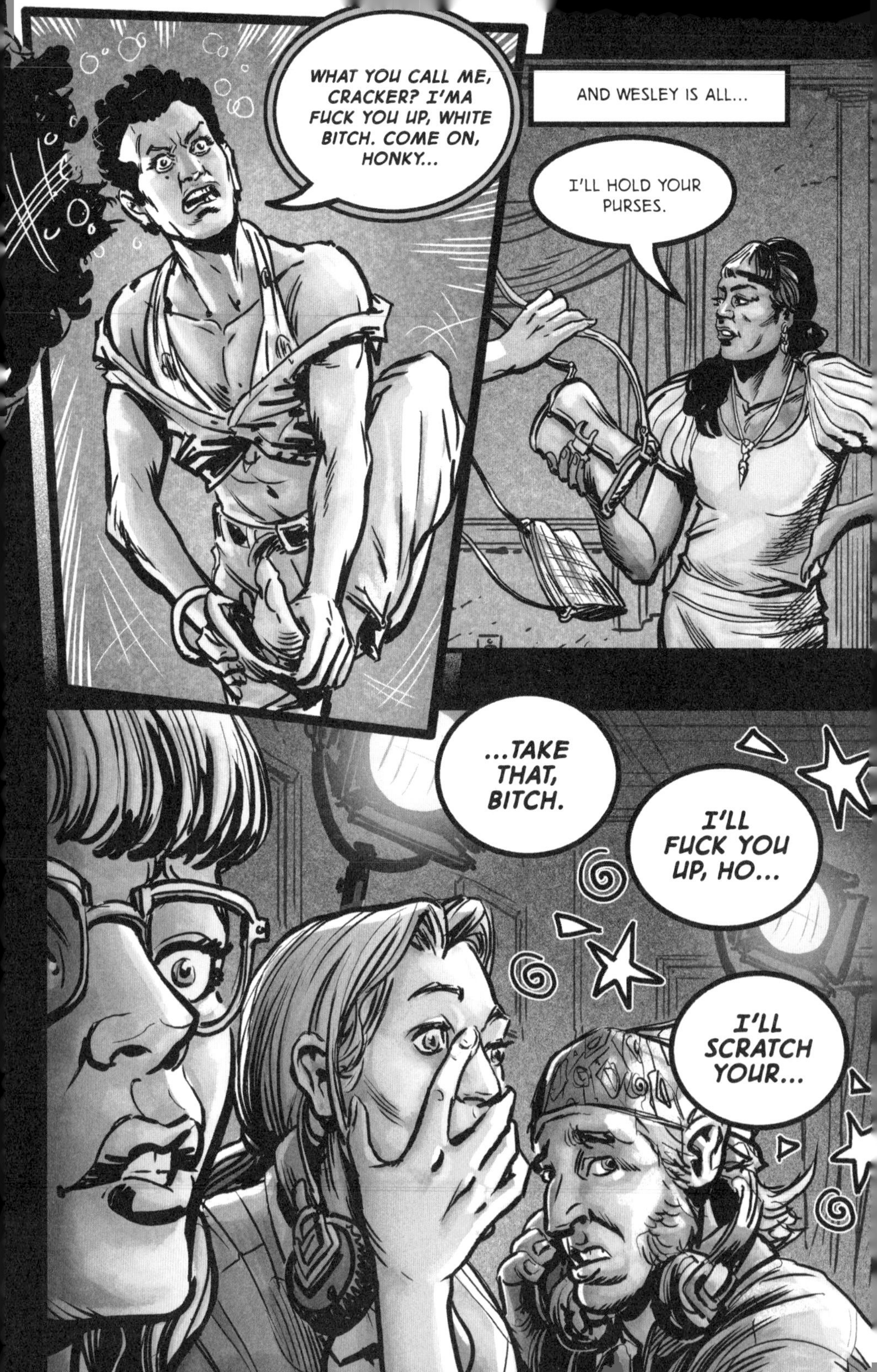
WHAT YOU CALL ME, CRACKER? I'MA FUCK YOU UP, WHITE BITCH. COME ON, HONKY...
AND WESLEY IS ALL...
I'LL HOLD YOUR PURSES.
...TAKE THAT, BITCH.
I'LL FUCK YOU UP, HO...
I'LL SCRATCH YOUR...

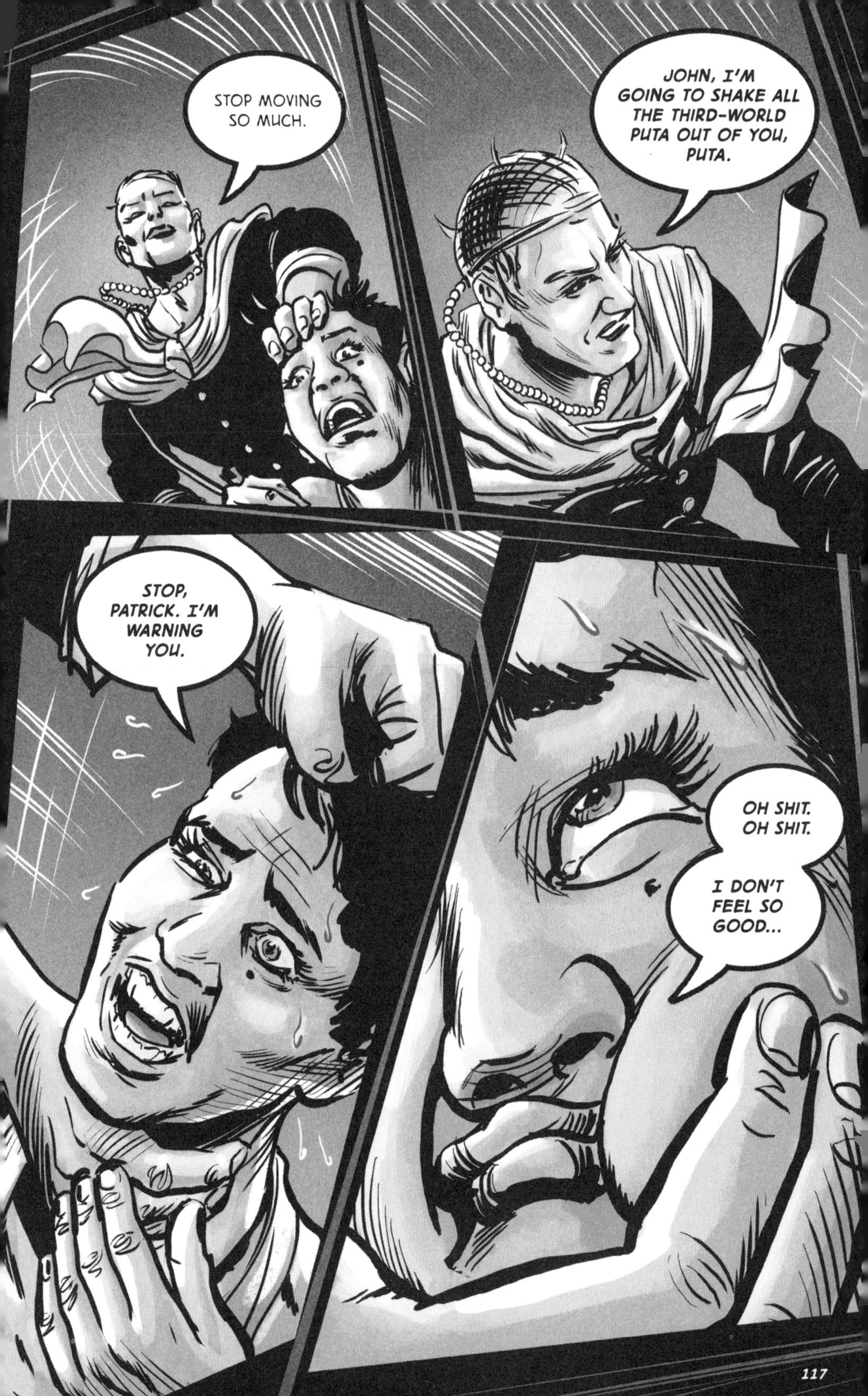
STOP MOVING SO MUCH.
JOHN, I'M GOING TO SHAKE ALL THE THIRD-WORLD PUTA OUT OF YOU, PUTA.
STOP, PATRICK. I'M WARNING YOU.
OH SHIT. OH SHIT.
I DON'T FEEL SO GOOD...

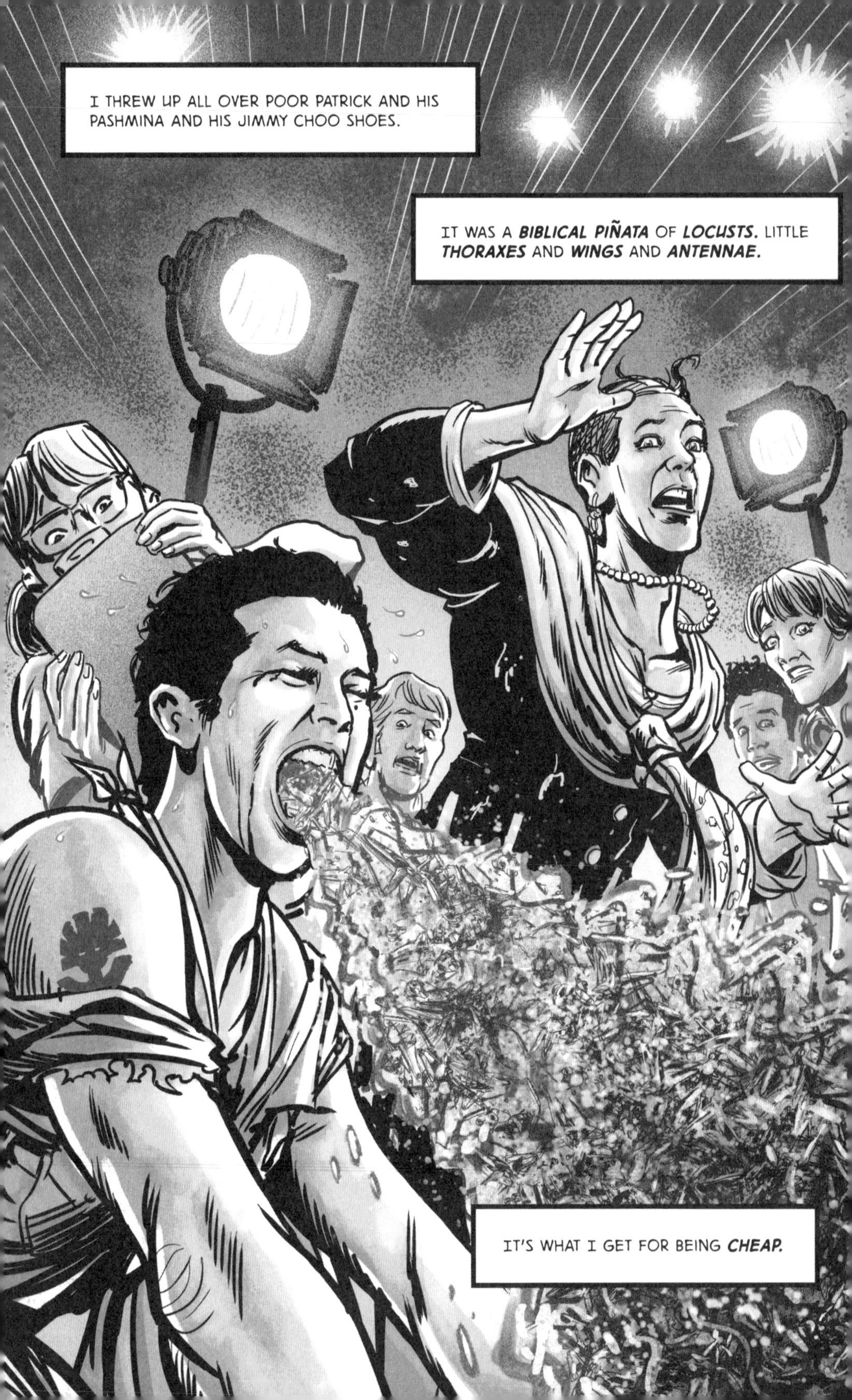
I THREW UP ALL OVER POOR PATRICK AND HIS PASHMINA AND HIS JIMMY CHOO SHOES.
IT WAS A ***BIBLICAL PIÑATA*** OF ***LOCUSTS.*** LITTLE ***THORAXES*** AND ***WINGS*** AND ***ANTENNAE.***
IT'S WHAT I GET FOR BEING ***CHEAP.***

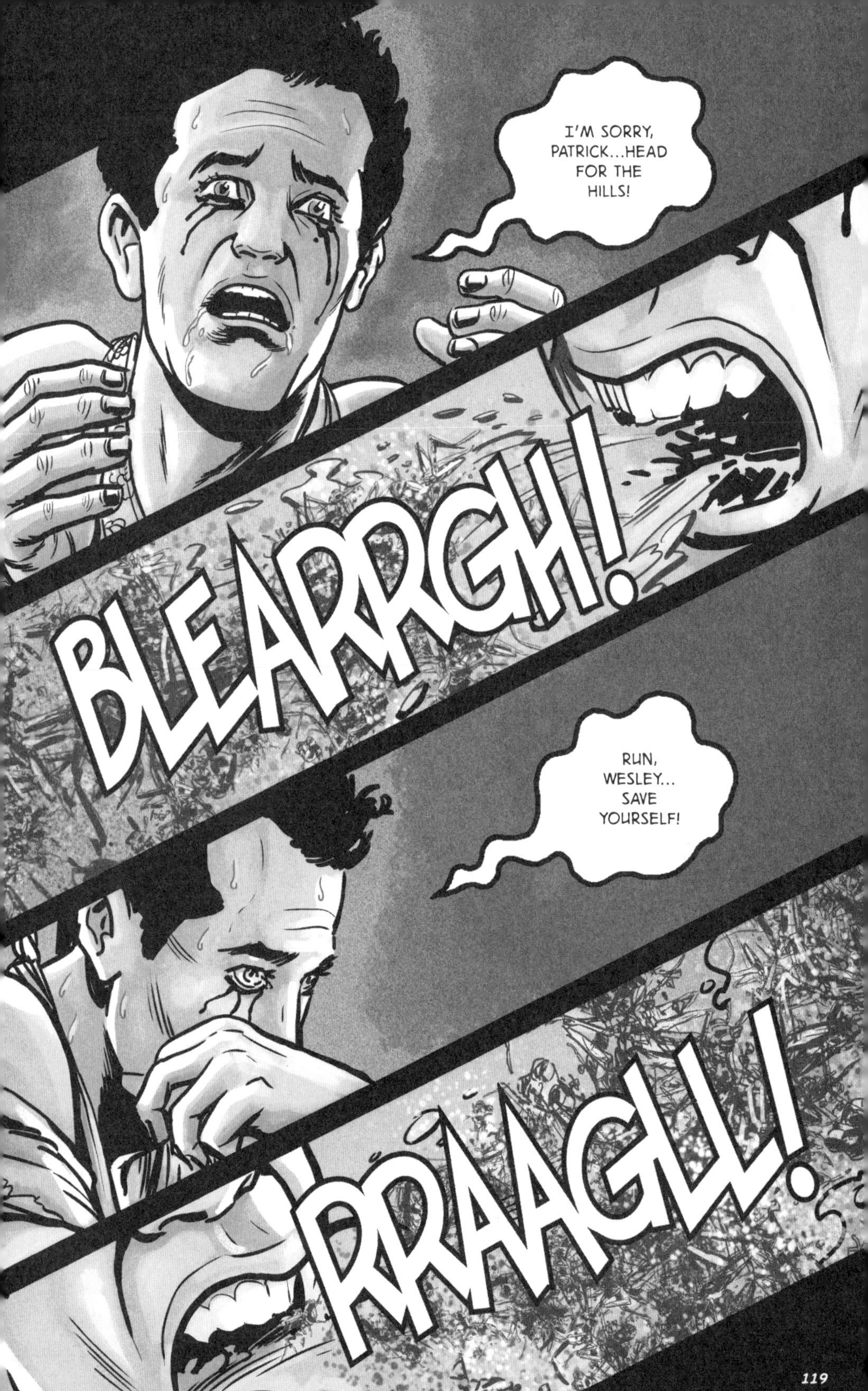
I'M SORRY, PATRICK...HEAD FOR THE HILLS!
BLEARRGH!
RUN, WESLEY... SAVE YOURSELF!
RRAAGLL!

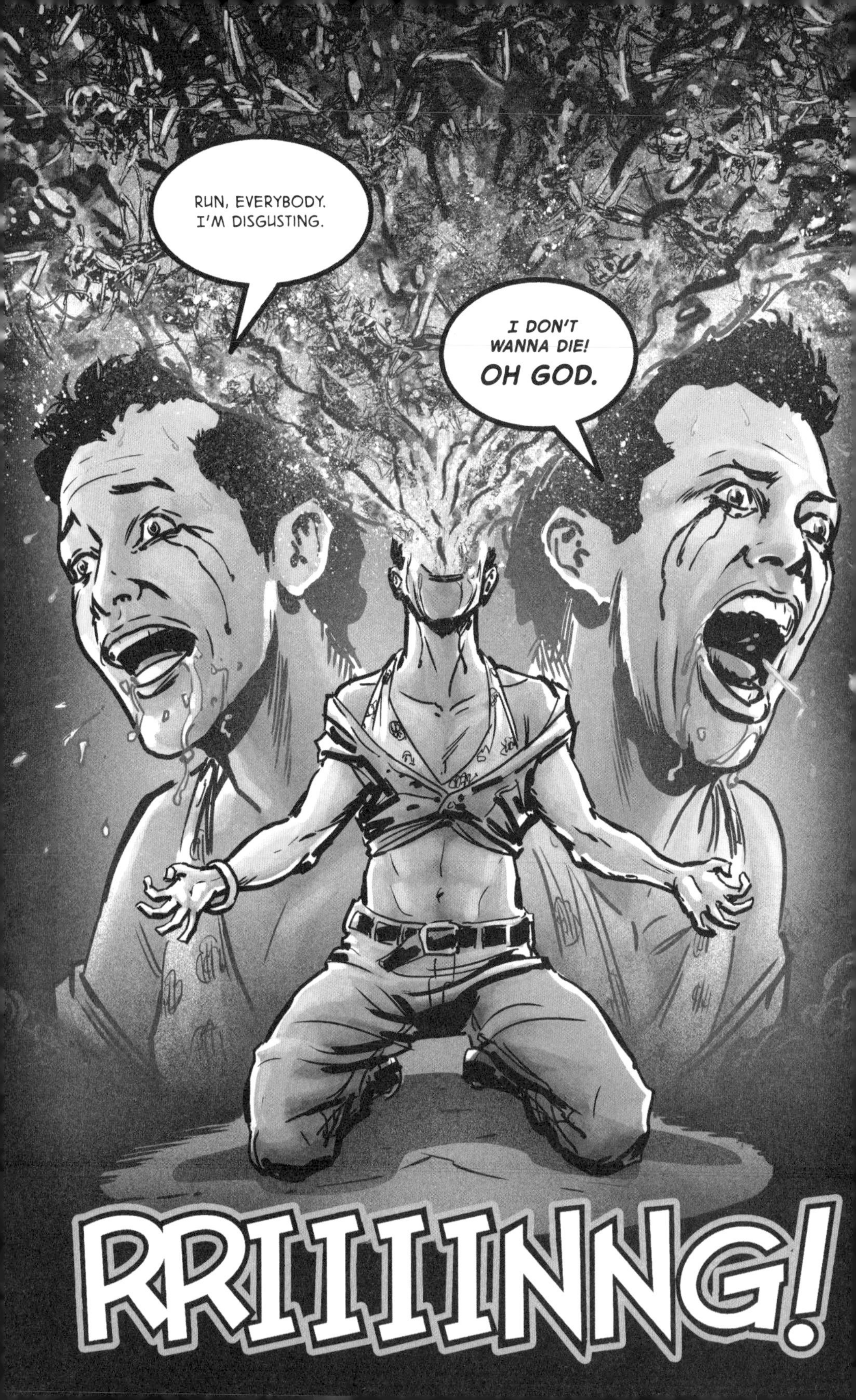
RUN, EVERYBODY.
I'M DISGUSTING.
I DON'T
WANNA DIE!
OH GOD.
RRIIIINNG!

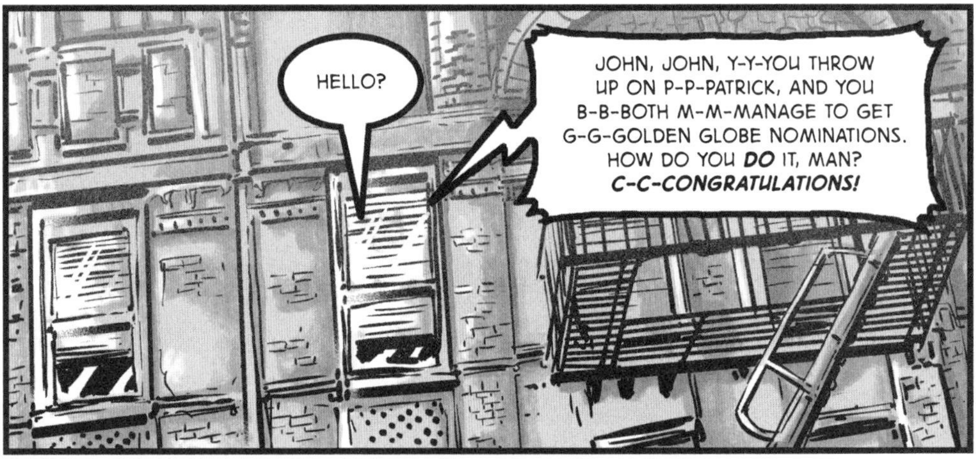
HELLO?
JOHN, JOHN, Y-Y-YOU THROW UP ON P-P-PATRICK, AND YOU B-B-BOTH M-M-MANAGE TO GET G-G-GOLDEN GLOBE NOMINATIONS. HOW DO YOU ***DO*** IT, MAN? ***C-C-CONGRATULATIONS!***

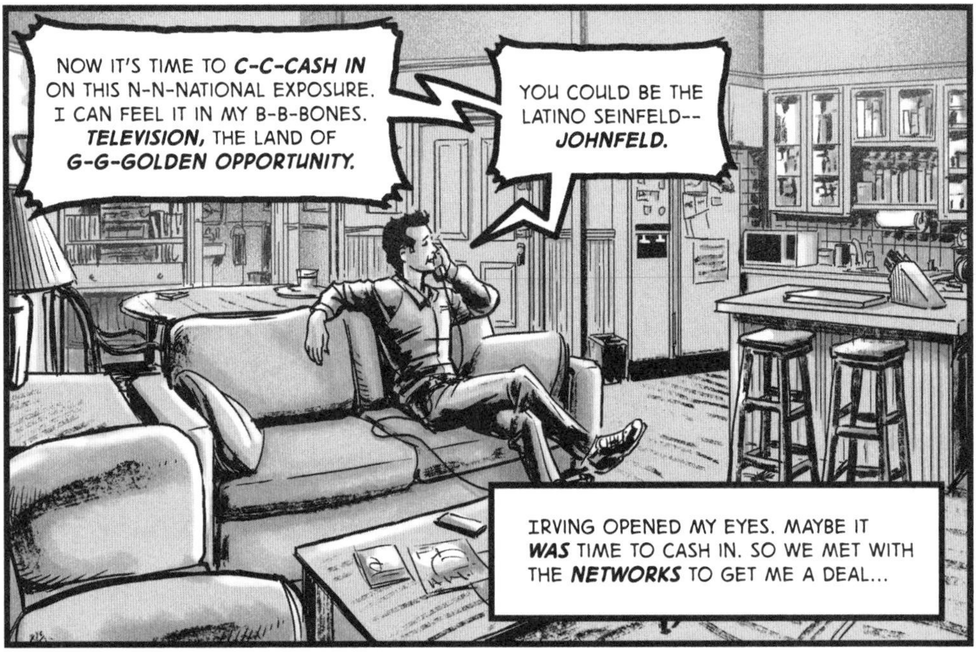
NOW IT'S TIME TO ***C-C-CASH IN*** ON THIS N-N-NATIONAL EXPOSURE. I CAN FEEL IT IN MY B-B-BONES. ***TELEVISION,*** THE LAND OF ***G-G-GOLDEN OPPORTUNITY.***
YOU COULD BE THE LATINO SEINFELD-- ***JOHNFELD.***
IRVING OPENED MY EYES. MAYBE IT ***WAS*** TIME TO CASH IN. SO WE MET WITH THE ***NETWORKS*** TO GET ME A DEAL...

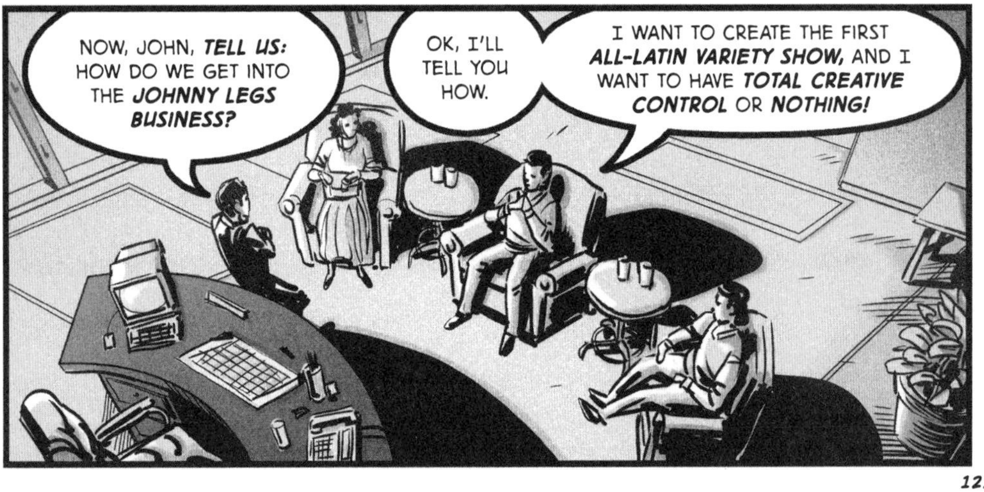
NOW, JOHN, ***TELL US:*** HOW DO WE GET INTO THE ***JOHNNY LEGS BUSINESS?***
OK, I'LL TELL YOU HOW.
I WANT TO CREATE THE FIRST ***ALL-LATIN VARIETY SHOW,*** AND I WANT TO HAVE ***TOTAL CREATIVE CONTROL*** OR ***NOTHING!***

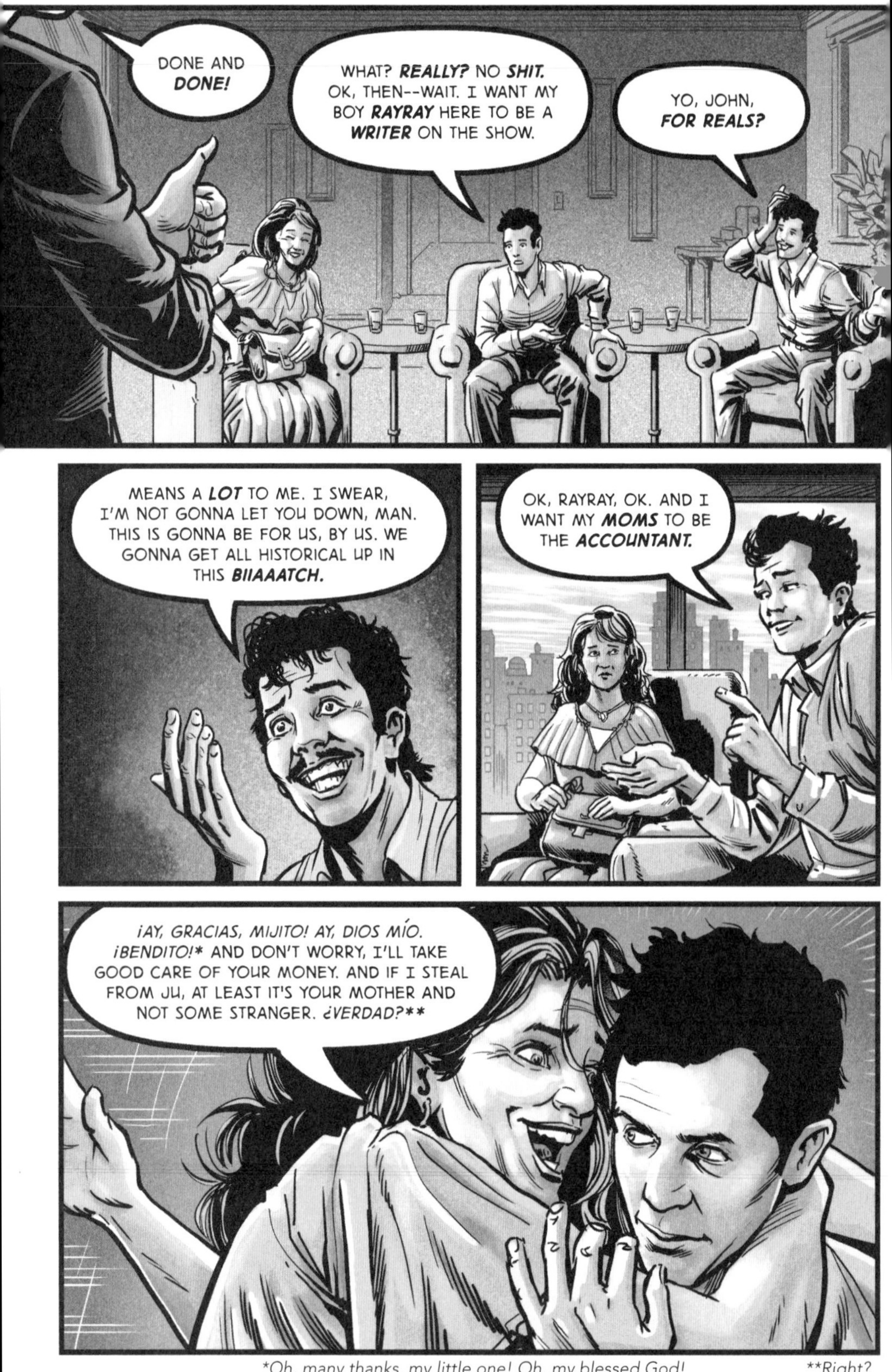
DONE AND DONE!
WHAT? REALLY? NO SHIT. OK, THEN--WAIT. I WANT MY BOY RAYRAY HERE TO BE A WRITER ON THE SHOW.
YO, JOHN, FOR REALS?
MEANS A LOT TO ME. I SWEAR, I'M NOT GONNA LET YOU DOWN, MAN. THIS IS GONNA BE FOR US, BY US. WE GONNA GET ALL HISTORICAL UP IN THIS BIIAAATCH.
OK, RAYRAY, OK. AND I WANT MY MOMS TO BE THE ACCOUNTANT.
¡AY, GRACIAS, MIJITO! AY, DIOS MÍO. ¡BENDITO!* AND DON'T WORRY, I'LL TAKE GOOD CARE OF YOUR MONEY. AND IF I STEAL FROM JU, AT LEAST IT'S YOUR MOTHER AND NOT SOME STRANGER. ¿VERDAD?**

**Oh, many thanks, my little one! Oh, my blessed God!* ***Right?*

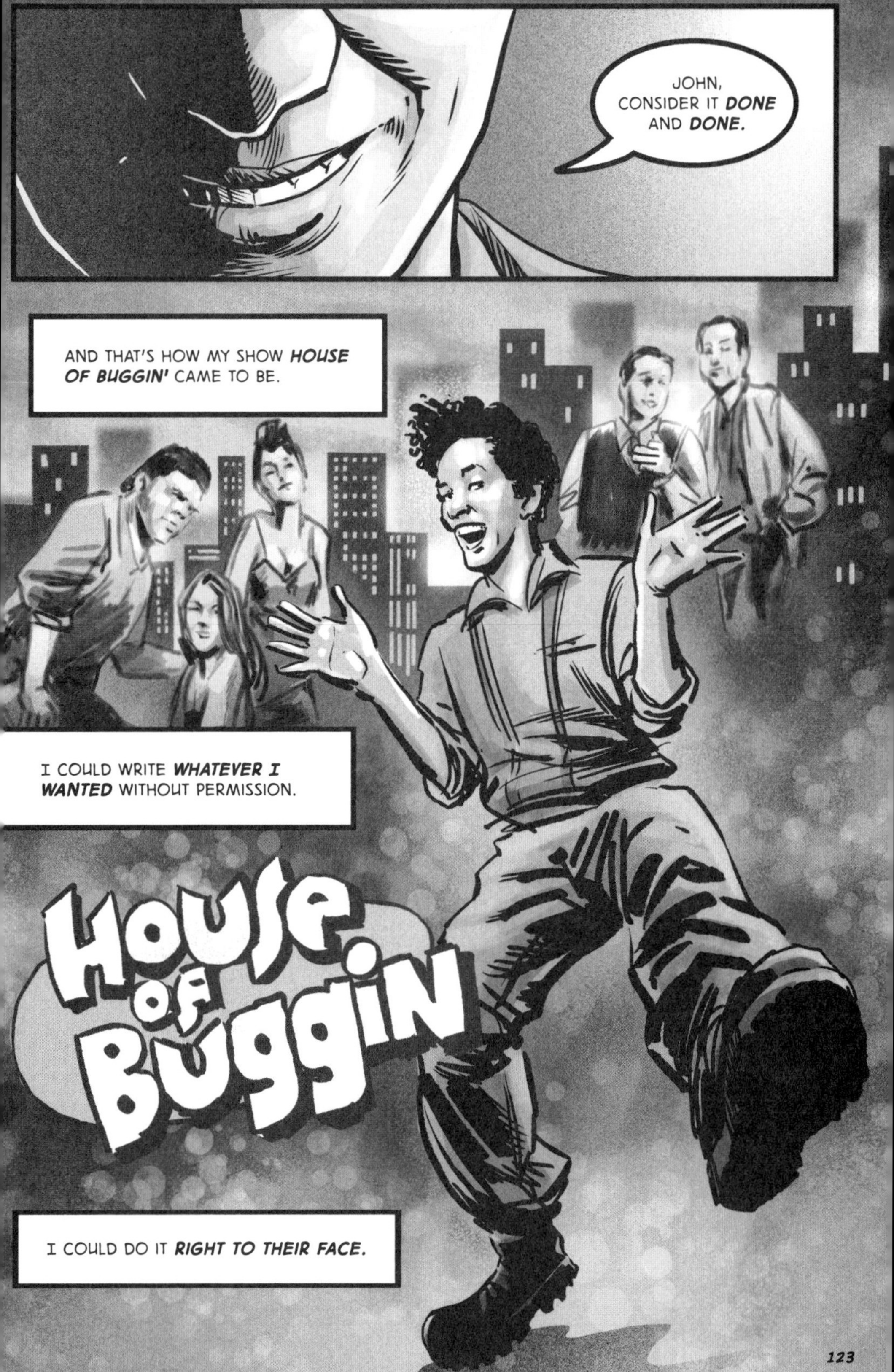
JOHN, CONSIDER IT DONE AND DONE.
AND THAT'S HOW MY SHOW HOUSE OF BUGGIN' CAME TO BE.
I COULD WRITE WHATEVER I WANTED WITHOUT PERMISSION.
HOUSE OF BUGGIN
I COULD DO IT RIGHT TO THEIR FACE.

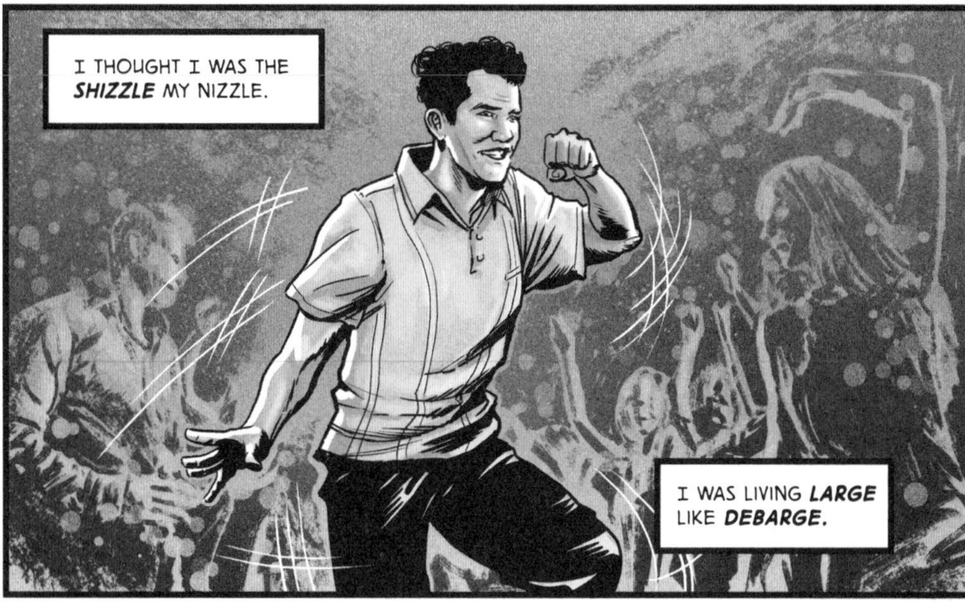
I THOUGHT I WAS THE SHIZZLE MY NIZZLE.
I WAS LIVING LARGE LIKE DEBARGE.

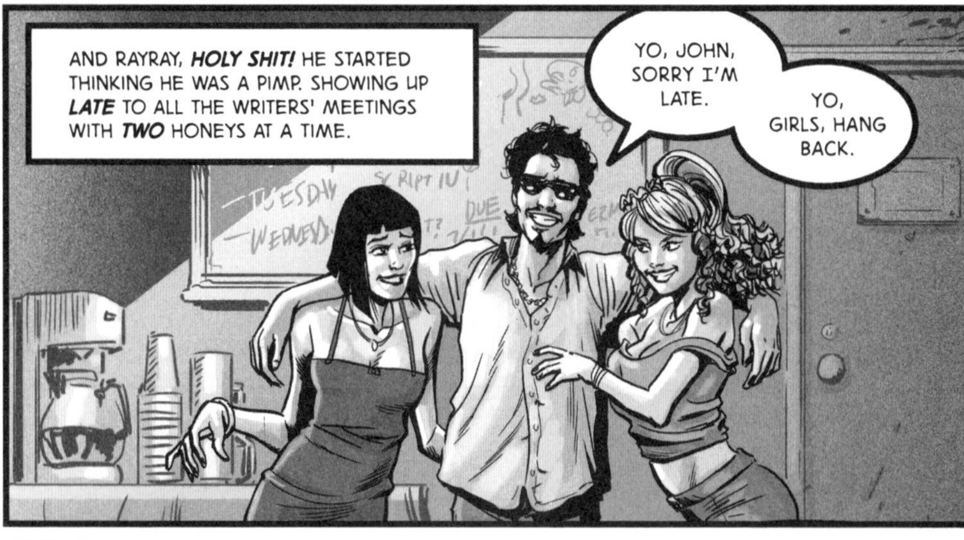
AND RAYRAY, HOLY SHIT! HE STARTED THINKING HE WAS A PIMP. SHOWING UP LATE TO ALL THE WRITERS' MEETINGS WITH TWO HONEYS AT A TIME.
YO, JOHN, SORRY I'M LATE.
YO, GIRLS, HANG BACK.

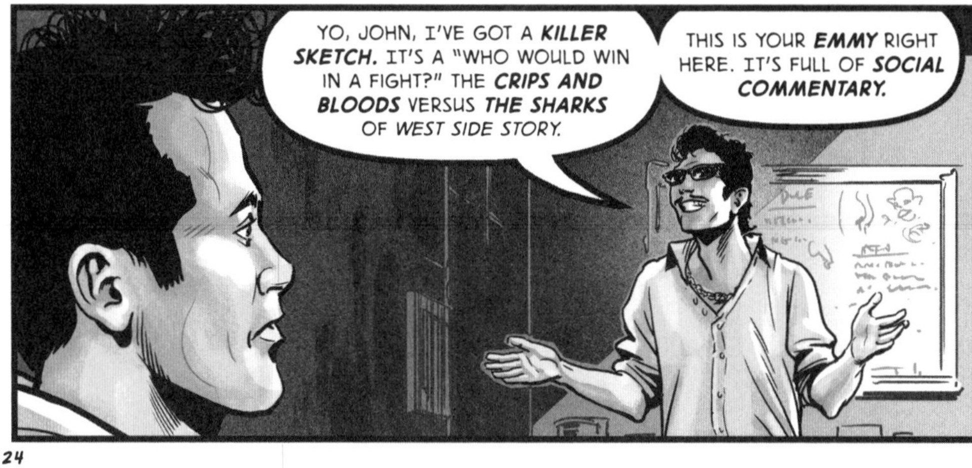
YO, JOHN, I'VE GOT A KILLER SKETCH. IT'S A "WHO WOULD WIN IN A FIGHT?" THE CRIPS AND BLOODS VERSUS THE SHARKS OF WEST SIDE STORY.
THIS IS YOUR EMMY RIGHT HERE. IT'S FULL OF SOCIAL COMMENTARY.

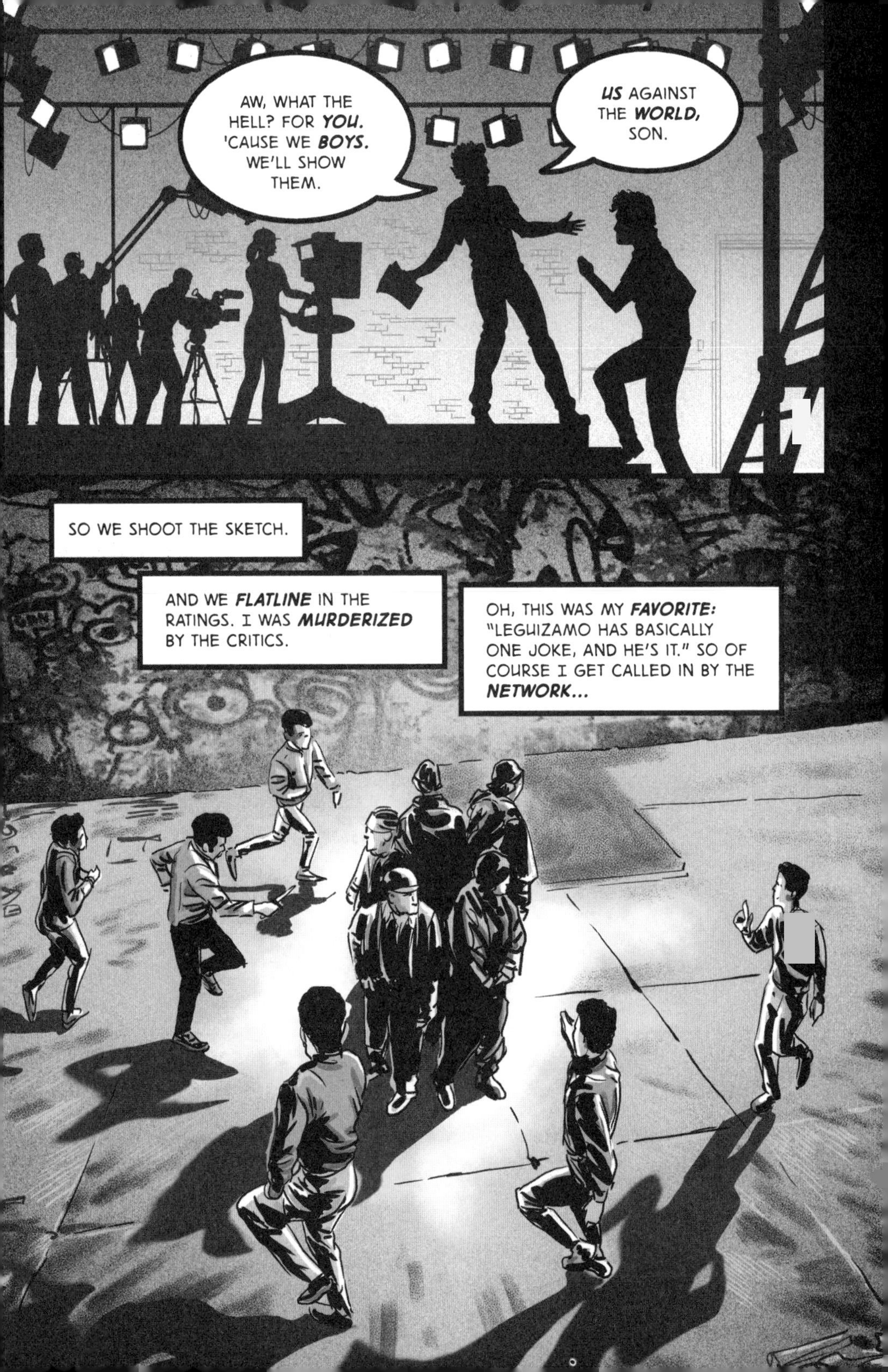
AW, WHAT THE HELL? FOR YOU. 'CAUSE WE BOYS. WE'LL SHOW THEM.
US AGAINST THE WORLD, SON.
SO WE SHOOT THE SKETCH.
AND WE FLATLINE IN THE RATINGS. I WAS MURDERIZED BY THE CRITICS.
OH, THIS WAS MY FAVORITE: "LEGUIZAMO HAS BASICALLY ONE JOKE, AND HE'S IT." SO OF COURSE I GET CALLED IN BY THE NETWORK...

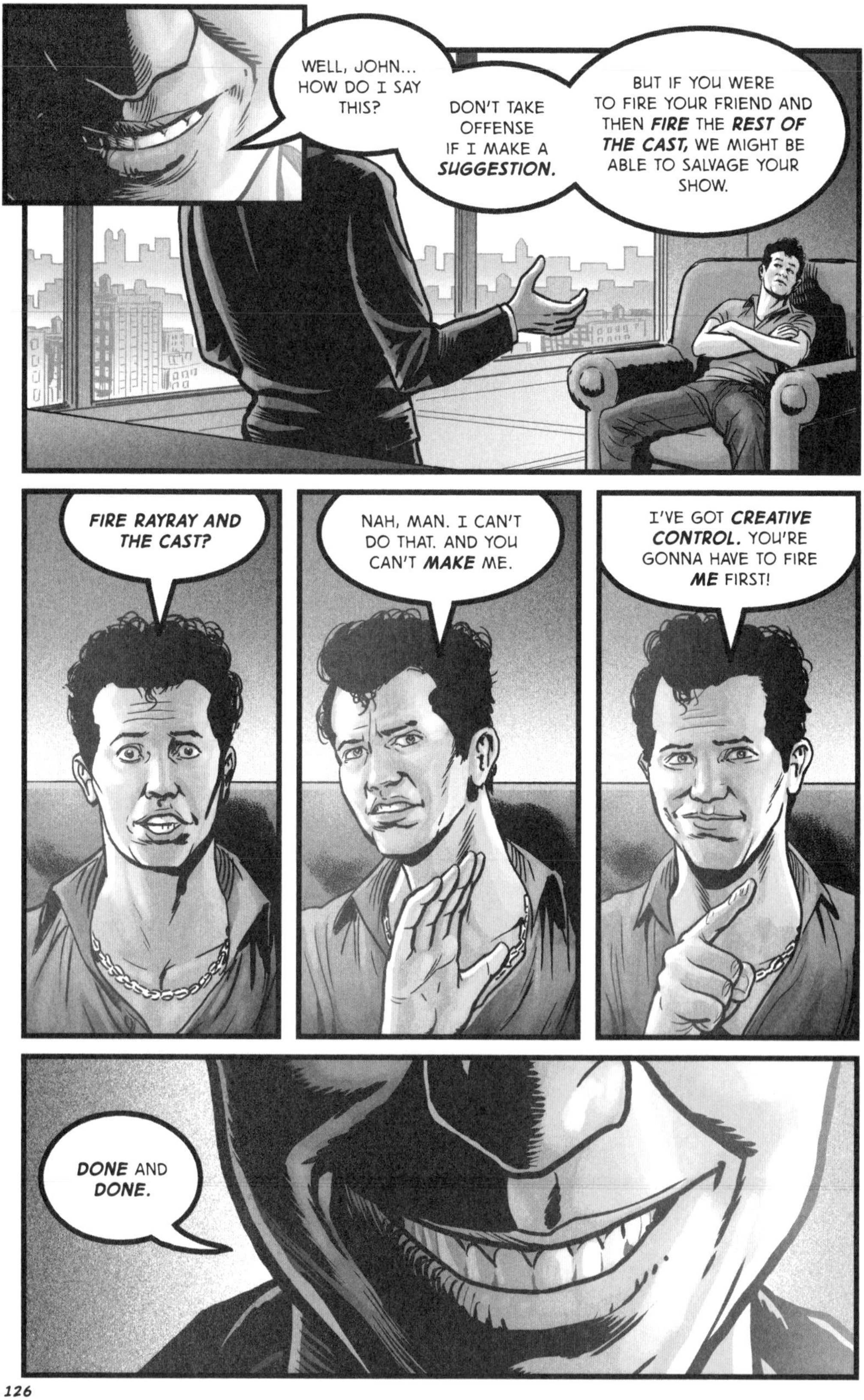
WELL, JOHN... HOW DO I SAY THIS?
DON'T TAKE OFFENSE IF I MAKE A *SUGGESTION.*
BUT IF YOU WERE TO FIRE YOUR FRIEND AND THEN *FIRE* THE *REST OF THE CAST,* WE MIGHT BE ABLE TO SALVAGE YOUR SHOW.
FIRE RAYRAY AND THE CAST?
NAH, MAN. I CAN'T DO THAT. AND YOU CAN'T *MAKE* ME.
I'VE GOT *CREATIVE CONTROL.* YOU'RE GONNA HAVE TO FIRE *ME* FIRST!
DONE AND *DONE.*

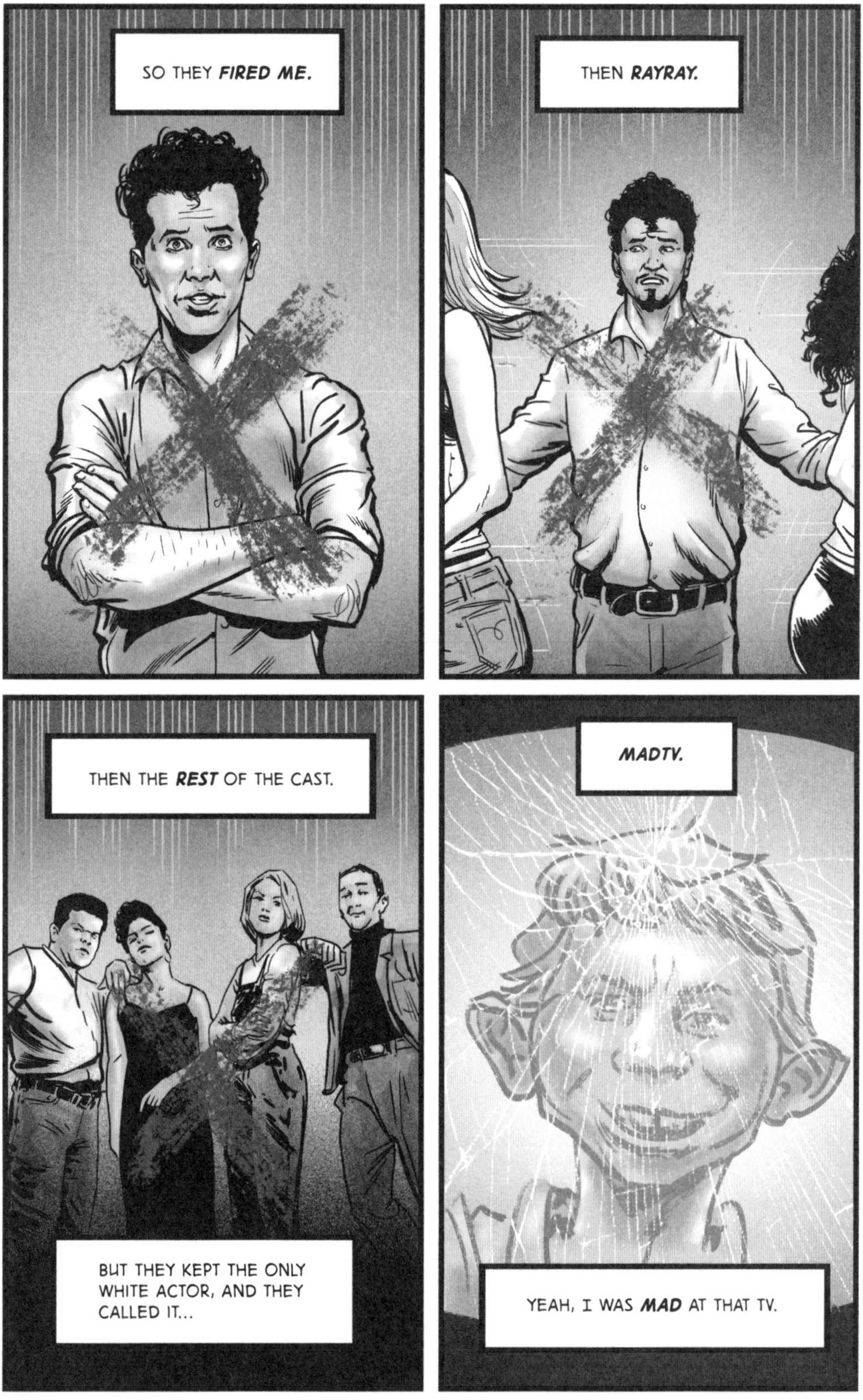
SO THEY **FIRED ME.**
THEN **RAYRAY.**
THEN THE **REST** OF THE CAST.
BUT THEY KEPT THE ONLY WHITE ACTOR, AND THEY CALLED IT...
MADTV.
YEAH, I WAS **MAD** AT THAT TV.

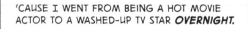

'CAUSE I WENT FROM BEING A HOT MOVIE ACTOR TO A WASHED-UP TV STAR *OVERNIGHT.*

HEY, IRVING, DID YOU CALL THE STUDIO? WHY CAN'T I BE IN *APOLLO 13*? GIVE ME ONE GOOD REASON WHY I CAN'T BE AN *ASTRONAUT.*

BUT NOW I HAD MY *MOMS* AND *RAYRAY* ON PAYROLL...

JOHN, 'C-C-CAUSE THERE WERE NO SPICS IN *SPACE.*

BUT I G-G-GOT A HOT LEAD. THEY'RE REMAKING *ROMEO AND JULIET,* AND YOU'D B-B-BE *P-P-PERFECT* FOR TYBALT.

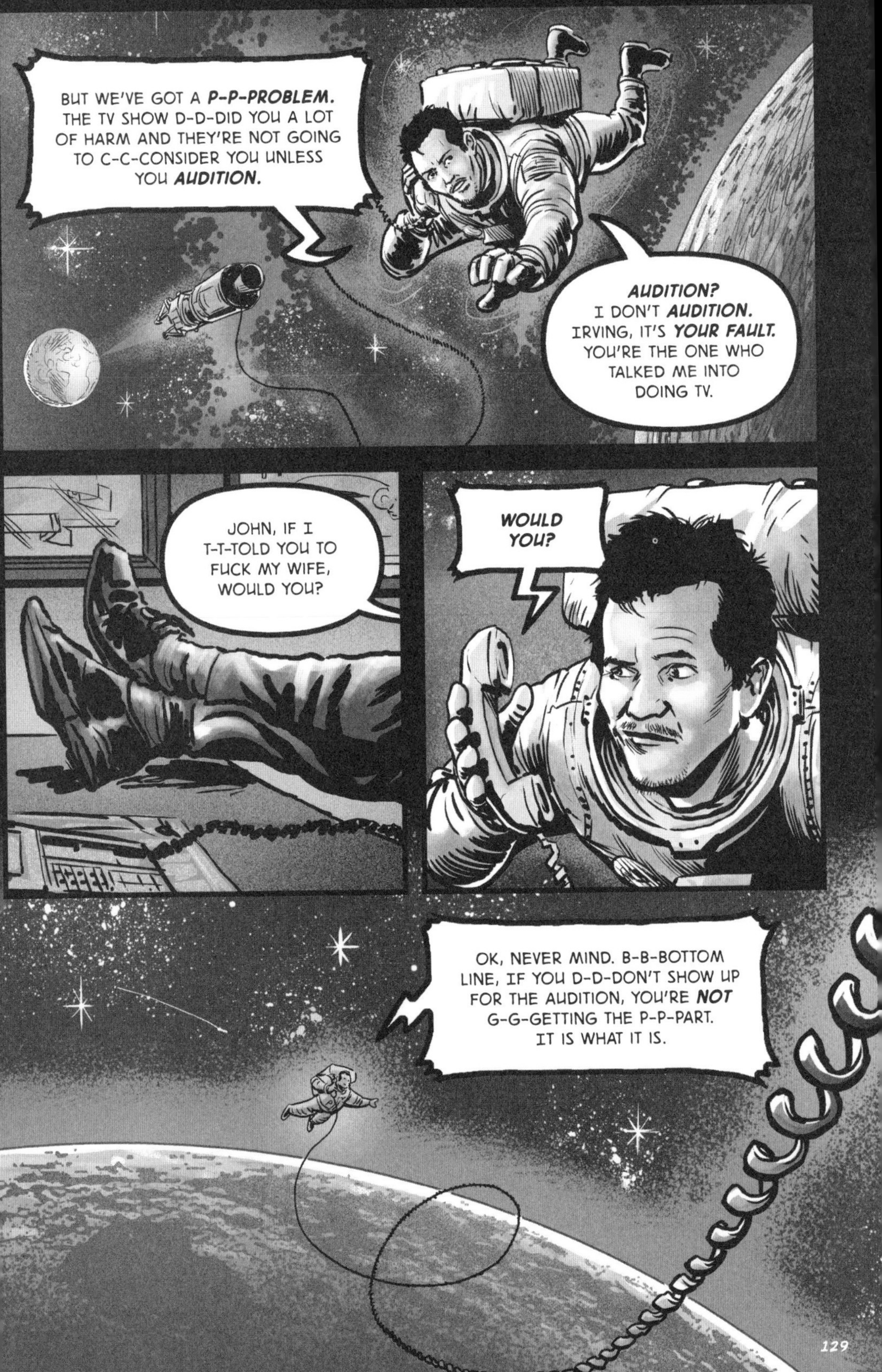
BUT WE'VE GOT A P-P-PROBLEM. THE TV SHOW D-D-DID YOU A LOT OF HARM AND THEY'RE NOT GOING TO C-C-CONSIDER YOU UNLESS YOU AUDITION.
AUDITION? I DON'T AUDITION. IRVING, IT'S YOUR FAULT. YOU'RE THE ONE WHO TALKED ME INTO DOING TV.
JOHN, IF I T-T-TOLD YOU TO FUCK MY WIFE, WOULD YOU?
WOULD YOU?
OK, NEVER MIND. B-B-BOTTOM LINE, IF YOU D-D-DON'T SHOW UP FOR THE AUDITION, YOU'RE NOT G-G-GETTING THE P-P-PART. IT IS WHAT IT IS.

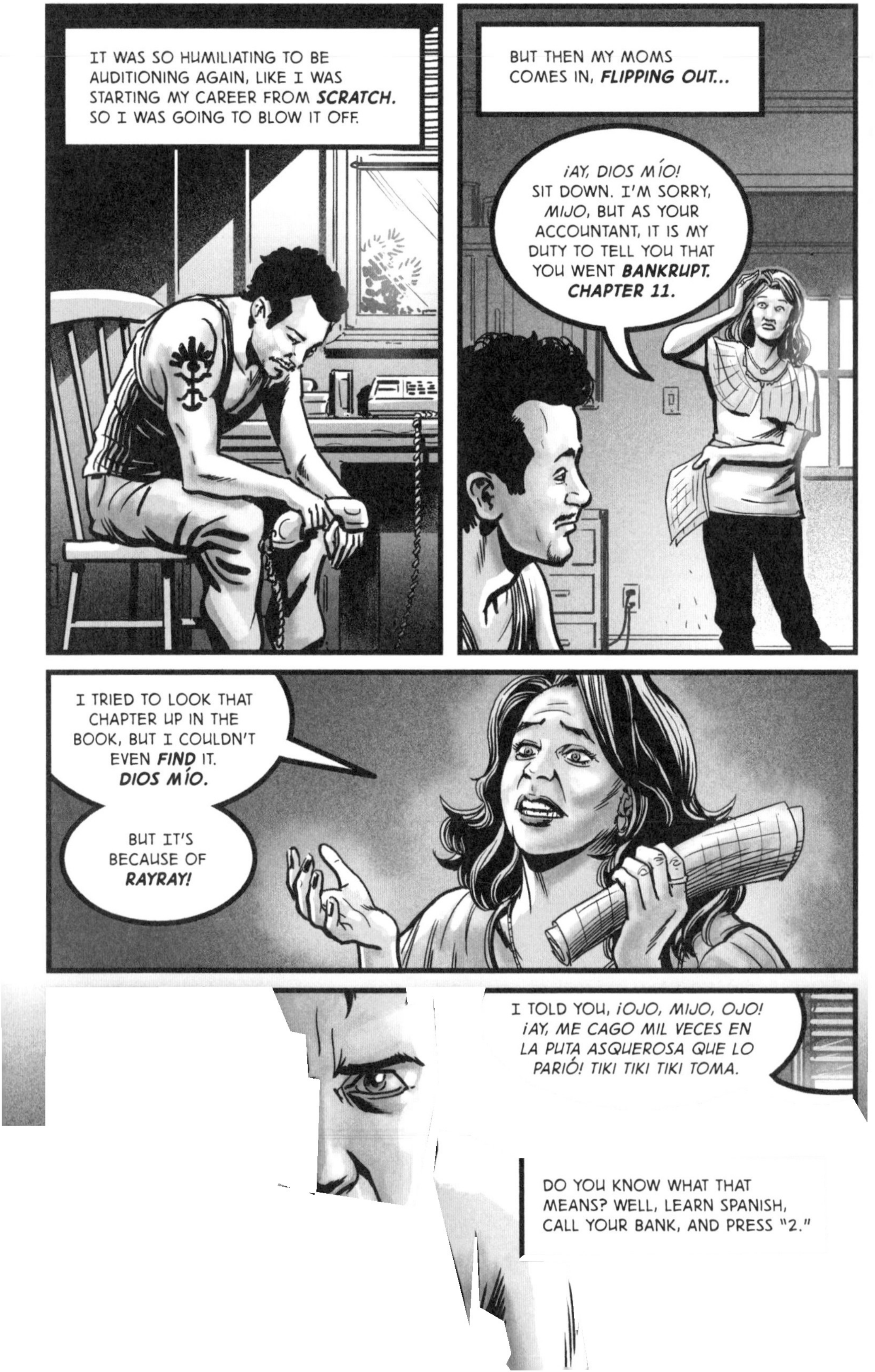
IT WAS SO HUMILIATING TO BE AUDITIONING AGAIN, LIKE I WAS STARTING MY CAREER FROM SCRATCH. SO I WAS GOING TO BLOW IT OFF.
BUT THEN MY MOMS COMES IN, FLIPPING OUT...
¡AY, DIOS MÍO! SIT DOWN. I'M SORRY, MIJO, BUT AS YOUR ACCOUNTANT, IT IS MY DUTY TO TELL YOU THAT YOU WENT BANKRUPT. CHAPTER 11.
I TRIED TO LOOK THAT CHAPTER UP IN THE BOOK, BUT I COULDN'T EVEN FIND IT. DIOS MÍO.
BUT IT'S BECAUSE OF RAYRAY!
I TOLD YOU, ¡OJO, MIJO, OJO! ¡AY, ME CAGO MIL VECES EN LA PUTA ASQUEROSA QUE LO PARIÓ! TIKI TIKI TIKI TOMA.
DO YOU KNOW WHAT THAT MEANS? WELL, LEARN SPANISH, CALL YOUR BANK, AND PRESS "2."

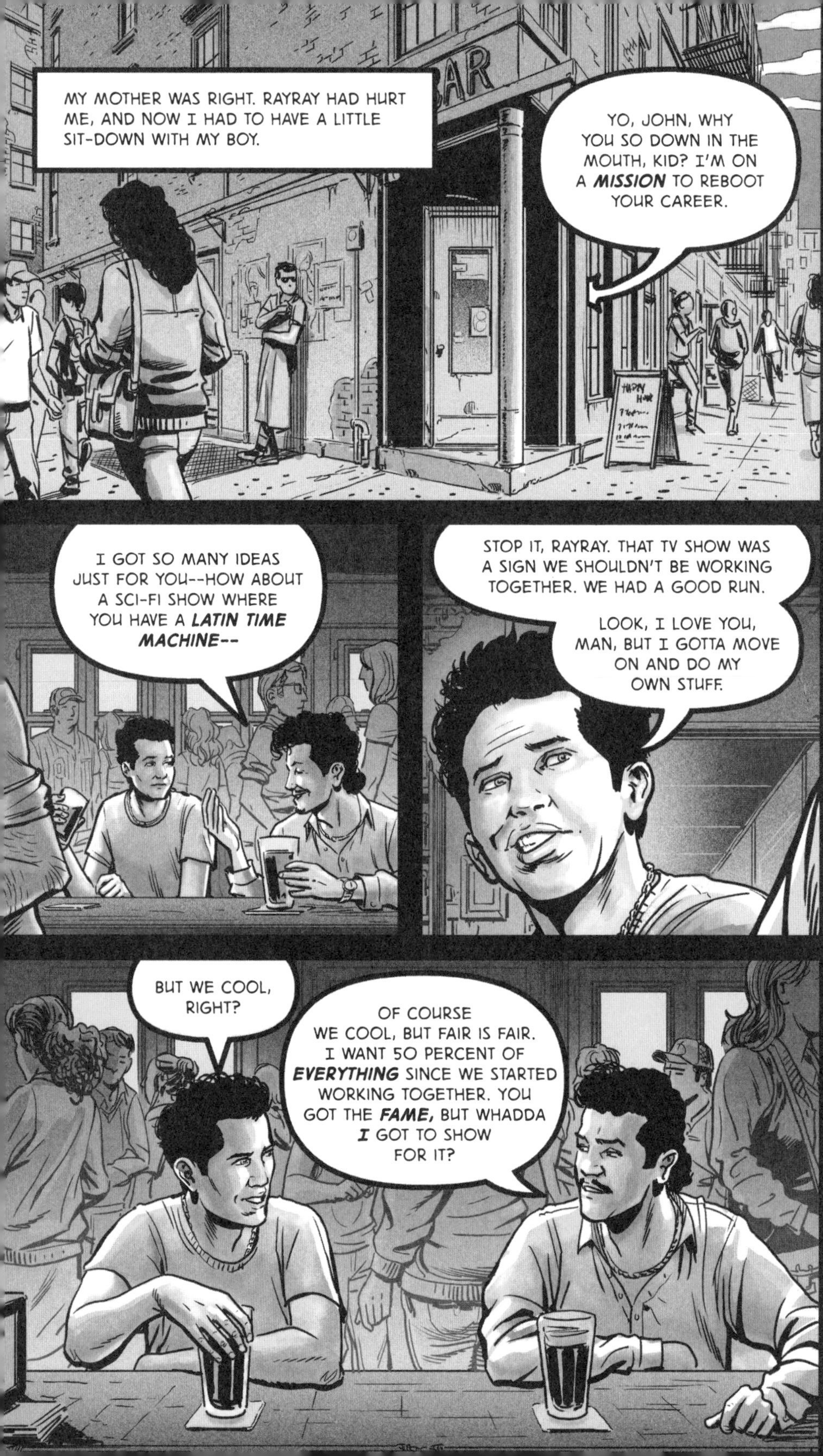
MY MOTHER WAS RIGHT. RAYRAY HAD HURT ME, AND NOW I HAD TO HAVE A LITTLE SIT-DOWN WITH MY BOY.
YO, JOHN, WHY YOU SO DOWN IN THE MOUTH, KID? I'M ON A **MISSION** TO REBOOT YOUR CAREER.
BAR
I GOT SO MANY IDEAS JUST FOR YOU--HOW ABOUT A SCI-FI SHOW WHERE YOU HAVE A ***LATIN TIME MACHINE--***
STOP IT, RAYRAY. THAT TV SHOW WAS A SIGN WE SHOULDN'T BE WORKING TOGETHER. WE HAD A GOOD RUN.
LOOK, I LOVE YOU, MAN, BUT I GOTTA MOVE ON AND DO MY OWN STUFF.
BUT WE COOL, RIGHT?
OF COURSE WE COOL, BUT FAIR IS FAIR. I WANT 50 PERCENT OF ***EVERYTHING*** SINCE WE STARTED WORKING TOGETHER. YOU GOT THE ***FAME,*** BUT WHADDA ***I*** GOT TO SHOW FOR IT?

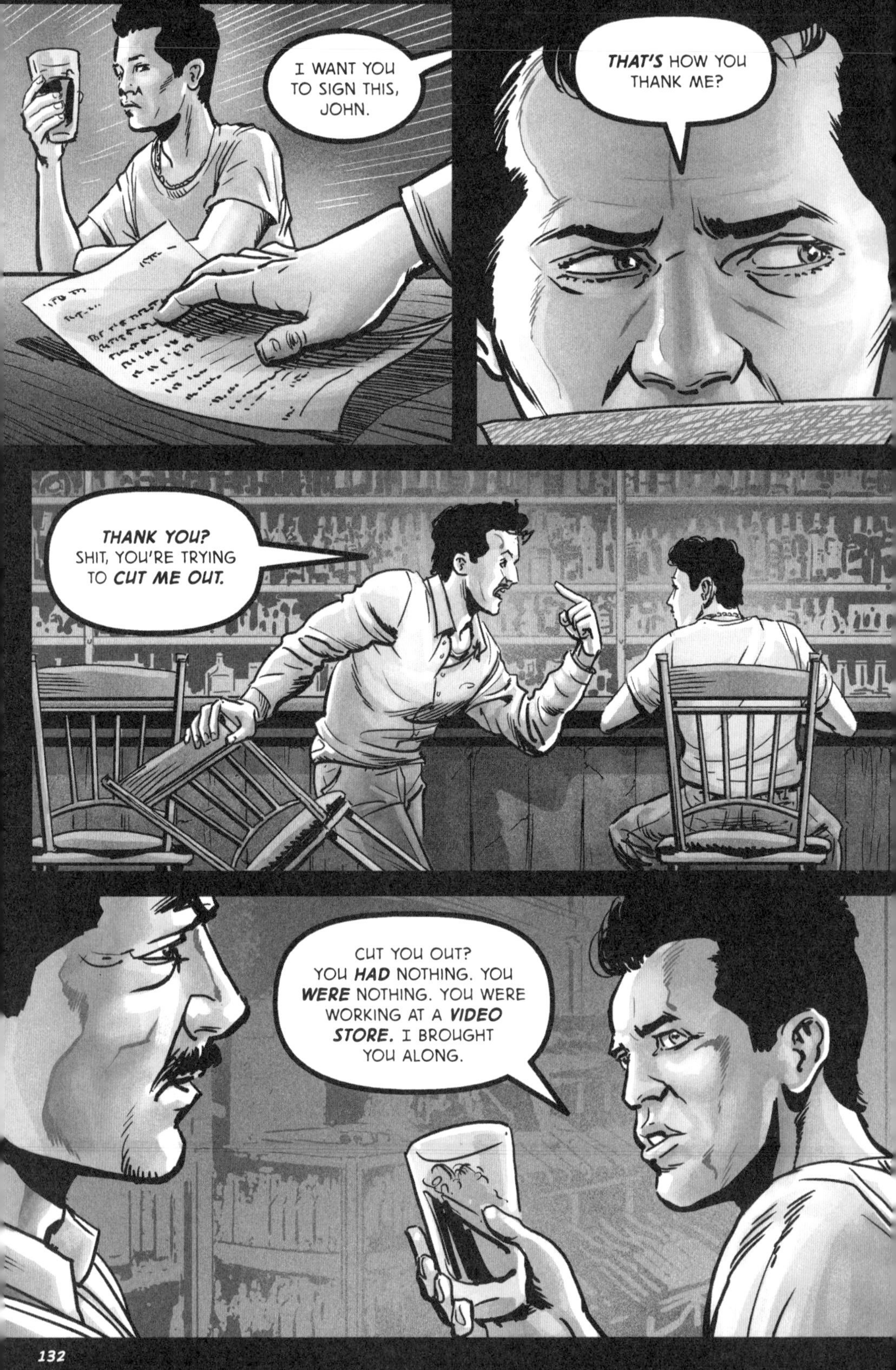
I WANT YOU TO SIGN THIS, JOHN.
THAT'S HOW YOU THANK ME?
THANK YOU? SHIT, YOU'RE TRYING TO CUT ME OUT.
CUT YOU OUT? YOU HAD NOTHING. YOU WERE NOTHING. YOU WERE WORKING AT A VIDEO STORE. I BROUGHT YOU ALONG.

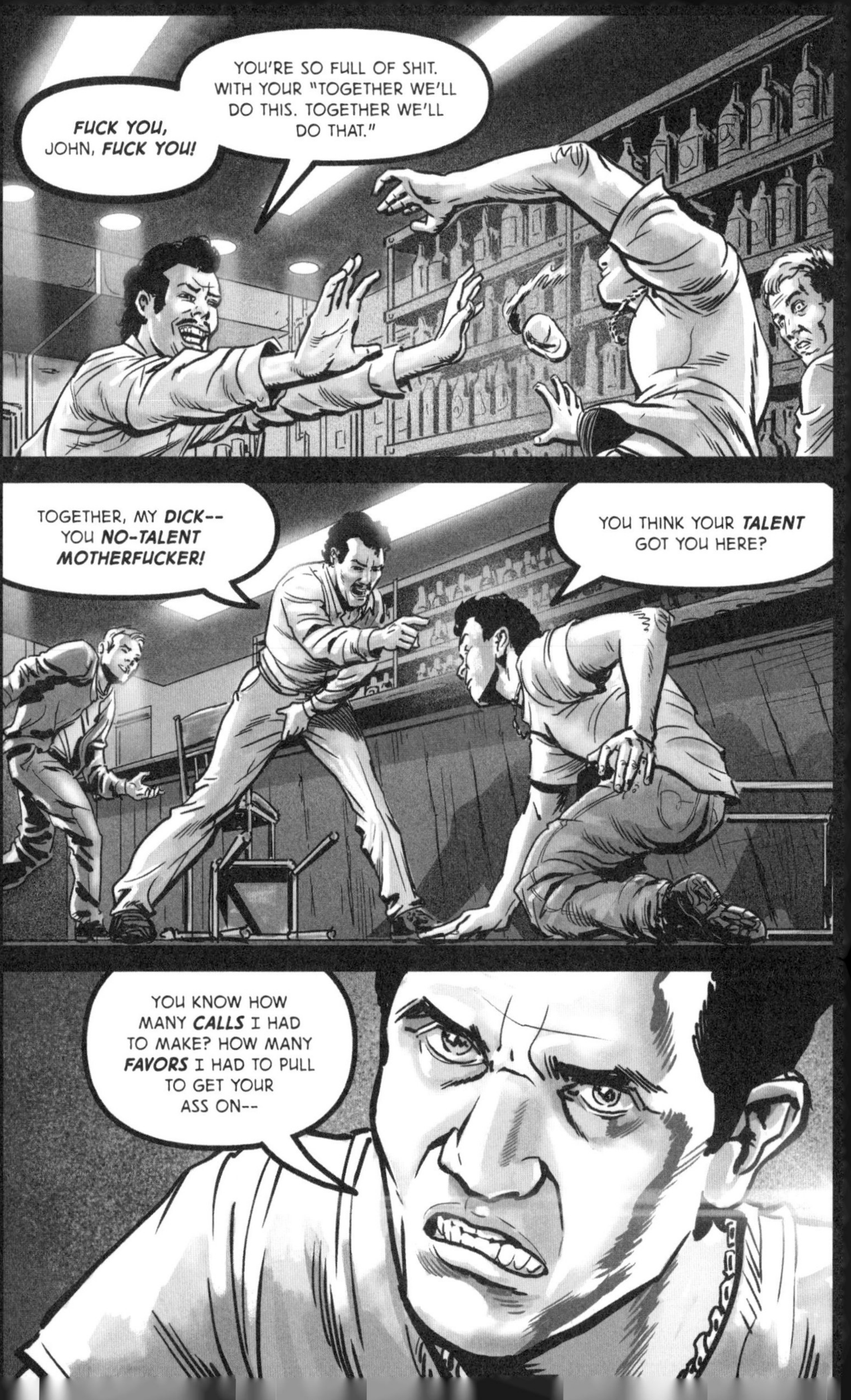
FUCK YOU, JOHN, FUCK YOU!
YOU'RE SO FULL OF SHIT. WITH YOUR "TOGETHER WE'LL DO THIS. TOGETHER WE'LL DO THAT."
TOGETHER, MY DICK-- YOU NO-TALENT MOTHERFUCKER!
YOU THINK YOUR TALENT GOT YOU HERE?
YOU KNOW HOW MANY CALLS I HAD TO MAKE? HOW MANY FAVORS I HAD TO PULL TO GET YOUR ASS ON--

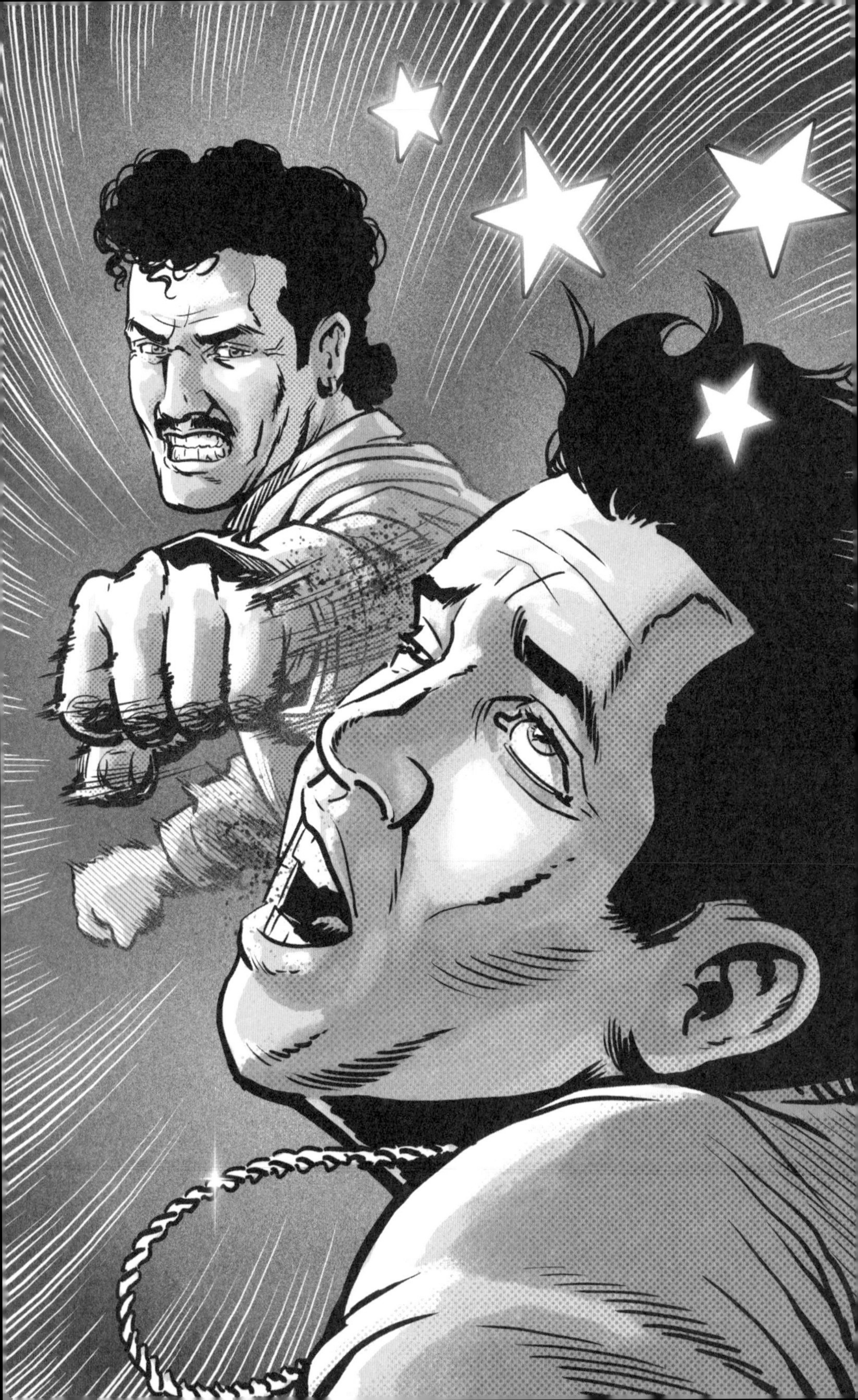

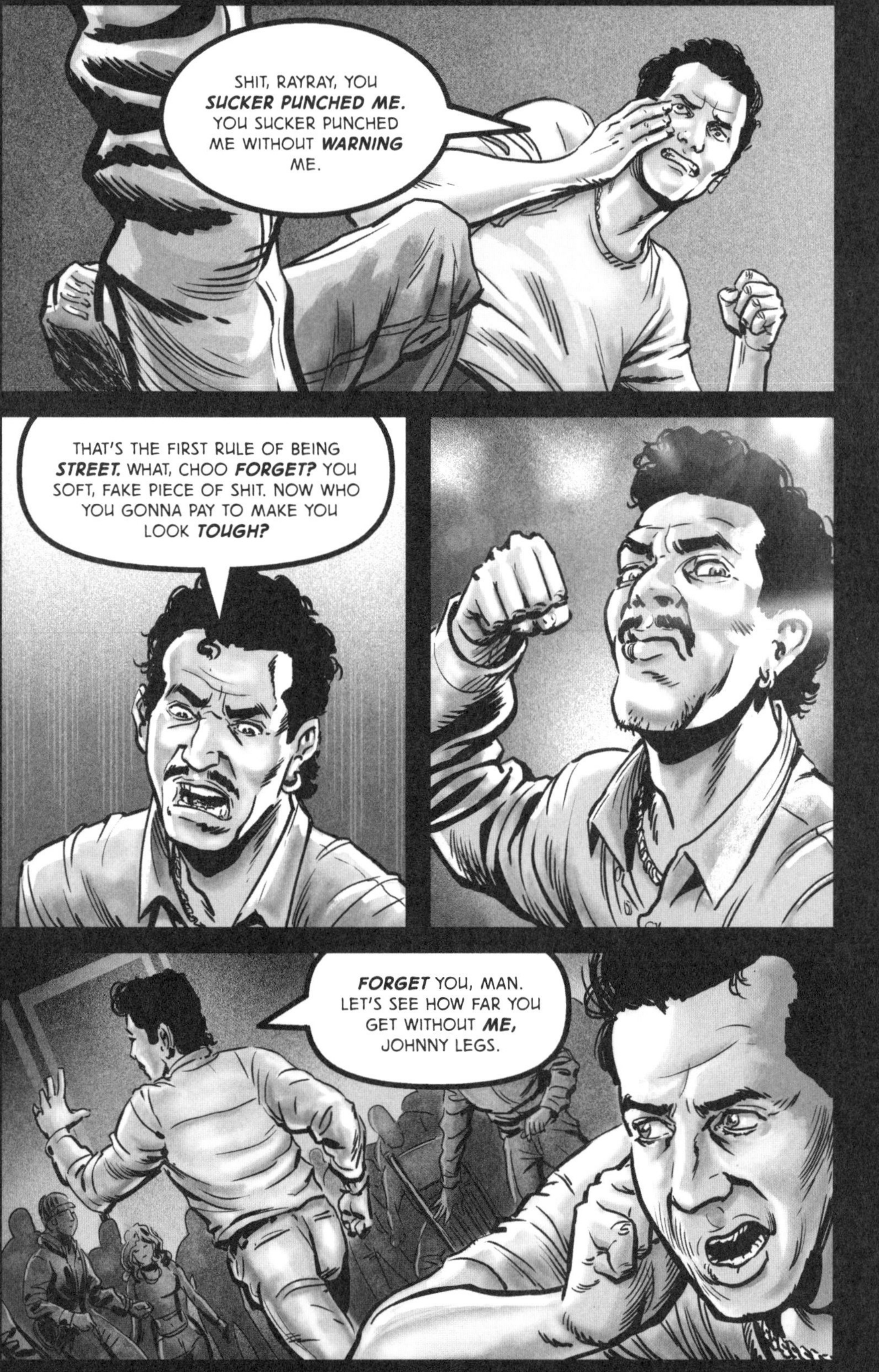
SHIT, RAYRAY, YOU **SUCKER PUNCHED ME.** YOU SUCKER PUNCHED ME WITHOUT **WARNING** ME.
THAT'S THE FIRST RULE OF BEING **STREET.** WHAT, CHOO **FORGET?** YOU SOFT, FAKE PIECE OF SHIT. NOW WHO YOU GONNA PAY TO MAKE YOU LOOK **TOUGH?**
FORGET YOU, MAN. LET'S SEE HOW FAR YOU GET WITHOUT **ME,** JOHNNY LEGS.

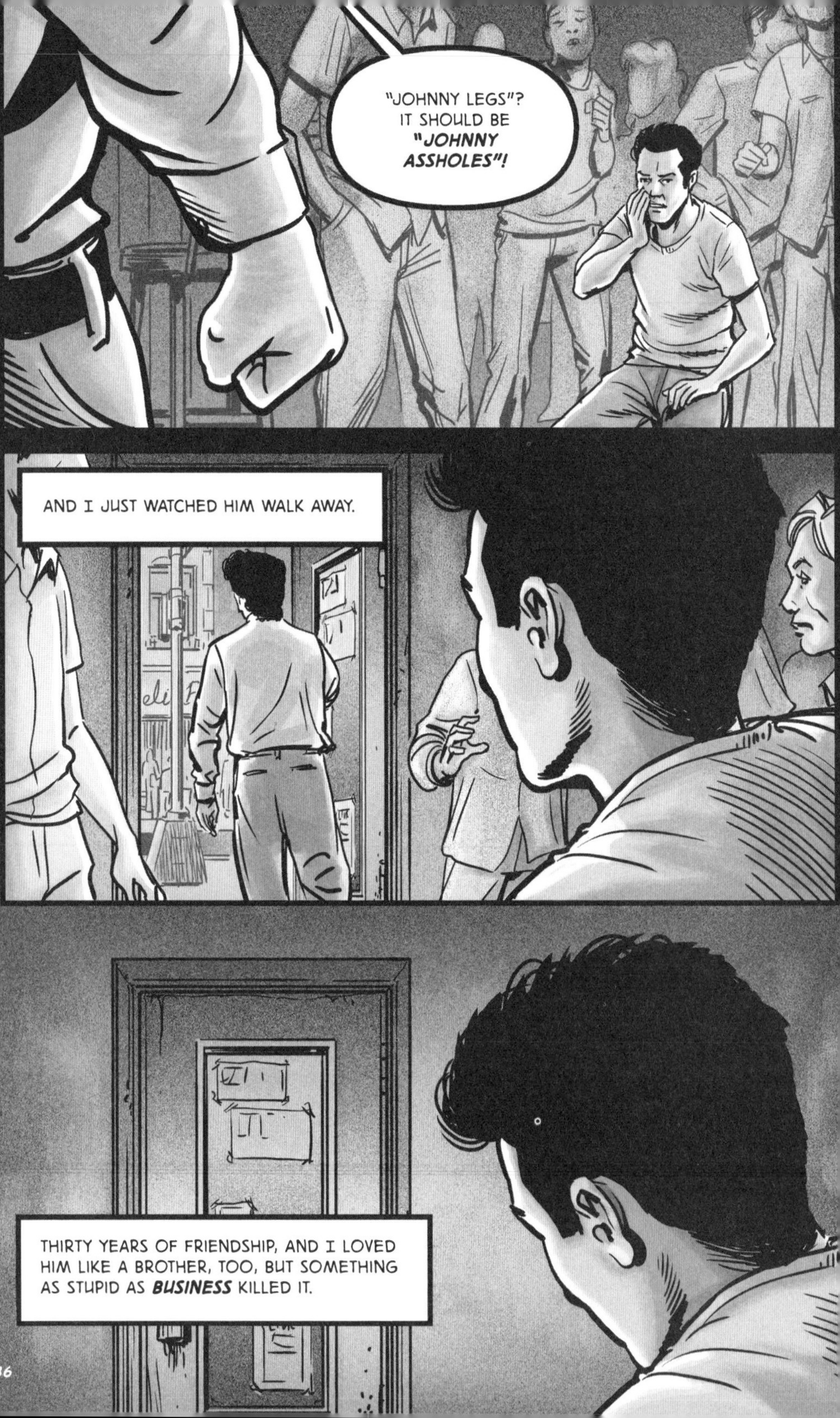
"JOHNNY LEGS"? IT SHOULD BE **"JOHNNY ASSHOLES"!**
AND I JUST WATCHED HIM WALK AWAY.
THIRTY YEARS OF FRIENDSHIP, AND I LOVED HIM LIKE A BROTHER, TOO, BUT SOMETHING AS STUPID AS ***BUSINESS*** KILLED IT.

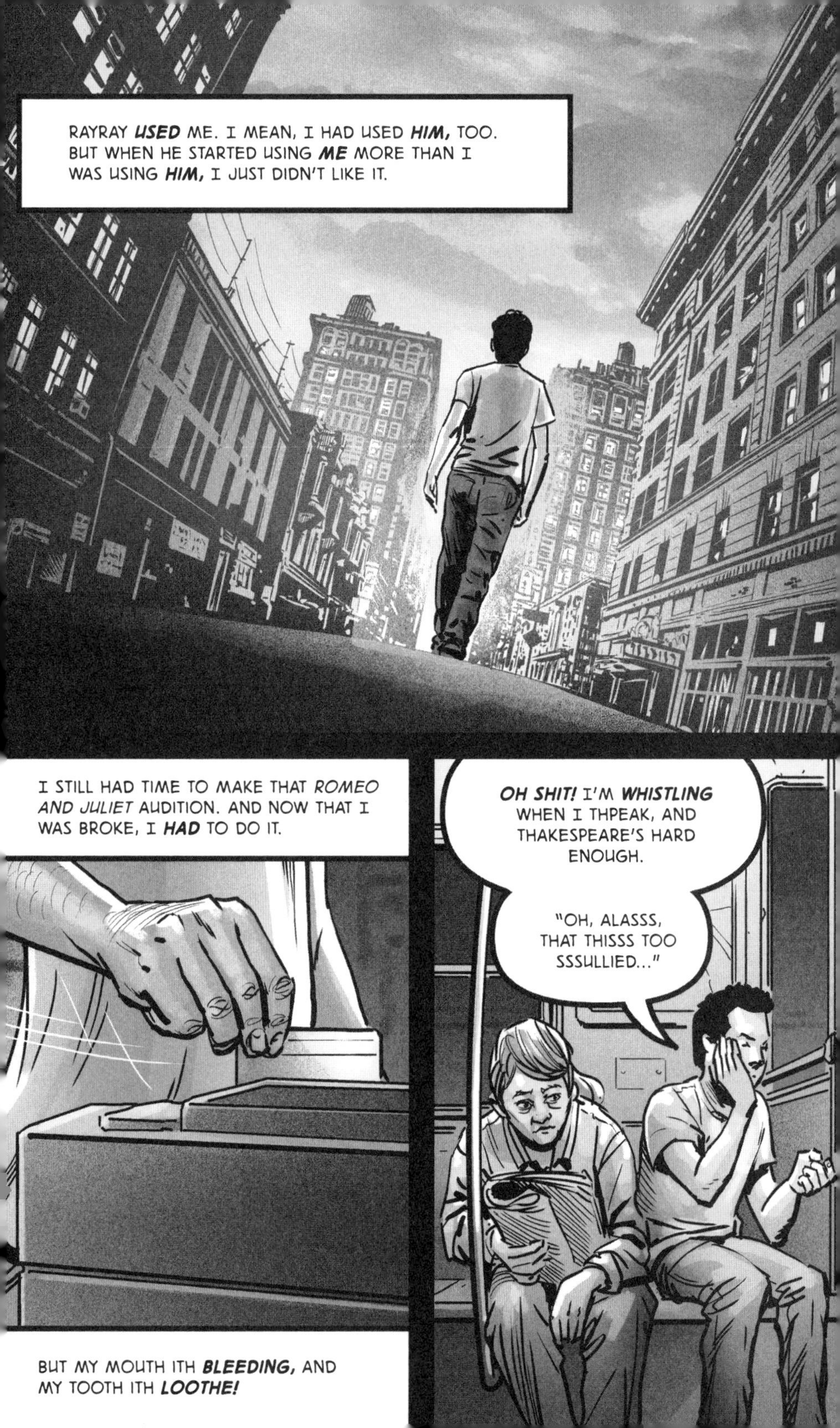
RAYRAY ***USED*** ME. I MEAN, I HAD USED ***HIM,*** TOO. BUT WHEN HE STARTED USING ***ME*** MORE THAN I WAS USING ***HIM,*** I JUST DIDN'T LIKE IT.
I STILL HAD TIME TO MAKE THAT *ROMEO AND JULIET* AUDITION. AND NOW THAT I WAS BROKE, I ***HAD*** TO DO IT.
BUT MY MOUTH ITH ***BLEEDING,*** AND MY TOOTH ITH ***LOOTHE!***
OH SHIT! I'M ***WHISTLING*** WHEN I THPEAK, AND THAKESPEARE'S HARD ENOUGH.
"OH, ALASSS, THAT THISSS TOO SSSULLIED..."

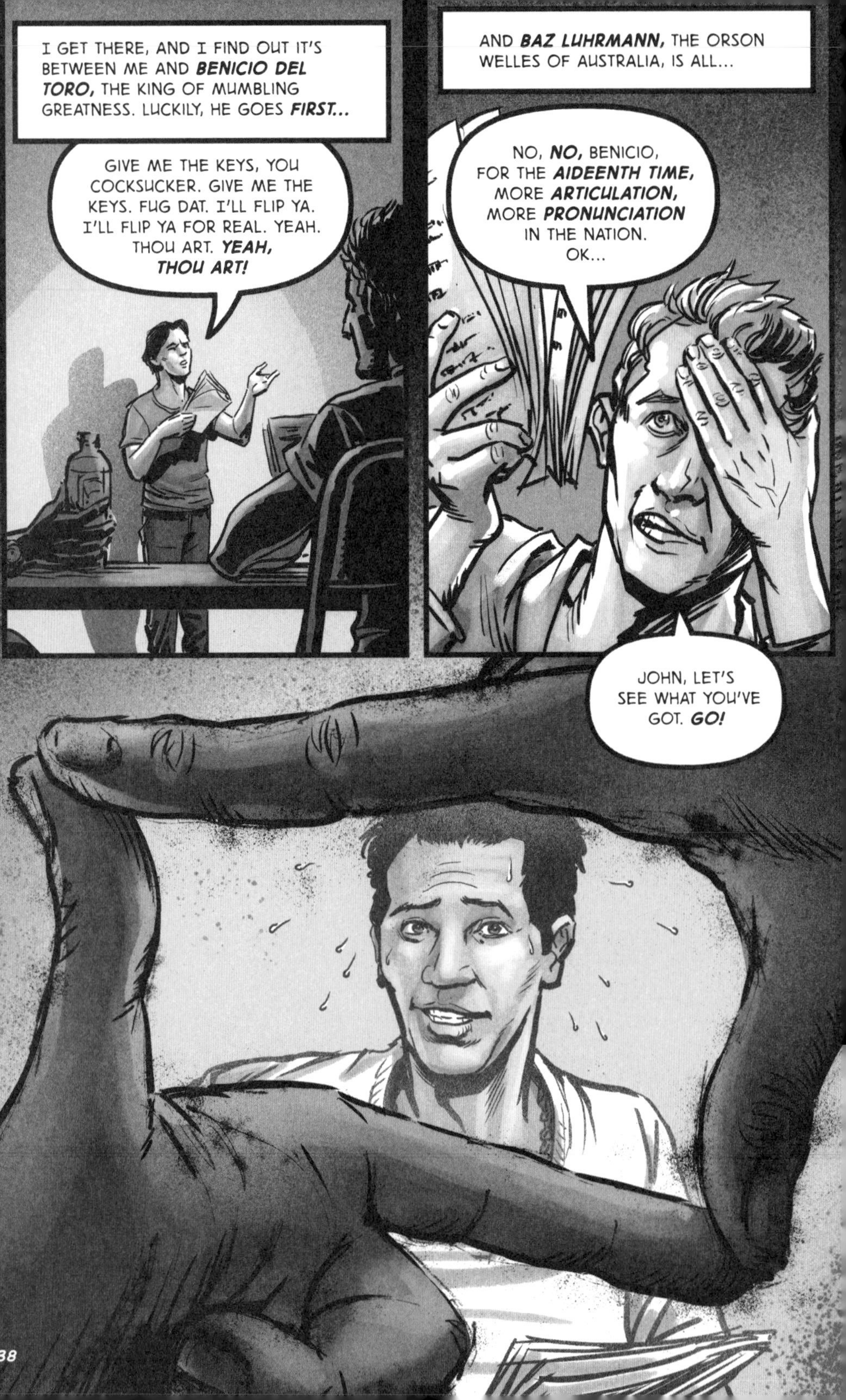
I GET THERE, AND I FIND OUT IT'S BETWEEN ME AND ***BENICIO DEL TORO,*** THE KING OF MUMBLING GREATNESS. LUCKILY, HE GOES ***FIRST...***
GIVE ME THE KEYS, YOU COCKSUCKER. GIVE ME THE KEYS. FUG DAT. I'LL FLIP YA. I'LL FLIP YA FOR REAL. YEAH. THOU ART. ***YEAH, THOU ART!***
AND ***BAZ LUHRMANN,*** THE ORSON WELLES OF AUSTRALIA, IS ALL...
NO, ***NO,*** BENICIO, FOR THE ***AIDEENTH TIME,*** MORE ***ARTICULATION,*** MORE ***PRONUNCIATION*** IN THE NATION. OK...
JOHN, LET'S SEE WHAT YOU'VE GOT. ***GO!***

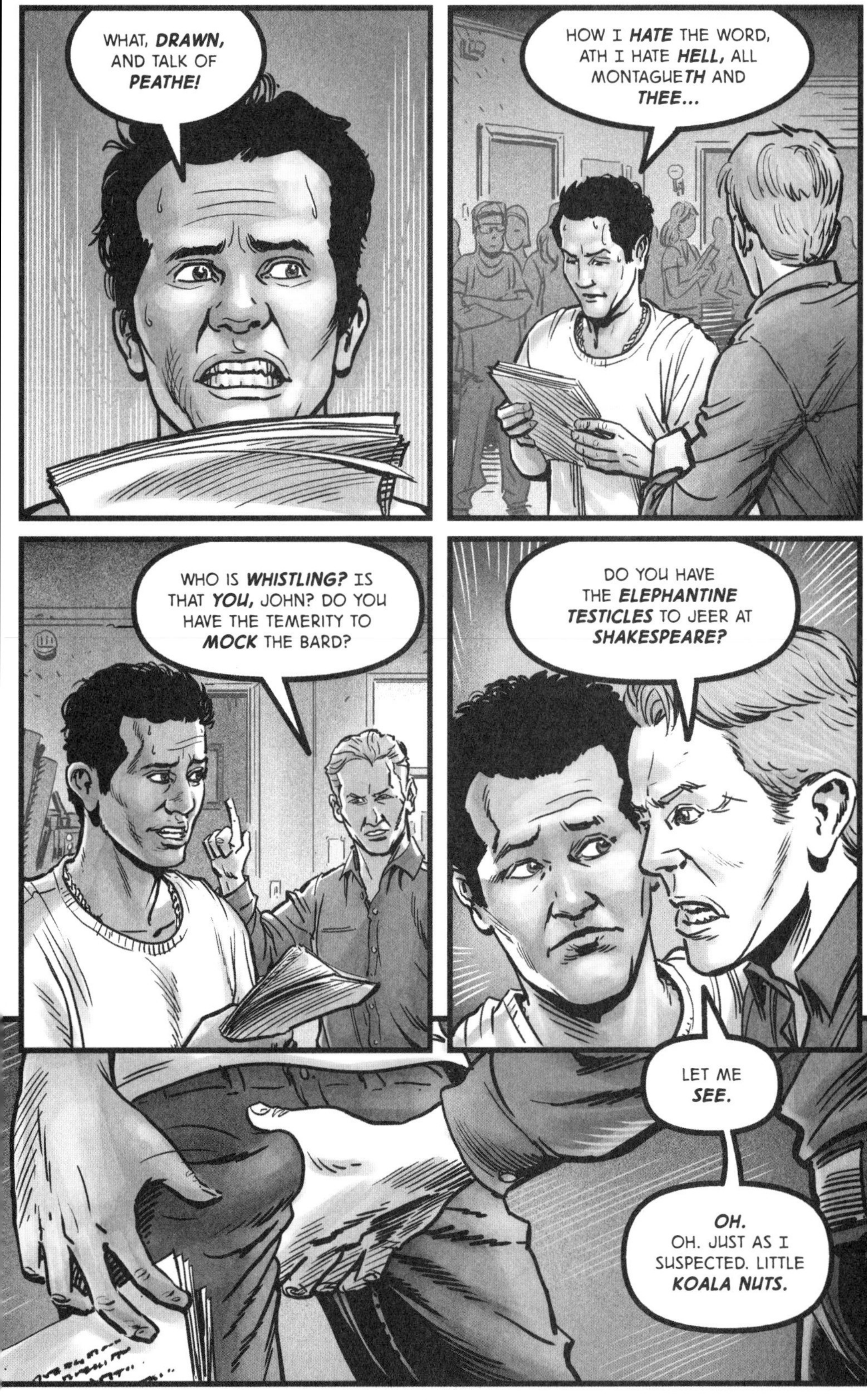
WHAT, DRAWN, AND TALK OF PEATHE!
HOW I HATE THE WORD, ATH I HATE HELL, ALL MONTAGUETH AND THEE...
WHO IS WHISTLING? IS THAT YOU, JOHN? DO YOU HAVE THE TEMERITY TO MOCK THE BARD?
DO YOU HAVE THE ELEPHANTINE TESTICLES TO JEER AT SHAKESPEARE?
LET ME SEE.
OH.
OH. JUST AS I SUSPECTED. LITTLE KOALA NUTS.

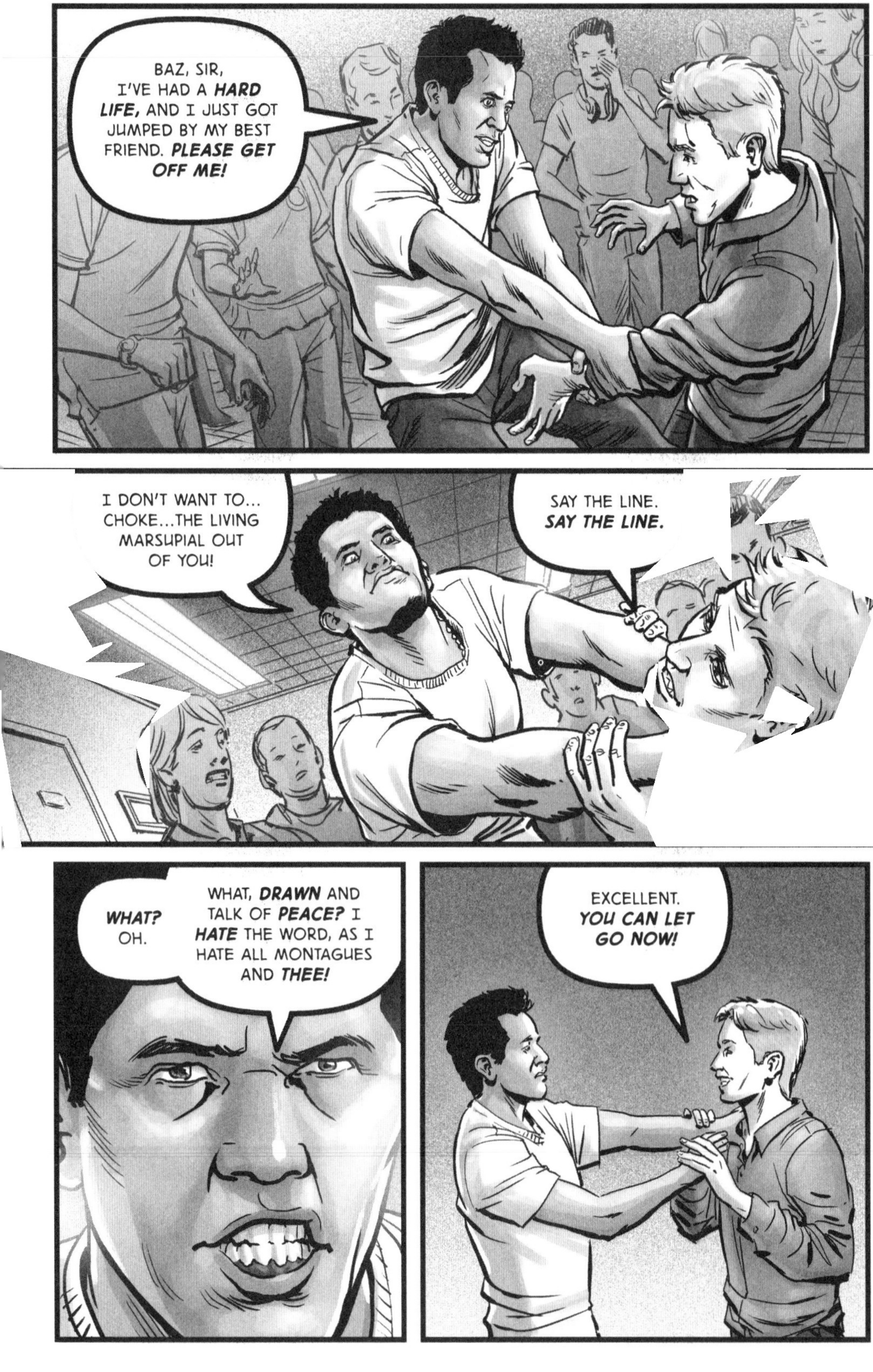
BAZ, SIR, I'VE HAD A **HARD LIFE,** AND I JUST GOT JUMPED BY MY BEST FRIEND. **PLEASE GET OFF ME!**
I DON'T WANT TO... CHOKE...THE LIVING MARSUPIAL OUT OF YOU!
SAY THE LINE. **SAY THE LINE.**
WHAT? OH.
WHAT, **DRAWN** AND TALK OF **PEACE?** I **HATE** THE WORD, AS I HATE ALL MONTAGUES AND **THEE!**
EXCELLENT. **YOU CAN LET GO NOW!**

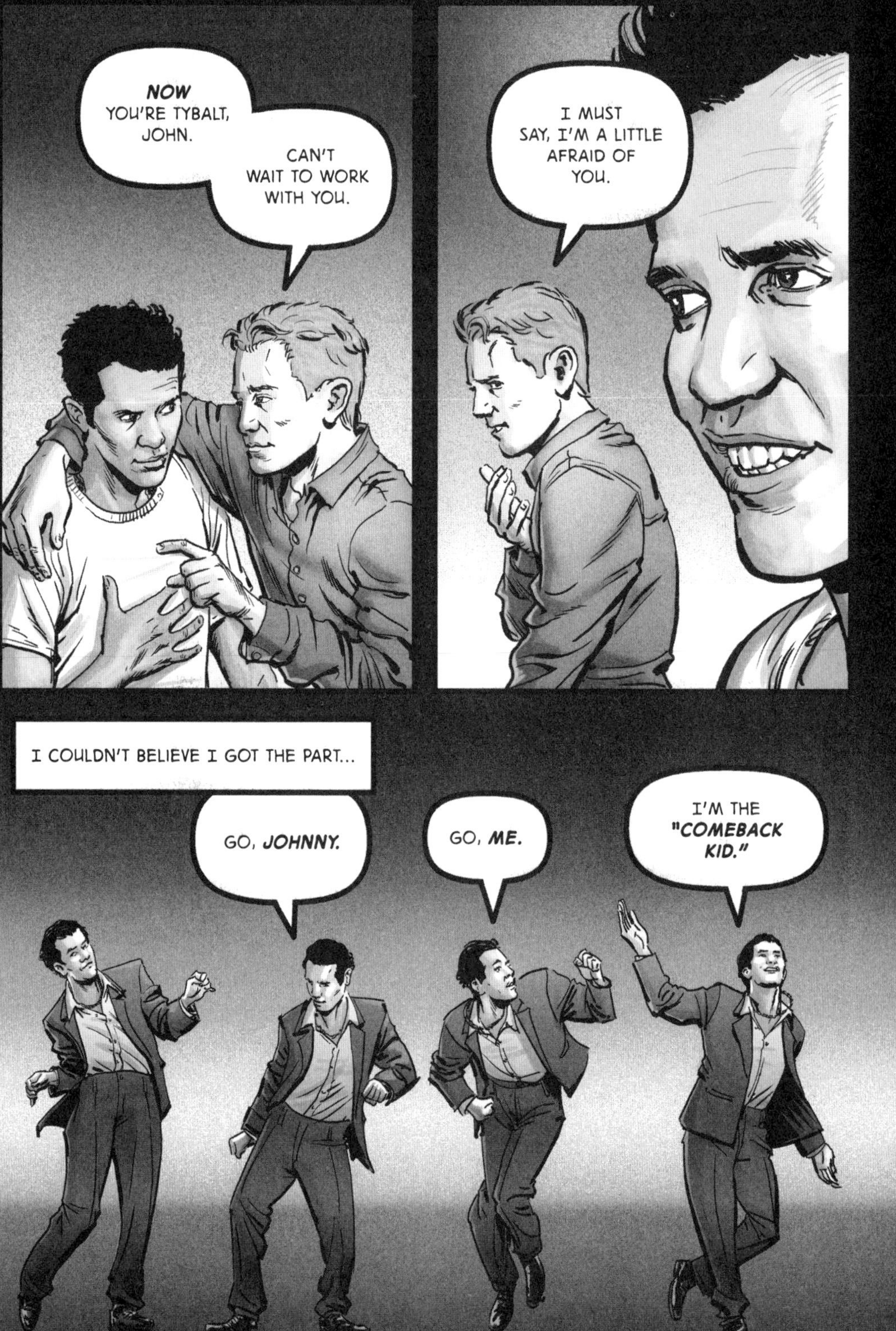

NOW YOU'RE TYBALT, JOHN.
CAN'T WAIT TO WORK WITH YOU.
I MUST SAY, I'M A LITTLE AFRAID OF YOU.
I COULDN'T BELIEVE I GOT THE PART...
GO, ***JOHNNY.***
GO, ***ME.***
I'M THE ***"COMEBACK KID."***

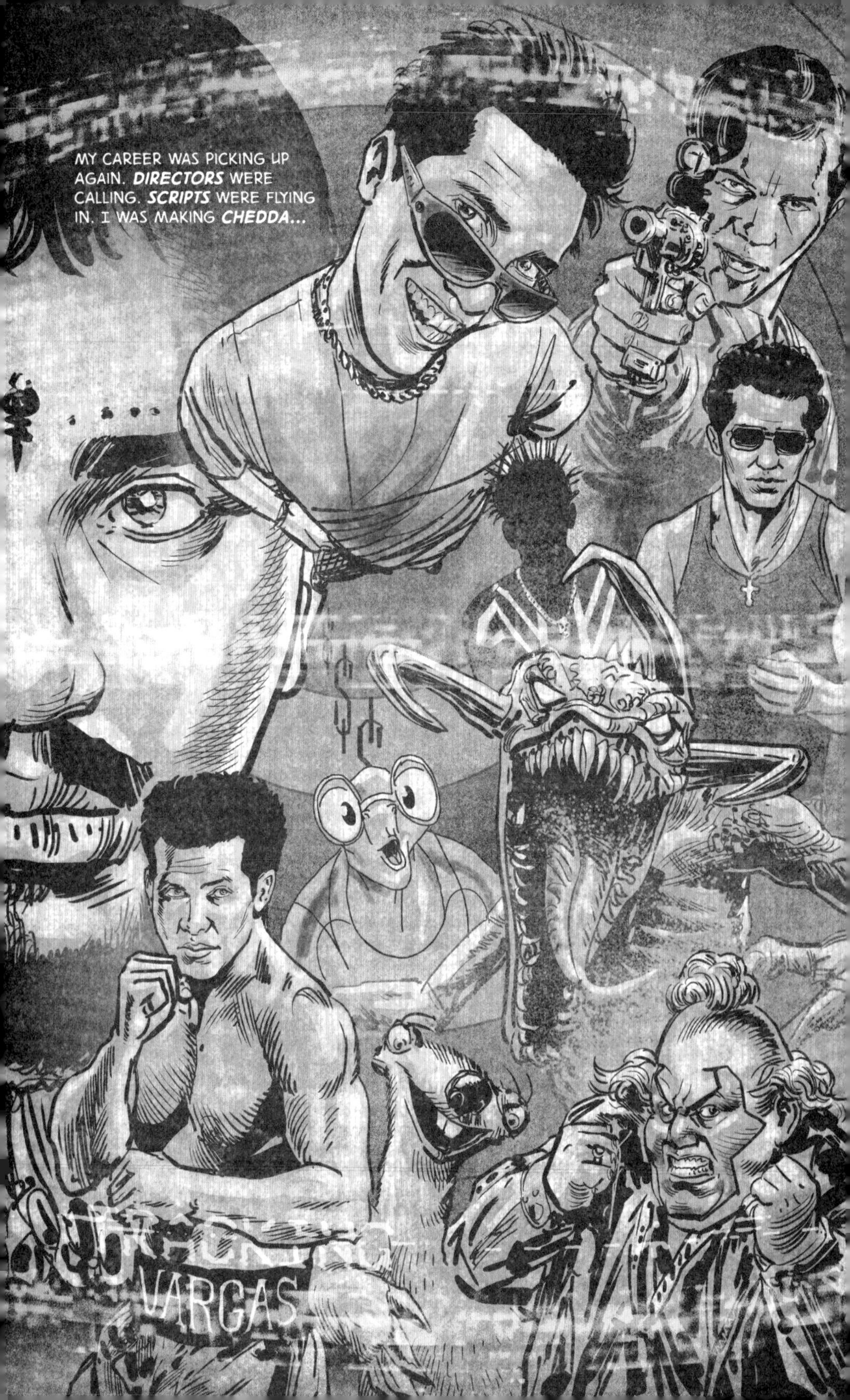
MY CAREER WAS PICKING UP AGAIN. **DIRECTORS** WERE CALLING. **SCRIPTS** WERE FLYING IN. I WAS MAKING **CHEDDA...**
VARGAS

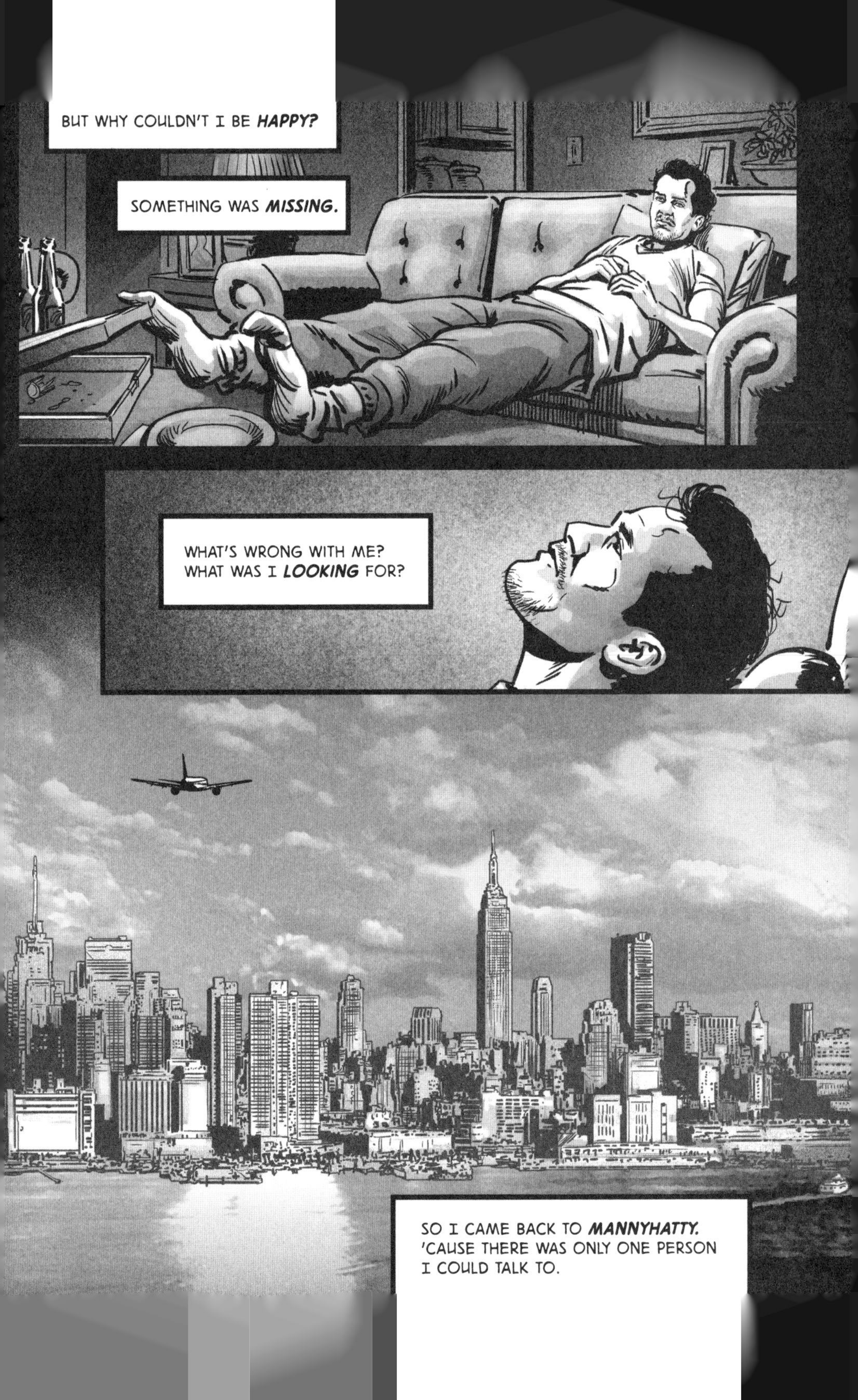
BUT WHY COULDN'T I BE HAPPY?
SOMETHING WAS MISSING.
WHAT'S WRONG WITH ME? WHAT WAS I LOOKING FOR?
SO I CAME BACK TO MANNYHATTY. 'CAUSE THERE WAS ONLY ONE PERSON I COULD TALK TO.

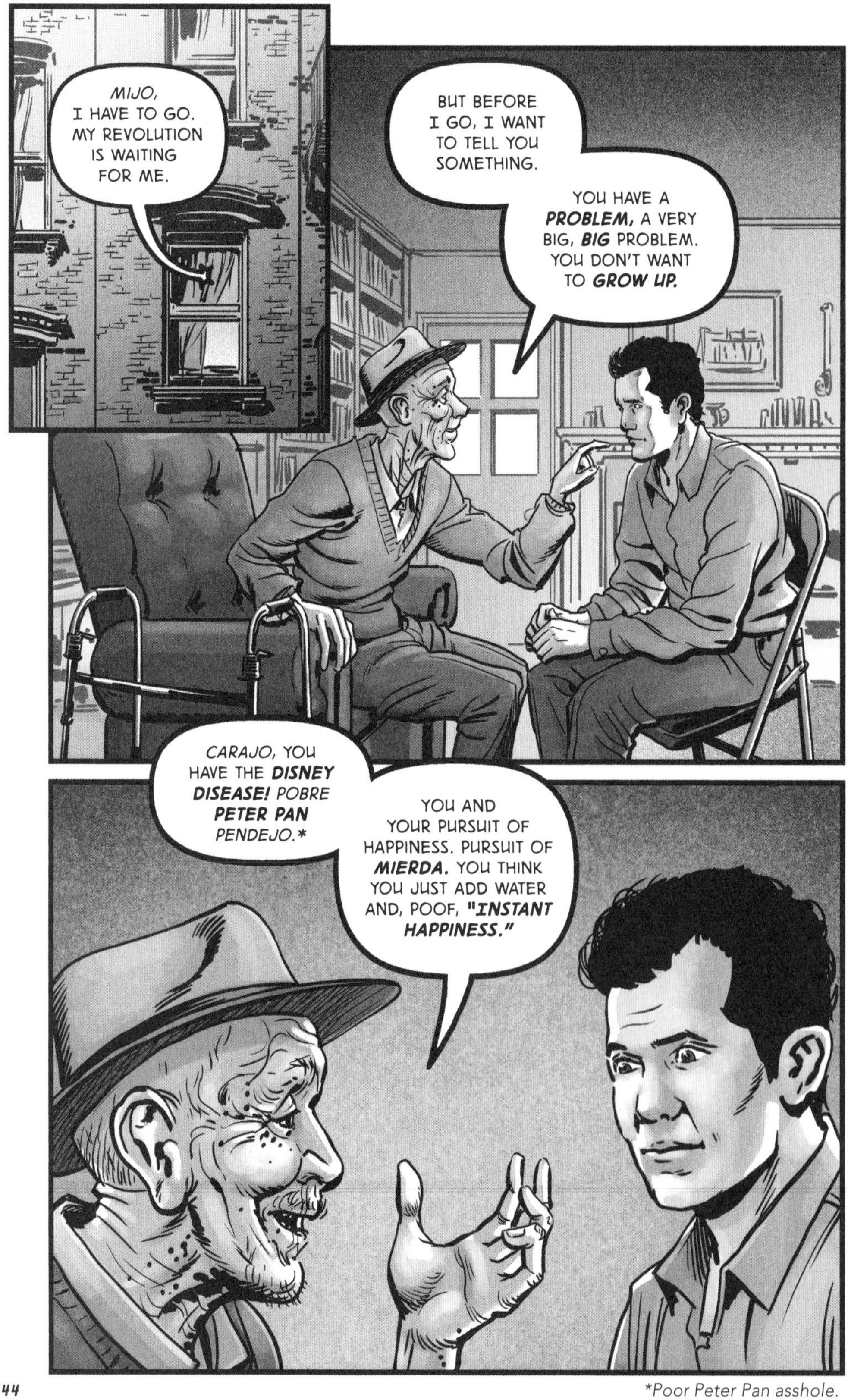
MIJO, I HAVE TO GO. MY REVOLUTION IS WAITING FOR ME.
BUT BEFORE I GO, I WANT TO TELL YOU SOMETHING.
YOU HAVE A ***PROBLEM,*** A VERY BIG, ***BIG*** PROBLEM. YOU DON'T WANT TO ***GROW UP.***
CARAJO, YOU HAVE THE ***DISNEY DISEASE!*** *POBRE* ***PETER PAN*** *PENDEJO.**
YOU AND YOUR PURSUIT OF HAPPINESS. PURSUIT OF ***MIERDA.*** YOU THINK YOU JUST ADD WATER AND, POOF, ***"INSTANT HAPPINESS."***

*Poor Peter Pan asshole.

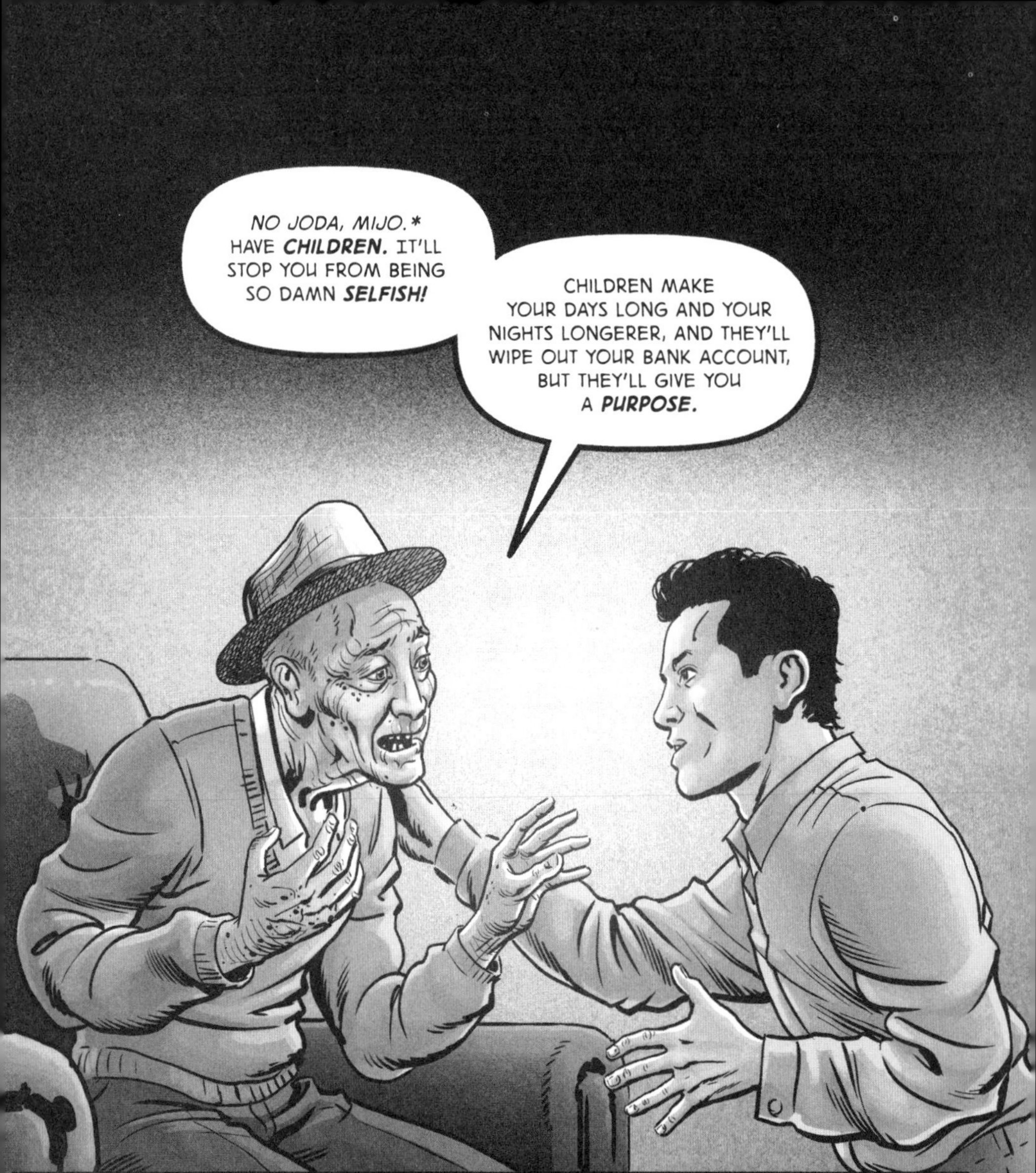
NO JODA, MIJO.* HAVE CHILDREN. IT'LL STOP YOU FROM BEING SO DAMN SELFISH!
CHILDREN MAKE YOUR DAYS LONG AND YOUR NIGHTS LONGERER, AND THEY'LL WIPE OUT YOUR BANK ACCOUNT, BUT THEY'LL GIVE YOU A PURPOSE.

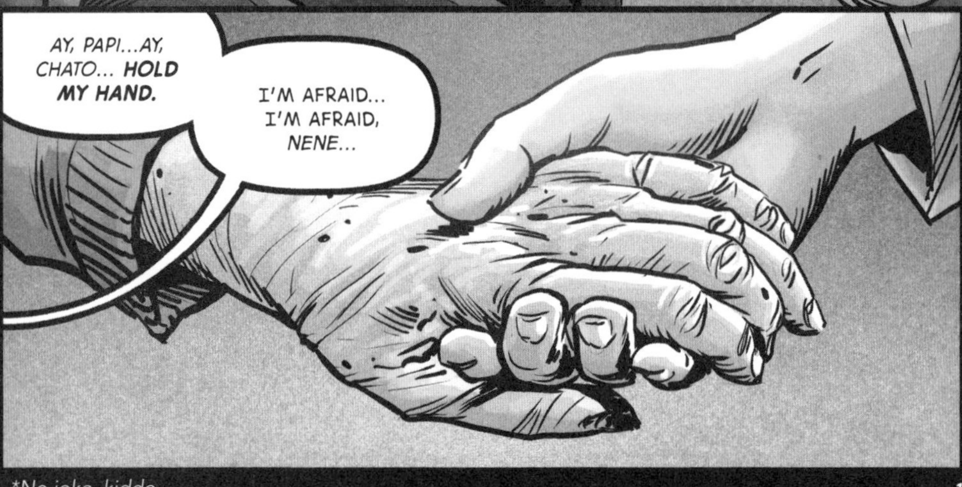
AY, PAPI...AY, CHATO... HOLD MY HAND.
I'M AFRAID... I'M AFRAID, NENE...

*No joke, kiddo.

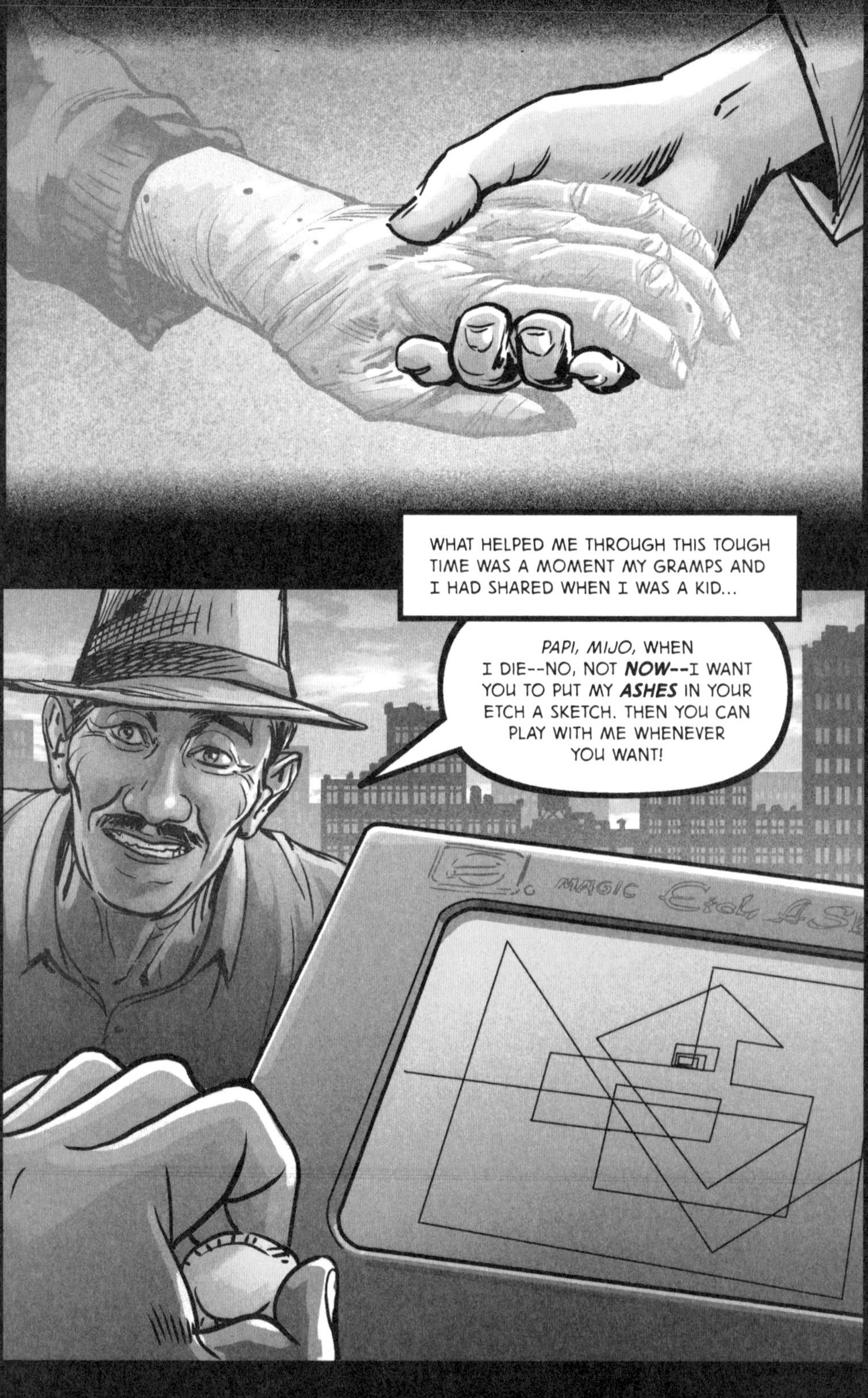

WHAT HELPED ME THROUGH THIS TOUGH TIME WAS A MOMENT MY GRAMPS AND I HAD SHARED WHEN I WAS A KID...
PAPI, MIJO, WHEN I DIE--NO, NOT ***NOW***--I WANT YOU TO PUT MY ***ASHES*** IN YOUR ETCH A SKETCH. THEN YOU CAN PLAY WITH ME WHENEVER YOU WANT!
MAGIC

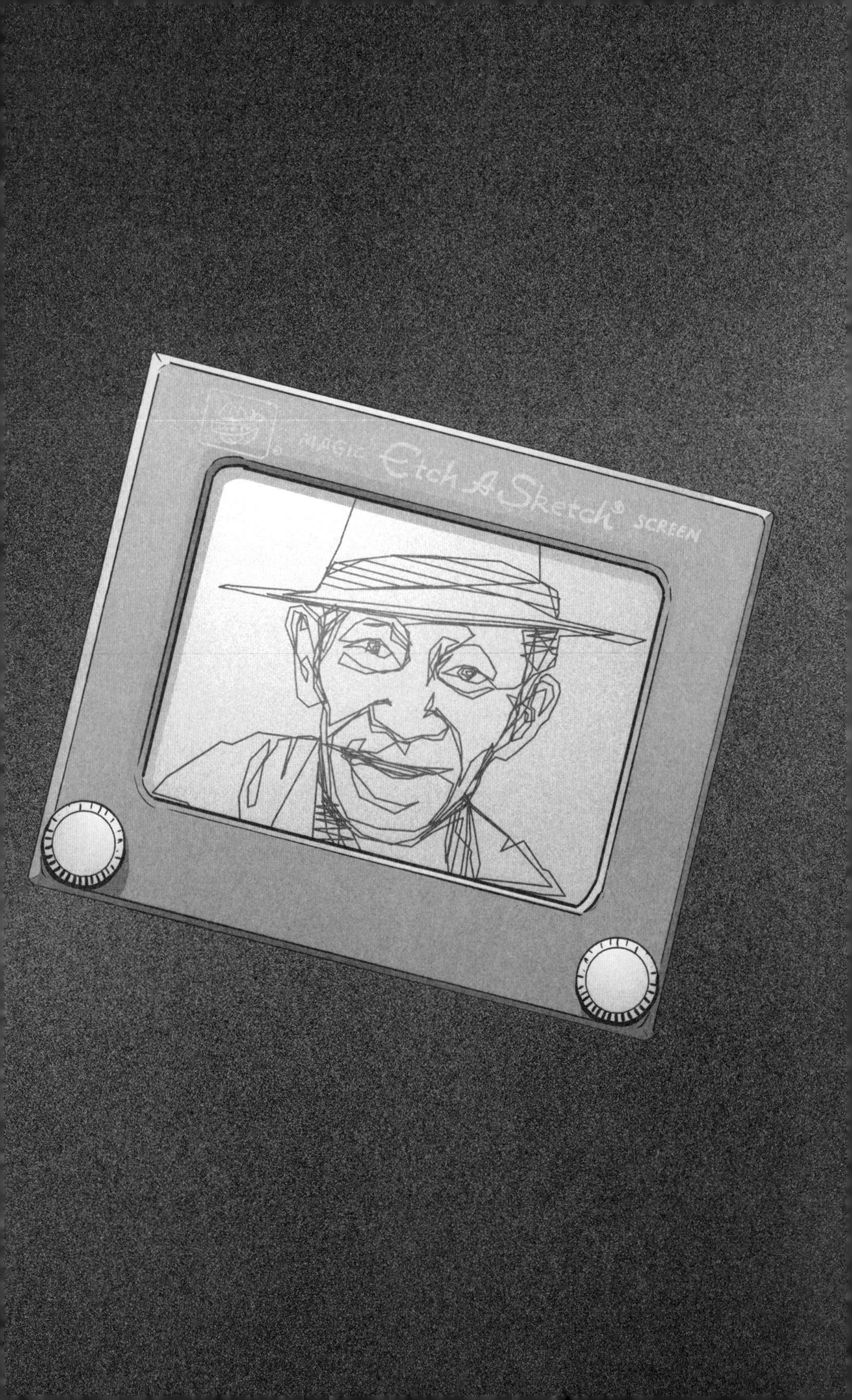

MAGIC Etch A Sketch® SCREEN

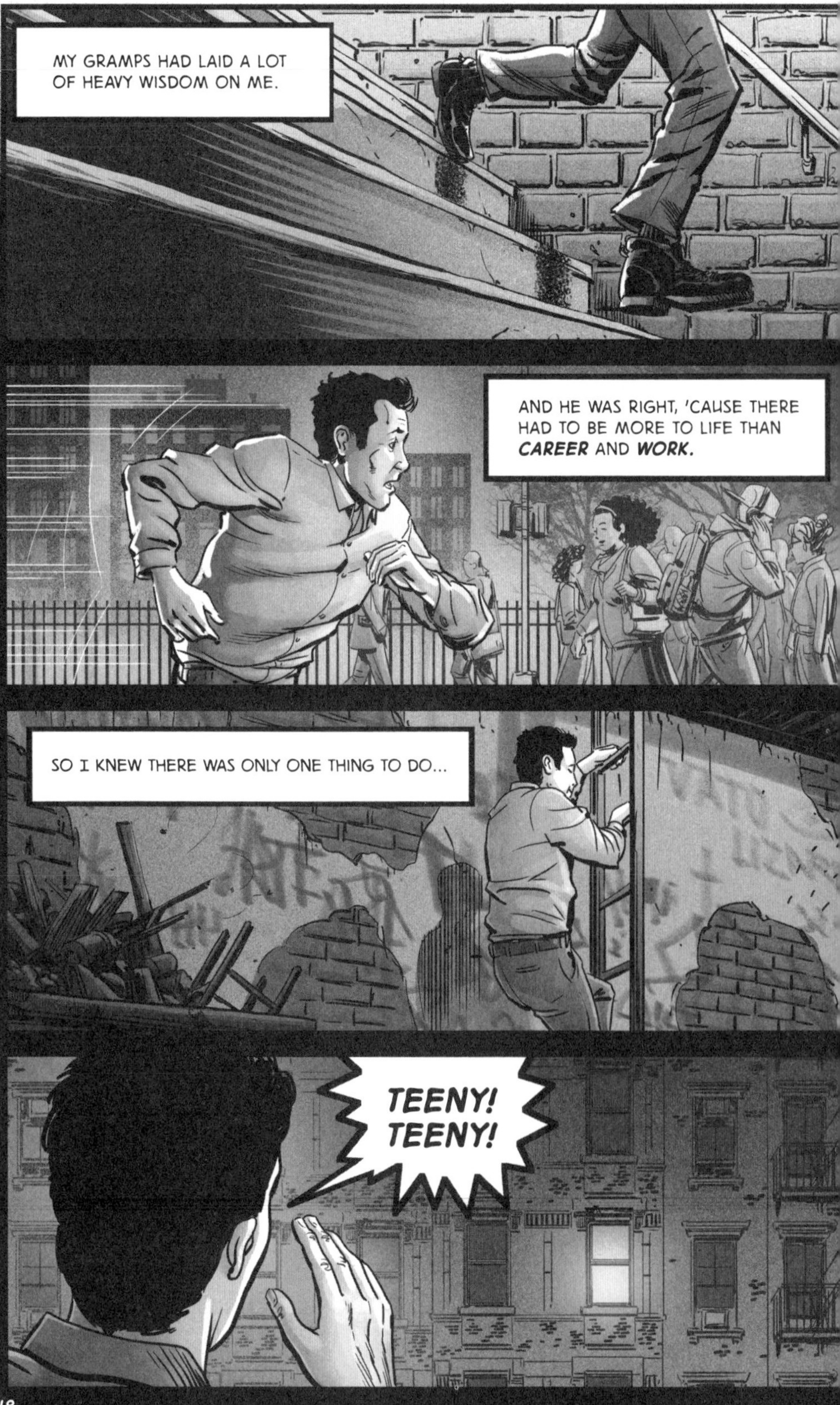
MY GRAMPS HAD LAID A LOT OF HEAVY WISDOM ON ME.
AND HE WAS RIGHT, 'CAUSE THERE HAD TO BE MORE TO LIFE THAN *CAREER* AND *WORK.*
SO I KNEW THERE WAS ONLY ONE THING TO DO...
TEENY! TEENY!

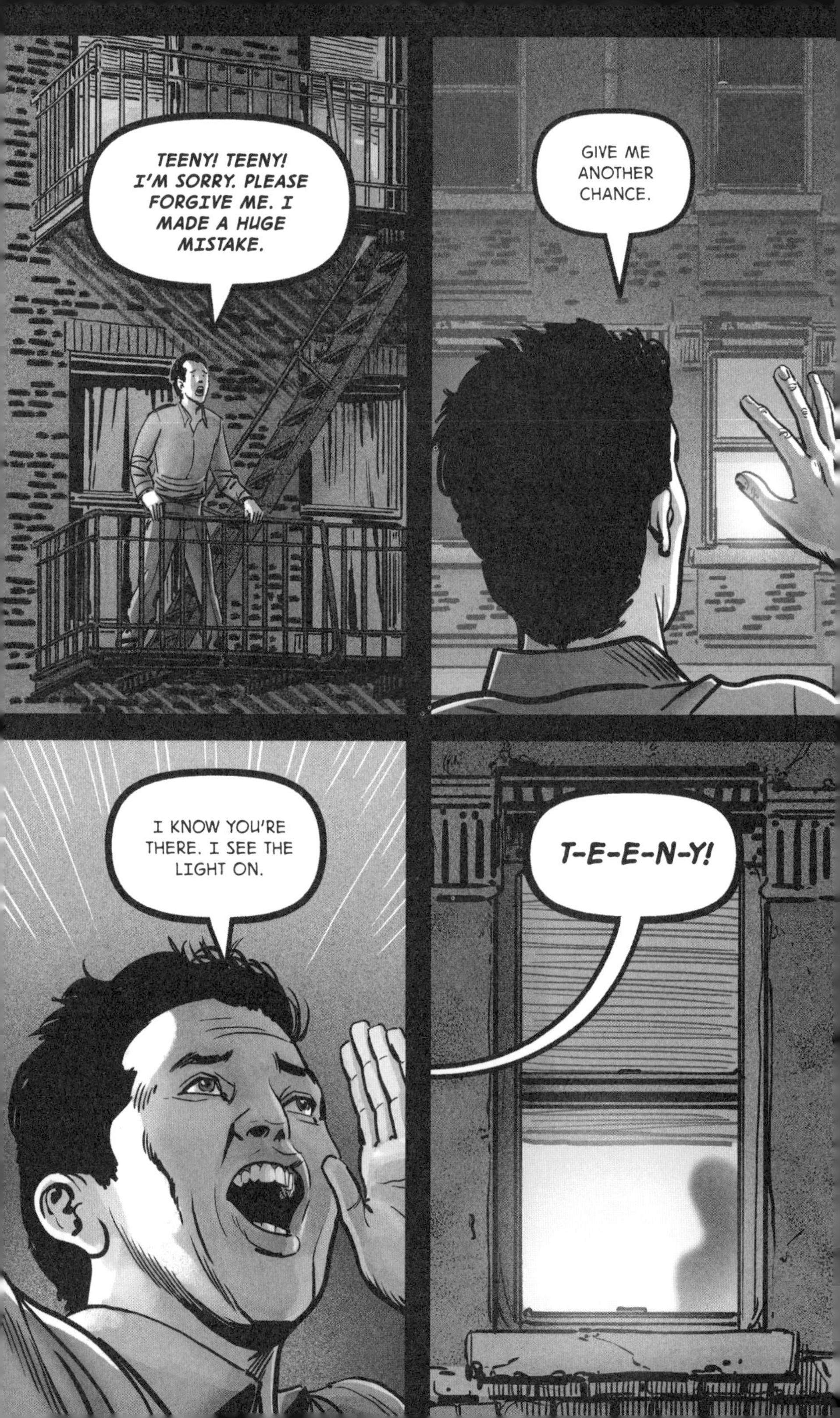
TEENY! TEENY! I'M SORRY. PLEASE FORGIVE ME. I MADE A HUGE MISTAKE.
GIVE ME ANOTHER CHANCE.
I KNOW YOU'RE THERE. I SEE THE LIGHT ON.
T-E-E-N-Y!

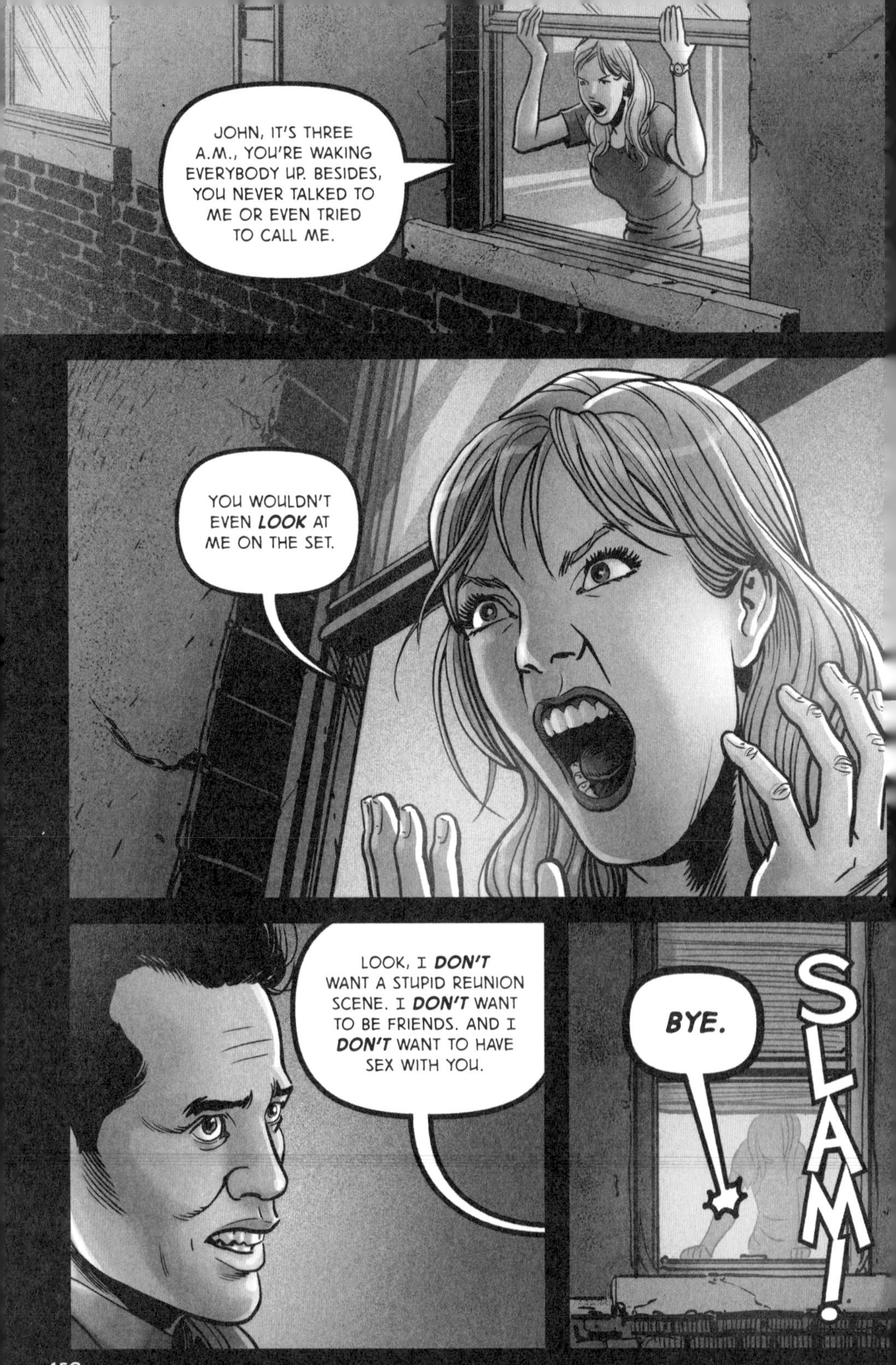

JOHN, IT'S THREE A.M., YOU'RE WAKING EVERYBODY UP. BESIDES, YOU NEVER TALKED TO ME OR EVEN TRIED TO CALL ME.
YOU WOULDN'T EVEN ***LOOK*** AT ME ON THE SET.
LOOK, I ***DON'T*** WANT A STUPID REUNION SCENE. I ***DON'T*** WANT TO BE FRIENDS. AND I ***DON'T*** WANT TO HAVE SEX WITH YOU.
BYE.
SLAM!

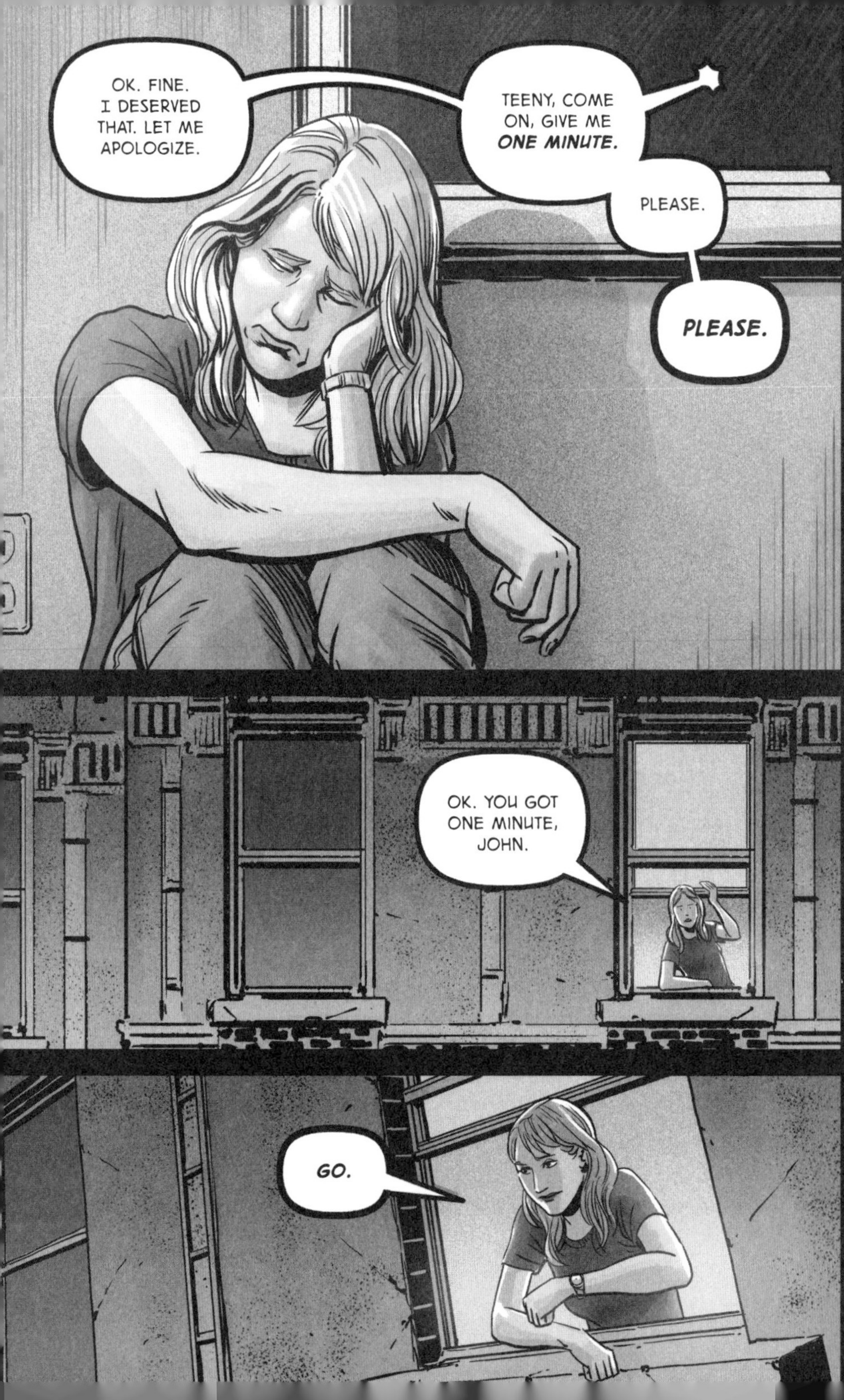
OK. FINE. I DESERVED THAT. LET ME APOLOGIZE.
TEENY, COME ON, GIVE ME ONE MINUTE.
PLEASE.
PLEASE.
OK. YOU GOT ONE MINUTE, JOHN.
GO.

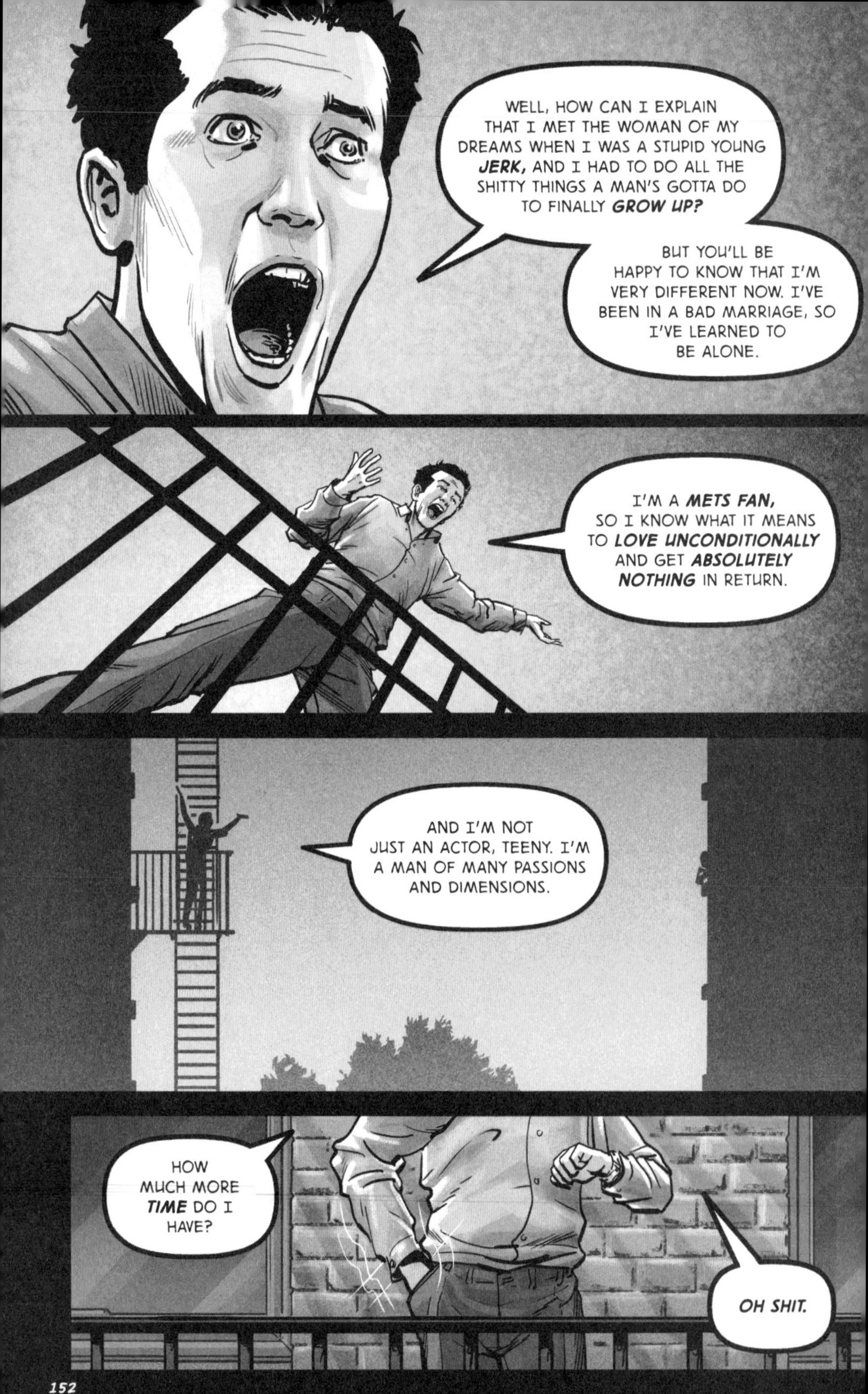
WELL, HOW CAN I EXPLAIN THAT I MET THE WOMAN OF MY DREAMS WHEN I WAS A STUPID YOUNG **JERK,** AND I HAD TO DO ALL THE SHITTY THINGS A MAN'S GOTTA DO TO FINALLY **GROW UP?**
BUT YOU'LL BE HAPPY TO KNOW THAT I'M VERY DIFFERENT NOW. I'VE BEEN IN A BAD MARRIAGE, SO I'VE LEARNED TO BE ALONE.
I'M A **METS FAN,** SO I KNOW WHAT IT MEANS TO **LOVE UNCONDITIONALLY** AND GET **ABSOLUTELY NOTHING** IN RETURN.
AND I'M NOT JUST AN ACTOR, TEENY. I'M A MAN OF MANY PASSIONS AND DIMENSIONS.
HOW MUCH MORE **TIME** DO I HAVE?
OH SHIT.

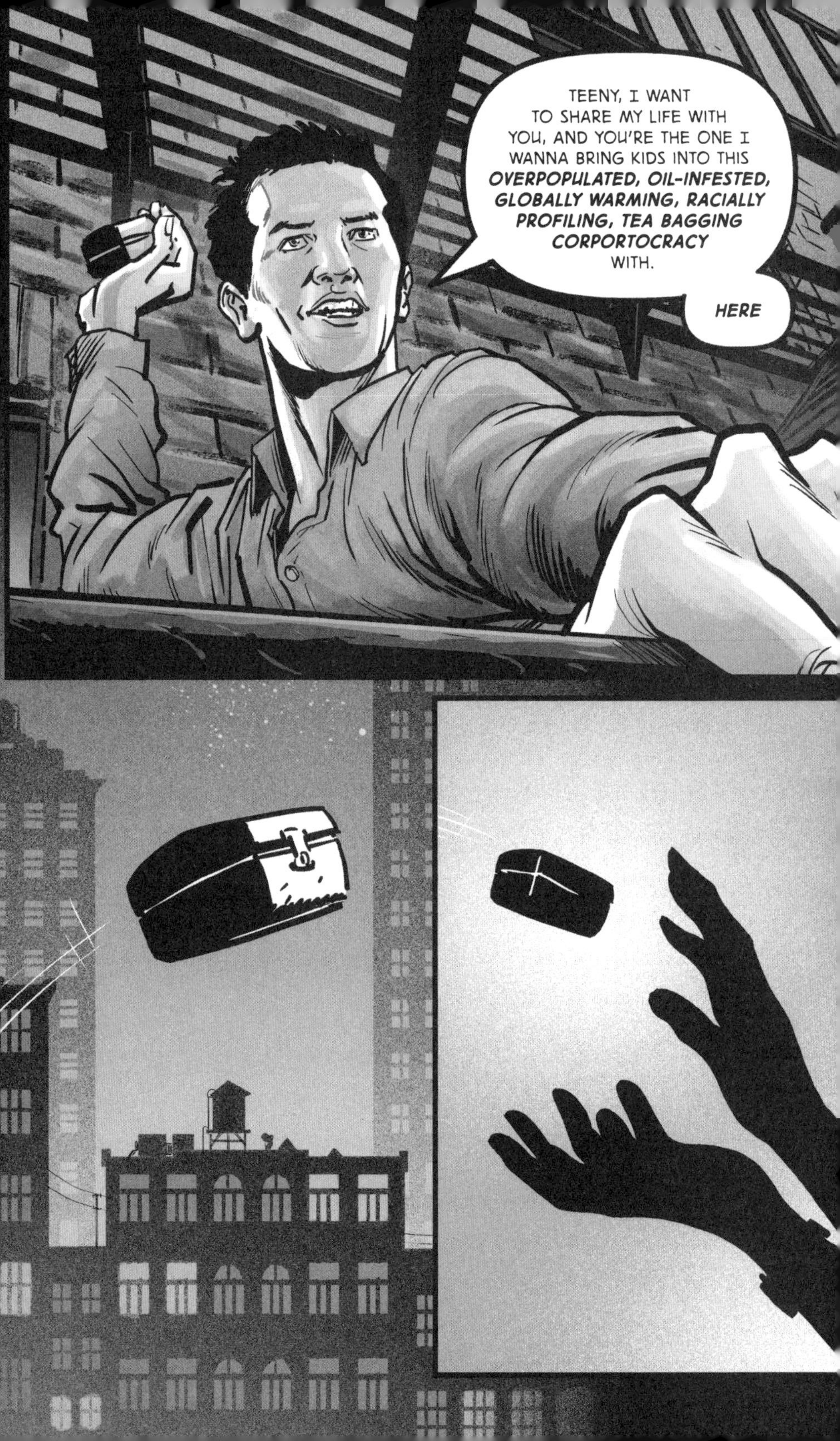
TEENY, I WANT TO SHARE MY LIFE WITH YOU, AND YOU'RE THE ONE I WANNA BRING KIDS INTO THIS **OVERPOPULATED, OIL-INFESTED, GLOBALLY WARMING, RACIALLY PROFILING, TEA BAGGING CORPORTOCRACY** WITH.
HERE

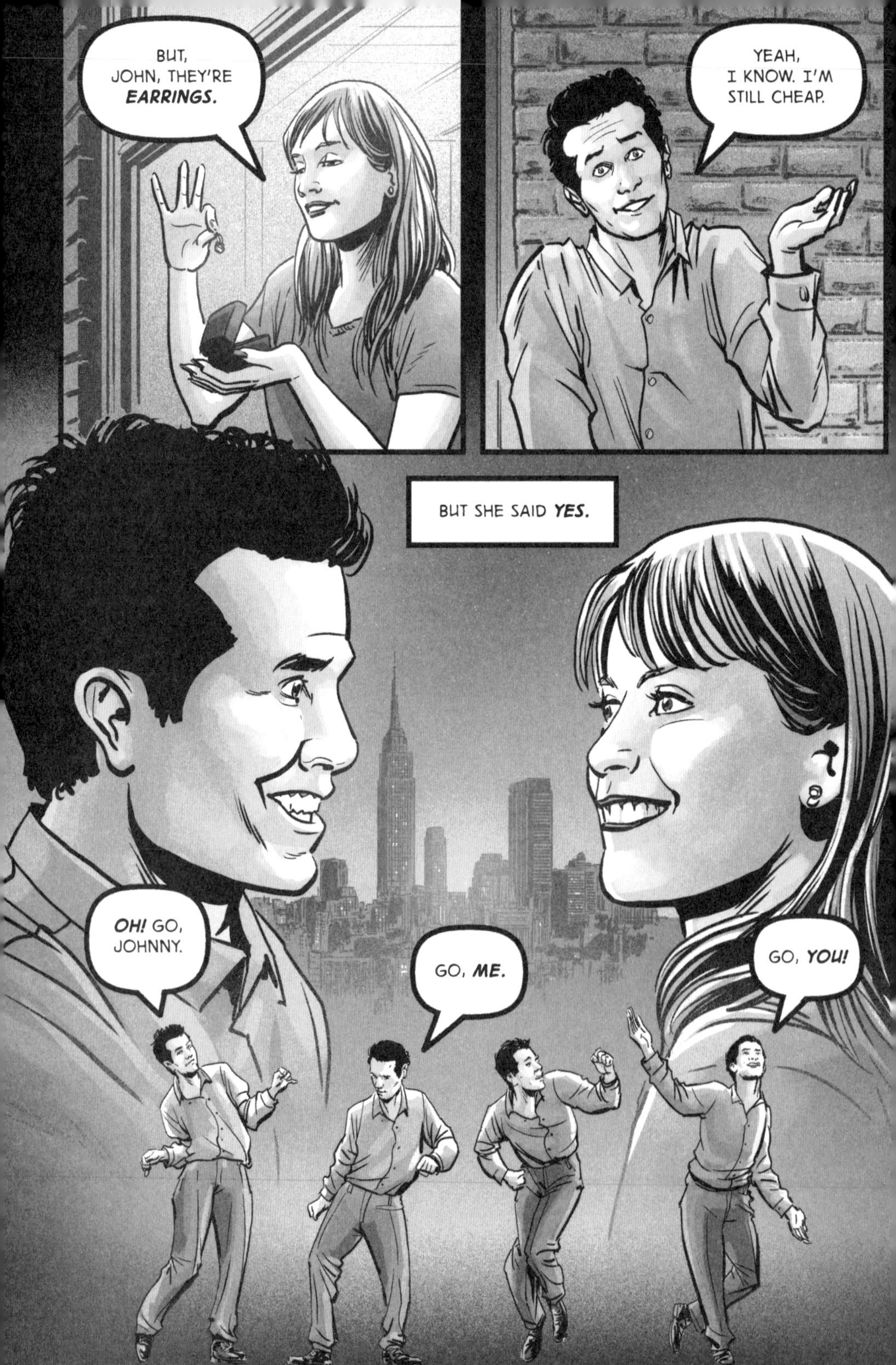
BUT, JOHN, THEY'RE **EARRINGS.**
YEAH, I KNOW. I'M STILL CHEAP.
BUT SHE SAID **YES.**
OH! GO, JOHNNY.
GO, **ME.**
GO, **YOU!**

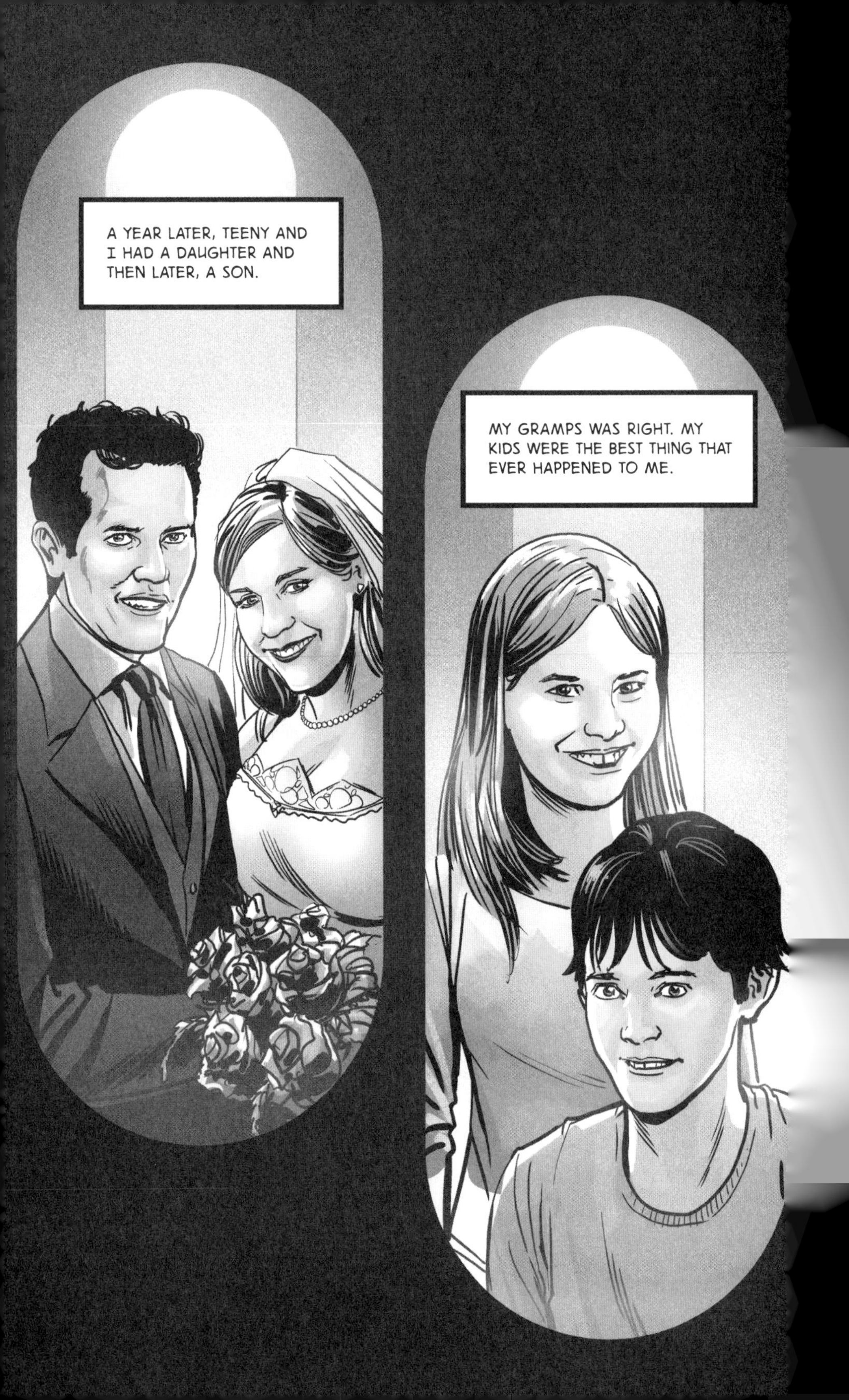
A YEAR LATER, TEENY AND I HAD A DAUGHTER AND THEN LATER, A SON.
MY GRAMPS WAS RIGHT. MY KIDS WERE THE BEST THING THAT EVER HAPPENED TO ME.

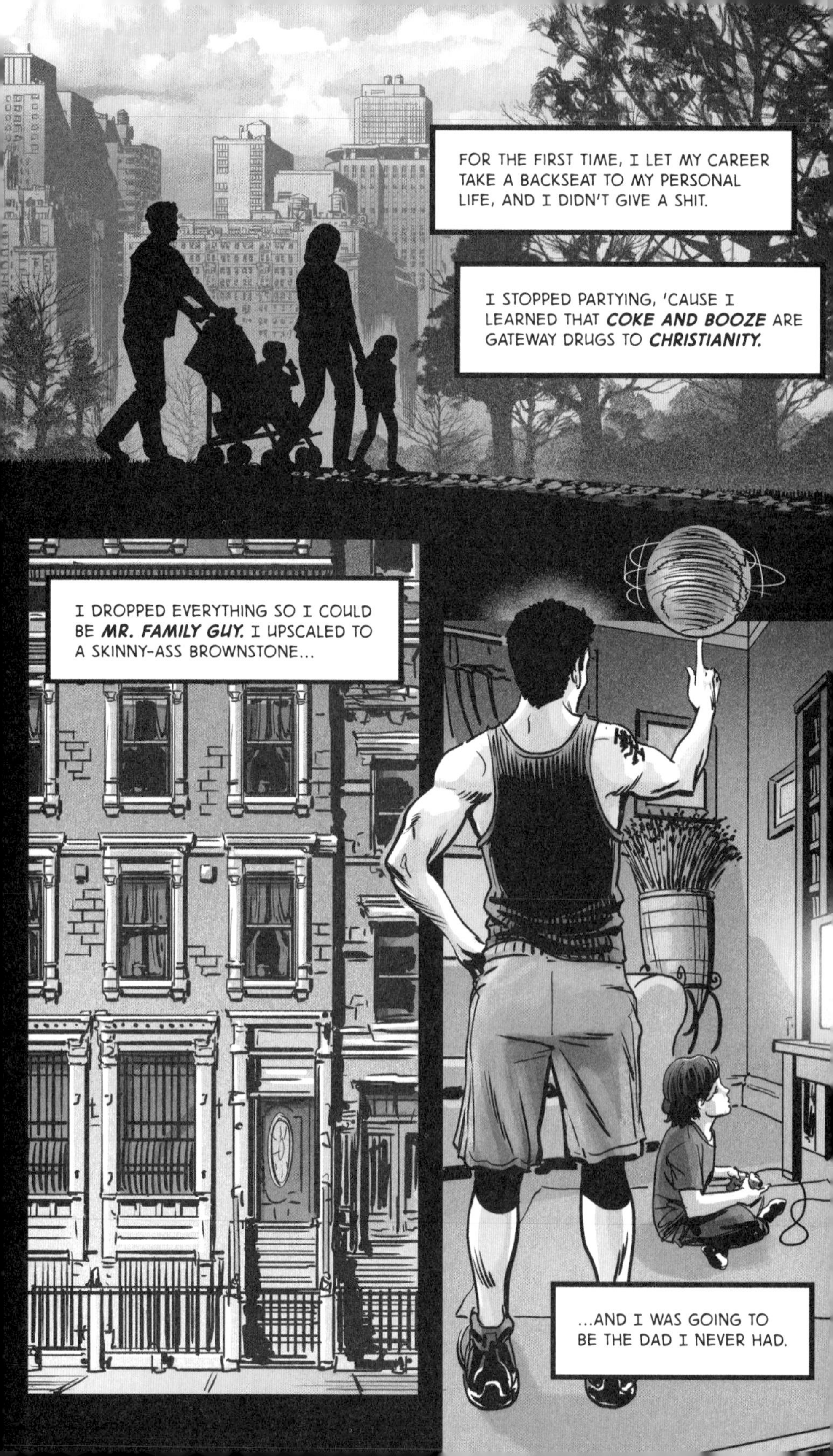
FOR THE FIRST TIME, I LET MY CAREER TAKE A BACKSEAT TO MY PERSONAL LIFE, AND I DIDN'T GIVE A SHIT.
I STOPPED PARTYING, 'CAUSE I LEARNED THAT ***COKE AND BOOZE*** ARE GATEWAY DRUGS TO ***CHRISTIANITY.***
I DROPPED EVERYTHING SO I COULD BE ***MR. FAMILY GUY.*** I UPSCALED TO A SKINNY-ASS BROWNSTONE...
...AND I WAS GOING TO BE THE DAD I NEVER HAD.

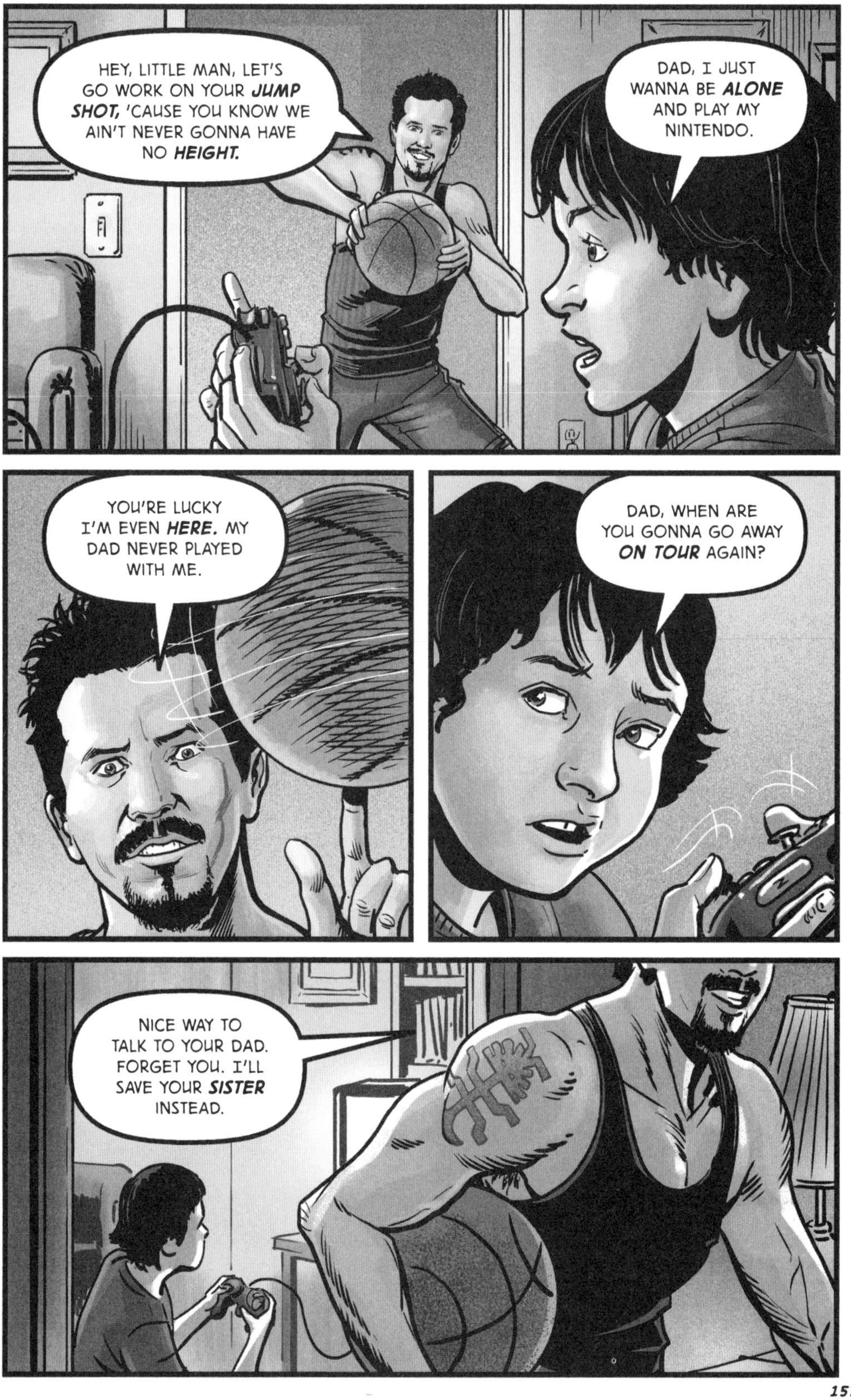
HEY, LITTLE MAN, LET'S GO WORK ON YOUR JUMP SHOT, 'CAUSE YOU KNOW WE AIN'T NEVER GONNA HAVE NO HEIGHT.
DAD, I JUST WANNA BE ALONE AND PLAY MY NINTENDO.
YOU'RE LUCKY I'M EVEN HERE. MY DAD NEVER PLAYED WITH ME.
DAD, WHEN ARE YOU GONNA GO AWAY ON TOUR AGAIN?
NICE WAY TO TALK TO YOUR DAD. FORGET YOU. I'LL SAVE YOUR SISTER INSTEAD.

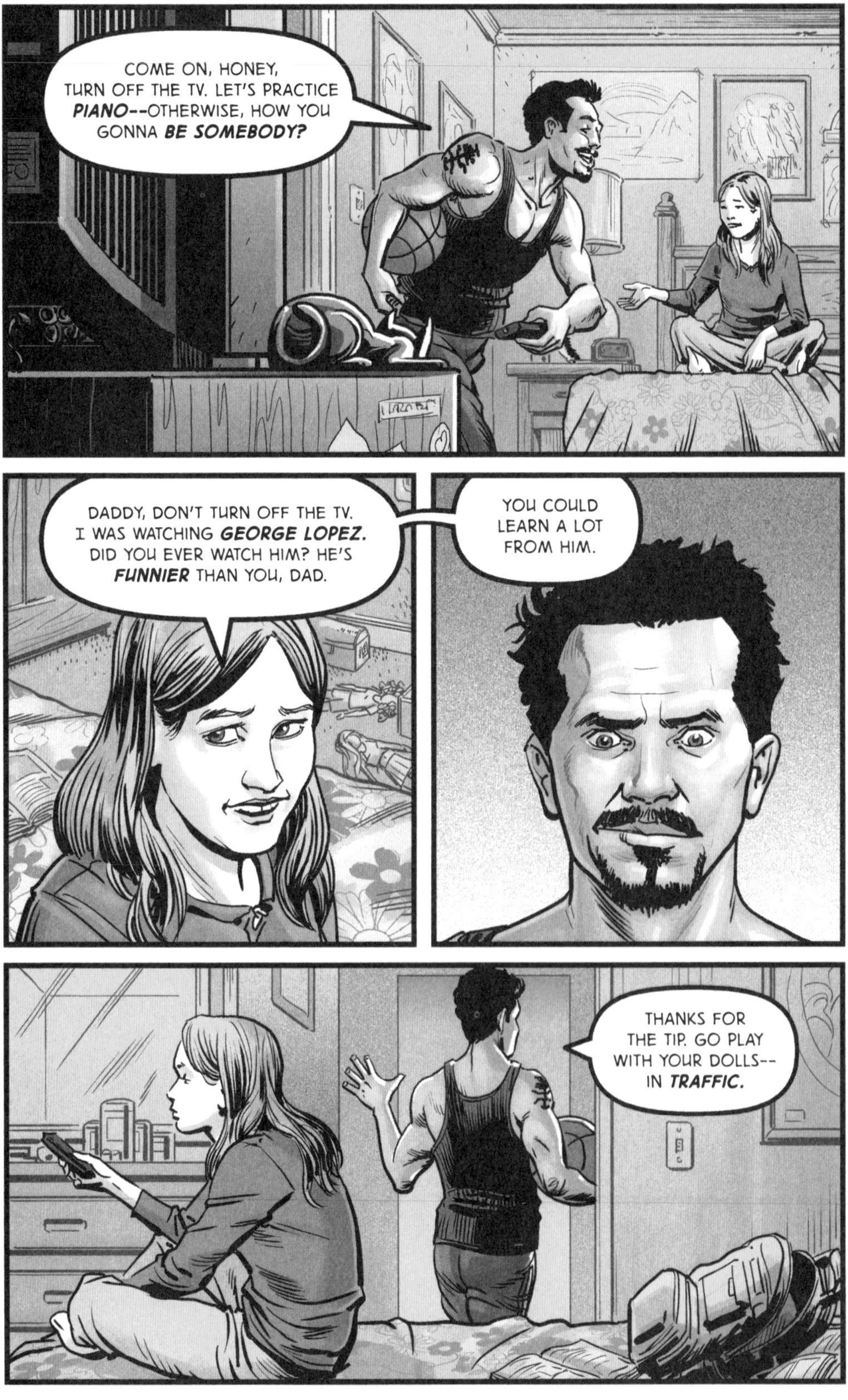
COME ON, HONEY, TURN OFF THE TV. LET'S PRACTICE PIANO--OTHERWISE, HOW YOU GONNA BE SOMEBODY?
DADDY, DON'T TURN OFF THE TV. I WAS WATCHING GEORGE LOPEZ. DID YOU EVER WATCH HIM? HE'S FUNNIER THAN YOU, DAD.
YOU COULD LEARN A LOT FROM HIM.
THANKS FOR THE TIP. GO PLAY WITH YOUR DOLLS-- IN TRAFFIC.

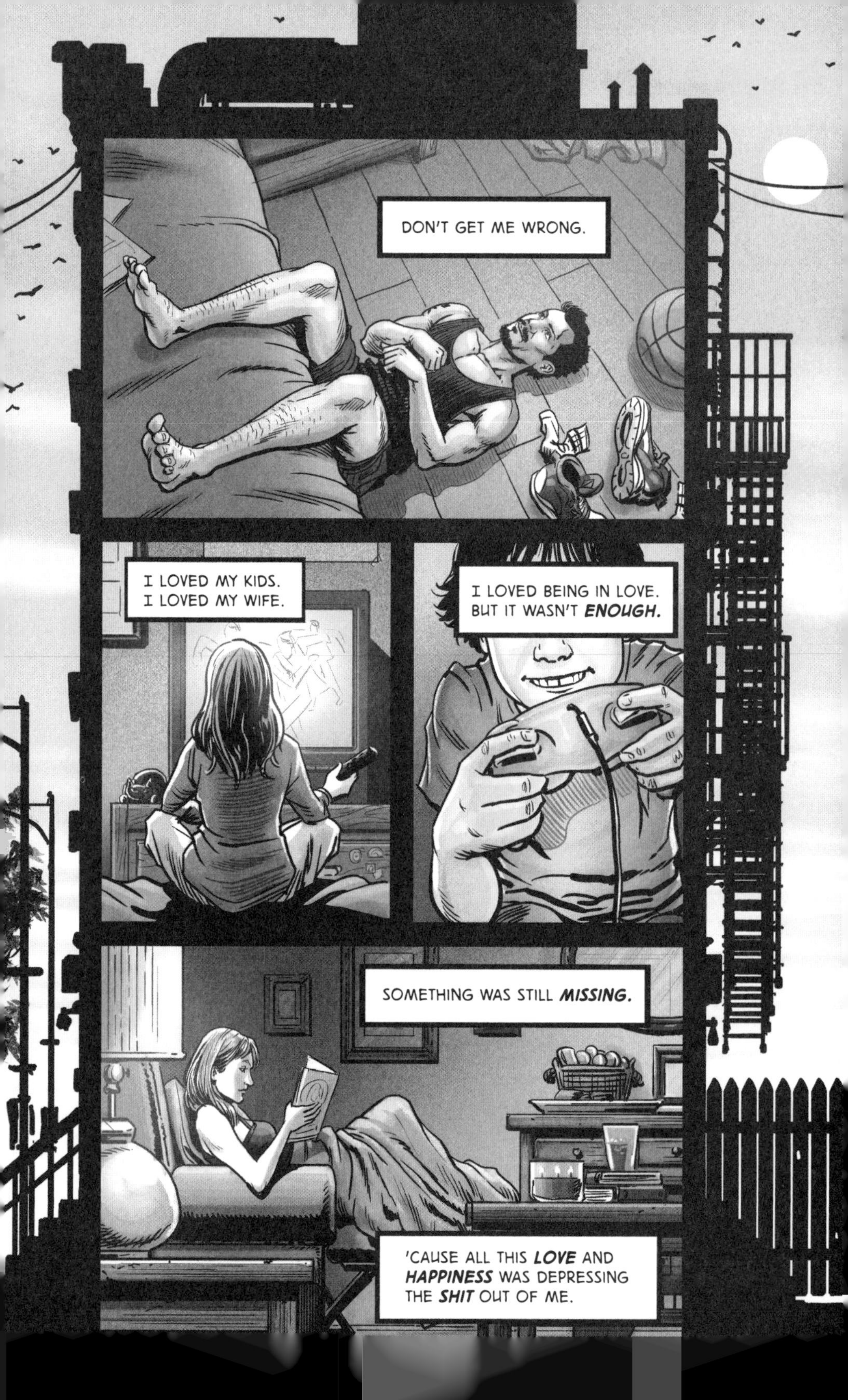
DON'T GET ME WRONG.
I LOVED MY KIDS. I LOVED MY WIFE.
I LOVED BEING IN LOVE. BUT IT WASN'T ENOUGH.
SOMETHING WAS STILL MISSING.
'CAUSE ALL THIS LOVE AND HAPPINESS WAS DEPRESSING THE SHIT OUT OF ME.

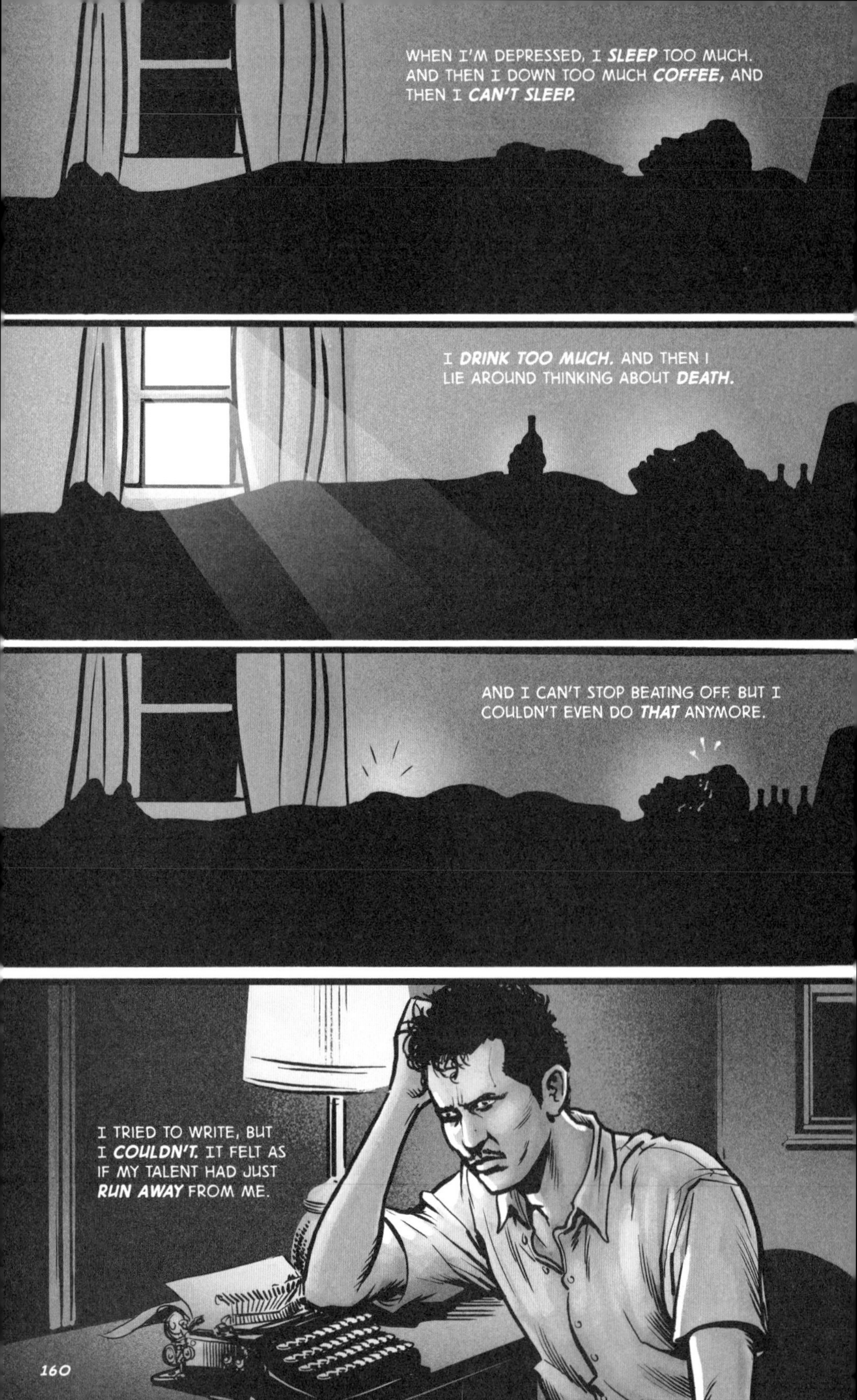
WHEN I'M DEPRESSED, I SLEEP TOO MUCH. AND THEN I DOWN TOO MUCH COFFEE, AND THEN I CAN'T SLEEP.
I DRINK TOO MUCH. AND THEN I LIE AROUND THINKING ABOUT DEATH.
AND I CAN'T STOP BEATING OFF. BUT I COULDN'T EVEN DO THAT ANYMORE.
I TRIED TO WRITE, BUT I COULDN'T. IT FELT AS IF MY TALENT HAD JUST RUN AWAY FROM ME.

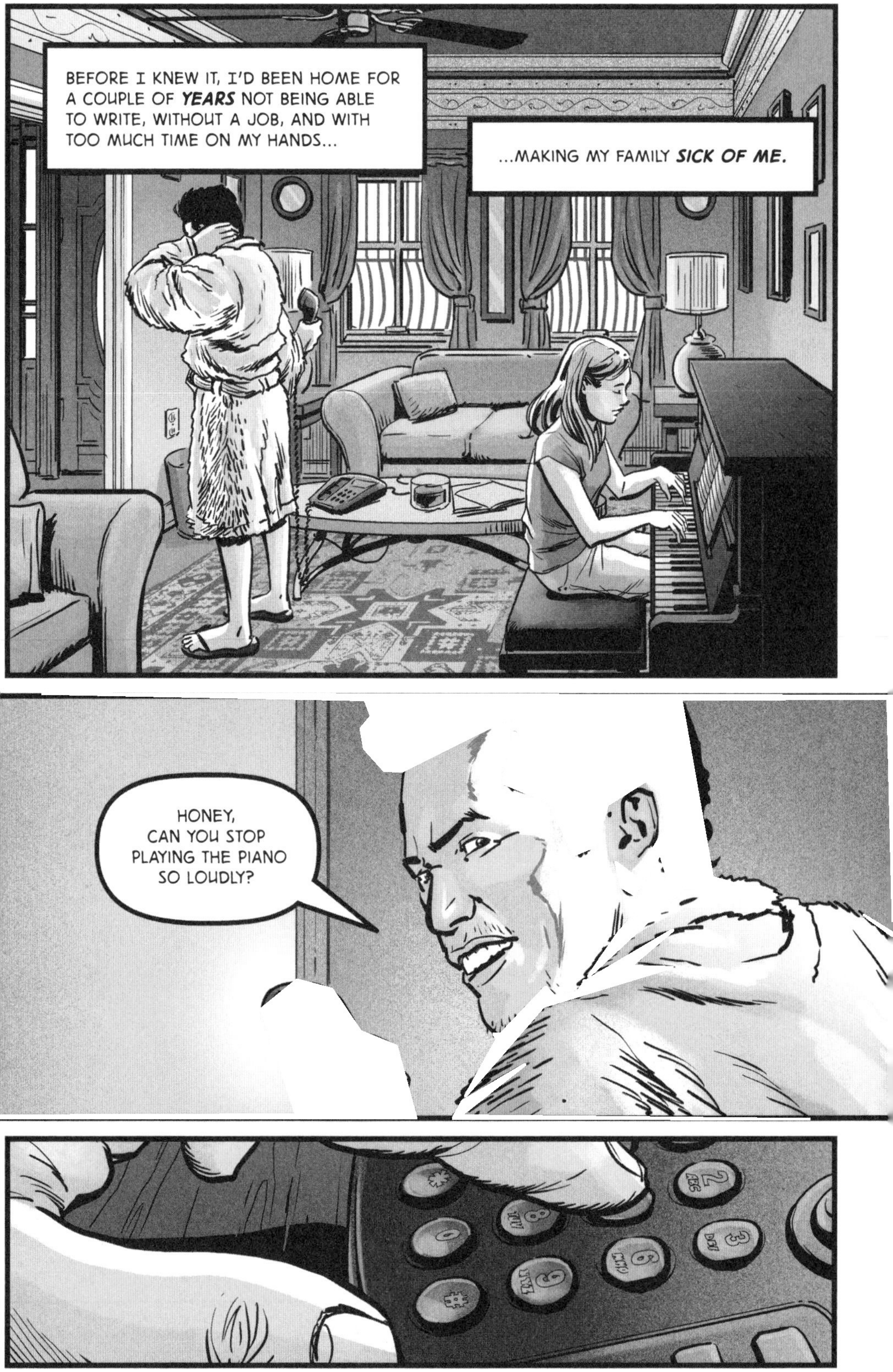
BEFORE I KNEW IT, I'D BEEN HOME FOR A COUPLE OF *YEARS* NOT BEING ABLE TO WRITE, WITHOUT A JOB, AND WITH TOO MUCH TIME ON MY HANDS...
...MAKING MY FAMILY *SICK OF ME.*
HONEY, CAN YOU STOP PLAYING THE PIANO SO LOUDLY?

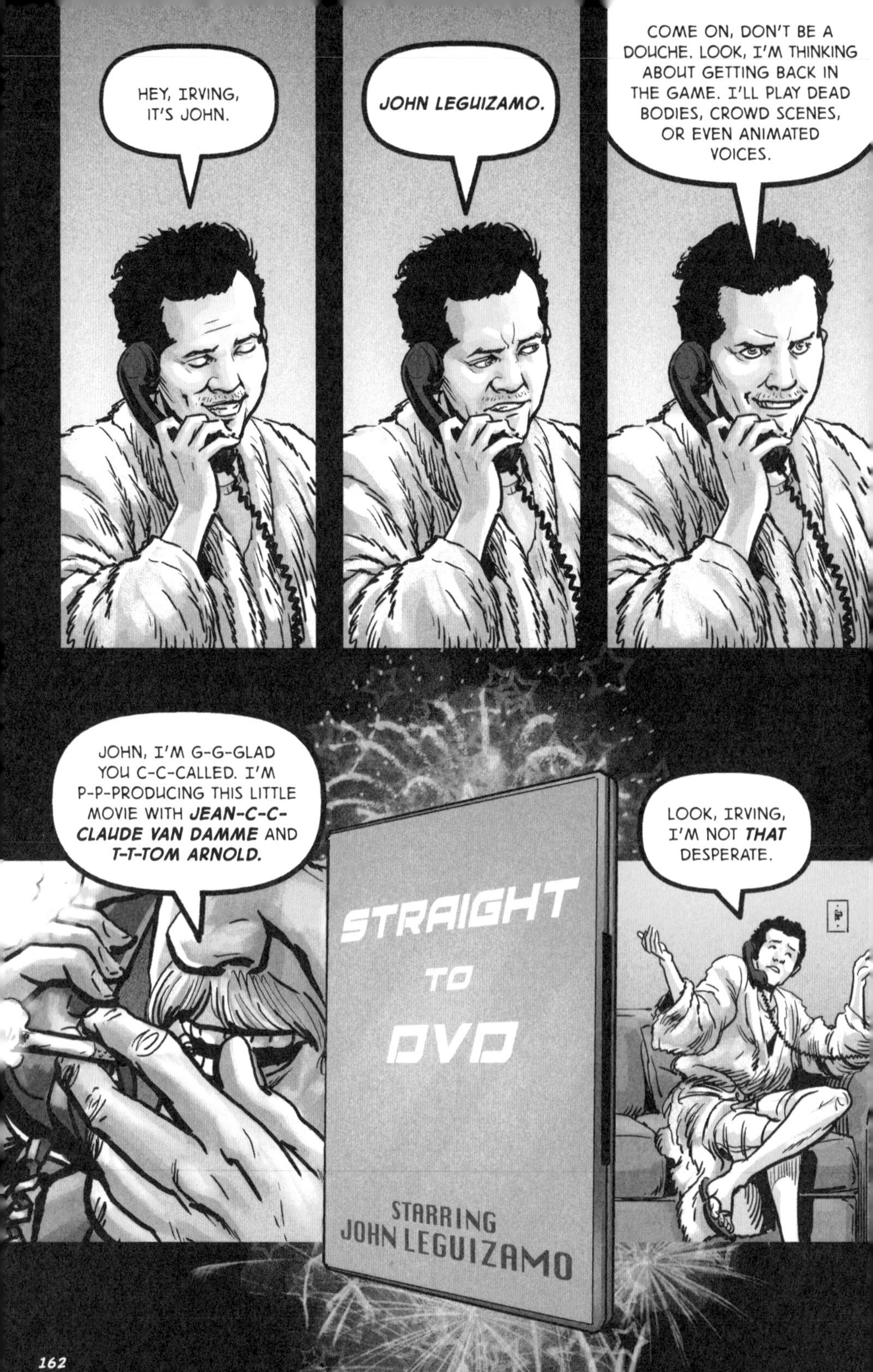
HEY, IRVING, IT'S JOHN.
JOHN LEGUIZAMO.
COME ON, DON'T BE A DOUCHE. LOOK, I'M THINKING ABOUT GETTING BACK IN THE GAME. I'LL PLAY DEAD BODIES, CROWD SCENES, OR EVEN ANIMATED VOICES.
JOHN, I'M G-G-GLAD YOU C-C-CALLED. I'M P-P-PRODUCING THIS LITTLE MOVIE WITH JEAN-C-C-CLAUDE VAN DAMME AND T-T-TOM ARNOLD.
STRAIGHT TO DVD
STARRING JOHN LEGUIZAMO
LOOK, IRVING, I'M NOT THAT DESPERATE.

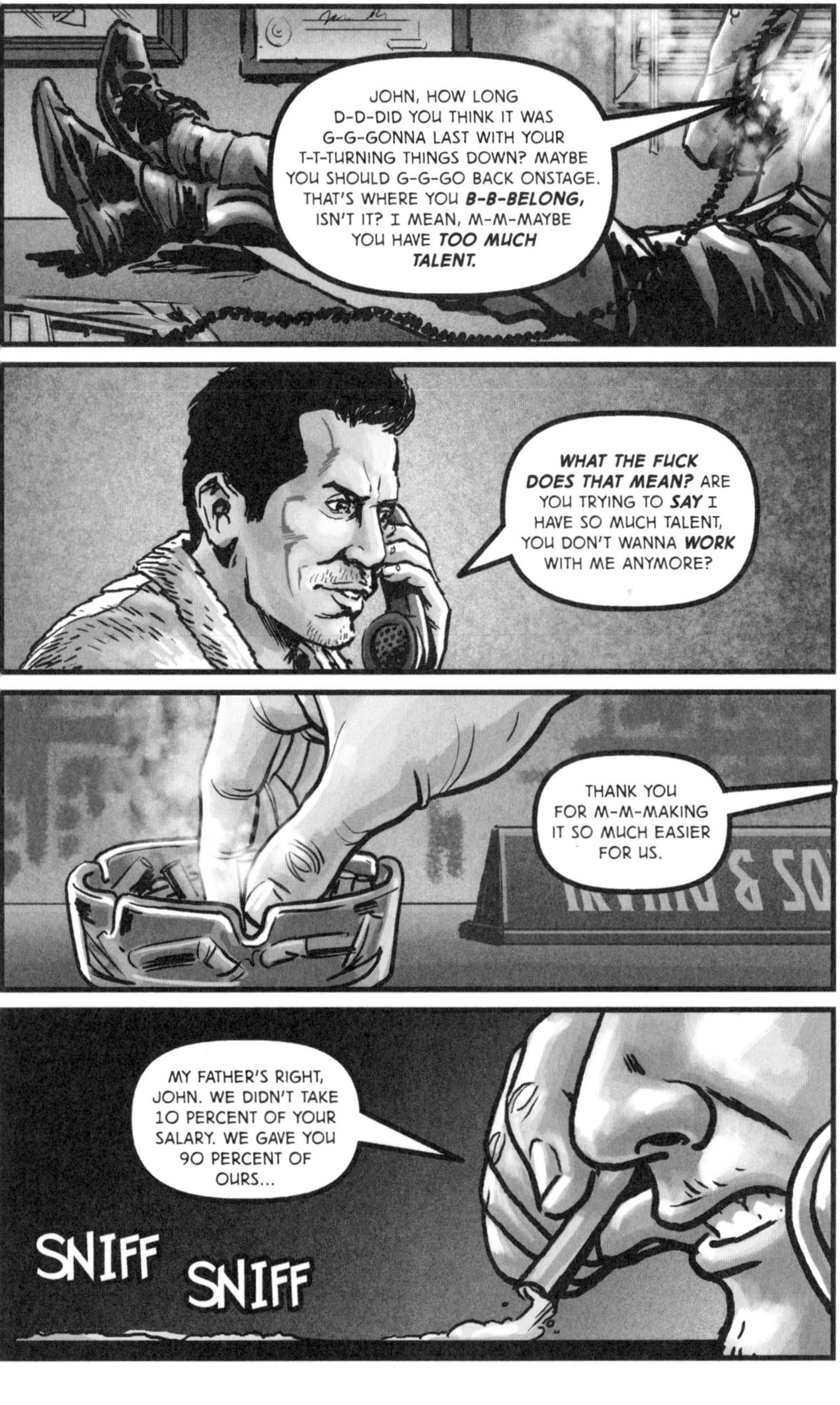
JOHN, HOW LONG D-D-DID YOU THINK IT WAS G-G-GONNA LAST WITH YOUR T-T-TURNING THINGS DOWN? MAYBE YOU SHOULD G-G-GO BACK ONSTAGE. THAT'S WHERE YOU **B-B-BELONG,** ISN'T IT? I MEAN, M-M-MAYBE YOU HAVE **TOO MUCH TALENT.**
WHAT THE FUCK DOES THAT MEAN? ARE YOU TRYING TO **SAY** I HAVE SO MUCH TALENT, YOU DON'T WANNA **WORK** WITH ME ANYMORE?
THANK YOU FOR M-M-MAKING IT SO MUCH EASIER FOR US.
MY FATHER'S RIGHT, JOHN. WE DIDN'T TAKE 10 PERCENT OF YOUR SALARY. WE GAVE YOU 90 PERCENT OF OURS...
SNIFF
SNIFF

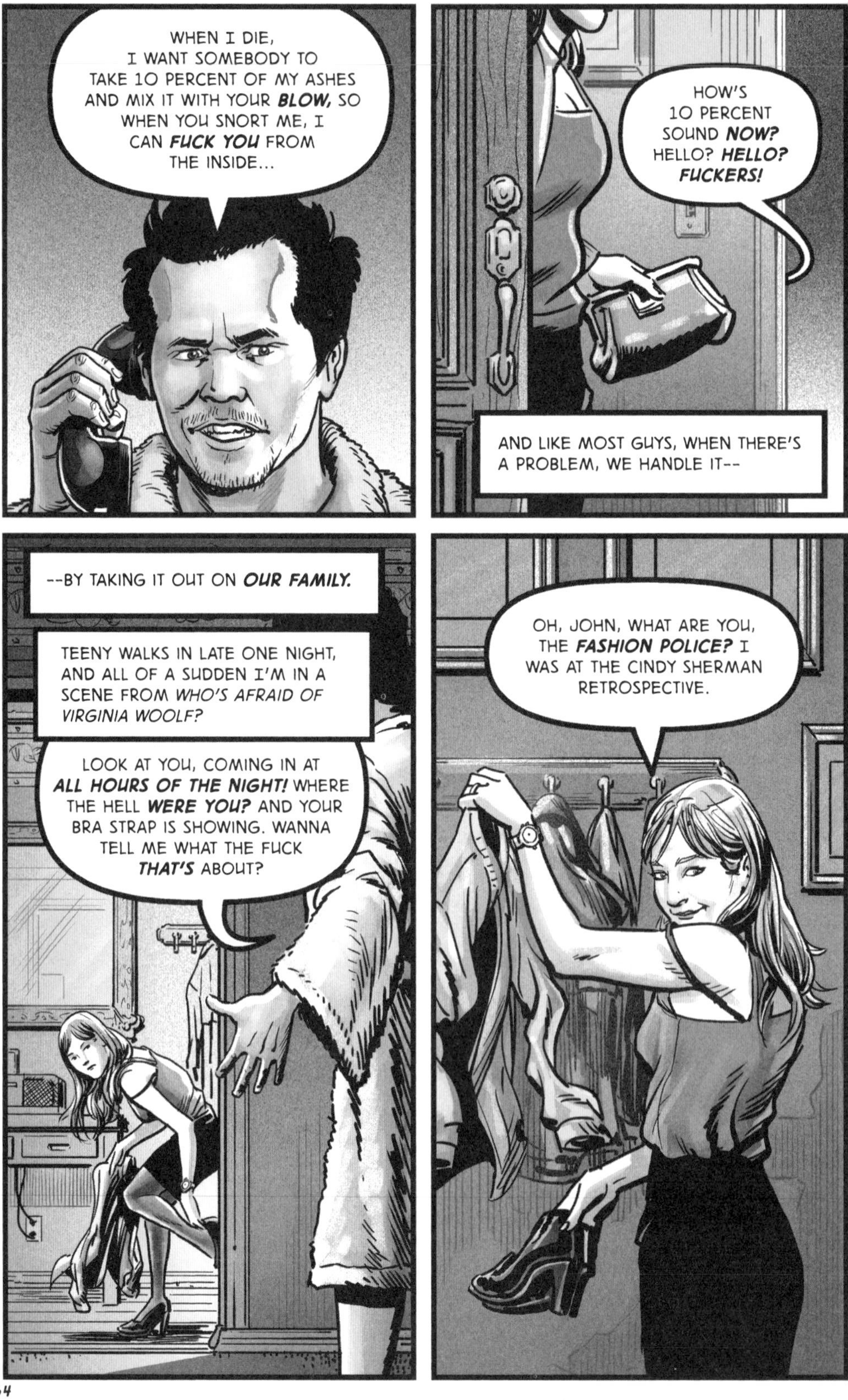
WHEN I DIE, I WANT SOMEBODY TO TAKE 10 PERCENT OF MY ASHES AND MIX IT WITH YOUR BLOW, SO WHEN YOU SNORT ME, I CAN FUCK YOU FROM THE INSIDE...
HOW'S 10 PERCENT SOUND NOW? HELLO? HELLO? FUCKERS!
AND LIKE MOST GUYS, WHEN THERE'S A PROBLEM, WE HANDLE IT--
--BY TAKING IT OUT ON OUR FAMILY.
TEENY WALKS IN LATE ONE NIGHT, AND ALL OF A SUDDEN I'M IN A SCENE FROM WHO'S AFRAID OF VIRGINIA WOOLF?
LOOK AT YOU, COMING IN AT ALL HOURS OF THE NIGHT! WHERE THE HELL WERE YOU? AND YOUR BRA STRAP IS SHOWING. WANNA TELL ME WHAT THE FUCK THAT'S ABOUT?
OH, JOHN, WHAT ARE YOU, THE FASHION POLICE? I WAS AT THE CINDY SHERMAN RETROSPECTIVE.

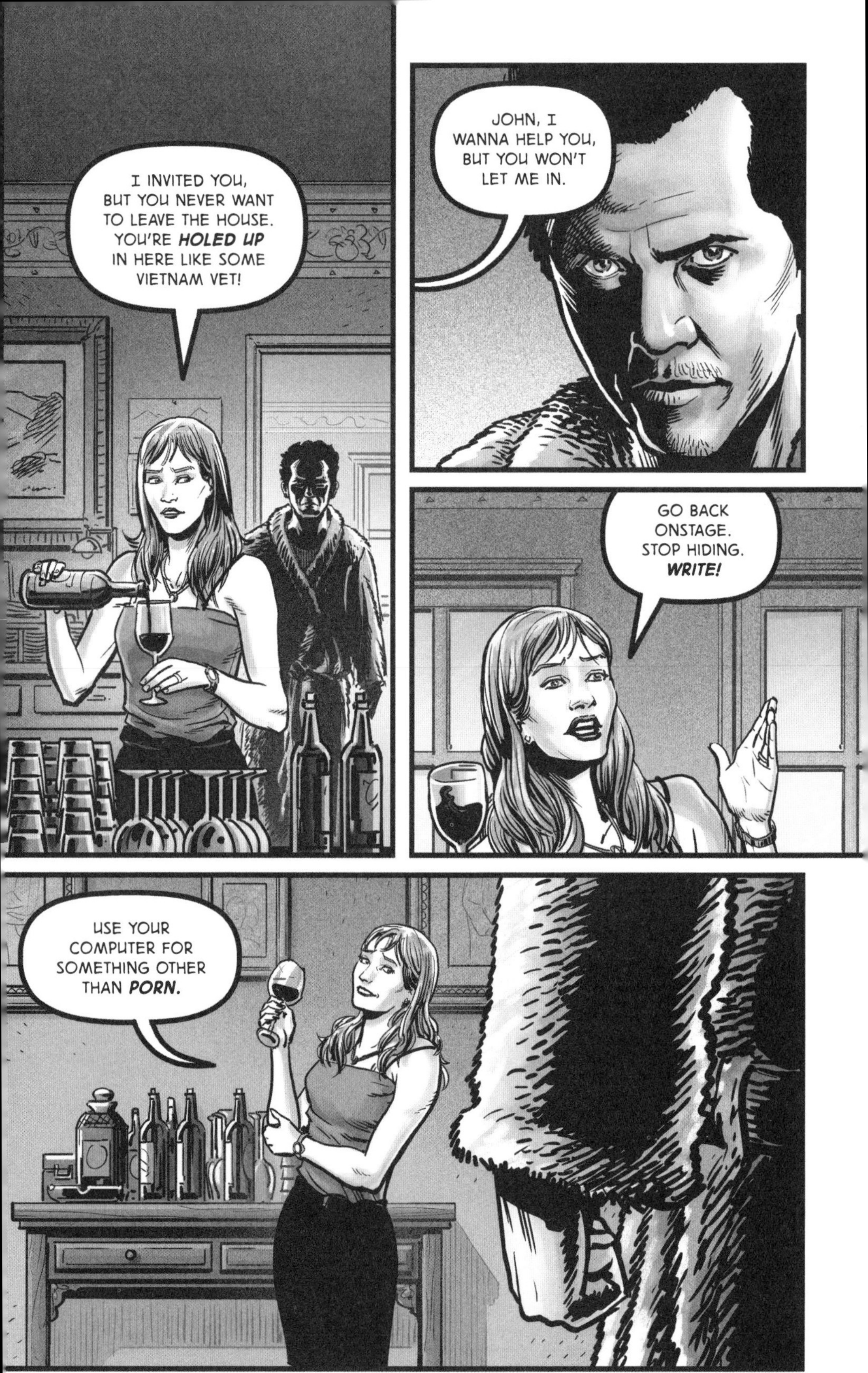
I INVITED YOU, BUT YOU NEVER WANT TO LEAVE THE HOUSE. YOU'RE ***HOLED UP*** IN HERE LIKE SOME VIETNAM VET!
JOHN, I WANNA HELP YOU, BUT YOU WON'T LET ME IN.
GO BACK ONSTAGE. STOP HIDING. ***WRITE!***
USE YOUR COMPUTER FOR SOMETHING OTHER THAN ***PORN.***

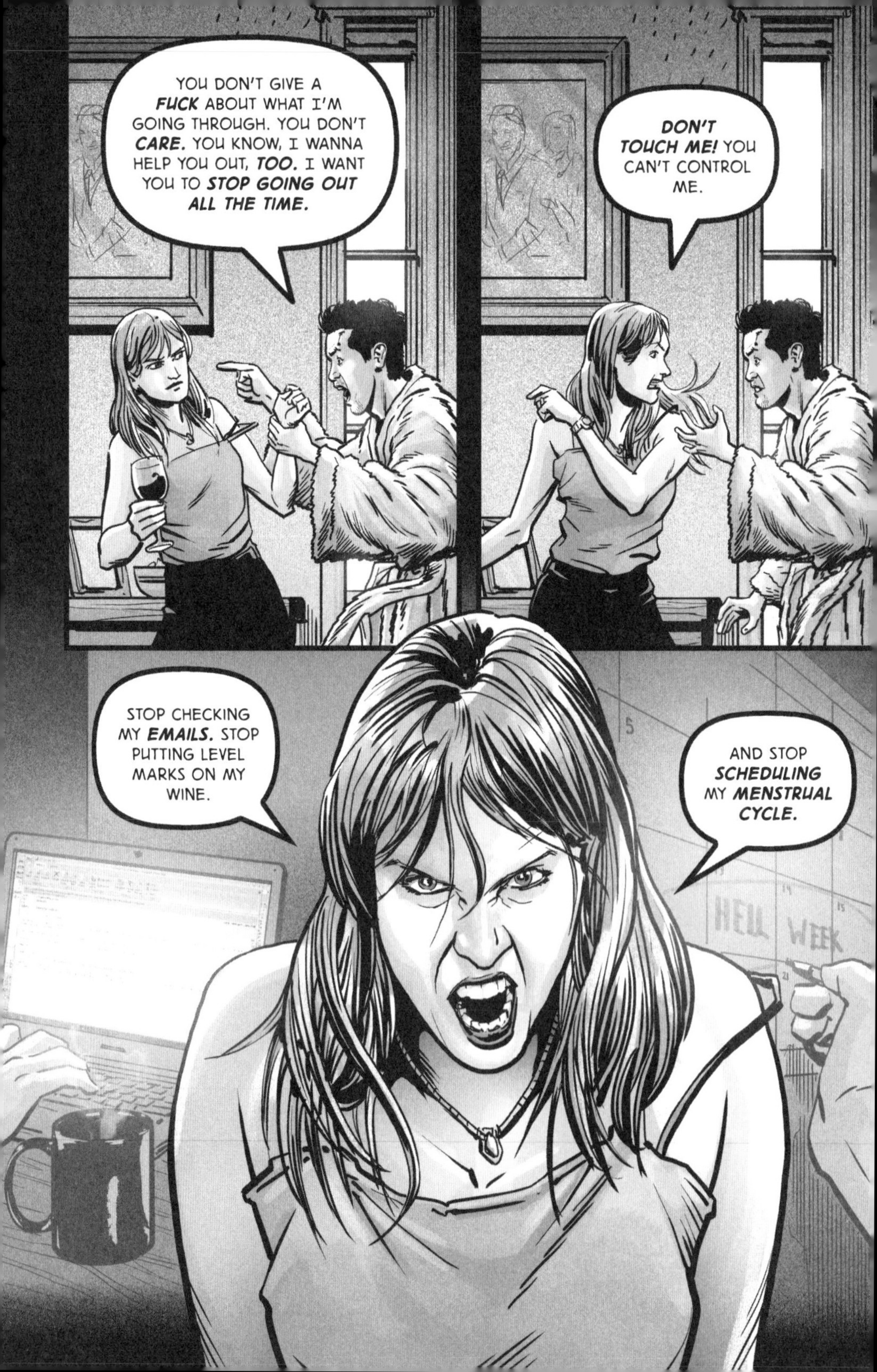
YOU DON'T GIVE A FUCK ABOUT WHAT I'M GOING THROUGH. YOU DON'T CARE. YOU KNOW, I WANNA HELP YOU OUT, TOO. I WANT YOU TO STOP GOING OUT ALL THE TIME.
DON'T TOUCH ME! YOU CAN'T CONTROL ME.
STOP CHECKING MY EMAILS. STOP PUTTING LEVEL MARKS ON MY WINE.
AND STOP SCHEDULING MY MENSTRUAL CYCLE.
HELL WEEK

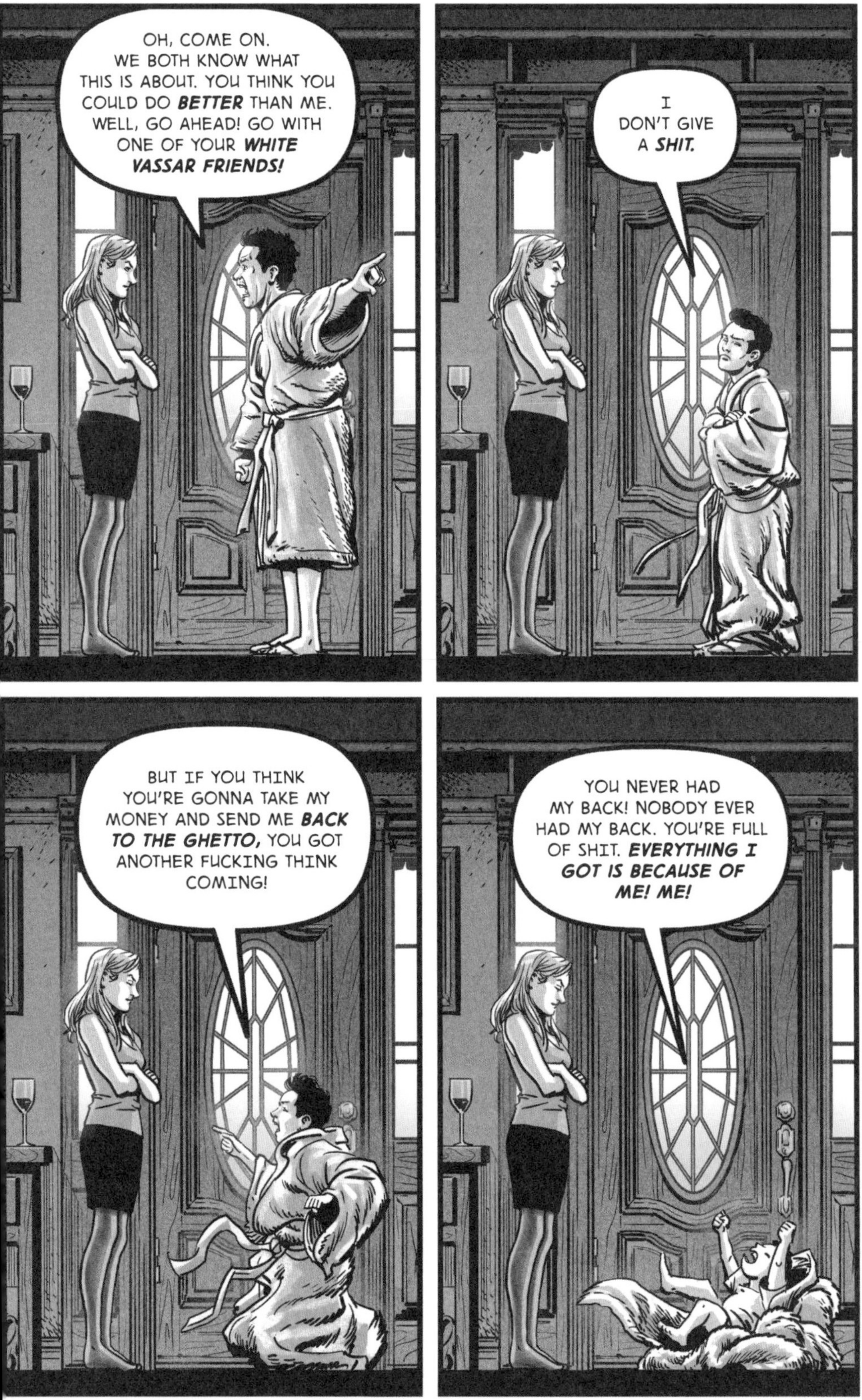

OH, COME ON. WE BOTH KNOW WHAT THIS IS ABOUT. YOU THINK YOU COULD DO **BETTER** THAN ME. WELL, GO AHEAD! GO WITH ONE OF YOUR **WHITE VASSAR FRIENDS!**
I DON'T GIVE A **SHIT.**
BUT IF YOU THINK YOU'RE GONNA TAKE MY MONEY AND SEND ME **BACK TO THE GHETTO,** YOU GOT ANOTHER FUCKING THINK COMING!
YOU NEVER HAD MY BACK! NOBODY EVER HAD MY BACK. YOU'RE FULL OF SHIT. **EVERYTHING I GOT IS BECAUSE OF ME! ME!**

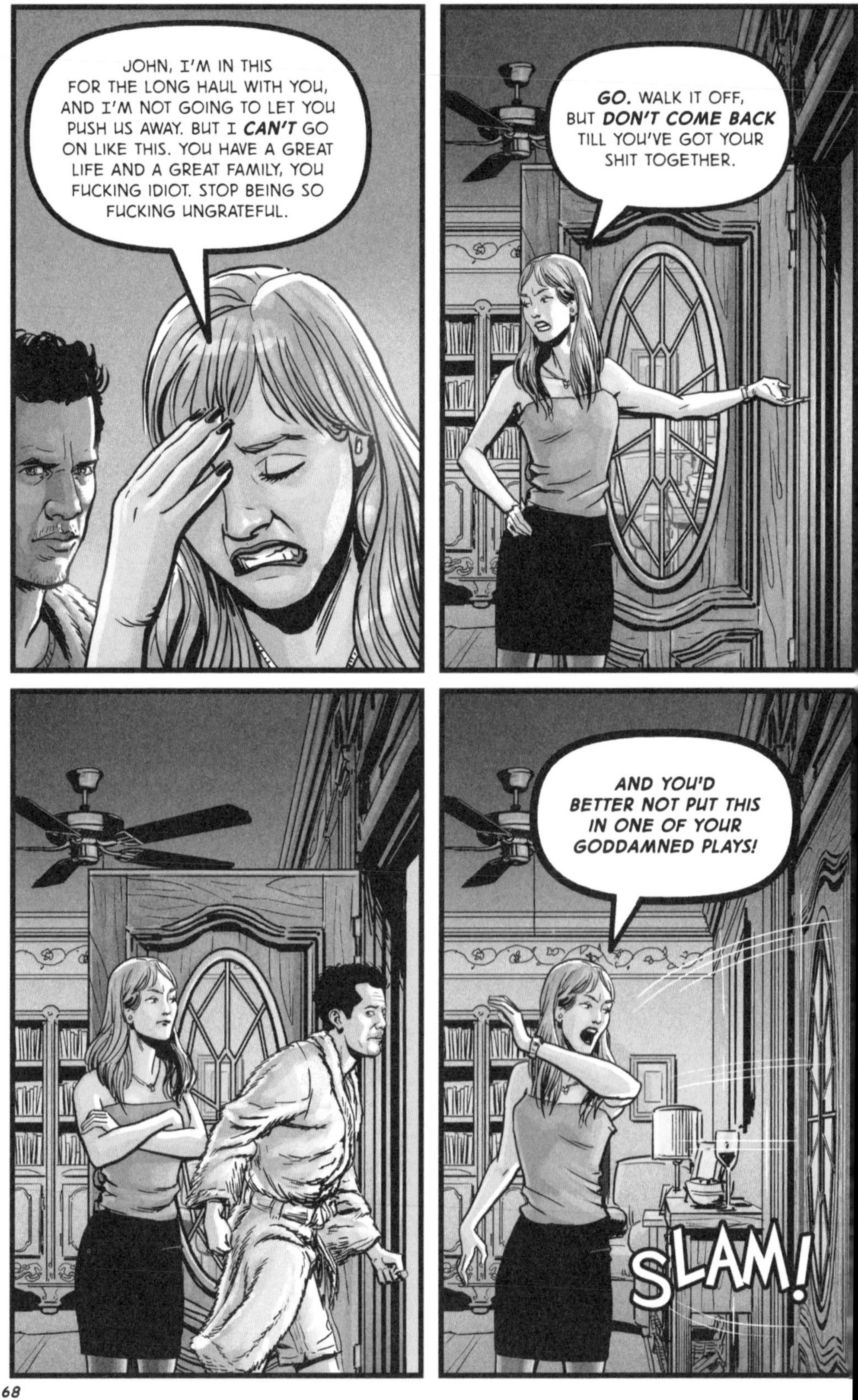
JOHN, I'M IN THIS FOR THE LONG HAUL WITH YOU, AND I'M NOT GOING TO LET YOU PUSH US AWAY. BUT I **CAN'T** GO ON LIKE THIS. YOU HAVE A GREAT LIFE AND A GREAT FAMILY, YOU FUCKING IDIOT. STOP BEING SO FUCKING UNGRATEFUL.
GO. WALK IT OFF, BUT **DON'T COME BACK** TILL YOU'VE GOT YOUR SHIT TOGETHER.
AND YOU'D BETTER NOT PUT THIS IN ONE OF YOUR GODDAMNED PLAYS!
SLAM!

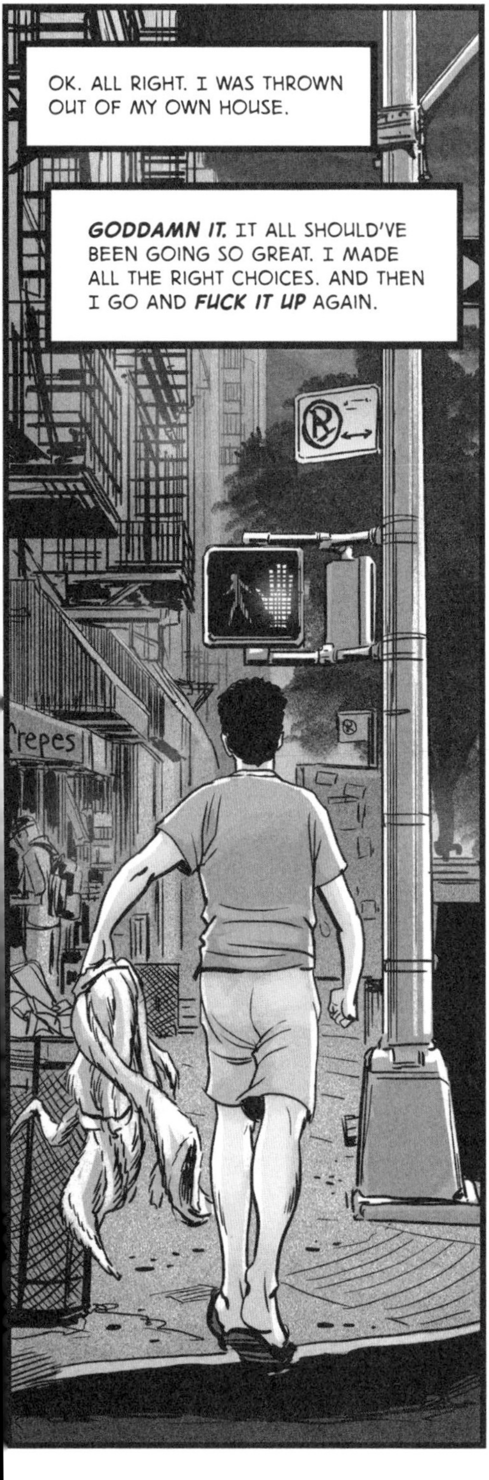
OK. ALL RIGHT. I WAS THROWN OUT OF MY OWN HOUSE.
GODDAMN IT. IT ALL SHOULD'VE BEEN GOING SO GREAT. I MADE ALL THE RIGHT CHOICES. AND THEN I GO AND **FUCK IT UP** AGAIN.
Crepes

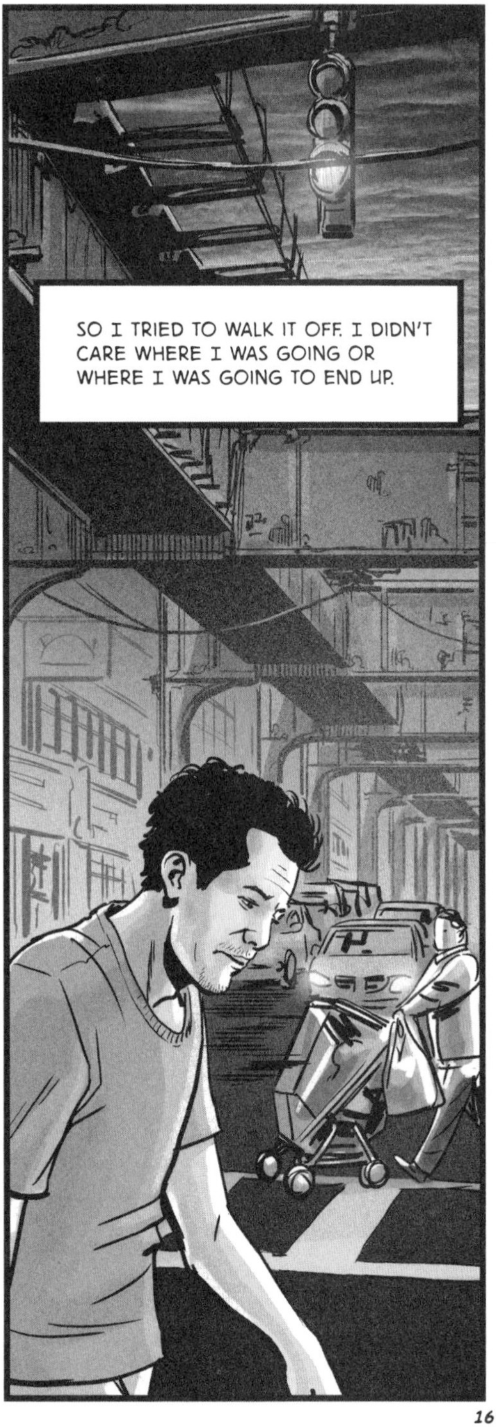
SO I TRIED TO WALK IT OFF. I DIDN'T CARE WHERE I WAS GOING OR WHERE I WAS GOING TO END UP.

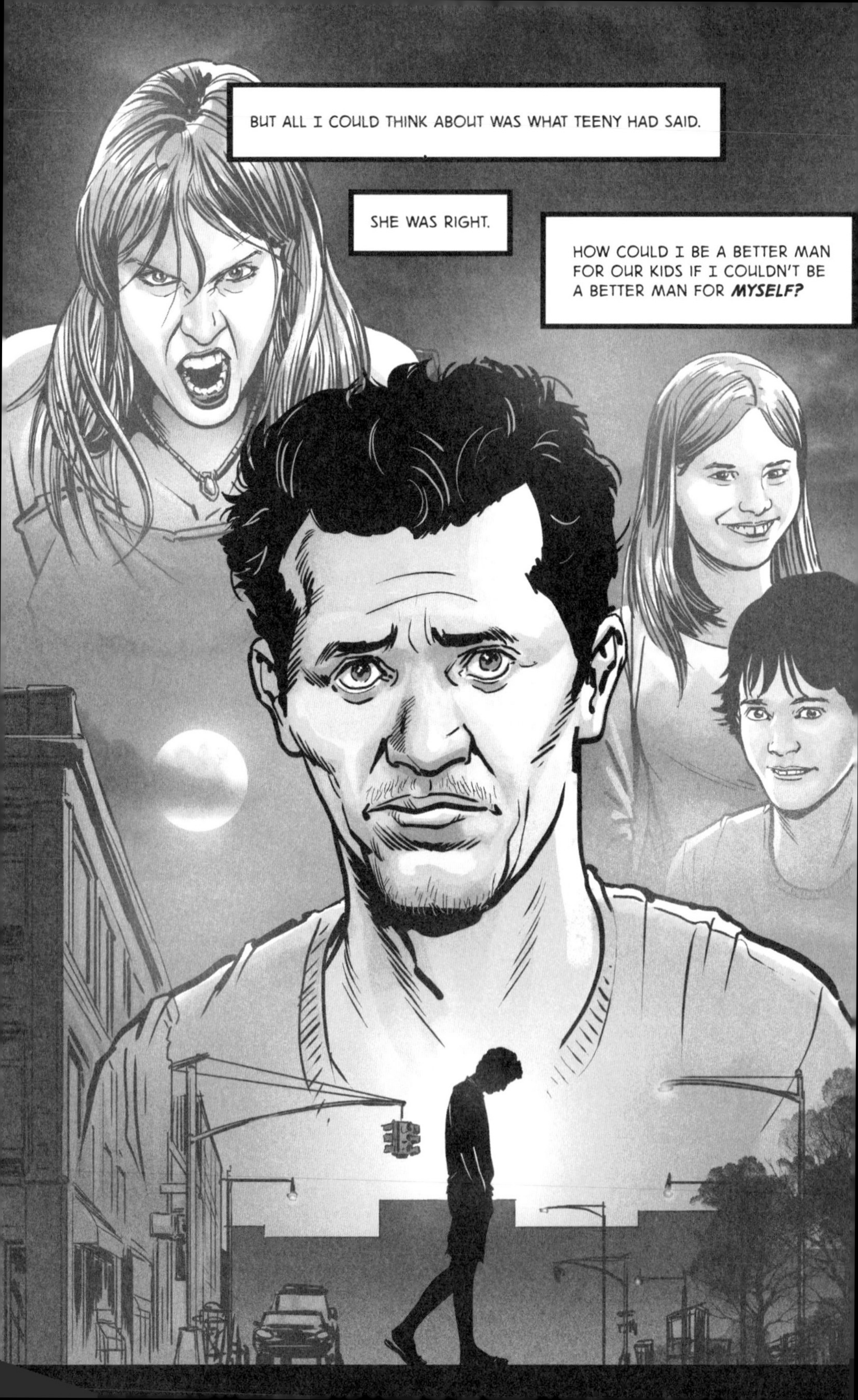
BUT ALL I COULD THINK ABOUT WAS WHAT TEENY HAD SAID.
SHE WAS RIGHT.
HOW COULD I BE A BETTER MAN FOR OUR KIDS IF I COULDN'T BE A BETTER MAN FOR ***MYSELF?***

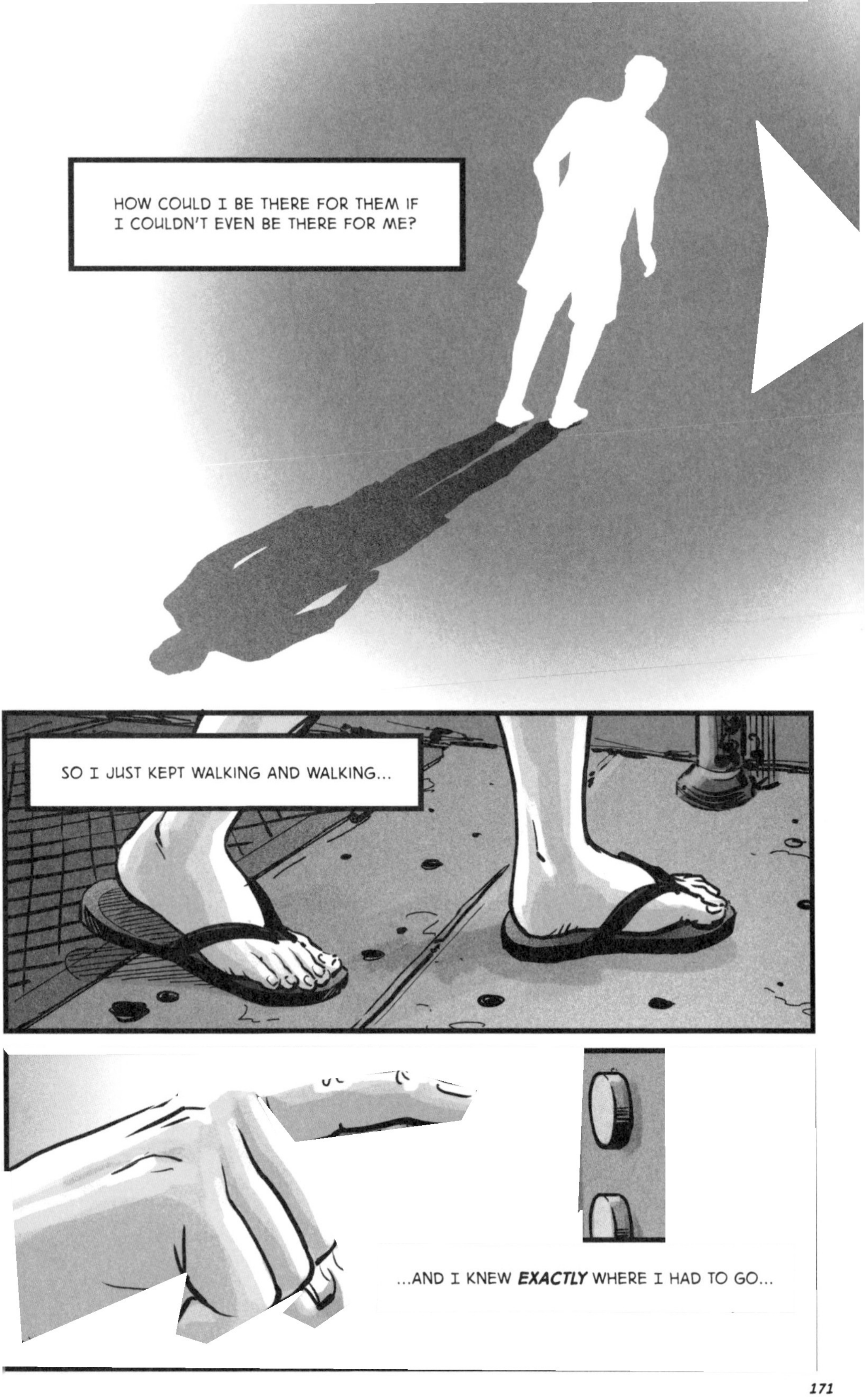
HOW COULD I BE THERE FOR THEM IF I COULDN'T EVEN BE THERE FOR ME?
SO I JUST KEPT WALKING AND WALKING...
...AND I KNEW ***EXACTLY*** WHERE I HAD TO GO...

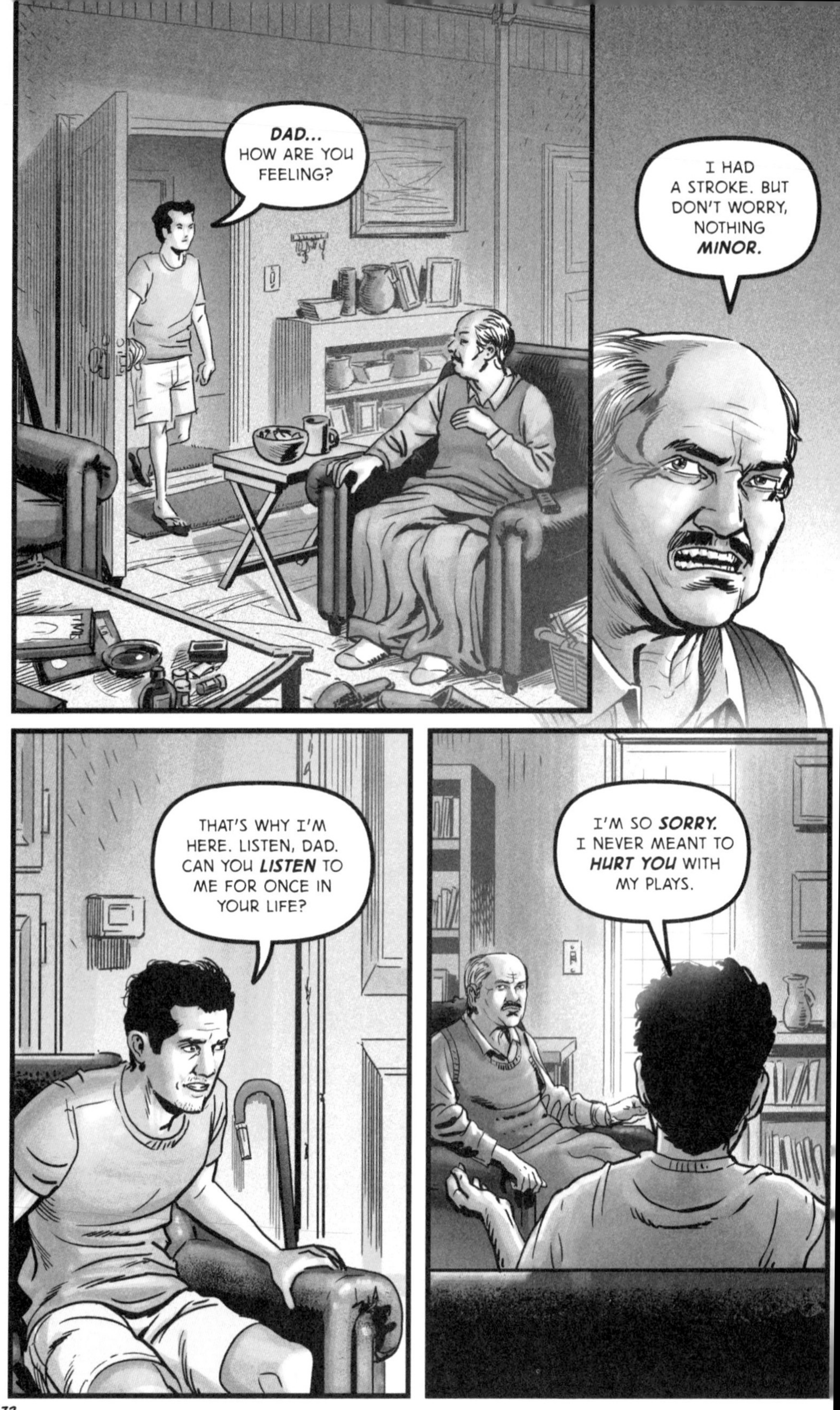
DAD... HOW ARE YOU FEELING?
I HAD A STROKE. BUT DON'T WORRY, NOTHING MINOR.
THAT'S WHY I'M HERE. LISTEN, DAD. CAN YOU LISTEN TO ME FOR ONCE IN YOUR LIFE?
I'M SO SORRY. I NEVER MEANT TO HURT YOU WITH MY PLAYS.

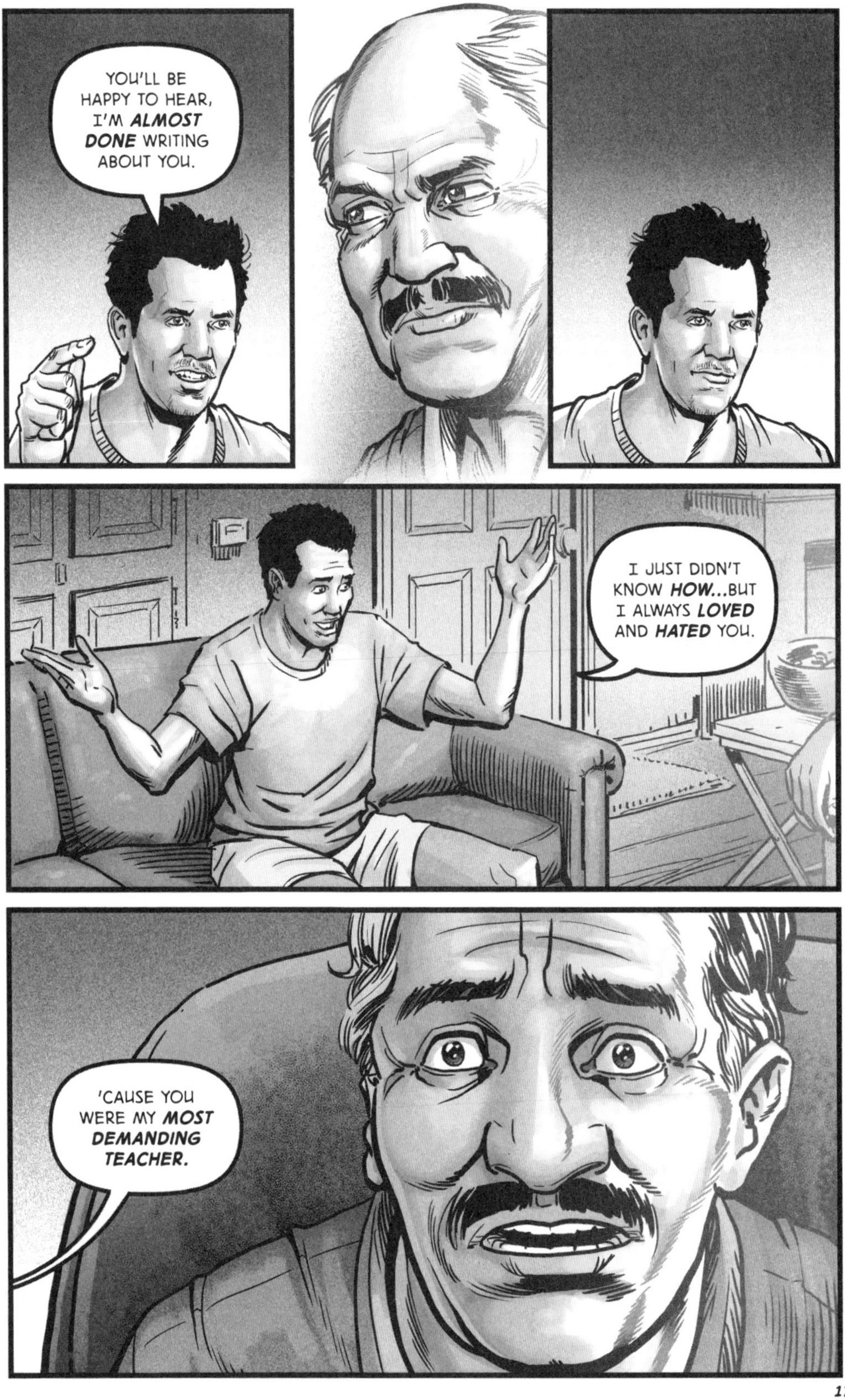
YOU'LL BE HAPPY TO HEAR, I'M **ALMOST DONE** WRITING ABOUT YOU.
I JUST DIDN'T KNOW **HOW...**BUT I ALWAYS **LOVED** AND **HATED** YOU.
'CAUSE YOU WERE MY **MOST DEMANDING TEACHER.**

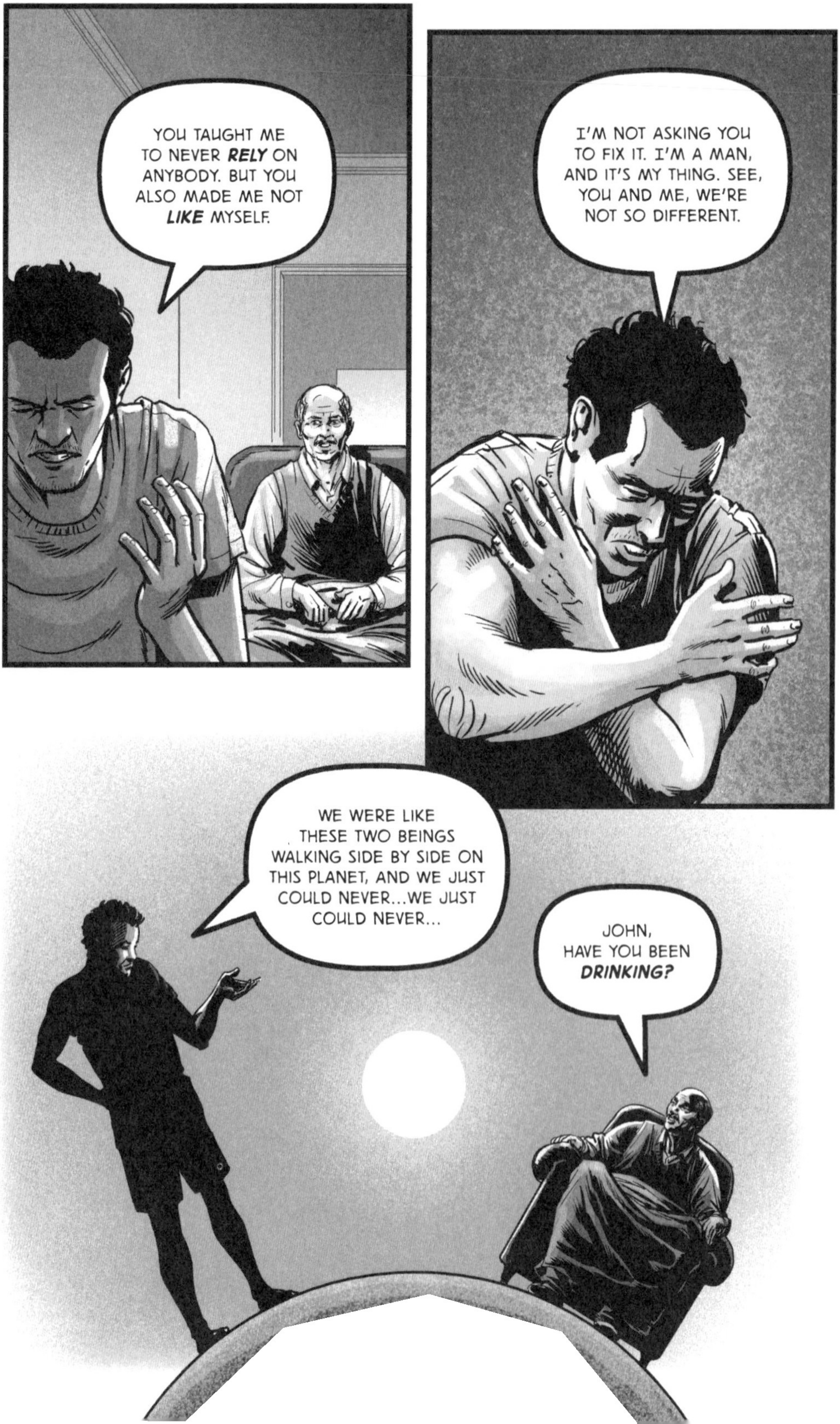
YOU TAUGHT ME TO NEVER **RELY** ON ANYBODY. BUT YOU ALSO MADE ME NOT **LIKE** MYSELF.
I'M NOT ASKING YOU TO FIX IT. I'M A MAN, AND IT'S MY THING. SEE, YOU AND ME, WE'RE NOT SO DIFFERENT.
WE WERE LIKE THESE TWO BEINGS WALKING SIDE BY SIDE ON THIS PLANET, AND WE JUST COULD NEVER...WE JUST COULD NEVER...
JOHN, HAVE YOU BEEN **DRINKING?**

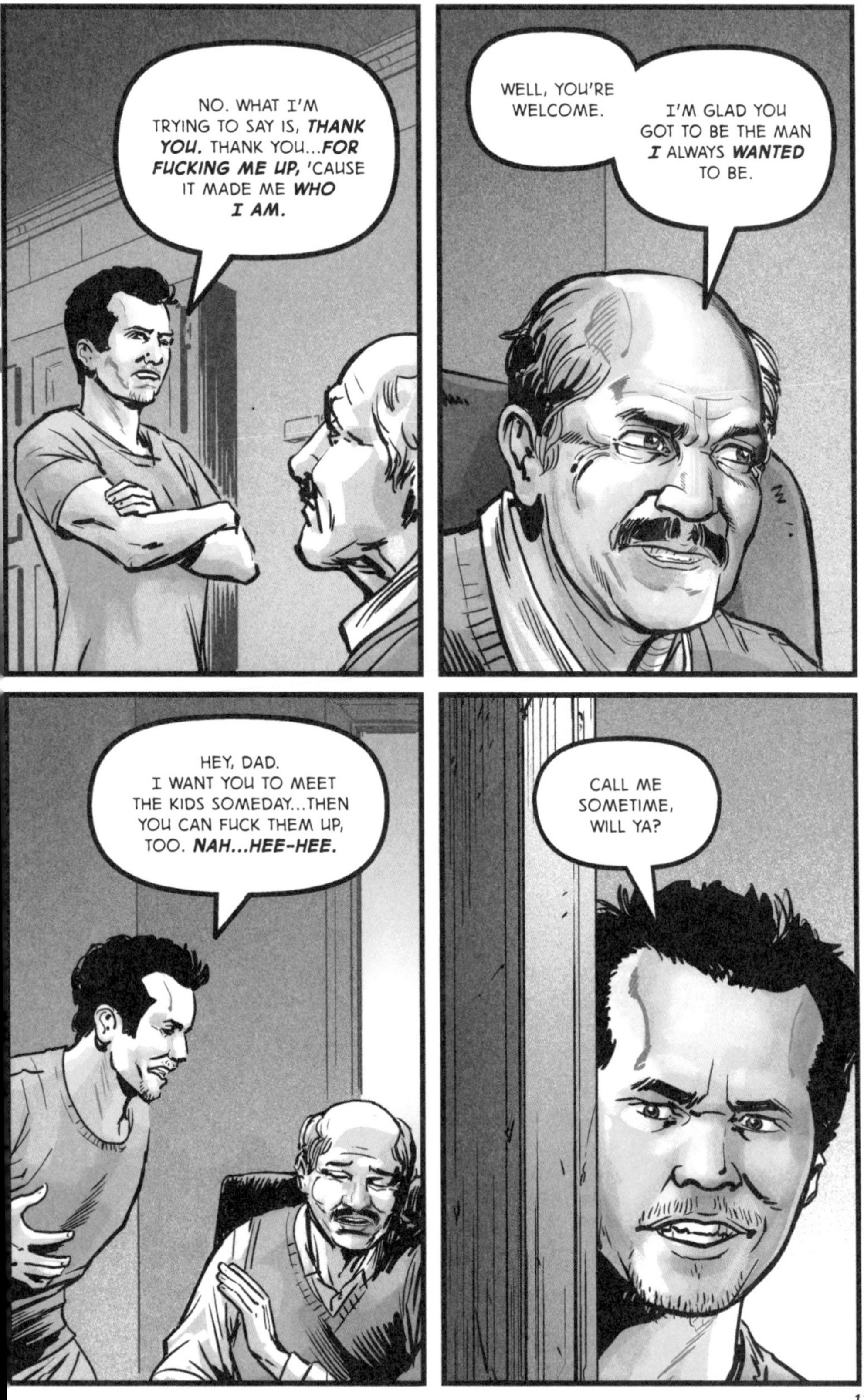
NO. WHAT I'M TRYING TO SAY IS, THANK YOU. THANK YOU...FOR FUCKING ME UP, 'CAUSE IT MADE ME WHO I AM.
WELL, YOU'RE WELCOME.
I'M GLAD YOU GOT TO BE THE MAN I ALWAYS WANTED TO BE.
HEY, DAD. I WANT YOU TO MEET THE KIDS SOMEDAY...THEN YOU CAN FUCK THEM UP, TOO. NAH...HEE-HEE.
CALL ME SOMETIME, WILL YA?

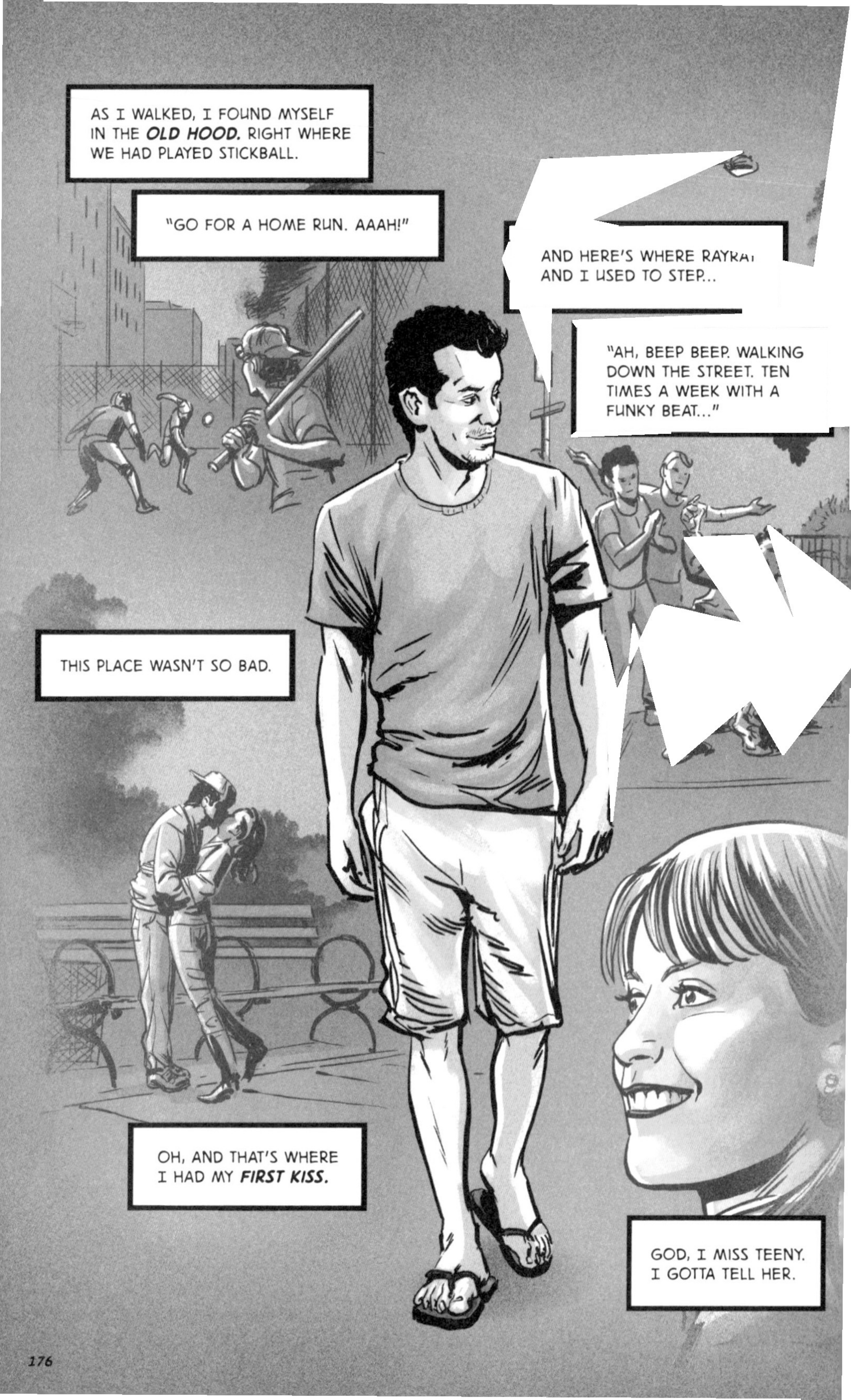
AS I WALKED, I FOUND MYSELF IN THE OLD HOOD. RIGHT WHERE WE HAD PLAYED STICKBALL.
"GO FOR A HOME RUN. AAAH!"
AND HERE'S WHERE RAYRA
AND I USED TO STEP...
"AH, BEEP BEEP. WALKING DOWN THE STREET. TEN TIMES A WEEK WITH A FUNKY BEAT..."
THIS PLACE WASN'T SO BAD.
OH, AND THAT'S WHERE I HAD MY FIRST KISS.
GOD, I MISS TEENY. I GOTTA TELL HER.

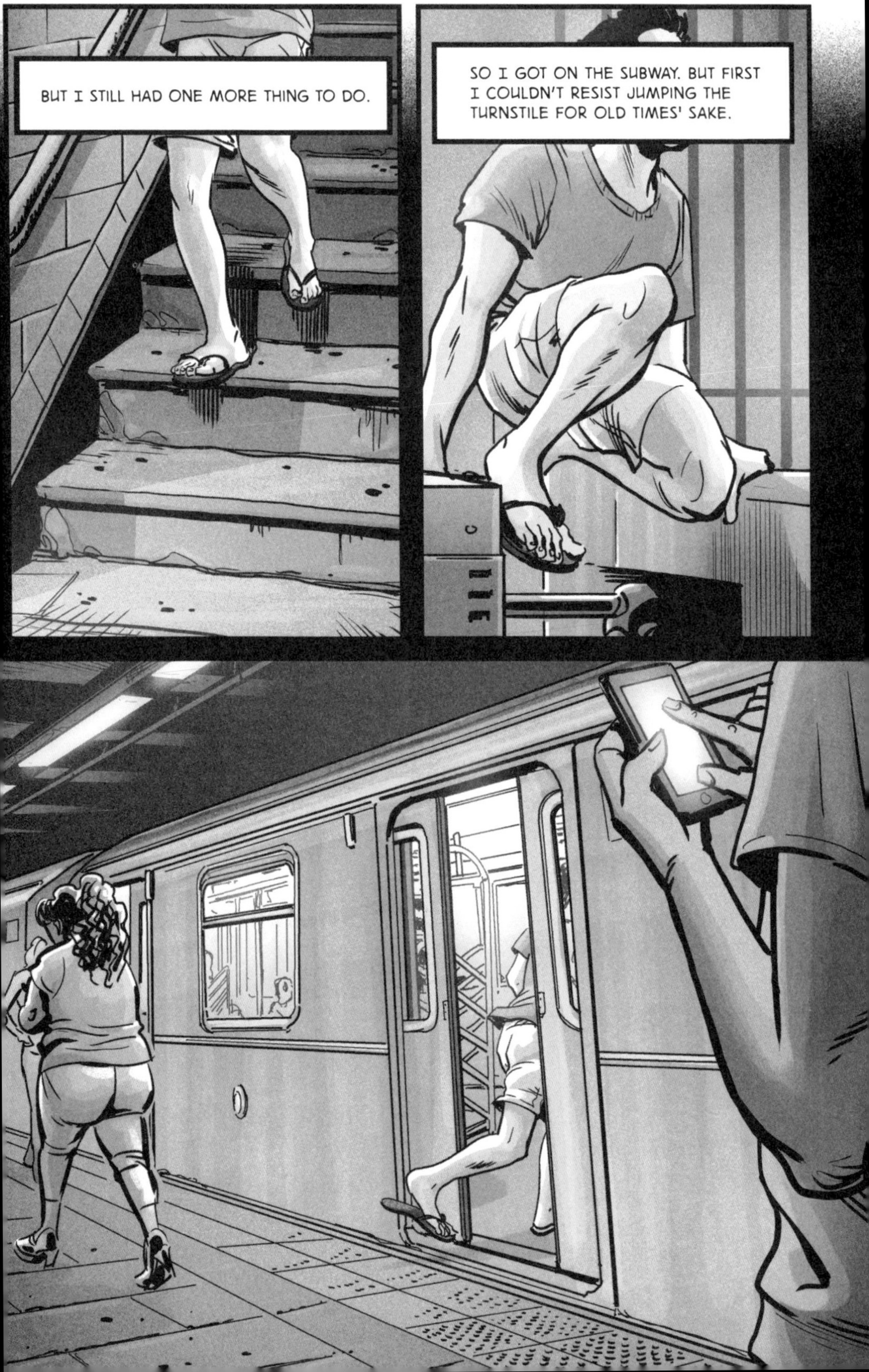
BUT I STILL HAD ONE MORE THING TO DO.
SO I GOT ON THE SUBWAY. BUT FIRST I COULDN'T RESIST JUMPING THE TURNSTILE FOR OLD TIMES' SAKE.

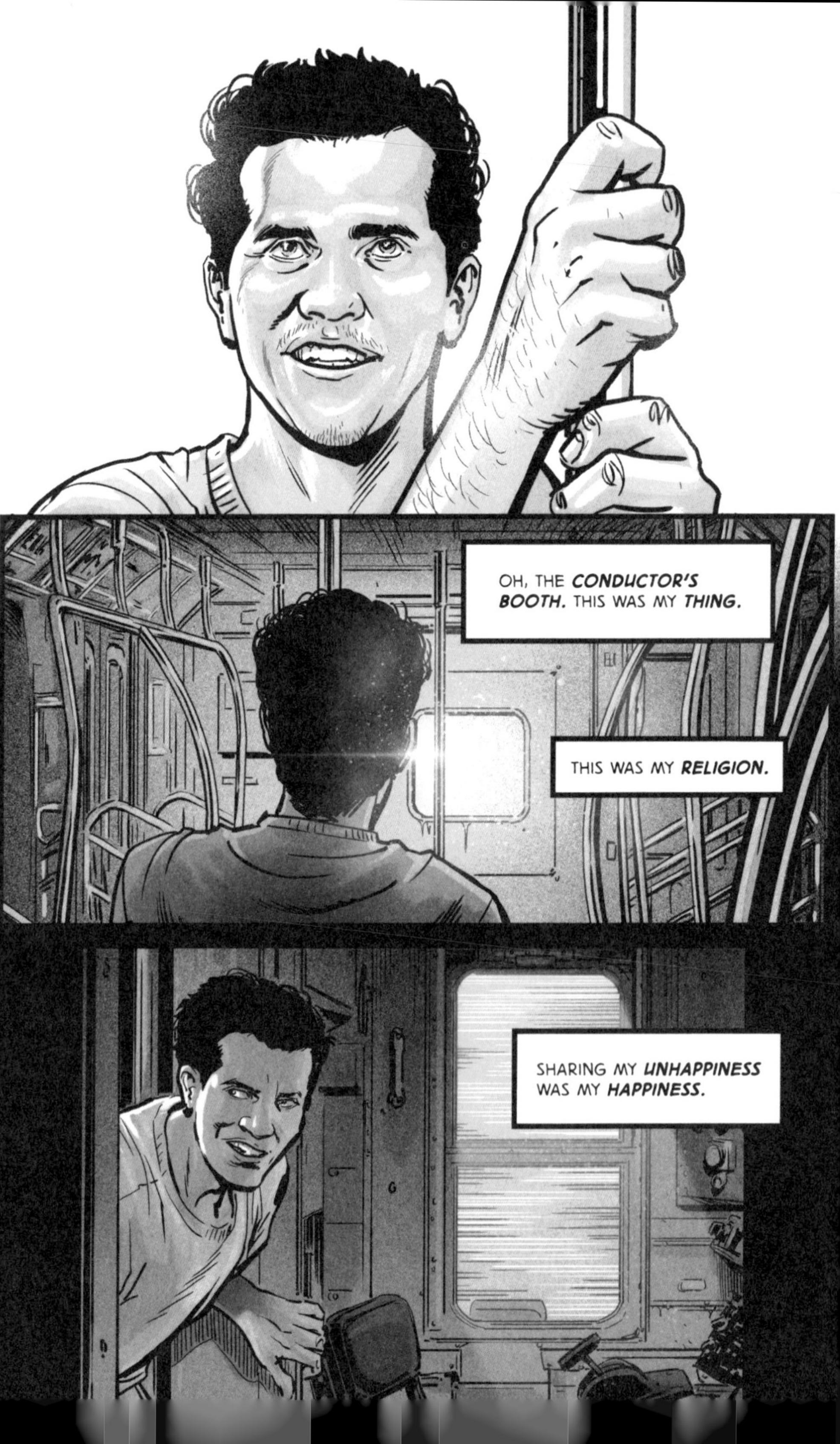
OH, THE CONDUCTOR'S BOOTH. THIS WAS MY THING.
THIS WAS MY RELIGION.
SHARING MY UNHAPPINESS WAS MY HAPPINESS.

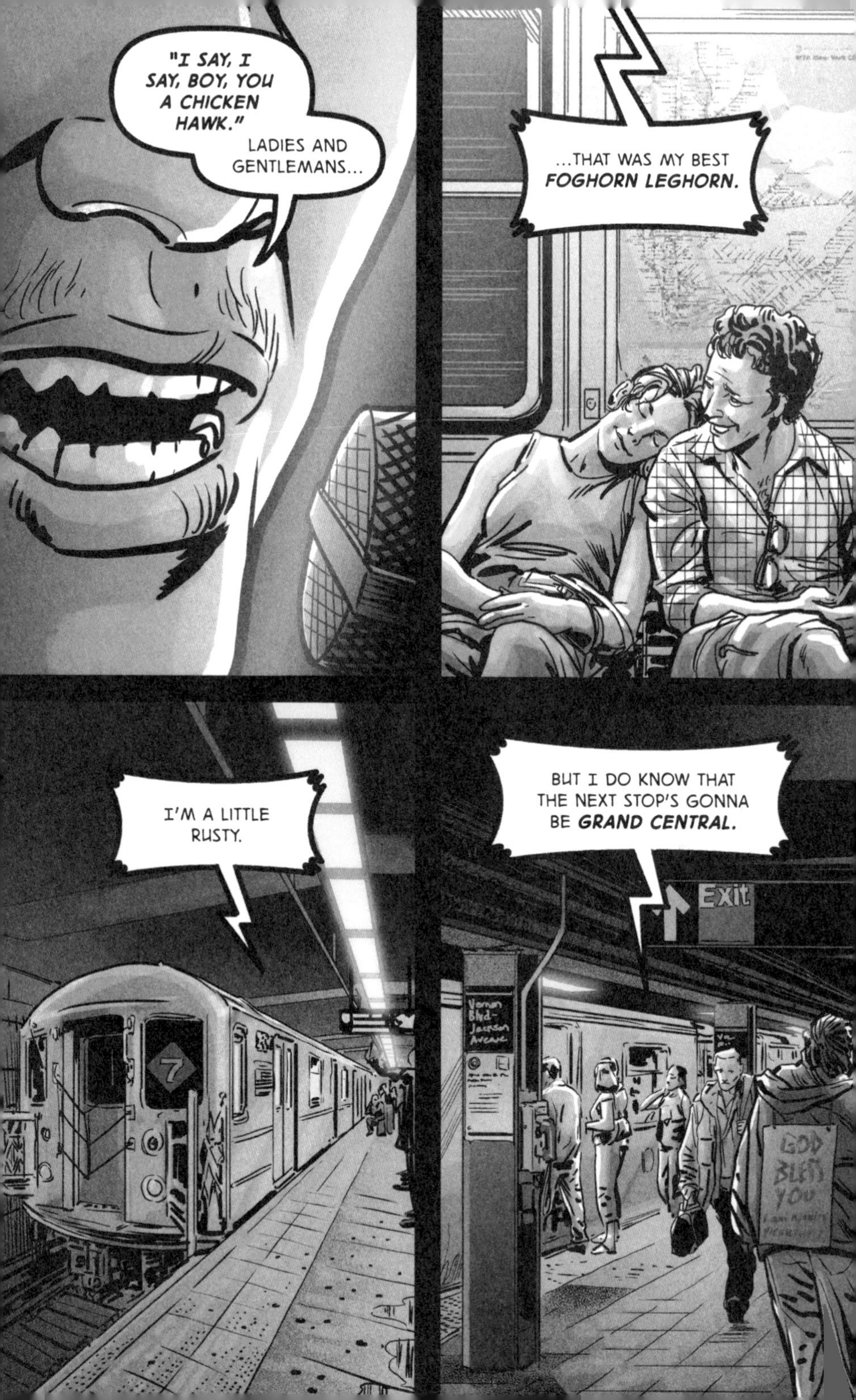
"I SAY, I SAY, BOY, YOU A CHICKEN HAWK."
LADIES AND GENTLEMANS...
...THAT WAS MY BEST **FOGHORN LEGHORN.**
I'M A LITTLE RUSTY.
BUT I DO KNOW THAT THE NEXT STOP'S GONNA BE **GRAND CENTRAL.**
Exit

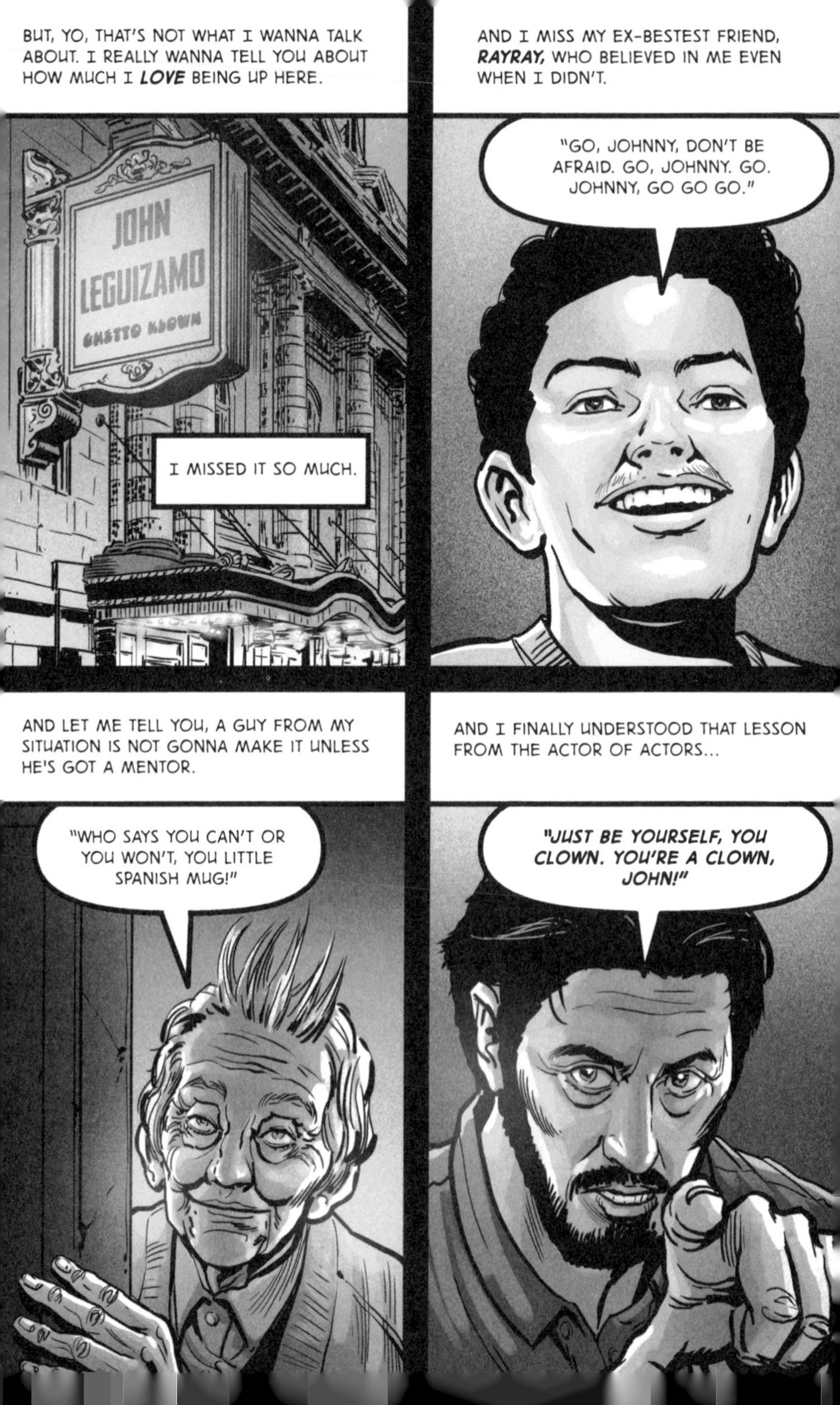
BUT, YO, THAT'S NOT WHAT I WANNA TALK ABOUT. I REALLY WANNA TELL YOU ABOUT HOW MUCH I *LOVE* BEING UP HERE.
JOHN LEGUIZAMO
GHETTO KLOWN
I MISSED IT SO MUCH.
AND I MISS MY EX-BESTEST FRIEND, *RAYRAY,* WHO BELIEVED IN ME EVEN WHEN I DIDN'T.
"GO, JOHNNY, DON'T BE AFRAID. GO, JOHNNY. GO. JOHNNY, GO GO GO."
AND LET ME TELL YOU, A GUY FROM MY SITUATION IS NOT GONNA MAKE IT UNLESS HE'S GOT A MENTOR.
"WHO SAYS YOU CAN'T OR YOU WON'T, YOU LITTLE SPANISH MUG!"
AND I FINALLY UNDERSTOOD THAT LESSON FROM THE ACTOR OF ACTORS...
"JUST BE YOURSELF, YOU CLOWN. YOU'RE A CLOWN, JOHN!"

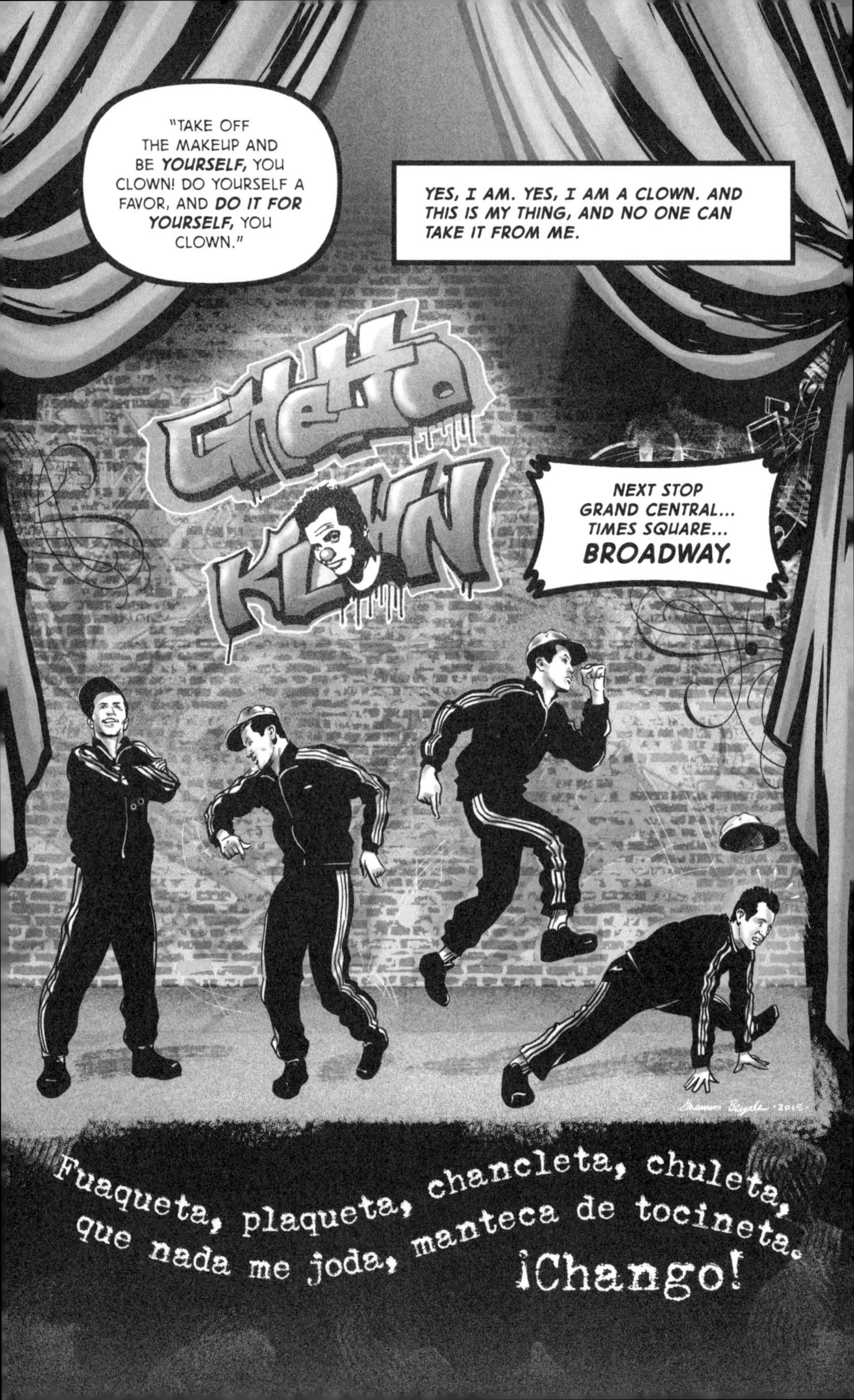
"TAKE OFF THE MAKEUP AND BE *YOURSELF,* YOU CLOWN! DO YOURSELF A FAVOR, AND *DO IT FOR YOURSELF,* YOU CLOWN."
YES, I AM. YES, I AM A CLOWN. AND THIS IS MY THING, AND NO ONE CAN TAKE IT FROM ME.
GHETTO KLOWN
*NEXT STOP GRAND CENTRAL... TIMES SQUARE... **BROADWAY.***
Fuaqueta, plaqueta, chancleta, chuleta, que nada me joda, manteca de tocineta.
¡Chango!

ACKNOWLEDGMENTS

This book is for anyone who has struggled just a little bit more along the way in life but because of it learned to value every moment and view any move—even laterally—as a triumph. I have to thank the many people on my journey who believed in me, even when I stopped believing in me, and who offered hope and faith in things unseen and yet to materialize: My wife, Justine, who is a pillar of strength and keeps my life free from chaos and is the muse I always longed for; my mother, who is the most positive woman on earth—she loves life, and life loves her, and it's that miracle that frequently gives me the courage to go on; my brother, Sergio, the intellectual pioneer in our family, who by age eighteen had read Dante, Homer, Dostoyevsky, and Nietzsche, and understood them—he set the bar and I limbo-danced underneath it; and my kids, Allegra and Lucas, who inspire in me a great need to be better than I can possibly be, if only to live up to the person they think I am.

I want to thank all the great playwrights whose bloodstained words saved me in my troubled youth: Eugene O'Neill, Sam Shepard, Arthur Miller, Miguel Piñero; and all the great monologists before me who unknowingly passed the baton of one of the oldest storytelling methods known to mankind and let me mutate it into my own bastardized autobiographical plaything: Eric Bogosian, Lily Tomlin, Spalding Gray, and Whoopi Goldberg. An artist is only as good as his heroes, and I have many just in case: Richard Pryor, the greatest comic who ever lived and who is the barometer to everything I ever do; Jonathan Winters, whose skills set the bar for anyone doing more than one voice at a time and also hearing them talk back; and Lenny Bruce, for it all.

I also want to thank all the many unsung Latin lives that should never have been left unsung.

I am grateful to my manager, Jeff Golenberg, for his loyalty and fiduciary skills; my director, Fisher Stevens, whose vision and deep, deep soul helped me delve further and reveal more than I wanted anyone to know; Charlie Kochman, for his faith in this project and because he creates beauty in everything he does; David Cashion, for his tireless editing and daring to drop off the galleys through my mail slot while my dog tried to chew his hands off; the graphic artists Christa Cassano and Shamus Beyale, for their artistry and sensitivity in turning mere words into the actual worlds I lived—their fine motor skills crush my motormouth; Dean Haspiel of Hang Dai Studios in Gowanus, for leading me to Christa and for his support; Arnold Engelman, for being a protector of and producer for the goals I had in mind; and all my acting teachers, including Wynn Handman, who was the very first to tirelessly put up with my constant testing of my work in his class and who finally put together my shows and gave me a venue for *Mambo Mouth*, *Spic-O-Rama*, and *Freak*.

Thanks also to Peter Askin, who has been one of the best directors of my work; Spike Lee, Aaron Gonzales, Arabella Powell, Ari Pineda, Marlene Ortiz, Jenaro Diaz, Ben DeJesus, Fred Golding, Michael Lombardo, Chris Albrecht, Emanuel Hernandez, Tony Taccone at Berkeley Rep, Christopher Ashley at La Jolla Playhouse, Nelle Nugent, David Frazier, and Eric Gordon.

Romans 12:6: Having gifts that differ according to the grace given to us, let us use them.